THE BIG BOOK
OF
PET NAMES

More than 10,000 Pet Names!
The Most Complete Guide
to Pet Names & Meanings

by
Eugene Boone

DEDICATION

The Big Book of Pet Names is dedicated to the memory of my mother – *Macy Boone* – who was always supportive of me and my writing endeavors.

ACKNOWLEDGMENT

I owe much gratitude to my friend and fellow writer,
the late *Faith A. Senior*, an active animal rights
spokesperson, whose encouragement and contributions
helped to make **The Big Book of Pet Names**
possible.

Special Thanks to *Sharon Coy* for the cover
photograph of cockatiels ("*Margarita & Poncho*").

I also give a Special Thanks to: *J.T.H.*
I could not have completed this book without you
and your unconditional support.

The Big Book of Pet Names

Contents

"I shall write a book some day about the appropriateness of names. Geoffrey Chaucer has a ribald ring, as is proper and correct, and Alexander Pope was inevitably Alexander Pope. Colley Cibber was a silly little man without much elegance and Shelley was very Percy and very Bysshe."

- **James Joyce**, 1882-1941

The Big Book
of
Pet Names

Introduction

Welcome to **The Big Book of Pet Names**. Naming a new pet can
often prove a difficult task as the pet lover tries to choose a name
that is just right, perfectly suited to both owner and pet. To make
the task a bit easier, I have compiled **The Big Book of Pet
Names**, a guide that offers thousands of names for birds, cats,
dogs, fish, hamsters, reptiles, and other types of pets.

The Big Book of Pet Names has more than 10,000 potential
names for your new pet. These names are listed alphabetically in
twenty-five categories, plus the **"Did You Know?"** boxes. Al-
though I have tried to keep repetition to a minimum, some repetition is necessary because many names fit into more than one category.

In my opinion, pet names should be chosen with the same regard
animal lovers use when choosing their pets. Thus, more than just
a few moments thought should be put into naming a new pet. This
is especially important when you realize that the name you
choose for your pet will inevitably be repeated hundreds of times,
often in rapid succession, so the name decided upon should not

be a name that will grow tiresome after a period of time has passed.

Likewise, even though names can be changed if necessary, it is a good idea to choose a name that will still be suited to your pet through various stages of growth: from the time the animal is in its infancy until it is well into adulthood. As time passes, you will be grateful that you've chosen a name that doesn't grow tiresome and still suits your pet.

I have learned from my years of experience naming pets that it is often a good idea to wait a few days before deciding on a permanent name for a new pet. This will give you the time to carefully choose a name that is well suited to the animal's personality, physical appearance and behavior. In fact, it is sometimes a good idea to select several names and practice calling the pet each of these names over a period of several days to determine the name to which the animal is most responsive.

When choosing a name, keep in mind that it is important to choose a name for your pet (this is particularly true for cats and dogs) that is easy to pronounce when it is necessary to call the animal home (of course, your pet should not be roaming the neighborhood in the first place, but that's besides the point!)

Names of one-syllable, such as *Satch, Duke* or *Spot* are easy to pronounce and to call as are many two-syllable names like *Dusty, Felix* or *Rocky*. Longer names can often be shortened for the purpose of making them easier to call. Also, you should give your pet a name that is fairly short or can be shortened if the pet is for a small child or there is a small child in your household.

Naming a pet after a child's favorite character from a TV series, a movie or a book will often make it easier for the child to remember the new pet's name as well as making it easier for the child to pronounce the name.

In most cases, it seems to lack imagination to give the same name to pet after pet. However, there is an exception: The naming of offspring or an animal of the same breed after another pet as a way of carrying on the name of a cherished pet. In this instance, the passing of the name takes on a special significance and is not merely a means of sticking a quick name on the animal.

Speaking of choosing a meaningful name for your pet, sometimes a pet owner's surname can inspire a pet's name. For example, if your last name is *Rogers*, you might choose to name your pet *Buck*, thus *Buck Rogers*. Or, if your last name is *Brown*, you might choose to name your pet *Charlie*, thus *Charlie Brown*. My last name is *Boone*, and I could name a pet *Daniel*, thus *Daniel Boone*, but I haven't, mainly because I have relatives with that name! Of course, whether your last name corresponds or doesn't, you can still name your pet *Buck Rogers* or *Charlie Brown* or any combination of names as you like. But, if you have the same last name as a famous person or well-known character, you might want to use this idea as a unique way to combine your last name with the given name of your pet.

Another way to add a personal touch to a pet name is to use an initial. For example, you can use the first letter of your last name (or your first name, if you prefer) and a title – like *Mr. B*, *Mrs. K*, *Miss M*, etc. When appropriate, this is an especially easy way to name a pet – and add a personalized touch as well.

At times pet lovers may want to appeal to a sense of irony when naming a new pet. For instance, giving the name *Mangler* to a tiny Chihuahua when the pet hardly appears vicious (of course, the Chihuahua thinks it's a much bigger dog!)

DID YOU KNOW? - Many celebrities are pet lovers just as you and I, and they must choose names for their pets just as we do. **The Big Book of Pet Names** includes the names of many celebrities' pets (and those of historical figures) in each chapter and in the **"Did You Know?"** boxes found at the end of each chapter. The twenty-five chapters and the **"Did You Know?"** boxes include the names of pets belonging to the following stars and others:

Marilyn Monroe
Brad Pitt
Jennifer Aniston (star of "Friends" and motion pictures)
Leonardo DiCaprio
Clay Aiken (of "American Idol")
Shaquille O'Neal
Sheryl Crow
Stephen King
Alyssa Milano (star of "Who's the Boss" and "Charmed")
Sylvester Stallone
Kate Jackson (star of "Charlie's Angels" and "Dark Shadows")
Slash (guitarist for rock band *Guns 'N' Roses*)
Judge Judy
Bill Murray (star of *Ghostbusters* and other motion pictures)
Kristi Yamaguchi
Fran Drescher (star of "The Nanny")
Elvis Presley
Whitney Houston
Suzanne Somers (star of "Three's Company" and other TV series and movies)

Beck (musician)
Gloria Estafan
Angelina Jolie (star of the *Lara Croft* movie series)
Fred Durst (of the band *Limp Bizkit*)
Melissa Joan Hart (star of "Sabrina, the Teenage Witch")
David Hasselhoff (star of "Knight Rider" and "Baywatch")
Barbara Eden (star of "I Dream of Jeannie")
Julio Iglesias
Drew Barrymore (star of *E.T.* and other motion pictures)
Clayton Moore (the Lone Ranger)
Tisha Campbell (star of "Martin" and "My Wife and Kids")
Martina Navratilova
Tom Green (star of movies and MTV's "The Tom Green Show")
Michael Jackson
Renee Zellweger (star of movies - including *Bridget Jones's Diary*)
John F. Kennedy, Jr.
David Boreanaz (star of the TV series "Angel")

Even though you may spend a great deal of time and effort selecting the perfect name for your pet, there are times when a pet name has to be changed, sometimes a name fails to fit the animal after a period of time. Whatever the reason, keep in mind that a pet's name can often be changed with very little resistance on the part of the animal, especially if the animal is relatively young. This is true even of cats, dogs and other pets that learn to respond to their names.

Recently, my family decided to change the name of a Chihuahua that was nearly a year old and there wasn't any noticeable resistance to the new name. In fact, the puppy seems to respond better to his new name, perhaps because it's easier to pronounce and to call. If, however, you are changing the name of an older pet, it may be wise to choose a name that has a sound similar to the name the animal is used to. That way, there may be less time for adjustment to the new name. Please be aware that if you have aspirations of your pet taking part in animal shows, such as dog shows or horse shows, there may be restrictions concerning the names selected. For information on any such limitations, consult the sponsors of the animal shows in which you hope to have your pet participate.

Besides a carefully chosen name, there are other requirements for having a happy pet: Lots of love and attention (which almost goes without saying!), proper feeding and grooming (there are a few exceptions, such as fish, reptiles and similar pets, but keep in mind that these animals often have their own special needs, like freshly cleaned bowls and cages!), and medical attention when necessary. There are books on these and other subjects related to pets and pet care available from libraries, bookstores, and pet shops. The saying "animals are people, too" is very true in that animals have the same rights as we do to live long, safe and healthy lives. Most animal lovers are, fortunately, aware of this and would never think of neglecting or otherwise abusing their pets. In fact, true animal lovers often treat their pets like a part of the family, which is, in essence, what most pets become.

In addition to previously mentioned dedications, **The Big Book of Pet Names** is dedicated to all animal lovers.

Best,

Eugene Boone

Favorite Pet Quotes

"The smallest feline is
a masterpiece."

- Leonardo Da Vinci

"Be as a bird perched on a frail branch
that she feels bending beneath her, still
she sings away all the same, knowing
she has wings."

- Victor Hugo

"My dog is worried about the
economy because Alpo is up to
99 cents a can. That's almost
$7.00 in dog money. "

- Joe Weinstein

Favorite Pet Quotes

"We give dogs time we can spare, space we can spare and love we can spare. And in return, dogs give us their all."

- M. Facklam

"Animals are such agreeable friends - they ask no questions, they pass no criticisms."

- George Eliot

"A cat pent up becomes a lion."

- Italian Proverb

Favorite Pet Quotes

"Animals are reliable, many full of love, true in their affections, predictable in their actions, grateful and loyal."

- Alfred A. Montapert

"Dogs need to sniff the ground; it's how they keep abreast of current events. The ground is a giant dog newspaper, containing all kinds of late-breaking dog news items, which, if they are especially urgent, are often continued into the next yard."

- Dave Barry

"Dogs and cats instinctively know the exact moment their owners will wake up. Then they wake them 10 minutes sooner!"

- Unknown

Favorite Pet Quotes

"I think dogs are the most amazing creatures; they give unconditional love. For me they are the role model for being alive."

- Gilda Radner

"He is your friend, your partner, your defender, your dog. You are his life, his love, his leader. He will be yours, faithful and true, to the last beat of his heart. You owe it to him to be worthy of such devotion."

- Unknown

"I wonder if other dogs think poodles are members of a weird religious cult."

- Rita Rudner

Favorite Pet Quotes

"A dog is the only thing on earth
that loves you more than he loves
himself."

- *Josh Billings*

"Cats always seem so very
wise, when staring with their
half-closed eyes. Can they be
thinking, I'll be nice, and
maybe she will feed me
twice?"

- *Bette Midler*

"You can say any fool thing to a
dog, and the dog will give you this
look that says, `My God, you're
RIGHT! I NEVER would've
thought of that'!"

- *Dave Barry*

DALBY

Chapter 1

Appearance: Breed, Color, Size

One of the most common (and the easiest) ways of naming a pet is by the appearance of the animal: **Breed** (*Angora, Collie, Shepherd*), **Color** (*Blackie, Calico, Goldie*), **Size** (*Tiny, Little Bit, Mammoth*), or **distinctive markings** or **shape** (*Freckles, Fuzzy, Spot*).

ABALONE: Beautiful.
ABELE: White.
ADENA: Beautiful.
ADOLPH: Wolf.
ADRIAN: Black.
ADRIANA: Dark.
ADRIANE, ADRIENNE: Dark.
AKITA: A breed of large muscular dog of Japanese origin.
ALA: Having wings.
ALABASTER: Delicate; prized.
ALETTA: Having wings.
ALGERNON: Having whiskers.
ALGIE: Short for Algernon.
ALITA: Having wings.
ALIZA: Golden; joyous.
ALIZARIN: Golden or reddish.

ALKA: Of the water.
ALMOND: Tan or beige. The name of the beige Beanie Baby bear.
ALPINE: Tall.
ALPO: Honorable.
ALTA: Tall.
ALVAR: White.
AMARA: Eternally beautiful; loving.
AMBER: Brownish yellow or golden. The name of the gold Beanie Baby tabby kitty.
AMBERLY: Brownish yellow.
ANCHOVY: Small.
ANGORA: A kind of cat with long, silky fur.
ANT: Small; the runt. Often a pest.
ANTIA: Small.

AQUA: (Latin "water") A pet that lives in water. Also the color blue-green.

ARENA: Sandy. A place of physical competition. A show-off.

ARGYLE: Old-fashioned; silvery gray.

ARROW: A pointer; slender.

ARTIS: Creative; beautiful.

ARTISSA: Creative; beautiful.

ASHA: Gray or white-gray.

ASHEN: Gray or white-gray.

ASHER: Ash gray.

ASHLYN, ASHTYN: Gray or white-gray.

ASHTON: Gray.

ASPHALT: Black.

ASTOR: Bright yellowish color.

ASWAD: Black.

AUBREY: Tiny ruler.

AUBURN: Reddish brown.

AUGUSTA: Grand.

AUGUSTIN: Growing.

AUGUSTINE: Growing.

AUGUSTUS: Growing.

AURELIA: Golden.

AUREOLUS: Golden.

AUTUMN: Golden brown.

AVELINA, AVELINE: Light reddish brown.

BABETTE: Pretty.

BAGGY: Bulging.

BAIZE: Chestnut brown.

BALBOA: Silvery. A silver coin in Panama. The name Rupert gave the small, injured snake he found on "Survivor: Pearl Islands"; the snake was adopted by the Drake tribe as their mascot. The last name of the boxer, played by Sylvester Stallone, in the series of *Rocky* movies.

BALLERINA: A dancer; graceful.

BALLOON: Plump.

BAMBINO: Baby.

BANDICOOT: Ratlike.

BANDO: Pretty; shiny like ribbon.

BANGLES: Pretty.

BARBO: Bearded.

BAUBLE: Pretty.

BAY: Reddish brown.

BEADY: Having small dark eyes.

BEAGLE: A small, long-eared hunting dog.

BEAKY: A pet with a large or protruding beak.

BEANIE, BEANY: Small.

BEANO: Small.

BEAR: Furry; strong.

BEAUFORT: Handsome.

BEAUTY: Pretty; pleasing.

BEEBO: Handsome.

BEEFCAKE: Handsome.
BELLA: Beautiful.
BELLADONNA: Beautiful lady.
BELLAMY: Beautiful friend.
BELLO: Beautiful.
BELLY: Plump. A pet that loves to eat.
BELVA: Beautiful.
BERLIN: A fine, soft wool yarn. A soft, furry pet.
BIG BOY: Large.
BIG BRITCHES: Overgrown in size or ego.
BIG EYES: Watchful.
BIG GIRL: Large.
BIG MAN: Macho; large.
BIG RED: Large; golden or reddish brown.
BIG STUFF: Huge; egotistic.
BIG WIG: A leader. Furry or shaggy.
BIRDIE: A bird or birdlike.
BITSY, BITSEY: Itsy-bitsy or tiny.
BITTY: Little one.
BITZ: Small.
BJORN: (Scandinavian) "bear" Pronounced "be-orn."
BLACK BEAR: Black and ferocious.
BLACK KNIGHT: Dark; mysterious.
BLACK ROSE: Dark flower.

BLACKBERRY: Black, dark.
BLACKIE: The dark one; black. The name of a Beanie Baby bear.
BLACKJACK: Tar-colored.
BLAINE: Thin.
BLARNEY: Smooth; lucky.
BLAZE: Fiery; red-haired.
BLIMP: Large.
BLIZZARD: Unpredictable; white.
BLOB: Huge.
BLUBBER: Babylike; plump.
BLUE: Melancholy; grayish-black.
BLUE EYES: Having eyes of blue.
BLUEBELLE: Blue or blue-eyed. John F. Kennedy, the 35th President of the United States, had a parakeet with this name.
BLUSH: Rosy; shy.
BO: Handsome.
BOBSY, BOBSIE: Tiny.
BOCEAN: (Pronounced "bo-shawn") Tiny and gracious.
BOCHEE: Small; playful.
BODEAN: Handsome; leader.
BON BON: Tiny; dark; good.
BONES: Skinny.
BONNIBELLE: Beautiful; good.
BONZ: Bony.

BOOTIES: A pet who appears to be wearing boots. Sure-footed.

BOOTS: A pet who appears to be wearing boots. Sure-footed.

BOOTSY: A pet who appears to be wearing boots. Sure-footed.

BOUFFANT: Puffy.

BOW: Tidy.

BOWLEGS: A pet whose legs are crooked.

BOWS: Beautiful.

BOWSER: Large dog.

BOXER: Sturdy.

BOY: Youthful.

BOYD: Fair-haired.

BRAMBLE: Prickly.

BRAND: A pet with distinguishing marks.

BRANT: Dark.

BRANTLEY: Dark.

BRASS: Golden.

BRAWNY: Strong; muscular.

BRENESSE: Little raven; dark.

BRENNA: Streaked or spotted with a darker color.

BRENNAN, BRENNEN: Streaked or spotted with a darker color.

BRIA: Thorny; prickly.

BRICK: Clay-colored; strong; sturdy.

BRIE: Light-colored.

BRINDLE: Streaked or spotted with a darker color. Well-mannered.

BRIQUETTE: Dark gray.

BRISTLE: Short-haired.

BRISTOL: Short-haired.

BRIT: Of English descent. Red-haired.

BRONSON: Dark.

BRONZE: Reddish brown.

BROWN BEAR: Brown and ferocious.

BROWNIE, BROWNY: Brown.

BUFF, BUFFY: Golden.

BUG: Small.

BUGGLES: Small and playful; mischievous; zany.

BULGIE: Enormous.

BULKY: Large; hulking; muscular.

BUNNY: Fluffy, soft. Usually a rabbit, but can be used for any pet that hops or jumps.

BUNZI, BUNZY: Small; nestling.

BURDOCK: Strong.

BURLY: Heavy; muscular.

BURNETTA, BURNETTE: Brown; small.

BUSHBY: Like a bush, bushy.

BUSHKIN: Short.

BUSHY: Thick, overgrown; long-haired.

BUSHYTAIL: A pet with a fluffy tail.

BUTCH, BUTCHIE: Short-haired, brisk. Butch, the name of a bull terrier Beanie Baby.

BUTTERBALL: Plump.

BUTTERCUP: Blonde, tan.

BUTTERFLY: Beautiful; winged.

BUTTERMILK: Yellowish-white or tan-colored.

BUTTERSCOTCH: Golden.

BUTTERWORTH: Precious; golden.

BUTTON, BUTTONS: Tiny.

CABOODLE: The whole kit and caboodle. Any large pet.

CABOOSE: The runt.

CADDIE, CADDY: Small.

CADWALLER: Tidy.

CALICO: Spotted; multicolored.

CALLI, CALLIE: Beautiful.

CALLIS: Beauty; strength.

CALLISON: Beauty; strength.

CAMEO: Ivory-colored; small.

CANDIDA: White; pure.

CARETTA: Little maiden.

CARLITA: Little woman.

CARMEN: Rosy.

CARMINE: Passionate; red-haired.

CARNELIA: Reddish; precious.

CATLIN: Feline.

CELLA: (Latin: "cell") Small.

CEPHAS: Sturdy.

CHADWICK: Stately.

CHALLIE: Soft.

CHALLIS: Soft.

CHAMMY: Soft.

CHAMOIS: Soft.

CHARA: Gray. charcoal. A dark-colored pet.

CHARCOAL: Dark gray or black.

CHARKY: Dark as charcoal.

CHARLA: Short for Charlene. Little; ladylike.

CHARLANE, CHARLENE: Little; ladylike.

CHARMING: Attractive; enchanting.

CHEENO: Soft.

CHELINDA: Pretty.

CHENICE: Soft.

CHERISE: Slinky.

CHERUB: An angel; beautiful; chubby.

CHET: Small.

CHEWINK: Small.

CHIA: Full; creative.

CHICLET: Tiny.

CHINA: White; fragile; exotic.

CHINTZ: Bright; spotted.
CHIPA: Small.
CHIPETTA: Small.
CHIQUAPIN: Sturdy.
CHOW CHOW: A pet with a hearty appetite. Also, chow is a Chinese breed of dog.
CHRISTA: Fair one.
CHRISTABELLE: Fair one.
CHUB, CHUBS: Well-nourished.
CHUBBLES: Well-nourished.
CHUBBY: Well-nourished.
CHUD, CHUDNEY: Pudgy.
CHUNKY: Large.
CINDA, CYNDA: Light to dark gray.
CINDER: Light to dark gray.
CINNEBAR: Red-haired.
CIPRIANNA: Small.
CIRUS, CYRUS: White.
CLANCY: Green or green-eyed. Lucky.
CLARET, CLARETTE: Reddish.
CLARETHA: Reddish.
CLARETTA: Reddish.
CLARINDA: Fair one.
COCO: Light brown, dark brown, or reddish brown.
COFFY: Coffee-colored.
COLLIE: For the large, long-haired Scottish sheep dog with a long, narrow head.

COLT: Young male.
COLTON: Young male.
CON: Small.
CONCHA, CONCHO: A pet the color of a seashell.
CONCHITA: Small.
CONELLA: Furry.
CONEY: Furry.
CONLEY: Small.
CORBET, CORBIN, CORBY: A raven.
CORNEL: Small.
COTTON: White, soft.
COTY: Small.
COUGAR: A tawny-brown animal of the cat family, with a long, slender body.
COYOTE: Small wolf.
CRETA: (Latin: "chalk") Light-colored.
CRICKET: Energetic or long-legged.
CRIMSON: Red-haired.
CRINKLE: Having ripples, such as wavy fur, or wrinkles.
CRISPIN: Curly.
CRUM: Tiny.
CRUMBSY: Tiny.
CUB: A baby animal.
CUBBY: Small.
CUDDY: Small.
CUMQUAT: Tiny.
CUPCAKE: Tiny, sweet.
CURLICUE: Curly.

CURVES, CURVY: Shapely.
CUTIE: Pretty.
CUTIE PIE: Pretty.
CYBELLE: Showy.
CYLUS: Large.
DABNEY: Tiny.
DACEAN, DACEANA: Small.
DACEY: Small.
DAHVEE: Pretty.
DAINTY: Delicately pretty.
DAL: Small.
DALBELLO: Small; beautiful.
DALBY: Short for Dalmatian.
DALIA: Pretty.
DALLY: Short for Dalmatian.
DANDIE: Short for Dandie Dinmont terrier, a breed of terriers with short legs, a long body, floppy ears, and a full silky topnotch.
DANE, DAYNE: Short for Great Dane.
DAPHENA, DAPHENE: Showy.
DAPPER: Small and active, tidy.
DAPPLE: Spotted.
DAPPLEGRAY: Gray spotted with darker gray.
DARK-EYES: Soulful.
DART: Small. On target.
DEE: (Welsh) "black or dark."

DEEDA: Dark.
DEEDEE, DIDI: Black, dark.
DEEDRE: Dark.
DEEGE: Dark.
DEKE: Dark.
DELL: (Anglo-Saxon) "small valley."
DEMETRA: Healthy-looking.
DEMETRI: Healthy-looking.
DEMETRIA: Healthy-looking.
DEMPSEY: Small.
DEWDROP: Small; prized.
DIMITY: Small, pretty.
DINGO: An Australian wild dog.
DINKY: Small.
DOBIE: Short for Doberman, a breed of dog.
DODIE, DODY: Dainty.
DOEDA: Soft.
DOLL: Pretty.
DOLPH: Wolflike.
DOMINO: Black and white.
DONELLA: Ladylike.
DONELLE, DONNELL: Ruler.
DONETTE: A lady.
DONIA: A lady.
DOODLEBUG: Small.
DORY: Small. A good-hearted blue tang fish voiced by Ellen DeGeneres in the Disney animated movie *Finding Nemo*.

DOT, DOTS: A pet with spots.

DOTTIE: Dotted. A pet with spots.

DOUGH BOY: Cute. Plump.

DOUGIE: Gray.

DOUGLAS: (Celtic) "dark or gray."

DRAKE: A male duck.

DREAMY: Soft-eyed, soothing as a melody.

DRESDEN: Fine as china.

DRIBLET: Small.

DROLL: Short, stout fellow.

DUFFY: Dark.

DUMPLING: Small.

DUMPY: Unkempt.

DUNC: Brown warrior.

DUSKA: Dark.

DUSKY: Dark.

DUSTER: Golden.

DUSTIN: Golden.

DUSTY: Golden.

DWARF: Tiny.

EBONY: Black.

ECLIPSE: A large or dark-colored pet.

ELDEN, ELDON: Small.

ELDORA: Golden.

ELDWIN: Tiny.

ELVIA: Small.

ELVIN: Small.

EMERALD: Green-colored or green-eyed pet.

ERLIE: Elf-king. Small.

EULABELLE: Pretty; gentle.

EXQUISITE: Very beautiful.

EYES: Having large eyes; watchful.

FABIA: Pretty.

FALLON: Golden.

FALLY: Golden.

FANG, FANGS: A pet that has sharp teeth.

FANGORA: Sharp teeth.

FAT CAT: Plump, large. The name of a character in the novel The Adventurers by Harold Robbins.

FAYBER: Tiny elf.

FAYIA: Elf.

FAYLENE: Tiny.

FECIE: Soft. Woolly.

FEDOREE: Soft.

FIFI: Fluffy.

FILLY: Young, wild, usually a colt or mare.

FILO: Young.

FINIAN: Colorful.

FINN: Having fins.

FINNY: Having fins.

FINWICK: Having fins.

FISHBONE: Skinny.

FLABBY: Overweight.

FLATFOOT: Firm and uncompromising.

FLATTOP: A pet that has a flattened head, a low brow.

FLAVE, FLAVIA: Yellowish.

FLAVIAN: Yellowish.

FLAVIOUS: Yellow.

FLAWLESS: Perfect.

FLEA: Small.

FLECK, FLECKS: Spotted.

FLEDGLING: Young animal, especially a baby bird.

FLEECE, FLEECY: Woolly, furry.

FLEX: A muscular, very fit pet.

FLINT: Grayish or brown.

FLOP, FLOPPY: A pet with long ears.

FLORABELLE: Pretty flower.

FLOSSIE, FLOSSY: Light, fluffy. A flower.

FLOWER: Colorful. The name of the skunk in Disney's animated movie *Bambi*. Also, the name of a pet skunk at Walt Disney World, Florida.

FLUBBER: Large, plump.

FLUFF, FLUFFO: Soft and light.

FOXIE, FOXY: Slang for attractive. Clever.

FOZ: Fuzzy.

FRAZER: (Old English) "curly-haired."

FRAZZLE: Shabby. Tired.

FRECKLES: Spotted.

FRIZZ, FRIZZY: Curly haired.

FRIZZLE: Curly.

FROST: Cool; light-colored.

FROTHY: Light.

FRU-FRU: Adorned.

FUCHIA: Reddish colored.

FULVIA: Yellowish.

FUNNYFACE: Jolly, any pet with a comical face.

FURBALL: Furry.

FURRY: Hairy.

FUZZ: Soft. The name of a brown-colored Beanie Baby bear.

FUZZBALL: Puffy, soft.

FUZZER: Soft.

FUZZFACE: A pet with a fuzzy face.

FUZZY: Soft.

FUZZYFACE: A pet with a fuzzy face.

GALENA: Silvery.

GARISHA: Garish, flashy.

GARLAND: Pretty, colorful.

GENEVIEVE: Wavy.

GENTLE GIANT: Enormous but kind.

GEORGETTE: Silky.

GERMANIA: The name of a brown-colored Beanie Baby bear.

GIANT: Huge.

GIB, GIBBER: Tiny; noisy.
GIBBLER: Tiny; noisy.
GIBBY: Tiny; noisy.
GIBLET: Tiny.
GIGANTA: Giant.
GILAD: Golden.
GILDEROY: Golden.
GIMPY: Silky; accident prone.
GINGERLEE: Gangly; timid.
GLADSTONE: Stately.
GOATEE: A small, pointed beard on the chin. Any pet who seems to have a goatee. The name of a Beanie Baby mountain goat.
GODDESS: Female god. Charming; beautiful.
GOLD DUST: Golden; tiny.
GOLD, GOLDEN: Golden.
GOLDIE: Gold-colored.
GORGEOUS: Stunningly beautiful.
GRALEN: Gray-colored.
GRAND: Beautiful; large; important.
GRANDEE: Large; important.
GRANDESS: Large; important.
GRAY WOLF: Gray-colored; wolflike.
GRAY, GREY: Gray-colored.
GRAYBEARD: Gray-colored. Like an old man.

GRAYCLOUD: Gray-colored; moody.
GRAYFEATHER: Gray-colored.
GRAYLEY: Gray-colored.
GRAYSON: Gray.
GREASER: Shiny.
GREYLING: Gray-colored.
GRIFF, GRIFFY: Ruddy.
GRIFFITH: Red-haired.
GRISSLY: Gray.
GRIZZ, GRIZZY: Gray.
GRIZZLE: Gray.
GRIZZO: Gray.
GUNNY: From gunny sack. A pet that is baggy like a sack.
GWEN: White.
GWENA: White.
GWENDA: White.
GWENNIE: White.
HAIRBALL: Furry, fluffy.
HAIRY: Furry, fluffy.
HAKU: Haiku. Short, small.
HALF-PINT: Small.
HEAVEE: Heavy.
HEBE: Young.
HEFTY: Large and powerful.
HENNA: Reddish brown.
HER: Female. Lyndon Baines Johnson, the 36th President of the United States, had a dog named this during his years in the White House. He also had a dog named Him at this time.

HERVY: Serpentlike.
HILMA: Tidy.
HIM: Male. Lyndon Baines Johnson, the 36th President of the United States, had a dog named this during his years in the White House. He also had a dog named Her at this time.
HOBIE: An elf.
HOJO: Golden.
HOLLAN: Soft.
HOLLIS: Prickly.
HONEY: Tan-colored; sweet.
HONEYBEAR: Large but lovable.
HOT LEGS: Any pet with noticeably long or short legs.
HOURI: Young, beautiful.
HULKENSTEIN: Enormous; ferocious.
HULKY: Huge.
HUNK, HUNKY: Handsome; large.
HUSKY: Rugged, large, strong. An Eskimo dog.
HYA: Blue or blue-eyed.
IKO: Bearlike.
INCH: Very small. The name of a Beanie Baby worm.
INDIGO: Dark blue to grayish purple.
INKLING: Small.
INKSPOT: Dark.

INKY: Dark. The name of a Beanie Baby octopus.
IOTA: Tiny. The ninth letter of the Greek alphabet. A very small quantity.
ISOBEL: Beautiful.
IVOR: White.
IVORY: Creamy white.
JABON: Attractive; clean.
JABOT: Pretty; frilly.
JADA: Green-colored or green-eyed.
JAMBU: Leggy.
JAMOCA: Tan-colored.
JELLY BELLY: Plump.
JEN: White, fair.
JENNA: White, fair.
JERZY: Small.
JETA: Black.
JEWEL: Beautiful; treasured, valuable.
JIGGER: Small.
JIMBO: Large; scheming.
JITNEY: A token; small.
JOLENE: Colorful.
JOLETTA, JOLETTE: Colorful.
JORI, JORY: Short for Jorinda. Beautiful.
JUM JUM: Enormous.
JUMBO: Huge.
JUNE BUG: Large, brownish.
JUNIOR: Tiny; the runt; the smallest of the litter.

KADA: Small.
KALA: Black.
KALEA: Beautiful, black.
KALEI: Beautiful.
KARA: Black.
KASHTIN: Soft.
KATLIN: Feline.
KEAH: Fair.
KEANE: Fair.
KEANO: Fair.
KEBO: Handsome.
KEEBIE: Handsome.
KELVIN: Beautiful newborn.
KENJI: Handsome.
KENSA: Attractive.
KENSELLA, KENSELLE: Attractive.
KENSIE, KENSY: Handsome.
KENTON: Light-colored.
KENZI: Handsome.
KERNEL: Small.
KEWPIE: Cute. A caricatured picture or doll of a cherub.
KIA: Reddish.
KIANTI: Reddish.
KIBBLE: Small.
KIBBLER: Small.
KICKAPOO: Undefeated. Also, a mixed breed of dog: poodle and Pekinese.
KIKU: Noble flower.
KILROY: Vicious redhead.
KIRL: Curly.

KITTEN: A young cat.
KITTY: A pet name for a cat of any age.
KIWANI: Known.
KLAUS: Bearded.
KNEES: Noticeably knobby-kneed.
KY: Handsome.
KYKO: Handsome.
KYLA: Attractive.
KYLIE: Attractive.
KYRA: Attractive.
KYRIE: Attractive.
LACY: Beautiful, delicate.
LAD: Young male.
LADA: Young.
LADDIE: Young as a young boy. Warren Gamaliel Harding, the 29th President of the United States, had a dog named Laddie Dog.
LADONNA: Ladylike.
LADYBELLE: Beautiful lady.
LADYLOVE: A sweetheart.
LADYNE: Ladylike.
LALA: Colorful, pretty as a flower.
LAMBKIN: Furry, soft as a lamb.
LAMBSY: Gentle; innocent, woolly.
LAMONT: Tall.
LANKY: Long-legged.

LANNY: Muscular.

LARAMIE: Shining.

LARUE: Reddish.

LEA, LEAH: Small.

LEAF, LEAFIE: A green pet, such as a tropical bird or a lizard.

LEDO: Sparkling.

LEGGY: Lanky.

LEGS: Lanky. The name of a Beanie Baby frog.

LEIF: Dark.

LEILA: Dark.

LELA: Dark.

LELU: Dark.

LEROUX: Red-haired.

LES: Small.

LESHIA, LISHIA: Small.

LESLIE: Small.

LESSIE: Small.

LIDA: Sparkling.

LIL' BIT: Small.

LILIAS: Delicate.

LINDY: Pretty.

LIRA: (Latin: "libra," meaning a pound) The monetary unit and a silver coin of Italy. Silver-colored, valuable.

LISETTE: Playful.

LITA: Small. The real name of the boxer who played Wilson in the movie *Good Boy!*

LITTLE BIT: Small.

LITTLE BUDDY: Small pal.

LITTLE ONE: Tiny.

LITTLE RASCAL: Tiny, mischievous.

LITTLE SHEBA: Tiny queen.

LITTLE SHEP: Small shepherd.

LITTLE STAR: Small, distant.

LIZABET: Dainty.

LONGLEGS: Gangly.

LUBA: Smooth.

LUBIE: Smooth.

LULABELLE: Beautiful warrior.

LUZETTA, LUZETTE: Sparkling.

LYON: Like a lion.

MACAW: Variety of parrots of South and Central America including the largest and most spectacular birds. James Madison, the 4th President of the United States, had a pet parrot with this name.

MAGENTA: Passionate. Purplish red.

MAHOGANY: Reddish brown.

MAITLIN: Beautiful.

MALLOY: Colorful.

MAME: Graceful.

MAMIE: Mother. Graceful.

MAMMOTH: Enormous.

MANX: For the Manx, a tail-less cat.

MARAH: (Old French: "horse") A large pet.

MARCEAN, MARCEANA: White.

MARE: A female horse.

MARSALA: White.

MARSTON: Tidy.

MAYFAIR: Attractive.

MAYLENE: Attractive.

McDUFF, McDUFFY: Black.

MERLEE: Blackbird; dark.

MERLENE: Blackbird. A dark-colored pet.

MIDGE: Small. The name of Barbie's best friend.

MIDGET: Small.

MIDNIGHT: Dark gray or black.

MIGHTY MITE: Small but powerful.

MILKY: White.

MING: Delicate as a Ming vase, from a Chinese dynasty ruling 1368–1644.

MINI: Short for miniature; tiny.

MINNOW: Small.

MITE: Tiny.

MOIRA: Silky; wavy.

MOKEY: Brown.

MONGREL: A pet of mixed breed.

MONSTER: Huge animal.

MOOSEY: Mooselike.

MOP: Shaggy.

MORSEL: Small as bite-size.

MOTLEY: Consisting of or wearing a combination of different colors.

MUDDY: An unkempt pet or a pet that is a muddy color. Any pet that frequents mud puddles.

MUFF: Soft.

MURKLE: Dark.

MUSA: Mousy.

MUTSEY: A mutt.

MUTT, MUTTA: A mongrel; pet of mixed breed.

NAPPY: Hairy; sleepy.

NARITA: Beautiful pearl.

NATTY: Tidy appearance. A neat pet.

NEEDLES: Prickly.

NEWELL: Small.

NIBBLET: Tiny.

NIBBLING: Small, a morsel.

NIBBY: Tiny.

NIGHT: Dark-colored.

NIGUEL: Dark-colored.

NOBBY: Bow-legged.

NOMI: Homebody.

NOZZLE: A pet with a noticeable nose.

NUB, NUBBY: Tiny.

NUBBIN: A small or imper-

fect ear of corn. A tiny pet.
NUGGET: A lump of gold, precious. A pet that is golden-colored or small.
NUGGY: Tiny.
OLD WHITEY: White. Zachary Taylor, the 12th President of the United States, had a horse with this name.
OLE BLUE EYES: A nick name for singer Frank Sinatra. A blue-eyed pet.
OLEE: Shiny.
OLENE: Shiny.
OLIVER: Small soldier.
ORAN: Light-colored.
OREN, ORIN: White.
ORENDA, ORINDA: Golden.
OREO, ORIO: A black-and-white pet.
ORIANA: (Latin) "dawning, golden."
ORINA: Golden-haired.
ORLENA: Golden-flecked.
ORMAND, ORMOND: Bear.
OSCY: Bearlike.
OSITO: The name of a Beanie Baby bear, a reddish colored Mexican bear.
OSSIE: Bearlike. When they were kids, Donny Osmond and his brothers had a dog named Ossie, short for Osmond.

OX: Huge.
PAISLEY: Soft; colorful.
PALE FACE: Light-colored.
PALOMINO: A pale yellow horse with a white mane and tail.
PANZO: Plump.
PAPAG: Small.
PASTEL: Soft, pale colored.
PATCH, PATCHES: Scruffy.
PAULIE: Small.
PAWS, PAWLEY: A four-footed animal with claws.
PEABO: Handsome.
PEETO: Little.
PEKITO: Dark.
PENNYWORTH: Small amount. A tiny pet.
PERFECT: Flawless.
PERFECTA, PERFECTO: Flawless.
PERO: Dog.
PETITE: Small, pretty.
PHELAN: A wolf.
PINHEAD: Tiny.
PINTO: Marked with spots or more than one color, especially a pinto horse or pony.
PIP: Short for Pipsqueak. Very small. Slang for something remarkable. When Donny Osmond was a kid, he and his brothers had a brown Labrador with this name.

PIPKIN: A small earthenware pot. Any pet that is small.
PIPPER: Small, cute.
PIPSQUEAK: Anything or anyone regarded as small.
PIPSY: Small.
PIXIE, PIXY: Tiny. A fairy, a sprite.
PIXLEY: Small.
PLENTY: Plump.
PLUMPERFECT: Small; excellent.
POCKETS: A plump pet that appears to be stuffed; full pockets.
POCO: Little.
PODGY: Pudgy; short.
POLKADOT, POLKA-DOTS: Spotted.
POLLIWOG: A tadpole. A small pet.
POM POM, POM PON: A ball of feathers, fur. Soft, fluffy.
POMEROY: Red-haired.
POMPADOUR: Bushy-haired.
PONGEE: A soft, thin silk cloth, usually left in its natural light brown color.
POOCH: Slang for a dog, especially a mongrel.
POOCHI, POOCHIE: Any pet of mixed breed.

POOPSI, POOPSY, POOPY: Unkempt; messy.
POPPET: Golden red. Joe Namath, a former football star quarterback, has a cat named Poppet.
PORKO: Plump.
POTBELLY: Having a round, plump belly.
POTSIE, POTSY, POTTS: Plump.
POUND: One pound. Small.
PRETTY BOY: Attractive male.
PRETTY GIRL: Attractive female.
PRINCE GALLANT: Handsome; chivalrous.
PUDGY: Short and stout.
PUFFBALL: Puffy.
PUFFNSTUFF: Plump, fluffy.
PUFFY: Soft, fluffy.
PUG: A small, short-haired dog with a wrinkled face, snub nose, and curled tail.
PUGNOSE, PUGO, PUGSY: Having a short nose or snout.
PUP: Young dog.
PUTTY: Soft; manageable.
PYGMY: Any small, dwarflike pet.
QUINCE: Golden.
RAGAMUFFIN: A small, un-

kempt pet.

RAGGEDY: Unkempt. For the classic rag dolls Raggedy Ann and Raggedy Andy.

RAGS: An unkempt pet.

RAINDROP: Small. A good name for a fish.

RATINA: Frizzy.

RECELLA: Small.

REDDY: Reddish or rust-colored.

REDEYE: A pet with red eyes or whose eyes flash red in certain light.

REDFOX: Reddish or rust-colored; clever.

REDHEAD: Reddish or rust-colored.

REMMY: Small.

REX: (Latin: "king") A breed of curly-haired cat. Also, a common name for dogs. Ronald Reagan, the 40th President of the United States, had a King Charles spaniel named this.

REXI, REXY: Curly-haired.

RHINESTONE: Bright, pretty.

RIBBON, RIBBONS: Pretty, silky.

RIZZ, RIZZY: Frizzy.

RIZZO: Frizzy.

ROACH: From the insect, the cockroach. A small, untidy pet.

ROANY: Reddish brown with a thick sprinkling of gray or white.

ROENA: Small; graceful.

ROLLY, ROLY POLY: Short and plump; pudgy.

ROSABELLE: Beautiful rose.

ROSALIE: A rose.

ROSALITA: A tiny rose.

ROSAMOND: Clean rose.

ROSEBUD: The bud of a rose. Beautiful, precious, tiny.

ROSELLA, ROSELLE: A rose.

ROSE PETAL: Rose leaf.

ROSETTE: Small rose.

ROSY: Blushing.

ROYCE: Red-haired.

RUBINOOS: Red nose.

RUDD, RUDDY: Reddish.

RUDYARD: Reddish.

RUFFLES: A frilly, well-groomed pet.

RUGGLES: Strong, rugged.

RUGRAT: A young pet.

RUNT, RUNTY: The smallest animal of the litter. A tiny pet, with stunted growth.

RUSSO: Red-haired.

RUSTY: A rust-colored pet. Actor David Hasselhoff, the former star of the TV series "Knight Rider" and star of

"Baywatch," has a Shih Tzu with this name.

SABINA: Young.

SABLE: Dark, black.

SACK: Large.

SAFFY: Golden.

SAFIRE: Sapphire, a gem.

SAGS: A pet with loose skin.

SALANA: Soft.

SAMBO: Small, dark.

SAN: Sandy-haired; saintly.

SANDY: Blonde.

SASHA: Cute, petite.

SATINA: Silky.

SAVONNE: Clean.

SCANT: Tiny. Short.

SCHNOZZE, SCHNOZZLE: Any pet with a large nose, beak, or snout.

SCHWATZIE: Black.

SCRAGGY: Lean, bony.

SCRUBBY: Small.

SCRUFF: Unkempt.

SCRUMBLE: Soft.

SCRUMPY: Excellent, gorgeous.

SCRUPLES: (Latin: "a small sharp stone") A very small amount; a tiny pet.

SCUZZBALL: Unkempt.

SCUZZY: Unkempt.

SEBAY: Reddish brown.

SEPIA: Dark brown.

SHABBY: Unkempt.

SHADAI: Dark.

SHALANA, SHALENA, SHALENE: Soft; exotic.

SHALISE: Soft.

SHAMOO: Large.

SHANI: Pale.

SHANICE: Small; wise.

SHARLA, SHARLANE, SHARLEE: Little, ladylike.

SHARLENA, SHARLENE: Charlene. Little, ladylike.

SHARNA: Little, ladylike.

SHARONA: Pretty flower.

SHASHA: Cute, petite.

SHAUGHNESSEY: Lean, tidy.

SHAVER: Short-haired.

SHEALY: Ladylike.

SHEENA: An Irish form of Jane. Shiny.

SHEP: Short for shepherd.

SHEPHERD: For German Shepherd, a breed of dog often trained as police dogs.

SHERILEE, SHERILYN: Little, womanly.

SHERM: Fair-haired.

SHERMIE: Fair-haired.

SHINER, SHINY: Radiant.

SHORT LEGS: A small pet.

SHORTSTUFF: Short.

SHORTY: Having short legs.

SHOT: Fast.

SIENNA: Yellowish brown,

golden.

SILKY: Smooth and flowing.

SILVERADO: Valuable, silver and gold.

SILVERBELLE: Gray or silvery.

SILVER DOLLAR: Valuable, gray or silvery.

SKIFF: Small.

SKIMP, SKIMPY: Very little; stingy.

SKINNER: Lean, thin.

SKINNY: Lean, thin.

SLATER: Gray.

SLIPPERS: A pet that appears to be wearing shoes or slippers. Theodore Roosevelt, the 26th President of the United States, had a cat with this name.

SLOPPY: Untidy.

SMALLFRY: Small fish. Also, small children.

SMIDGEN: A small amount, a bit.

SMIDGET: From smidgen. A small amount, a bit.

SMITHEREEN: A small amount, a bit.

SMOKY: Gray.

SMUDGE: Unkempt, messy.

SMUDGY: Soiled.

SMUTT, SMUTTY: Soot-colored, black.

SNAKEY: Snakelike.

SNAZZ, SNAZZY: Great-looking.

SNIP, SNIPPY: A small, young pet.

SNOW, SNOWY: White as snow, fluffy.

SNOWBALL: A fluffy, solid-white pet.

SNOWDRIFT: A pet that has heaps of soft, white fur.

SNOWDROP: Small, solid-white pet.

SNOWFIRE: Bright white or golden white.

SNOWFLAKE, SNOWFLAKES: A fluffy, solid-white pet.

SNOWSER: A pet of mixed breed, usually a dog.

SNOWY: White.

SNUBNOSE: A pet with a short or flat nose.

SOCKS: A pet that appears to be wearing socks. President Clinton, the 42nd President of the Unites States, had a cat with this name during his years in the White House.

SONNIE: Young. Herbert Hoover, the 31st President of the United States, had a fox terrier with this name.

SONNY: Little son.

SOOTY: Black.

SPADO: Dark.
SPARK: Little but fiery tempered. Also, a gallant young man.
SPAZZY: Attractive.
SPECK: Tiny.
SPECKLES: A pet with small spots, speckled.
SPIFF, SPIFFY: Fine-looking.
SPOT: A pet with spots. President George W. Bush, the 43rd President of the Unites States, has a dog with this name. Spot is returning to the White House; as a pup, Spot enjoyed life at Pennsylvania Avenue with his mother, Millie, the English springer spaniel of former President George Bush.
SPOTS: A spotted pet.
SPOTTY: A spotted pet. The name of the pet leopard of Prince Memnon of Ethiopia.
SPRECKLES: Speckled.
SPRIG: A little twig, tiny.
SPRINGER: Short for springer spaniel. Any highly active pet.
SPROUT: A bud, a small pet.
SPUD: Slang for a potato. A small pet.
SQUIRT: Fast, small.
SQYDEL: Small.

STALKY: Tall, thin.
STALLION: A male horse.
STANTON: Colorful.
STARBUCK: Bright.
STARDUST: Bright, small.
STARLA: Bright, starry-eyed.
STARLET: Tiny star, bright.
STARLIGHT: Lighted as a star.
STARRY: Shining like a star, bright.
STARSHINE: Shining like a star.
STICKY: Prickly.
STIGG, STIGGY: Prickly.
STOCKARD: Sturdy.
STOCKINGS: A pet that appears to be wearing stockings because of a change in coloration.
STOCKY: Heavily built, sturdy.
STODGY: Bulky.
STRINGBEAN: Thin, lean.
STRINGY: Thin, lean.
STRIPE, STRIPES, STRIPER: A pet that appears to have stripes.
STUBBY: Short. A pet with short legs.
STUD: Attractive male.
STUFFIN': Well-nourished, stuffed, plump.
STUMPY: Short.

SUEBELLE: Pretty lily.
SUEDE: Short-haired.
SULLY: Unkempt.
SUNDOWN: Golden as the setting sun.
SUNLIGHT: Golden.
SUNNY: Bright, golden.
SUNRISE: A pet that gets up at the break of dawn.
SUSU: Lily; pretty.
SUZANNE: Pretty.
SUZE: Pretty.
SUZETTE: A form of Susan. Pretty.
SUZISUE: (Pronounced "soozy-soo") Pretty.
SUZY: Pretty. The object of a lover's affection in the song titled "Suzy Q" by Creedence Clearwater Revival.
SWARTHY: Dark.
SY: Solid-looking.
SYRUS: White.
TAB: Tiny.
TABBA: Tabby.
TABBY: A striped cat or kitten.
TACITA: Small.
TAD, TADDY: Tiny.
TANA, TANNA, TANDY, TANE: Tan or light brown.
TANESHA, TANISHA: Tan.
TANGERINA: From Tangier. Reddish yellow.

TANGIE: Tart. Reddish yellow.
TANGLES: A pet that often appears unkempt.
TANITA: Tan.
TANNER, TANNY, TANO, TANSY: Tan.
TAR BABY: Black.
TARPO, TARRIA, TARRY: Dark.
TARRY: Black.
TASSEL, TASSIE: Pretty, well-groomed.
TATTERS: Unkempt.
TAWNA, TAWNY: Brownish yellow or tan.
TEE CEE: Small.
TEENIE, TEENY, TENNY, TINNY: Tiny.
TERRA: From terracotta, a hard, brownish red, usually unglazed earthenware used for pottery. Terra also means "earth," from which terracotta is derived.
TEX: Short for Texas. Big.
TEXY: Big.
THIMBLENA: Tiny.
THOM: Little.
THORNE: Prickly.
TIAN: Red.
TIANA: (Pronounced "tee-ena") A red or rust-colored pet.
TIARA: Pretty as a jeweled

crown.

TIDBIT: Little thing, tiny.

TIGE: Tiger.

TIGERA: Tiger.

TIGRA: Tiger.

TIMBO: Handsome.

TINY: Petite, very small. Franklin Delano Roosevelt, the 32nd President of the United States, had an English sheepdog with this name.

TIP, TIPPER: Small present.

TIPPY: Small present.

TITIAN: Auburn.

TOBIAS: Stout.

TOBIN: Stout.

TOBY: Stout.

TOGA: Baggy. A loose garment outer garment as that of the ancient Romans.

TOGE, TOGY: Well-groomed.

TONETTE: Attractive, stylish.

TONI, TONY: Handsome, stylish.

TONIO: Handsome, stylish.

TONITA: Dark.

TONKA: Sturdy. The name of a popular brand of toy truck.

TONYA: Attractive, stylish.

TOT: A very small amount;

TOTSY: Tiny.

TOUKIE: Brightly colored.

TOUSLE: Disorder, unkempt mass of hair.

TOWSER: Blond.

TOWY: Blond.

TOYA: Pretty; tiny.

TRACKS: Messy.

TREG: Trim, neat.

TRESS, TRESSA: Curly-haired.

TRINKET: Pretty as a jewel.

TRIXIE: A pixie; a small pet.

TROY: Curly-haired. An ancient city in northwest Asia Minor.

TUBBY, TUBS: Pudgy.

TUFF, TUFFY: Solid, strong.

TULA: A beauty.

TUMMY: Plump.

TURQUOISE: A pale blue green, green-eyed.

TUTONE: Having shades of two colors.

TWIG: Small.

TWILIGHT: Gray or black.

TWILLA: Dark.

TWILLY: Sturdy, strong.

TWYLA: Dark.

TYKE: Wee one, tiny.

UNDINE: Flowing, curly, wavy.

URCHIN: A mischievous youngster.

VANILLA, VANILLI: Golden, light tan.

VELLUS: Shaggy-haired.
VELOTTA: Soft.
VERDI, VERDIE: Green, green-eyed.
VERMILLION: Red, red-haired, auburn.
VERTIE: Green, green-eyed.
VITTA: Striped.
WABBLES: A pet that wobbles while walking.
WADDLE, WADDLES: A pet that sways when walking. A good name for a duck or a rotund cat or dog.
WALDORF: Small ruler.
WANNETTA, WANNETTE: Pale one.
WAVY: Curly, wavy-haired.
WEE: Tiny.
WEEBO: Small, sturdy, and handsome.
WEEBY: Small.
WEENSIE: From teensie weensie, very small, tiny.
WENETTA, WENETTE: White.
WENNIE: White.
WENSLEY: White.
WESTIE: For the tiny breed of dog the West Highland White Terrier.
WHIFFET: Small; young. Benjamin Harrison, the 23rd President of the United States,

had a goat with this name.
WHISKERS: Long, bristly hairs on the lips or cheek of a cat, dog, or other pet. Benjamin Harrison, the 23rd President of the United States, had a goat with this name.
WHIT: Tiny.
WHITBY: Tiny.
WHITE, WHITEY: White, snowy.
WHITE TIP: A pet with a white tip on its tail or ears. Caroline Kennedy, daughter of the 35th President of the United States John F. Kennedy, had a puppy named this when her father was President.
WHITLEY: Tiny.
WHOPPER: Large, enormous.
WICKSY: Small.
WIDGET: Short, small.
WIGGY: Short.
WILLA: Thin, flexible.
WILLABELLE: Willowy, flexible, thin.
WILLO: Thin, willowy.
WILTON: Velvety.
WINFRED: White wave.
WISEGUY: Small fellow.
WOLFEN, WOLFIE, WOLFKA: Wolflike.
WOLFRAM: Brownish or

blackish.

WOOLLY: Furry, shaggy. For the woolly mammoth, a prehistoric elephant that is now extinct.

WOOLSY: Woolly, furry.

WORM: Wiggly.

WRINKLE, WRINKLES: A pet with folds of loose skin or fur.

WUZZY: From "fuzzy wuzzy," a pet that is furry.

WYNETTE: White, bright.

WYOMIE, WYONA: Large.

XANTHIA, XANTHE: Yellow.

YANA: (Spanish) "black."

YELLA: Yellow.

YOUNGSTER: A young animal.

ZAMBU: Young.

ZAR, ZAREK: Golden.

ZEPPELIN: A large pet. A zeppelin is a dirigible airship with a cigar-shaped bag.

ZINGY: Strikingly attractive.

ZUNIE, ZUNI: Sleek.

Did You Know?

MAF: The name of movie legend Marilyn Monroe's poodle.

FLOSSIE: Actress Drew Barrymore, star of the *Charlie's Angels* movies and others, has a lab-chow mixed dog with this name. Flossie alerted Drew and her then-fiancé actor Tom Green of a house fire in February 2001 and they and their hero Flossie escaped to safety!

THOR: (Scandinavian: "thunder") In Norse mythology, the god of thunder, war and strength. Also, the name of a popular comic book superhero. A very strong, loud pet. The name of Shaquille O'Neal's Rottweiler.

Dribbles

CORWIN AND ADDIE

Chapter 2

PERSONALITY AND BEHAVIOR

Just watching your new pet's behavior, including its personality and actions, may spark your imagination and inspire the perfect name. For example, a cheerful pet may be named *Smiley*, *Gayla*, *Rissa*; a mischievous pet: *Bandit*, *Rascal*, *Scampy*; and, of course, there are numerous other behavioral traits and mannerisms that inspire names, such as *Digger*, *Scratches*, *Dribbles*.

ADDIS: Aristocratic.

ADDISON: Aristocratic.

ADELA: Noble.

ADELAI: Noble.

ADELAIDE: Having nobility.

ADELBERT: Bright, noble.

ADELE: Noble.

ADELIA: Noble.

ADELINA, ADELINE: Noble, musical.

AFRA: Peaceful ruler. Also spelled Aphra.

AFTON: Upbeat, positive.

AIDAN: Humble. Adventuresome.

AILSA: Cheerful.

AINSLEY: Manly.

AINSWORTH: Bold.

AKEA: Bright.

AKEI, AKI: Bright.

AKIRA: Bright.

ALAI: Merry.

ALAINA: Harmonious.

ALAN: Harmonious.

ALANNA: Harmonious.

ALARICE: Leader.

ALBA: Bright, noble.

ALBERTO: Honorable.

ALBY: Bright.

ALDA: Good spirits.

ALDEA: Protector.

ALDEN: Protector.

ALDORA: Guardian.

ALEDA: Wise.

ALENA, ALENE: Noble; musical.

ALESSI: Helper.

ALESTEDE: Helper.

ALGER: Noble.

ALINA, ALINE: Noble; musical.

ALISE: Fiery. Temperamental.

ALLEGRO: Brisk, lively, musical.

ALLIE, ALLY: Friend. Ally, the name of a Beanie Baby alligator.

ALLURA: Alluring; full of charm.

ALPHONSINE: Feisty.

ALVY: Noble friend.

ALWIN: Noble friend.

AMIA: Friend.

ANAIS: Graceful.

ANALEAH: Graceful.

ANALISE: Graceful.

ANDON: Manly.

ANELLE: Graceful.

ANGUS: Strong.

ANIQUE: Graceful.

ANJOI: Grace and joy.

ANON: Graceful.

ANSEL: Defender.

ANSELM: Defender.

ANSLEY: Defender.

ANTSY: An energetic pet who can't sit still.

APHRA: Peaceful ruler.

ARABELLA, ARABELLE: Courageous heroine. In 1973, a spider named Arabella was sent into space to prove a high school kid's theory: spiders *can* build webs in space.

ARBY: Insightful.

ARDELIA: Devoted.

ARDELLA, ARDELLE: Enthusiastic, devoted.

ARGIE: An alert watcher.

ARIS: Intelligent.

ARISSA: Intelligent.

ARLANA: Beaming.

ARROGANCE: False pride.

ARSHA: Fiery.

ARTICUS: Brave.

ARVEL: Heartbreaker.

ARVILLE: Dazzlingly bright.

ATAKAPA: Ferocious.

ATAR, ATARA: Venomous.

AUDIE: Noble strength.

AUDRA, AUDRIA: Noble.

AURELIUS: A good listener.

AVANTI: Progressive.

AVARIS: Greedy.

BABOO: Respectful.

BAD BOY, BAD GIRL: Spoiled, rowdy.

BAD GUY: Spoiled, rowdy.

BALDWIN: Bold, friend.

BALKY: Stubborn; a pet who refuses to move.

BANDIT: An outlaw; a pirate.

BANDY: Careless.

BANNON: Bossy.

BARNETT: In command.

BARRON: Noble warrior.
BARTON: Dashing.
BASHFUL: A pet that is shy, likes to hide from strangers.
BATHSHEBA: Loyal.
BEAMER: Radiant; cheerful.
BECKET: Saintly.
BEE-BEE: Intelligent.
BELENA: Graceful.
BELITA: Graceful.
BENAY: Wise.
BERNARDO: Brave.
BERNIE: Brave. The name of a Beanie Baby St. Bernard.
BERTIE: Intelligent.
BETTE: Serene.
BEVAN: Youthful warrior.
BILLIE: Guardian.
BINKEY, BINKY: Good-natured, easygoing.
BIZ: Short for show biz. Any pet that behaves like a star.
BIZZY: Always busy.
BLADE: Sharp-witted.
BLAIR: Quiet.
BLAZER: Fiery.
BLENDA: Easygoing.
BLINK, BLINKER: Any pet that blinks a lot.
BLINKS, BLINKY: Any pet that blinks a lot.
BLISS: Joyful.
BLUE DEVIL: Moody.
BLUFF: Unpredictable.

BLYTHE: Cheerful.
BOBINA: Intelligent.
BONTE: Good.
BOOFUS: Frightening.
BOOGEDY: Scary.
BOOKI: (Pronounced "boo-ki") Bookish, intelligent.
BOOPERS: Clumsy.
BOOPIE: Accident-prone.
BOXCAR: Introverted.
BRACER: Strong-willed, firm.
BRADFORD: Open-hearted.
BRAINS: A very intelligent pet.
BRANDALL: Mellow.
BRAVO: Approving.
BRAZEN: Shameless.
BREN: Fiery.
BRIANNA, BRIANNE: Strong, graceful.
BRIGGITTE: Strong.
BRIGHT: Smart.
BRIGHTON: Intelligent.
BRIGID: Strong.
BRINA: Protector.
BRITCHES: Independent. Also spelled Breeches.
BRUBAKER: Strong-willed.
BRUNELLA, BRUNELLE: Smart.
BUB, BUD: A friend.
BUMBLE: Clumsy.
BUMBLEBEE: Busy.

BYRON: Homebody.
CAL: Trustworthy.
CAMILLA, CAMILLE: Elegant; pure.
CAMPY: Eccentric.
CANDACE: Gentle.
CANDRA: Bright.
CARA: A friend.
CARAS: Always friendly.
CAREME: Pleasing.
CAREY: Caring.
CARINA: (Latin: "keel") Level-headed.
CARLA: Easygoing.
CARLISLE, CARLYLE: Mysterious.
CARLY: Easygoing.
CASIMIR: Peace loving.
CASS: Helper.
CASSIDY: Innocent.
CASTOR: Industrious.
CATHARINA: Purity.
CATHERINE: (Greek) "pure."
CATO: Cautious.
CATRINA: Graceful.
CAVALIER: Gallant, especially a horse.
CECINDA: Trusting.
CEE: Good-natured.
CEE CEE: Good-natured.
CEEJAY, CJ: Good-natured; playful.
CELLE: Tempestuous.

CHADNEY: Hot-tempered.
CHAFEE: Warm.
CHANCY: (Scottish) "lucky."
CHANDA: Bright.
CHANDELLE: Bright.
CHANDLER: Bright.
CHANDRA: Bright.
CHANGE: Moody.
CHAPPY: Friendly fellow. The name of the smelly poodle at Phoebe's wedding in the TV series "Friends."
CHARELLE: Strong.
CHAZZ: Self-assured.
CHESLEY: Intelligent.
CHESNEY: Intelligent.
CHESSIE: Intelligent.
CHESTLY: Proud.
CHEZZ: Intelligent.
CHI: Pronounced "chee", a Chinese word, meaning "natural energy of the universe."
CHICA: Clever.
CHIVALRY: Respectful. Protector.
CHRISTEL: Brave one.
CHUM, CHUMMY: Friend.
CHUMLEY: Chum, companion.
CID: Hero.
CIE: Good-natured.
CILLA: Trusting.
CILLAY: Trusting.

CIMARRON: Moody.
CIMONE: Attentive.
CLAIREE: Bright.
CLARENA, CLARENE: Bright.
CLARICE: Bright.
CLAUDIA, CLAUDIE: Frail.
CLAUDIO: Frail.
CLAUDIS: Frail.
CLAYTON: Easygoing.
CLEMEN, CLEMENT: Merciful.
CLEMENCY: Merciful.
CLEMENTINA: Merciful.
CLEMENTINE: Merciful. From the old song "Oh My Darlin' Clementine."
CLEMMY: (Latin) "merciful."
CLENICE: Kind.
CLEVE: Intelligent. Quick-witted. Short for Cleveland.
CLIVE: Lofty.
CLOTHILDA: Feisty.
CLOTILDA: Feisty.
CLOVIS: Spicy.
COLBY: Hard worker.
COMPADRE: Companion.
COMPANION: Friend.
CONROY: Intelligent.
CONSTANCE: Faithful.
CONSTANT: Faithful.
CONSUELA: Comforting.
COOKIE, COOKY: Smart, sweet.
COOLEY: Pleasing; excellent.
COOT: Set in his or her ways.
CORENA, CORENE: Warm-hearted.
CORETA: Warm-hearted.
CORITA: Warm-hearted.
CORLISS: Warm-hearted.
CORLY: Warm-hearted.
CORNELIA: Noble.
CORNELLA, CORNELLE: Noble.
CORNELLIA: Heavenly, noble.
CORWIN: Devoted.
COURAGE: Heroic protector; fearless.
COURTLAND: Dignified.
COURTLY: Dignified.
COY: Shy, bashful, quiet.
CULLY: Fellow, pal.
CYANNA: Graceful.
CYCLONE: Temperamental.
CYRELLE: Serene.
CYRENE: Serene.
DAGO: Sharp.
DALTON: Dedicated.
DAMAR: Gentle.
DAMARIA, DAMARIS: Gentle.
DAME: Ladylike.
DAMIAN: Tame.
DANCY: A dancer.

DANITA: Trusting.
DANON: Confident.
DARA, DARAH: Wise.
DARBY: Harmonious.
DARCEL: Protector.
DARCY: Protector.
DARGO: Courageous.
DARNEL, DARNELL: Ill-tempered.
DARNELLA: Ill-tempered.
DARVIN: Noble.
DARVISH: Noble.
DAX: Intelligent.
DEACON: Servant.
DEANNA, DEANNE: Bright.
DEBS: Busy.
DEELE: Honest.
DELAMETRI: Noble, godly.
DELLA: Noble.
DELLO: Noble.
DELPHE: Serene.
DELPHINA, DELPHINE: Temperate.
DEMURE: Serious.
DEMYRA: Rebellious.
DENNY: Mellow.
DERA: Daring.
DESHAUN: Gracious.
DESMA: Trusted.
DESMOND: Faithful.
DEVERE: Honest.
DEVIN: Divine.
DEVINA: Divine.
DEVITA: Divine.

DEVLIN: Mischievous.
DEVO: Short for devoted. A name for any loyal pet. The name of a futuristic 1980s rock band and short for "de-evolution."
DEVOLA: Devoted.
DEVOTION: Devoted, very loyal.
DEX: Short for Dexter. Skillful.
DEXI, DEXY: Short for Dexter. Skillful.
DEXTER: (Latin) "right; skillful."
DIGGER: A pet that loves to dig.
DIGGY, DIGS: A pet that loves to dog.
DIGNA, DIGNI: Short for dignified.
DINGUS: Humorous.
DINGY: Absentminded.
DIRCE: Alluring.
DITZY: Unpredictable.
DIVA: (Latin: "goddess") Prima donna, spoiled.
DIVIA: Goddess-like.
DOBBIN: A patient horse.
DOBBY: Patient.
DOBIE, DOBY: Quiet. This can be an excellent name for a Doberman Pinscher.
DOBRY: Good.

DOEBY: Patient.
DOGBERT: Bright doggie.
DOLBY: Clear.
DOLDRUMS: Calm; bored.
DOMINA: Ladylike.
DOMINIE: (Latin: "lord") A master.
DOMINION: (Latin: "lord") Ruler.
DONA: Lady.
DONATA: Charitable.
DONDRE: Ruler.
DORCAS: Full of grace.
DORCY: Graceful.
DORUS: Talented one.
DOSSIE: Docile.
DOVE: Gentle, innocent.
DOZER: Overbearing.
DRIBBLES, DRIBBLER: A pet that drools.
DRIZZLY: Carefree.
DUCI: Leader.
DUFFER: Awkward.
DUKENHEIMER: Leader.
DYNAST: Ruler.
DYNASTY: Ruler.
EASY: Easygoing.
EB: Courageous.
ECSTASY: Rapture. Passionate.
EDA: Ruler.
EDAN: Hot-tempered.
EDANA: Hot-tempered.
EDBERT: Bright one.

EDELINA, EDELINE: Simple.
EDELLE: Simple.
EDEN: (Hebrew) "delight."
EDENA, EDDENA: Delight.
EDREA: Helpful.
EDRED: Helpful.
EDRIC: Ruler.
EDSON: Protector.
EDWALD: Strong.
EDWARD: Valued guardian.
EDWARDINE: Valued guardian.
EFREM: Shameless.
EGAN: Glowing.
EGBERTA: Bright.
EGMONT: Strong protector.
EGO: (Latin: "I") Self-centered.
ELANA: Warm.
ELBERT: Bright, noble.
ELBERTA: Bright.
ELDRED: Wise.
ELENA, ELENE: Warm.
ELFREDA: Friendly.
ELISKA: Reverent.
ELISSA: Honest.
ELKE: A form of Alice or Alexandra. Truthful.
ELLBY: Glowing.
DOC: Caring.
DOCEAN: Gracious.
DOCIE: Docile.
DOCILLA: Docile.

ELLI, ELLIE: Gentle.
ELLSMERE: Glowing.
ELRICA: Quiet.
ELVINA: Stubborn.
EMBER: Hot-tempered.
EMMILOU: Nurturing.
ENCHANTRESS: Charming; delightful.
ENOCH: Dedicated. Calvin Coolidge, the 30th President of the United States, had a goose with this name.
ENOS: Earnest.
ENRICO: Leader.
ERASMA: Friend.
ERGON: Worker.
ERICA: Ruler.
ERIE: Frightening.
ERLENE, ERLINE: Trusted.
ERNA: Strong willed.
ERVIN: Friend.
ERWIN: Friend.
ESMOND: Protector.
ESSIE: Attentive.
ESTEE: Highly esteemed.
ETTA: Ruler.
EULA: Gentle.
EULACIA: Gentle one.
EULAMAE: Gentle, trustful.
EULESS: Good. Gentle.
EVALD: Powerful.
EVERLY: Pleasant.
EXXI: Outgoing.
EZZI: Helpful.

FAITH: Hope, trust.
FAITHFUL: Loyal, keeping the faith. Ulysses S. Grant, the 18th President of the United States, had a Newfoundland with this name.
FALA: Bright.
FALANA: Musical; bright.
FALLA: Deceptive.
FANG: Vicious. Common name for a Chihuahua.
FARNSWORTH: Distant.
FARQUHAR: Manly.
FAZON: Pesky.
FELICE: Happy one.
FELICITY: Happiness, blissful.
FELIPA: Horse-lover.
FELIPE: Horse-lover.
FENNI: Defensive.
FENWICK: Aristocratic.
FICKLE: Moody.
FIDO: (Latin: "faithful") Well-known name for a dog.
FINI: Short for finicky. Fussy.
FINICKY: Fussy.
FINKLE: Fussy.
FINOLA: Joyful.
FIOLA: Ladylike.
FIONA: Ladylike.
FITZ: Temperamental.
FONDA: Resolute.
FOXWORTH: Sly.
FRANCOIS: Friendly.

FREDO: Ruler.
FRESIA: Refreshing.
FREYA: Refreshing.
FRIAR: Nurturing.
FRIEND: Companion.
FRIENDLY: Warm, loving.
FRITZI: Peaceful ruler.
FURY: Rage. Temperamental.
FUSSY: Argumentative.
FYVISH: Stubborn.
GABE: Devoted, strong.
GALE: Happy, easygoing.
GAR: (Anglo-Saxon: "spear")
Sharp-witted.
GARDA: Strong.
GARDINER: Guardian.
GARRISON: Defensive;
watchful.
GASPER: Sensitive.
GASTON: Stubborn.
GAY: Joyous and lively.
GAYDEN: Happy.
GAYLA, GAYLENE: Joyful.
GAYLEY, GAYLY: Happy.
GAYLON: Cheerful.
GAYLOR: Cheerful.
GAYLYNN: Joyful.
GERALL: Ruler.
GERBER, GERBERT:
Growing.
GERDA: Protector.
GERINA: Growing.
GIELGUD: Giving.
GIFF: Short for Gifford.

Courageous.
GIFFORD: Courageous.
GIFFY: Short for Gifford.
Courageous.
GIL: Bright.
GILBERT: Bright.
GILBERTINA: Bright.
GILBY: Short for Gilbert and
Gilbertina. Bright.
GILFORD: Devoted.
GINGER BOY: Spicy, spir-
ited fellow. General Omar
Bradley, who led the U.S. 1st
Army in the invasion of Nor-
mandy during World War II,
had a dog with this name.
GINGY: Spicy.
GOODFELLOW: Likeable.
GORDIE: Considerate.
GORDON: Considerate.
GORMON: Brave.
GRACEFUL: Beautiful
movement or expression.
GRACIA: Graceful, attractive.
GREGOR: Watchful.
GRIEF: A complainer.
GRISSELA, GRISSEL: Res-
olute.
GRITTY: Brave.
GROWL: Ill-mannered.
GRUMBLE,
GRUMBLES: Stubborn, argu-
mentative.
GRUMPY: Bad-tempered.

GUARDIAN: Protector.
GUISEPPE: A worker.
GUTSY: Brave.
GUY: Leader.
GUYLA: Leader.
GUYLON: Leader.
HAAKON: Loyal family member.
HAIDEE: Humble.
HAISIE: Moody.
HAKEEM: Wise, learned.
HALBERT: Bright, strong.
HARLAN: Leader.
HAROD: Leader.
HARRON: Home ruler.
HATTIE, HATTY: Ruler.
HEDDA: Prissy.
HEDDIE, HEDDY: Prissy; resting.
HEDIA: Agreeable.
HEDRA: Agreeable.
HEDWIG: Protective.
HELENA: Bright.
HELENUS: Bright.
HELOISE: Helpful.
HELSA: Loyal, faithful.
HENRIKA: Modest.
HEROD: Ruler.
HERSCHEL: Watchful.
HEYWARD: Attentive.
HEYWOOD: Attentive.
HIRAM: Noble.
HIRO, HIROSHI: Generous.
HOBART: Smart.

HOKUM: Sentimental.
HONEST: Truthful.
HONESTINE: Honorable.
HONESTY: Honorable, truthful.
HONOR: Respectful.
HONORA: Honorable.
HONORE: (Pronounced "ON-ree") Honorable.
HONORIA: Honorable.
HORATIO: Honorable.
HOT STUFF: Self-assured, egotistical.
HUBIE: Bright.
HUCKABY: Bright.
HUCKLEBERRY: Free-spirited boy in *The Adventures of Huckleberry Finn* by Mark Twain.
HUFF, HUFFY: Hot-tempered.
HUZZA: Cheerful.
IBBY: Smart.
IDA: Goddess of youth.
IDALINE: Goddess.
IDAMAE: Goddess.
IDELLA, IDELLE: Happy.
IGGY: Short for Igneous. Fiery. The name of the tie-dyed Beanie Baby iguana.
IGMAR: Fiery.
IGNACE: Fiery.
IGNACIA: Fiery.
IGNEOUS: Fiery.

ILEANA: Stubborn.
IMADENE: Likable.
INGA: Fiery.
INGMAR: Fiery.
ILSE: (Old German) "noble."
IMOGEN, IMOGENE: Likable.
INA: Considerate.
INEZ: Chaste.
IOLA: Passionate.
IRI: Peaceful.
IRMA: Warrior.
ISABELLA, ISABELLE: Beautiful.
JABEZ: Sensitive.
JACALYN: Graceful.
JACE: Healer.
JACINDA: Bright, shining.
JACOBI: A schemer.
JAKARI: Self-centered.
JAKO: Schemer.
JALENE: Jealous.
JAMILA: Schemer.
JAMILEE: Schemer.
JAMILLE: Schemer.
JANA: Gracious.
JANDI: Gracious.
JANECE: Gracious.
JANELLA, JANELLE: Gracious.
JANITA: Gracious.
JANNA: Gracious.
JANO: Gracious.
JANSON: Gracious.

JANU: Godlike.
JANZEN: Godlike.
JAREK: Ruler.
JARRETT: Watchful.
JARRIS: Watchful.
JARROD: Speared ruler.
JARVIS: Saintly.
JASTON: Healing.
JEALOUS: Envious.
JEALOUSY: Envious.
JEBE: Considerate.
JEMEZ: Imitative.
JEPH: Peaceful.
JEPTHAR: Peaceful.
JERA: Woeful.
JERELLE: Woeful.
JEREMIAD: A complainer.
JERICA: Ruler.
JERINA: Ruler.
JERINDA: Ruler.
JERLENE: Reverent.
JERMAINE: Akin.
JERON: Noble.
JERRILEE: Reverent.
JERVIS: Saintly.
JEZ: Flirtatious.
JOELLA,
JOELLE: Reverent.
JONESSY: Gracious.
JONESY: Gracious.
JON JON: Gracious.
JONNA, JONNE: Gracious.
JONSY: Gracious.
JORA: Open-minded.

JORDANA: Open-minded.
JORDY: Open-minded.
JUDGE: Authoritative.
JUDSON: Critical.
JUS: Righteous, proper.
JUSSIE: Justified.
JUSTICE: Righteous.
JUSTINA, JUSTINE: Righteous, just.
JUSTUS: Justice; righteous.
JUSTY: Justified.
KADI: Noble.
KADIN: Noble.
KAIMEE, KAYLEE: True friend. Playful, happy.
KALENA: Bright.
KANSA: Proud.
KASHA: Serene.
KASMIR: Serene.
KEEBO: Wise.
KEEGAN: Mischievous; wise.
KEEN: Wise.
KEENAN: Wise.
KEETI: Wise.
KENDA: Fiery.
KENNA: Bold.
KENNARD: Bold.
KERA: Sharp.
KIMBA: Ruler.
KIMBER: Ruler.
KIMBERLIN: Ruler.
KIMBRA: Ruler.
KIMMY: Ruler.
KIRY: Bright.

KIVA: Sacred.
KNAVE: Humble, serving.
KOOBY: Little.
KRINKLE: Wrinkled.
KYNDA: Fiery.
LAMBERT: Bright.
LANE: Solitary.
LANETTE: Solitary.
LANEY: Solitary.
LANGLEY: Distinguished.
LARINE: Flighty.
LASHANE: Gracious.
LASHAUN, LASHAUNA: Gracious.
LATISHA: Noble.
LAURENA: Brave.
LAVETTE: Impulsive.
LEANNA, LEANNE: Agreeable.
LENDI: Sharing.
LEOPOLD: Bold, strong.
LETA: Good-spirited.
LIANE: Charming.
LILLIBETH: Honest.
LINETTA, LINETTE: Graceful.
LIONHEART: Brave.
LISANNE: Honest, graceful.
LOLITA: Free spirit.
LOLLY: Jolly.
LOLLY ANN: Jolly, petite.
LONA: A loner.
LONE: A loner.
LONELY: A loner. Solitary.

LONER: Solitary.
LONESOME: Lonely. Solitary.
LONEWOLF: Loner, wild.
LONEY: Lonely, solitary.
LORE: Knowledgeable.
LOREDO: Knowledgeable.
LORELLE: Firm courage.
LORENA: Brave.
LORINDA: Courageous.
LORING: Commander.
LORIS: Shy.
LOWEY: Melancholy. Author William F. Buckley, Jr. had a spaniel with this name.
LOY: Loyal, loyalty.
LOYA: Loyal, loyalty.
LOYAL: Faithful.
LUCA, LUKA: Bright.
LUCAN: Bright. Shining.
LUCELLA: Free-spirited.
LUCIA: Bright. Shining.
LUCIANA: Bright. Shining.
LUCIEN: Bright. Shining.
LUCRETIA: Impulsive.
LUPE: Smart.
LURLENE: Bright.
LUVEN: Graceful.
LUVENIA: Graceful.
MACHO: (Spanish: "male, masculine, strong, tough") Actress Zsa Zsa Gabor has a dog with this name.
MACRINA: Obedient.

MACY: Sophisticated.
MADELLE: Devoted.
MADIGAN: Mischievous.
MADOC: Helpful.
MAJESTIC: Noble.
MAKO: Well-mannered.
MALAIKA: Ill-mannered.
MALARKEY: Pretentious.
MALEIAH: Strong.
MALLIE: Strong.
MANON: Hot-tempered.
MARA: Friendly.
MARABELLE: Friendly; pretty.
MARALINE: Easygoing.
MARCELLA: Warrior.
MARCELLE: Warrior.
MARCELLINA: Warrior.
MARCELLUS: Warrior.
MARCENE, MARCINE: Warrior.
MARELLA, MARELLE: Sensitive.
MARISOL: Bright. Noble.
MARISSA: Bright, easily understood.
MARLISS, MARLISSA: Bright; respectful.
MARLO: Respectful.
MARQUIS: Noble.
MARSE: Warrior.
MARY JANE: Rebellious; gracious.
MATO: Courageous.

MAURA: (Celtic-Gaelic) "dark."
MAURITA: Moody.
MAVEN: Independent.
MAVERICK: Independent.
MAVIE: Independent.
McKEEGAN: Playful, mischievous; wise.
MEANIE: Mischievous.
MEDWIN: Strong friend.
MEELA: Faithful.
MEESHA, MEISHA: Solitary.
MEKESHA: Faithful.
MELA: A friend.
MELAN: Short for melancholy. Gloomy.
MELANA: A friend.
MELANCHOLY: Gloomy.
MELENE: Gentle.
MELINA: Gentle.
MELVINA: A companion.
MIFFY: Temperamental.
MILBURN: Stubborn.
MINGA: Guardian.
MINGO: Guardian.
MITSY, MITZI: Rebellious.
MODESTA: Shy.
MODESTINE: Shy, modest.
MONIE: Solitary.
MOODY: Gloomy.
MOPEY: A brooder.
MORELLA, MORELLE: Rebellious.

MOREY: Rebellious.
MORILLA: Temperamental.
MORISSEY: Secure.
MORRIE: Secure.
MOUSEY: Quiet and timid like a mouse.
MOXIE: Spirited, brave.
MUTA: Moody.
MYRLIE: Obedient.
MYRON: Soothing.
NADA: Hopeful.
NADEE: Hopeful.
NALIA: Strong.
NALLIE, NELLIE: Bright.
NANNITA: Graceful.
NARCISSA: Self-absorbed.
NAYEE: Uncooperative.
NEDDA: Protector.
NEDDIE, NEDDY: Protector.
NEELY: Champion.
NEHEMIAH: Comforter.
NEILSON: Champion.
NELL, NELLA: Bright.
NELLWYN: Bright.
NELMA: Smart.
NESSA: Wise.
NETTA, NETTIE: Gracious.
NEULY: Nervous.
NICOLENA, NICOLINA: Victorious.
NICOLENE: Victorious.
NIGELLA: Champion.
NILES, NYLES: Humble.
NILLA: Humble.

NILLIE: Humble.
NOBLE: Having excellent qualities. Stately, excellent.
NOPEY: Disagreeable, stubborn.
NORBERT: Bright.
NORELL: Bright.
NORINDA: Obedient.
NORY: Bright.
OBERT: Smart.
OGILVY: Intelligent.
OLD FAITHFUL: Loyal.
OLD SAGE: Wise.
OLD SHEP: Protector, shepherd.
OLLA: Spicy; ill-mannered.
ONNIE: A loner.
ORRIE: Bright.
ORVILLE: Dazzlingly bright.
OSBERT: Bright.
OSMAN, OSMUND: Protective.
PADDY: Noble.
PANDITA: Wise.
PANGO: Temperamental.
PASCAL: Bright.
PASHA: Honorable. Richard Nixon, the 37th President of the United States, had a terrier with this name.
PATIA: Enduring, never complaining.
PATIENCE: Enduring, never complaining.

PATRICE: Noble.
PEPA: Spicy-tempered.
PEPPO: Spicy-tempered.
PERA: Arrogant.
PETRINA: Loyal, reliable.
PETRONELLA: Dependable.
PETULA: Impatient.
PHEBE: Bright one.
PHINEAS: Wise. One of the characters, Phineas T. Bluster, in the 1950s children's TV series "Howdy Dowdy."
POINDEXTER: Sharp.
POLENE: Rebellious.
PRISTINA: Unspoiled.
PRISTINE: Unspoiled.
PROTECTOR: Guardian.
QBERT: Intelligent.
QUINN: Wise.
RAE: Wise protector.
RAEANNE, RAYANNE: Wise protector.
RAFE: Natured as a wolf.
RAINE: (English) Wise ruler.
RALPHIE: Wolf-counselor.
RAMAH: Leader.
RAMON: Wise protector.
RAMONA: Wise protector.
RAMSEY: Intense.
RAPHAELA: Healer, nurturer.
RASCAL: Mischievous.
RASHAUN, RASHAUNA: Rash.

RASHELLA: Hasty.
RASTA: Likable.
RASTUS: Likable.
RAVEL: Clear.
RAYDO: Wise.
RAYMOND: Wise protector.
RAYNARD: Wise.
RAZZ, RAZZY: A teaser.
REANNA, REANNE: Gracious.
REB: Short for rebel or rebellious. Ulysses S. Grant, the 18th President of the United States, had a pony with this name.
REBA: Giving.
REBIE: Self-assured.
REDHOT: Hot-tempered, easily angered.
REDMOND: Protector.
REGALE: Delightful, pleasing.
REGENCE: Authoritative.
REGGIE: Strong ruler.
REGIS: Authoritative.
REJOICE: Happy.
RENORA, RENORE: Bright.
RHIANNON: Gracious.
RIDGE, RIDGLEY: Lofty.
RIDLEY: Timid.
RIMFIRE: Temperamental.
RISSA: Bright. Cheerful.
RIVAL: Competitive.
RIVALA: Competitive.
ROANNA: Easygoing.

ROBAIRE: Bright; wolflike.
ROBERTO: Bright.
ROLDO: Ruler.
ROLF: Wolflike.
ROLFIE: Wolflike.
ROMA: Chivalrous.
ROMAR: Chivalrous.
RORICK: Watchful protector, strong king.
RORY: Watchful protector.
ROSINA: Hopeful.
ROWENA: A friend.
ROTTEN: Mischievous; spoiled.
RUBERT: Ruler.
RUDE: Inconsiderate.
RUDELL: Inconsiderate.
RULER: Bossy.
RUMAR: Eccentric.
RUPY: Bright.
RUX: Pal.
RYKEN: Bright.
SABER, SABRE: Sharp-witted. A heavy cavalry sword with a slightly curved blade.
SABIN: Faithful.
SABON: Introverted.
SABRA: Sharp, intelligent.
SABRINA: Faithful.
SACHA: Considerate.
SADANA: Melancholy.
SAGE: Wise and perceptive.
SANARA: Comforting.
SANDRO: Helpful.

SANTANA: Saintly.
SANTE: Saintly.
SANTINA: Saintly.
SANTOS: Loyal.
SASHI: Imprudent.
SASKA: Imprudent.
SASS, SASSY: Imprudent.
SCAMP, SCAMPY: Rascally.
SCHAE: Easygoing.
SCHMO: Naive.
SCOOLY: Smart.
SCRATCHES: A pet that loves to scratch.
SCRIMPY: Stingy.
SEBOLT: Noble.
SEETHER: To seethe; easily agitated.
SELBY: Kindred, compatible.
SEMPLE, SEMPLETON: Simple; naïve.
SERGEANT: Authoritative.
SERLO: Protector.
SEWARD: Defender.
SHAKEY: Nervous, shy.
SHAME: Bashful.
SHAMEER: Guardian.
SHAMP: Mischievous.
SHARA, SHARE: Giving.
SHARETTA, SHARETTE: Giving.
SHARI: Honest.
SHARIF: Honest.
SHAUN, SHAWN: Gracious.

SHAUNA, SHAWNA: Gracious.
SHAYLA: A form of Sheila. Trusting.
SHEBRA: Noble.
SHEILA: Trusting.
SHERA: Noble.
SHERWIN: Kind.
SHIFTY: Tricky-natured.
SHIRLENA: Bright.
SHOO: Shy, timid.
SHUCKY: Disappointed.
SHUKA: Disappointed.
SHUKI: Disappointed.
SHY: Timid.
SHYLER: Shy; timid.
SHYLY: Timid.
SHYSTER: Tricky.
SIEDAH: Patient.
SIETTA: Patient.
SIGGY: Intellectual.
SIGNY: Intellectual.
SIMKINS: Naive.
SIMPLETON: Easily deceived.
SIR: Respectful.
SIZZLE: Hot-tempered.
SLICK: Clever.
SLICKER: Clever.
SLOAN: Giving.
SMARTIE: A highly intelligent pet. A smart alec, smarty pants.
SMILEY: A cheerful pet that

appears to always be smiling.
SNEAKY: A quiet, timid
pet.
SNOOKA: Clever.
SNOOKI, SNOOKY: Tricky.
SNOOKS: Interested.
SNOOKUM: Interested.
SNOOP, SNOOPER: Sneaky,
nosy.
SOFINA: Wise.
SOLAI, SOLAY: Bright.
SONDRA: Defender.
SOPHINE: Wise.
SOREHEAD: Temperamen-
tal.
SORESS: Ill-mannered.
SORI: Ill-mannered.
SOURPUSS: Gloomy, moody.
SPATZ: Argumentative.
SPICE, SPICY: A pet with a
lively, zestful personality.
SPITE: Temperamental.
SPITFIRE: A temperamental
female.
SPOOKY: Nervous, easily
scared.
STACIA, STASHA: Calm.
STING, STINGER: Tempera-
mental.
STONY: Hard, cool-headed.
STORMY: Moody.
STROKER: Affectionate.
STUBBORN: Hardheaded. A
pet that refuses to yield, obey,

or comply.
SULTRA: Sultry, fiery.
SUMMER: Warm.
SUMNER: Authoritative.
SUNBURST: A pet with a
bright, loving personality.
Golden.
SUNSHINE: Bright, a pet
with a sunny personality.
Golden.
SYRELLA, SYRELLE: No-
ble.
TAM: Gentle.
TAMA: Gentle, graceful
movements.
TAMALE: Hot-tempered.
TAMELA: Tame.
TAMESHA: Tame.
TANGY: Spicy. A hot-
tempered pet.
TANIA: Arrogant.
TANTRUM: Vicious, pout-
ing.
TEETE: Timid.
TEETRA: Timid.
TELMA: A form of Thelma.
Nurturing.
TEMPER: Temperamental.
TEMPERANCE: Moderation,
having self-discipline.
TEMPLE: Respectful.
TENA: Short for tenacious,
meaning persistent, stubborn.
TENILLE: Tender.

TESHON: Gracious.
THAD: Short for Thaddeus. Wise.
THADDEUS: Wise.
THADYS: Wise.
THANE: Trustworthy.
THELMA: Nurturing.
THERA: Nurturing.
THERON: Warm.
TIANNA: Graceful.
TIBB, TIBBY: Easygoing.
TIBBLES: Easygoing.
TICHIA, TISHA: Noble.
TIMBER: Strong of character.
TIMOTHEA: Honorable.
TINKA: Clever.
TISH, TISHA: Bright, sharp.
TITO: Leader.
TITUS: Protective.
TORESS: Hot-tempered.
TORINO: Temperamental.
TORREL, TORELL, TOR-RELL: Loyal.
TORY: Loyal, supportive.
TOSHAUN, TOSHAUNA: Gracious.
TOVA, TOVAH: Bright.
TRACE: Distant.
TRAPIS: Quiet.
TREAGUE, TRIGUE: Complex.
TREMAINE, TREMAYNE: Prudent.
TREVA: Wise.

TREVIN: Wise.
TREVOR: Wise, prudent.
TRISH, TRISHA: Noble.
TRISHKA: Noble.
TRISTA: Melancholy.
TRISTAN: Melancholy.
TRUBY: Honest.
TRUFFLES: Changeable.
TRUSTY: Trustworthy, dependable.
TRYVGE: True.
TUDIE, TUDDY: Content.
TWEAK, TWEAKY: Upbeat.
TWITCHY, TWITCHY: A nervous, fidgety pet.
TYCE: Temperamental.
TYNE, TYNETTE: Smart.
TYRA: Noble.
TYREE: Noble.
TYRELL: Noble.
TYRONE: Noble.
VENOM: Spiteful.
VENORA: Ill-tempered.
VERE: Honest.
VEREEN: Honest.
VERENA: Honest.
VIRAGO: Bold.
WHIDBY: Bold.
WHIDLEY: Bold.
WILEY: Clever.
WILLIS: Protector.
WILLOUGHBY: Delusive.
WILMER: Protector.
WINGARD: Guardian.

WINKS: A pet that blinks or winks. Franklin Delano Roosevelt, the 32nd President of the United States, had a Llewellyn setter with this name.

WINORA: Bright.

WOEBY: Woeful.

WOOBY: Woeful.

WOOSER: Woeful.

WORRY: Anxious, troubled.

WYLENE: Clever.

WYLON: Stubborn.

WYSTAN: Stubborn.

XAV: Bright.

XENIA: Kind.

YALE: Intelligent.

YAMINAH: Sweet.

YANCY: Humble.

YATES: Devoted.

YEOMAN, YEOMANLY: Brave; sturdy; faithful.

YOKEEN: Companion.

YSOLDE: Chaste.

ZABO: Bold.

ZASLO: Humble.

ZEB: Homebody.

ZELESTINE: Zealous.

ZELIA: Zealous.

ZELLA: Zealous.

ZELLY: Zealous.

ZENE: Introspective.

ZENIA: Kind-hearted.

ZENZEL: Introspective.

ZERA: Peaceful.

ZORA: Peaceful like the dawn.

ZORBA: Peaceful.

ZOREE, ZORY: Peaceful.

Did You Know?

ASHES: The name of one of author Mark Twain's pet cats.

RUFUS: (Latin: "red-haired") Popular actor Leonardo DiCaprio has a pet poodle with this name.

SCATTER: To throw about, sprinkle here and there. The King of Rock-n-Roll, Elvis Presley, had a chimpanzee named Scatter.

Oprah & Elvis

Matt

Cojo

Katie

Ann

Al

The Cast of the "Today" Show

Chapter 3

Famous People and Animals

The names of popular celebrities, past and present, provide excellent names for pets, especially if you are a fan of the celebrity who inspires the name: *J.Lo* (nickname for actress-singer Jennifer Lopez), *Elvis* (the King of Rock 'n Roll), *Cojo* (nickname for fashion guru Steven Cojocaru, *Roseanne* (the actress-comedian), *Cosby* (for actor-comedian Bill Cosby), *Oprah* (the daytime talk show queen), etc.

ABBOTT: One half the American comedy team Abbott and Costello.

AL: For Al Roker, weatherman on the NBC morning series "Today."

ANN: For journalist Ann Curry of the NBC morning series "Today."

ARETHA: (Greek: "the best") For legendary singer Aretha Franklin.

ARSENIO: For actor and former talk show host Arsenio Hall.

BAM BAM: The real name of the orangutan who played *Precious* in the daytime drama "Passions."

BELA: Honest. Known for late actor Bela Lugosi, who is best known for his starring roles in numerous horror movies. Also spelled Bella.

BEYONCÉ: For Beyonce Knowles, singer and former member of music group Destiny's Child.

BOGART: American film actor Humphrey Bogart starred in "Casablanca" and other motion pictures.

BOGIE: Nickname for Humphrey Bogart.

BOLTON: May be a very fast paced pet that "bolts," but the name is known for soulful pop singer Michael Bolton.

BORIS: (Slavic: "warrior") Known for Anglo-American actor Boris Karloff who appeared in "Frankenstein" and other horror motion pictures. Also, the villain, Boris Badenov, a Russian spy, in the cartoon TV series "Rocky and Bullwinkle."

BOSS: In charge, the chief. Nickname for rock star Bruce Springsteen.

BOWIE: Sharp. Name of English born pop singer and actor David Bowie.

CAGNEY: American film actor James Cagney who played the role of a sadistic tough guy in movies such as *Public Enemy*.

CARROT TOP: For the red-haired (nearly orange, hence carrot) and somewhat obnoxious comedian.

CARUSO: Italian operatic tenor Enrico Caruso.

CHARLIZE: For actress Charlize Theron star of *The Italian Job*.

CHEECH: For comedian-actor Cheech Marin, best known as half of the comedy team Cheech and Chong.

CHER: (French: "expensive") For the multi-talented performer Cher.

CHESNEY: For country music star Kenny Chesney.

CHEVY: To chase, hunt. Name of comedian and film actor Chevy Chase, who starred in the "Vacation" movie series as well as other films and TV series. Humorous.

CHICO: (Spanish: "small, boy") Peppy. The nickname of Leonard, the oldest brother of the comedy team the Marx Brothers.

CHONG: For Tommy Chong, half of the 1970s comedy team Cheech and Chong.

CLARK: Loyal. For actor Clark Gable who starred in "Gone With the Wind," *The Misfits*, and other movies.

COJO: Nickname for fashion guru Steven Cojocaru who appears on the "Today Show" and "Entertainment Tonight."

COS: Short for Cosby.

COSBY: For comedic actor Bill Cosby who starred in the TV series "The Cosby Show" and host of the TV series

"Kids Say the Darndest Things."

COSTELLO: One half the American comedy team Abbott and Costello.

CURLY: Curly-haired. For the most popular member of the American slapstick comedy team the Three Stooges.

DELTA: The fourth letter of the Greek alphabet. Friendly. For actress Delta Burke who starred in "Designing Women" and other TV series.

DEMI: Lady. For actress Demi Moore who starred in movies including *Ghost* with Patrick Swayze.

DENZEL: For actor Denzel Washington.

DEPP: For actor Johnny Depp who starred in the TV series "21 Jump Street" and movies including *Edward Scissorhands.*

DESI: For the actor Desi Arnaz who played Lucy's husband in the 1950s TV sitcom "I Love Lucy" and was the real-life husband of Lucille Ball.

DILLER: Comical after comedian Phyllis Diller.

DISNEY: American film producer and creator of the world's most famous mouse, Mickey Mouse, Walter Elias Disney, better known as Walt Disney.

DOLLY: A gift. The name of pop country music singer Dolly Parton, who also owns an amusement park (located in eastern Tennessee) called Dollywood.

DUKE: Ruler. Nickname for American film star John Wayne, who played tough heroes and was best known for his many roles in westerns. Rutherford B. Hayes, the 19th President of the United States, had An English mastiff with this name.

DYLAN: For American singer and composer Bob Dylan, who gained critical recognition and commercial success in the 1960s through his lyrics.

EARTHA: Down to earth. Nature lover. For actress and singer Eartha Kitt who played cat woman in the TV series "Batman."

EASTWOOD: Actor Clint Eastwood who starred in the *Dirty Harry* movie series and many westerns.

ELTON: Homebody. For pop

superstar Elton John, who recorded the soundtrack for the Disney animated feature *The Lion King*.

ELVIRA: Complete, fair one. The female entertainer who dresses in black and sometimes hosts macabre movies.

ELVIS: (Scandinavian: "all wise") For Elvis Presley, the King of Rock-n-Roll.

EMERIL: For Emeril Lagasse, the well-known chef and author.

ENGELBERT: Fiery. For pop singer Engelbert Humperdink.

ENYA: The name of a popular New Age vocalist.

FABIAN: Earthy. The name of a 1950s teen idol.

FALANA: For singer-actress Lola Falana.

FARRAH: (Middle English: "beautiful, pleasant") For Farrah Fawcett, an actress who appeared in "Charlie's Angels" and other TV series and movies, known for her thick, flowing mane of hair.

FLYNN: For actor Errol Flynn who starred in The Charge of the Light Brigade (1936) and other films. The real name of the border terrier who played Hubble in the movie *Good Boy!*

GABLE: For American film actor Clark Gable who starred as Rhett Butler in the movie version of Margaret Mitchell's sweeping novel *Gone With the Wind*.

GALLAGHER: For the stand-up comedian who uses props such as watermelons in his act.

GARBO: (Italian: "elegance") For Swedish-American actress Greta Garbo who was noted for her beauty and dramatic intensity. She starred in *Anna Karenina* and *Camille*.

GILLESPIE: For American Jazz great Dizzy Gillespie.

GOLDIE: Blonde, golden haired. Know for comedic actress Goldie Hawn.

GROUCHO: Comical, sly, a prankster. The most famous of the Marx Brothers, an American family of comedians.

GUMMO: The nickname of Milton, one of the Marx Brothers, an American family of comedians.

GUTHERIE: For American folk singer and guitarist.

HARDY: Bold. For Oliver Hardy of the American film

comedy team Laurel and Hardy.

HALLE: Loving. For Oscar-winning actress Halle Berry.

HAMILTON: The last name of actor George Hamilton.

HARLOW: For American film actress Jean Harlow, a wisecracking platinum blonde, who starred in *Blonde Bombshell* and other movies.

HARPO: The nickname of Arthur, one of the Marx Brothers, an American family of comedians.

HARRISON: For actor Harrison Ford who has starred in many movies including the action-adventure *Indiana Jones* series.

HAYLEY: Nature lover. For English actress Hayley Mills who starred in Disney movies including the immensely popular *The Parent Trap.*

HITCHCOCK: For Anglo-American film director Alfred Hitchcock, who was a master of suspense and made such films as *The Birds* and *Frenzy.*

HOPALONG: For cowboy star Hopalong Cassidy.

HUMPHREY: (Anglo-Saxon: "strength in peace") Known as the name of American actor Humphrey Bogart who starred in *The Maltese Falcon, Casablanca,* and other films. Also, the name of a Disney cartoon bear that lives in a wild-life park.

IGLOO: The troublesome fox terrier who traveled with Admiral Richard E. Byrd on his first trip to the Antarctic.

IONE: Radiant. For actress Ione Skye who starred in movie Wayne's World and others.

IVANA: For Ivanna Trump, former wife of wealthy Donald Trump.

J.LO: Nickname for singer-actress Jennifer Lopez.

JUDE: A saint. For one of the best-loved and best-known songs, "Hey, Jude," by the legendary rock band The Beatles. The song was inspired by the young son, Julian, of band member John Lennon.

JUDGE JUDY: For the outspoken judge who has her own TV series and the author of several books including Win or Lose By How You Choose and others.

KADEEM: Noble. For actor Kadeem Hardison who starred

in the TV series "A Different World."

KATIE: For Katie Couric, journalist and host of the NBC morning series "Today."

KEANU: For actor Keanu Reeves who has starred in movies including *Speed* and *Bill and Ted's Excellent Adventure.*

KEIKO: The real name of the Orca whale in the FreeWilly movies.

KENAN: For Kenan Ivory Wayans, star of movies and the TV series "In Living Color" and "My Wife and Kids." A name of Biblical origin.

KIKI: Lively, spirited. Known for singer Kiki Dee who has recorded hit duets with pop singer Elton John.

LANDAU: From German town. The surname of actor Martin Landau.

LANDON: "From the long hill." The surname of the late Michael Landon, who starred in the TV series "Bonanza" and "Little House On the Prairie."

LARRY: Short for Laurence, Lawrence. The name of one of the members of the American slapstick comedy team The Three Stooges. Also, the name of one of the Three Little Pigs in Disney's animated musical.

LATOYA: The name of one of Michael Jackson's sisters.

LAUREL: Conqueror. For Stan Laurel of the American film comedy team Laurel and Hardy.

LENO: For comedian and "Tonight" show host Jay Leno.

LETTERMAN: For comedian and talk show host David Letterman.

LON: Loner. Also the first name of the actor, Lon Chaney, who starred in numerous old horror movies.

LONI: For actress Loni Anderson, star of movies and the TV series "WKRP In Cincinnati."

LUCILLE: (Latin "light, lightbringer") The name of comic actress Lucille Ball, who starred in "I Love Lucy," "The Lucy Show," "Here's Lucy" and several other TV series and movies.

LUGOSI: For actor Bela Lugosi who starred in numerous horror movies.

MACAULAY: For former

child-actor Macaulay Culkin, who starred in the movies *Home Alone* and *My Girl.*

MADONNA: Divine mother. The name of the often controversial pop singer Madonna.

MARIAH: The wind. Rebellious. For popular singer Mariah Carey.

MARILU: Rebellious. Bright. For actress Marilu Henner, who starred in the TV series "Taxi" and "Evening Shade."

MARILYN: Rebel. For American movie actress Marilyn Monroe whose birth name was Norma Jean Baker.

MARK, MARKY: A form of Marcus. God of war. For rap musician and actor Marky Mark aka Mark Walberg.

MARLON: Respectful. For actor Marlon Brando who starred in popular movies including *A Streetcar Named Desire*, *Apocalypse Now*, and *The Godfather.*

MATT: For Matt Lauer, journalist and host of the NBC morning series "Today."

MICK: A form of Michael. Known as the name of Mick Jagger, lead singer of the popular British rock band The Rolling Stones. Any pet with large or protruding lips.

MO, MOE: Short for Moses and Maureen. Leader. Rebellious. The name of one of the members of the American slapstick comedy team The Three Stooges.

MONTGOMERY: The capital of Alabama. For actor Montgomery Clift who starred with Marilyn Monroe in the movie *The Misfits.*

MR. T: Strong; hulking. For the actor who starred in the TV series "The A-Team."

MUGSI, MUGSEY: Making faces, over-acting, attention seeker. The name of the dog on David Letterman's late night talk show.

NEVE: For actress Neve Campbell.

NIA: For actress Nia Peebles, who starred in the TV series "Fame."

NUGENT: For rock musician Ted Nugent.

OLIVER: (Latin: "olive tree") Scandinavian for kind, affectionate. The first name of Hardy in the American film comedy team Laurel and Hardy.

OLLIE: Nickname for Oliver and Olive. Stanley Laurel's nickname for Oliver Hardy in the American film comedy team Laurel and Hardy.

OPRAH: For TV talk show host Oprah Winfrey. Oprah's parents intended to name her "Orpha" from the Bible, but the name was misspelled on her birth certificate and became Oprah.

PAVAROTTI: For Italian operatic tenor Luciano Pavarotti, the most popular tenor of his generation.

PIA: (Italian: "devout") For actress Pia Zidora.

PLACIDO: For Spanish-born operatic tenor Placido Domingo.

PRESLEY: For Elvis Presley, the King of Rock-n-Roll.

RAQUEL: Beautiful. For actress Raquel Welch.

RAUL: For the late actor Raul Julia who starred as the father, Gomez Addams, in the series *The Addams Family.*

REESE: For actress Reese Witherspoon who starred in the "Legally Blonde" movie series.

RIPA: For Kelly Ripa, actress and co-host of a daytime talk show with Regis Philbin.

ROSEANNE: A form of Rosemary. Known for comedian Roseanne Arnold who starred in the series of the same name.

SCHAMP: The name of one of the later comedians to join The Three Stooges, an American comedy team widely known for their slapstick humor.

SCHULZ: The name of the cartoonist, Charles M. Schulz, who created the "Peanuts" comic strip.

SHAGGY: Long-haired. The name of Scooby Doo's master in the animated TV series "Scooby Doo." The name of a pop singer with Jamaican roots.

SHAKIRA: (Arabic: "thankful.") Known for the blonde Latin pop star from Columbia, South America.

SHAMU: Active. The name of the whale at Sea World in Florida.

SHANIA: (Native American) "I'm on my way." For pop singer Shania Twain.

SIGOURNEY: For actress Sigourney Weaver who starred

in *Alien* and other movies.

SIMON: (Hebrew: "he who hears") The name of the somewhat harsh and painfully honest judge on the TV series "American Idol." Also, the name of a boy in cartoon segments about the Land of Chalk Drawings in the children's series "Captain Kangaroo."

SLY: Clever. Nickname for actor Sylvester Stallone who starred as *Rambo* in a series of movies.

SOLEIL: (Spanish: "sun") For the actress, Soleil Moon Frye, who portrayed the character Punky Brewster in the TV series of the same name.

SOUPY: For comedian Soupy Sales.

TALLULAH: For American actress Tallulah Bankhead, who had a flamboyant personality and wit, and feisty roles in movies such as *The Little Foxes*, *By the Skin of Our Teeth*, and *Lifeboat* that made her a legend.

TANDY: American actress Jessica Tandy who starred in *Driving Miss Daisy* and other films.

TATUM: For actress Tatum O'Neal who starred in *Paper Moon* and other movies.

TRINI: For Latin entertainer Trini Lopez. Also, the name of one of the original rangers in the TV series "Mighty Morphin Power Rangers."

TRUMP: For wealthy Donald Trump. Also, short for trumpet. A musical pet.

VALENTINO: (Latin: "strong, healthy") For American film actor Rudolph Valentino, who starred in many romantic roles.

VAN DYKE: A closely trimmed, pointed beard, as seen in portraits painted by Sir Anthony Van Dyke. Also, the name of actor Dick Van Dyke. A closely trimmed pet.

VANNA: For Vanna White, the hostess on the TV game show "Wheel of Fortune."

VARNEY: Ruler. The last name of actor Jim Varney who starred in the series of movies about the lovable, bumbling character Ernest.

VIN: Active. For actor Vin Diesel who starred in *The Fast and the Furious* and other movies.

WAYLON: A pet set in its

ways. The name of country singer Waylon Jennings.

WHITNEY: (Old English: "from the white island; from fair water") For pop superstar Whitney Houston.

WHOOPI: For actress Whoopi Goldberg who starred in movies including *The Color Purple* and *Sister Act*.

WYNONNA: Long life. The name of popular country singer Wynonna Judd.

YAHOO: Ill-mannered. For actor Yahoo Serious, who starred in the movie *Young Einstein*. Also, in Jonathan Swift's Gulliver's Travels, any of a race of brutish creatures.

YAKOV: Supplanter. For Russian comedian Yakov Smirnoff.

YANNI: For the popular Greek born musician who is an accomplished keyboardist.

ZEPPO: The nickname of Herbert, one of the Marx Brothers, an American family of comedians.

ZSA ZSA: (Hungarian) A form of Susan. For actress Zsa Zsa Gabor. John F. Kennedy, the 35th President of the United States, had a rabbit with this name.

Did You Know?

ANNIE: Graceful. Known for Annie Oakley, the female rifle expert whose targets resembled punched tickets. Barbara Eden, actress and the star of the TV series "I Dream of Jeannie," has a poodle with this name.

BLUEGRASS: The name of Daniel Boone's family cat.

PLUTO: As a child Alyssa Milano, star of "Who's the Boss" and "Charmed," had a pup she named Pluto.

Tommy & Lucy

Mc Tabbish

Chapter 4

Playful and Whimsical

Many pet lovers always look on the funnyside of life (excuse the obvious pun! Sic.), and a name with a playful or whimsical ring often reflects the relationship you have established early on with your pet. Some names are just so off-beat, whimsical or downright silly, that they have to be placed in their own special category. Many of the names included in this chapter meet this criteria, no holds barred! These names are reserved for very special pets, that is, a pet just like yours – should you choose to use a name from this chapter! Give in to whimsy, let your creativity soar! Your pet will thank you for it.

ABEBI: A pet that comes when she is called.

A.C.: Abbreviation for Animal Control.

ACE: First-rate, the best.

AGOG: With anticipation, excitement, mirth.

AJ, AJAYE: Playful.

ALAZOO: Zany.

ALIAS: Any pet that is sneaky or secretive.

ALIBI: Always elsewhere, and thus always innocent.

ALIEN: Different, hostile.

AMBI: Short for ambidextrous.

ANTS: The name of a Beanie Baby anteater.

APRI: Early to rise in the morning.

AUDI: A pet that hears all.

AUSSIE: Slang for a person from Australia.

AWESOME: Inspiring wonder.

BACHELOR: Single guy.

BAFFLE: Easily confused.

BAGO: Short for winnebago; a traveler, a wanderer.

BALDERDASH: Silly.

BALLYHOO: Loud, uproar.

BAMBOOZLE: To trick or

confuse, mystify.

BANANAS: Zany.

BANDANA: Flashy.

BATTY: Funny, silly.

BAWDY: Irreverent.

BAXLEY: Domestic.

BB: Short for bad boy.

BEAK: The name of the tie-dye kiwi bird Beanie Baby.

BEANS: A pet that eats beans.

BEATNIK: Unconventional.

BEAU GESTE: A graceful gesture.

BEAV, BEAVE: Short for Beaver.

BEBOP: Jazzy. Upbeat.

BEEJAY, BJ: Blessed, noisy.

BEEPER: Noisy.

BET: Chance-taker.

BIBI: Repetitious.

BIFF: Jolly.

BIG SHOT: Egotistic.

BITTERSWEET: Both painful and pleasant.

BIZBY: A show-off.

BLINKER: Winking, twinkling.

BLINKIE, BLINKY: Twinkling, staring.

BLUNDER: Clumsy.

BOBALOO: To wag, wiggle.

BOBEE: Silly.

BODACIOUS: Southern and Midland slang for outright, un-mistakable, remarkable, or noteworthy.

BOFFY: A clown.

BOGGLES: Overwhelming.

BOIGER: Burger. A pet that enjoys hamburgers.

BOJO: Liking music.

BONANZA: Good; riches.

BONER: Prone to blunder.

BONKERS: To drive one crazy.

BOOBY: Silly.

BOODLES: Valuables.

BOOPSY: Zany.

BOOTER: A buccaneer, pirate.

BOPEEP: Peekaboo.

BOPPER: A dancer.

BOUNTY: Generous gift.

BOXIE: A pet that loves to play or sleep in boxes.

BUBBA: A southern slang term for brother. Friend.

BUCKAROO: A cowboy.

BUCKEYE: Male.

BUCKLES: Playful.

BUFFOON: A clown, prankster; zany.

BUGABOO: Bugbear; a pest; aggravating.

BUGGERS: Sometimes gross.

BUGLE: Loud, easily heard.

BUGSY: A prankster; zany. Any pet that eats bugs.

BUMMER: Slang for unfortunate occurrence.

BUMPER: Large; a daredevil.

BUMPKIN: A hillbilly. A pet that enjoys the simple country life and the great outdoors.

BUNKO: A cheat.

BUNKY: Nonsensical.

BURB: Short for suburbs.

BUREAUCAT: A play on bureaucrat. A name for a cat or a surname like Abigail von Bureaucat.

BURPY: Noisy.

CADE: A pet that parades about.

CAMBRIA: Poetic meaning Wales.

CAMOUFLAGE: In disguise; secretive.

CAPER: Playful, mischievous.

CAPRICE: Whimsical.

CARGO: A load.

CHAMP: Champion, a winner.

CHAMPION: A winner.

CHAOS: Disorderly.

CHAP: A fellow.

CHARADE: A show-off.

CHARGER: Commander.

CHARM, CHARMER: Lucky.

CHATTERBOX: A pet that is continually noisy.

CHATTERLY: Chatty.

CHATTY: A pet that is continually noisy.

CHECKERS: Colorful. The name of Richard Nixon's family dog referred to, with such heartfelt digression, in the historic "Checkers" speech that public opinion was turned in Nixon's favor and rescued his bid for Vice President in 1952.

CHEEKS: The name of the baboon Beanie Baby.

CHEEKY: Impudent.

CHEER, CHEERY: Lightly; bright; pleasant.

CHICK: Short for Chicken. A good name for a pet that is always timid or easily scared.

CHICKEN: A pet that is easily scared.

CHIRP: The short, shrill sound of a bird. A good name for a bird or any pet that makes this sound.

CHITCHAT: A chatterbox. Any pet that makes continuous and idle noise.

CHOMP, CHOMPER: Any pet that has a healthy appetite.

CHOO CHOO: Noisy.

CHOOSY: Very particular,

CHOU CHOU: A pet that repeats itself.

CHUCKLE: Mildly amused.

CHUCKO: Amused.

CHUGG: Loud.

CHUGGLE, CHUGGLES: Loud.

CIJI: Unconventional; offbeat.

CLAWS: Any pet who has sharp claws or is seemingly ferocious.

CLOWN, CLOWNY: A buffoon; zany.

CLUBBY: The name of a Beanie Baby bear.

CLUMSY: Lacking grace.

COBY: Tricky.

COCOMINO: Silly.

CODE: Secretive. Also a nickname for Cody.

CONKY: Easily exhausted.

COO COO: Zany.

COSY: Warm and comfortable.

COVET: Desired.

COWARD: Easily scared.

COWGIRL: A pet that enjoys the simple life and the great outdoors.

CRAWLER: A pet that crawls more often than it walks.

CREEPER: Sneaky.

CRITTER: Creature.

CROC: Short for crocodile.

CUPIE: Kewpie.

CURIOSITY: Interested, eager to learn.

CURMUDGEON: Ill-mannered.

DABBLE: To play in water.

DALLY: From "dilly dally," to waste time. Can also be short for Dalmatian.

DANCER: The name of one of Santa's eight reindeer.

DANDY: First class, good.

DARE: Courageous.

DAZZ: Pleasing, dazzling.

DAZZLE: Surprising, pleasing.

DAZZY: Pleasing.

DELIGHT: Pleasurable.

DERMOTT: Witty.

DEZ: Scatterbrained.

DIDDLE: A pet who just spends time idly doing nothing.

DILL: Sour.

DILLY: From dilly dally, to waste time hesitating. Dilly Dally was the name a character in the 1950s children's TV series "Howdy Dowdy."

DING-A-LING: Small, playful.

DINSMORE: Playful, affectionate.

DIPPY: Scatterbrained, carefree.

DITTO: A pet that repeats itself.

DIZZ: Dizzy.

DOCKY: Clever.

DODO: Silly.

DOGGIE: A dog or puppy. Not a name that requires a lot of imagination, but it is easy for a small child to remember.

DOGIE: A stray.

DOKO: Refreshing.

DOLTON: A dolt, silly.

DONDY: A prize.

DONSIE: Saucy.

DOOBY: Playful. From Frank Sinatra's song "Dooby Dooby Doo."

DOODLE, DOODLES: Playful.

DOOFUS: Clumsy, silly.

DOZY: A sleepyhead.

DREAMER: Sensitive.

DRIBBLE, DRIBBLES: A pet that drools.

DUCKY: Delightful.

DUDE: A laid-back, cool pet.

EARLY, EARLEE: Early to rise; up before dawn. Early is the name of a Beanie Baby, a robin.

EBBA: Echo, repetitious.

ELFIN: Fairylike.

ELJAY: The bluejay.

ELNORA: Playfully mischievous.

EMCEE: Very vocal.

ENDORA: A copycat.

ENJOI: (Pronounced "on-joy") To enjoy or bring joy.

ENVY: Jealous.

EPPY: Close-by.

ESPY: A pet that likes to be sneaky and spy on everyone.

EUSTACIA: Fruitful.

EWART: Wild one.

FABLE: A story meant to teach a moral lesson and in which most of the characters are animals.

FABOO, FABU: Short for fabulous.

FANCY: Whimsical, superior.

FANFARE: Show-off, noisy.

FAVE: Favorite.

FELLA: Slang for fellow, meaning companion.

FIB: Short for fibber. Tattletale.

FIBBER: A tattletale.

FIBERT: A tattletale.

FIFINE: Catty.

FILBERT: A pet with a healthy appetite.

FINESSE: Delicate. Clever.

FIRECAT: A name for a temperamental cat.

FLAME: Warm, excited.

FLAPPER: Noisy, bold.

FLAVO: Tasteful.

FLICKER: Bright, glowing as a flame; fast.

FLIRT: Playful.

FLITTER: The name of a Beanie Baby butterfly.

FLUTTER: Graceful; floating.

FOLLY: Nonsensical.

FOO FOO: Repetitious.

FOY, FOYE: Playful.

FRAIDY: Afraid, easily frightened.

FRANTIC: Greatly excited.

FREE: Freedom.

FREEBO: Ronald Reagan, the 40th President of the United States, had a dog with this name.

FRUSTY: Easily frustrated.

FUDGIE: Silly.

FUMBLE, FUMBLES: Clumsy.

FUNNY: Comical, amusing.

FUNNYBONE: Humorous.

FURBY: Furry little mechanical toys.

GABBIE, GABBY: Noisy.

GABY: Noisy.

GADABOUT: Fun-seeker.

GADDY: Fun-seeker.

GADEN: Exciting.

GAGA: Awestruck.

GAIETY: Cheerful.

GAMBI: Playful.

GANZA: Short for "extravaganza." Musical.

GENIUS: Intelligent, creative.

GIDDY: Fickle.

GIFT: A present.

GIG: Cheerful.

GIGGLE, GIGGLES: Cheerful.

GILLIE, GILLY: Boy; servant.

GIPPER: Gypsy.

GITZI: Amusing.

GLACIA: Cool.

GLAM: Short for glamour.

GLAMOUR: Bewitching charmer.

GLITTER: Sparkling.

GLITZ: Sparking.

GLOWIE, GLOWY: Beaming.

GLOW WORM: Beaming.

GODIVA: Independent-minded.

GOOCH: Messy.

GOOCHY: The name of the tie-dyed jellyfish Beanie Baby.

GOOEY: Sticky.

GOOF, GOOFY: Silly.

GOOFBALL: Silly.

GOOFUS: Goofy.

GOOLIE: Ghoulie.

GOONBA: Awkward.

GOONIE: Awkward.
GOSHI: (Pronounced "go-shee") Surprised.
GRAFFITI: Colorful.
GRANDEUR: Important; noble.
GREEDY: A pet who loves to eat but doesn't like to share.
GRIN: Humorous.
GROOVY: Hip; Marvelous, wonderful, excellent, enjoyable. The name of a Beanie Baby bear.
GRUNT: Noisy.
GUFFY: Silly.
GUILTY: A pet who is always getting into trouble.
GUMBA: Sticky.
GUZZLE, GUZZLER: Thirsty.
HABIT: Often seen; steady.
HALO: The name of the Beanie Baby bear angel, a white bear with wings.
HAPPINESS: Joyful.
HAPPY: Cheerful, easygoing. The name of the family dog in the TV series "7th Heaven."
HARDLUCK: Melancholy.
HARMLESS: Innocent, blameless.
HARMONY: Peaceful.
HARUM: From "harum-scarum," meaning careless.

HEX: Unlucky.
HEYA: Attention-getter.
HIPPY: A free spirit.
HIPSTER: Slang for hip, a beatnik.
HITCH: Short for Hitchcock. Any pet that seems very attached.
HIYA: Attention-getter.
HOCUS, HOCUS-POCUS: Magical. A phrase used by magicians when performing a feat of magic.
HODGE-PODGE: Helter-skelter; messy.
HODGY: Messy.
HOKEY, HOKEY POKEY: Hocus-pocus; magical.
HONCHO: Big shot.
HONKS: Loud, noisy pet. The name of a silver-colored goose Beanie Baby.
HOOEY: Silly.
HOOLIGAN: A pet that is usually up to no good.
HOOT: Echoic; loud. Often a reference to an owl or other bird but may refer to any noisy pet.
HOOTIE: Echoic.
HOPE: Trustworthy; cherished. The name of a gold-colored Beanie Baby, a praying bear.

HOPEFUL: A dreamer.
HOPIE: Trustworthy.
HOPPERGRASS: A pet that hops like a grasshopper.
HOT SHOT: Big shot.
HOUDI: Short for Houdini. Tricky pet.
HOWL, HOWLER: A pet that often howls.
HOYT: Playful.
HUB: Center of attention or interest.
HUBLEY: Center of attention or interest.
HUCK: Short for Huckleberry.
HUCKABUCK: A dancer.
HULA: A pet that dances. For the native Hawaiian dance the hula-hula, which is performed by women.
HULLABALOO: Noisy excitement.
HUMBLE: Down to earth. Unpretentious.
HYDE, HYDER: Playful, mischievous.
ICCA: Cool.
ICE: Cool; laid-back.
IDLE: Lazy, content.
IFFY: Indecisive.
IKARI: Silly.
IKKY: Sometimes gross.
ILBERT: Joyful.

ILKA: Akin.
ILONA: Creative.
ILSA: A daydreamer.
INDI, INDY: Short for Independence. Self-reliant.
ITSY: From "itsy bitsy," meaning tiny.
ITTY: From "itty bitty," meaning tiny, especially a small bird.
IZAR: Always late.
JABBER: Idle chatter. The name of a parrot Beanie Baby.
JACKAROO: Australian slang for a male kangaroo. A pet that hops.
JACKO: A nickname for pop star Michael Jackson.
JACKPOT: Lucky; valuable.
JARGO: Jargon; vocal.
JARGON: Vocal.
JASS: A show-off.
JASSALYN: A show-off.
JASSI, JASSEE: A show-off.
JASSU: A show-off.
JAYBEE, JAYCEE, JAYDEE: Silly.
JAY-JAY: Silly.
JEMA: A gem.
JESTER: Playful, a joker.
JIFF, JIFFY: Inattentive.
JIG, JIGS: A dancer.
JIGSAW: Puzzling.
JILLAROO: Australian slang

for a female kangaroo. A pet that hops.

JINGLE: Noisy.

JINGLES: Musical.

JINGO: Loud.

JINKIE: Jinx.

JINX: Unlucky.

JIP: Greedy.

JITTERBUG: A dancer.

JIVE: Cool, jazzy.

JOBI, JOBY: Thoughtful.

JOCUSE: Humorous.

JO JO: Prosperous; playful.

JOKER: Playful, mischievous.

JOLLY: Joyful. The name of a Beanie Baby walrus.

JOOLS: Jewels, precious.

JOSHER: Good-humored, a joker.

JOVA, JOVAN: Jovial.

JOVI: Jovial.

JOY: Happy.

JOYBELLE: Ringing with joy, happy.

JOYOUS: Happy.

JUBILEE: Jubilation.

JUBY: Jubilation.

JUJU: A charm.

KABLOOEY: Clumsy.

KAHUNA: Big shot.

KAZ: Short for kazoo. Musical.

KAZEE: Musical.

KAZOO: Musical.

KEEBLES: Food lover.

KEEJI: Playful.

KENDRA: Akin.

KENO: Chancy.

KESHIA: Clever.

KIBITZ: A kibitzer, a meddlesome onlooker.

KIDDIE: A young pet or a pet that is young at heart. Slang for a child.

KIDDO: Slang term for a child.

KIP: Chief.

KIPPER: Male.

KISMET: Destiny.

KLUTZ, KLUTZY: Clumsy.

KOKO: Amusing.

KOO: The sound a bird makes.

KOOCHIE: From Koochie Koo, an affectionate term often conveyed to babies and small children.

KOOKY: Fun-loving.

KORGIE: Fun-loving.

KRINGLE: Childlike. From Kriss Kringle, German for Santa Claus.

KUENA: Playful.

KUESTON: Playful.

KUKI: Playful.

KUKU: Zany, playfully fun. A Beanie Baby cockatoo.

KUSHY: Comfortable.
LALITA: Playful.
LARISSA: Joyful.
LAZY: Idle.
LAZYBONES: Idle, slow moving.
LAZYLEGS: A pet that loves to just lie around the house.
LEEZA: Having a good sense of direction.
LEFTY: Slang for someone who is left-handed. The name of a Beanie Baby donkey.
LEX: Vocal.
LEXA: Vocal.
LEXI: Vocal.
LIBEARTY: The name of a Beanie Baby bear.
LIBERTY: Freedom.
LIGHTFOOT: Quiet. A pet who walks quietly, softly.
LING: Heather.
LINGO: Vocal.
LINK: Bond.
LISI: A charmer.
LITTLE WONDER: Small and amazing.
LUDIE: Silly.
MADAME: A lady who has a mate.
MADCAP: Reckless.
MAGIC: Mysterious.
MAGICIAN: Tricky.
MARBLE, MARBLES: Playful; colorful.
MARMION: Twinkling.
MARVEL: Astonishing, wonderful.
MARVY: Short for marvelous.
MASCOT: Lucky.
MATE: Pal.
MATEY: Pal.
MAZE: A pet that is easily confused or often behaves in a puzzling manner.
MAZUMA: Slang for money.
MAZZY: Amazing.
McDEVILISH: Mischievous.
McTABBISH: A good name for a male tabby cat.
MEEPERS: Meek.
MEGABUCKS: Slang for "many dollars."
MELLOW: Good-humored.
MEMENTO: Memorable.
MENACE: Mischievous.
MERRY: Cheerful.
MIGHTY: Strong.
MILBY: Playful.
MIME: A clown. An ancient Greek or Roman farce in which people and events were mimicked.
MINTY: Cool, refreshing.
MINTZI: Cool.
MISCHIEF: Playful, mischievous.

MISFIT: Ill at ease.
MITTY: Warmth.
MODESTY: Humble.
MOJO: Spicy.
MOMENT: Fleeting.
MONEY: Valued.
MOOCH, MOOCHER:
Sulky. Mooch is the name of a Beanie Baby spider monkey.
MOOCHI: Sulky.
MOOLAH: Slang for money.
MOONDUST: A dreamer.
MOONIE, MOONY: A dreamer, silly.
MOONSTRUCK: Bemused.
MOSEY: A slowpoke.
MOTTO: Anything expressive of character, a principle of behavior.
MOUSER: A good name for a cat that excels at this skill.
MR. BIG: A big shot.
MR. NICE GUY: Friendly.
MUFFY: Clumsy.
MUGGINS: Making faces, overacting, attention seeker.
MUGGLES: A pet that loves attention.
MUGGS: Making faces, overacting, attention seeker.
MUMBLES: Noisy.
MUNCHI: A pet that loves to munch on food.
MUNGO: Worldly.

MUNZIO: Prosperous.
MUSKY: Odorous.
NAJEE: Cheerful.
NANON: Charming.
NARA: Cheerful.
NARDA: Fresh, clean.
NAUGHTY: Disobedient.
NAZ, NAZZY: Blessed.
NEB: The beak of a bird.
NEBELINA: Distant.
NEO: New, as a new pet or newborn.
NEON: Brightly colored. The name of a Beanie Baby seahorse.
NEONA: Brightly colored.
NERVY: Nervous.
NESSIE: Nickname for the Loch Ness Monster.
NEZZIE: Nosey.
NIBBLE, NIBBLES: To eat with quick, small bites as a mouse. A morsel.
NIBBLER: One who nibbles.
NICETY: Being nice, modest.
NICEY: Nice.
NIFTY: Slang for attractive, enjoyable.
NIGHTMARE: A demon, frightening dream. A mischievous pet.
NIGHT OWL: A pet that stays up nights.
NIP, NIPPY: A pet that some-

times tries to bite.

NIPSY: A pet that sometimes tries to bite.

NODDY: Agreeable.

NONA: Long life.

NONI, NONIE: Long life.

NONYA: Long life.

NOOFY: Songwriter-musician Burt Bacharach has a dog with this name.

NO SHOW: A pet that doesn't always come when called.

NUTTY: Silly.

OBIE: Playful.

OGGIE: Persistent.

O.J.: An abbreviation for orange juice.

OKEY: Agreeable.

OLD BILL: Calvin Coolidge, the 30th President of the United States, had a thrush with this name.

OLD BLUE: Melancholy.

OLD BONES: A slowpoke.

OLD BOY: Lethargic. Warren Harding, the 29th President of the United States had a bulldog with this name.

OLD FELLOW: Lethargic.

OLD IKE: Woodrow Wilson, the 28th President of the United States, had a ram with this name.

OLD POKEY: A slowpoke.

OLD SALTY: A pet that enjoys the beach or ocean.

OLD SHOE: Old-fashioned.

OLE BLUE: Melancholy.

OLEG: A show-off.

OLETA: Good-spirited.

OLGA: Blessed.

ONA: One and only.

OODLES: Slang for "great amount."

ORAL: A very loud, very vocal pet.

ORALIE: Loud, very vocal.

ORBIE: Orbit, any pet that chases its tail or moves in circles.

ORCO: Eccentric.

ORFIE: An orphan.

ORGA: Complex.

ORICE: Fragrant.

ORKY: Eccentric.

OSBIRD: Divine.

OTIE: Carefree.

OUISER: A complainer.

OUTLAW: A pet that is always on the run, especially after a period of mischief.

OVIE: Out-going.

PADWICK: Slow-moving.

PAJAMAS, PYJAMAS: A pet, especially a cat, that loves to lie around and takes frequent naps.

PAL, PALLY: A friend, a

companion.
PALOOKA: Clumsy.
PAMPER: Overindulged, coddled.
PANDI: Short for pandemonium, a wild uproar.
PAPPY: A father.
PARASITE: Selfish.
PARDENE: Giving.
PARDNER: Partner; companion.
PASO: Mexican coin.
PEACHY: Slang for fine, excellent.
PEEK-A-BOO: Playful, shy.
PEEPER: A pet that snoops or spies from a hiding place.
PEKE: A peeper.
PEST: Troublemaker, destructive.
PESTY: Troubling, pest.
PET: Liked, the favorite, a darling.
PHANTOM: Illusive.
PHENOM: Short for phenomenal, meaning extremely unusual; extraordinary.
PIDDLE PADDLE: A mischievous pet that sometimes wets.
PIDDLER: A pet that likes to lie around, mope about.
PIDDLES: A pet that likes to lie around, mope about.

PIPEY: A vocal, musical pet.
PIPPIN: Slang for something lovely.
PIRATE: A pet that sometimes takes what isn't his.
PITTER: From the "pitter patter of little feet." A pet that is a companion, always at your heels.
PI WACKET: Causing a racket.
P.J.: Short for pajamas. A name for a pet that likes to sleep most of the time.
PLEASURE: Delight, enjoyment.
PLINKO: Playful.
POCUS: From Hocus Pocus, words magicians use when performing their magic.
POESY: Old-fashioned for poetry.
POKINOOS: Slang for the "middle of nowhere." A pet that enjoys the simple country life.
PONCH: Short for poncho, an often colorful cloaklike blanket with a hole in the middle for the head.
POOBAH: Leader.
POOH-POOH: To make light of.
POOKA: Pukka, pucka. Good,

first-rate, real, genuine.

POOKIE: Playful.

POPPER: One that pops.

POPS: Slow-moving.

POSY: A flower or bouquet.

POW WOW: Festive. For the Native American ceremony of magic and feasting.

PRANCER: A pet that struts, swaggers. The name of one of Santa's eight reindeer.

PRANKSTER: A clever, cunning pet.

PREZ: In charge.

PRIDE: Dignity, respect.

PRIM: Proper.

PRIMPER: To primp;. prissy.

PRISS, PRISSY: Very prim.

PRIZE: Valued.

PRIZZY: Valued.

PROMISE: Bright future.

PROPER: Decent.

PROPHET: Perceptive.

PROUD BOY: Splendid fellow.

PSYCHO: A pet that is unpredictable.

PUDDLE, PUDDLES: A pet that wets.

PUKKA: First-rate; genuine.

PUPPET: A doll with strings, wires, or other means for producing movement. A pet easily controlled.

QUACK, QUACKS: Noisy. The sound a duck makes.

QUACKER: An off-beat pet.

QUAPAW: Water-lover.

QUIP: Witty. Sassy.

RADA: Radiant.

RAINA, RAYNA: Rain lover.

RAINDANCER: A pet that loves to play in the rain.

RAINEE, RAINY: Rain, rainy; stormy; moody. Perhaps a damp pet, such as a fish, turtle, or similar.

RANDA: A shield.

RANDO: Shield.

RANSS: A shield.

RASCAL: Playfully mischievous.

RASSLE: Slang for wrestle. A pet that likes to wrestle.

RATCHET: Forward.

RAZZLE: From razzle dazzle, slang for a state of confusion.

REA: Flexible.

REAL: (Pronounced "ree–al.") Real.

REBUS: Puzzling. A kind of puzzle consisting of pictures of things whose names suggest words or phrases (for example, a picture of a bee plus the figure 4 is a rebus for "before").

REE: Repetitious.

REECY: Repetitious.

REEGE: Repetitious.
REFLEX: Responsive.
RENATA: Reborn.
RENZO: Laurel.
REVEL: Noisily merry.
REWARD: Valued.
RICH: Wealthy. Short.
RIDDLES: Silly.
RIDER: A pet that loves to ride, especially on car trips.
RIFF: Musical.
RIGBY: Close-by.
RIGSBY: Close-by.
RINGO: Repetitious.
RITA: A pearl.
RITZ, RITZY: Slang for elegant.
ROCCO: Elaborate.
ROGO: Questioning.
ROLLO: Famed wolf.
ROOBINUZ: A pet that rubs its nose against you.
ROOKIE: A newcomer. Slang for an inexperienced recruit.
ROUSTABOUT: Inexperienced.
ROZ: Playful.
ROZZIE, ROZZY: Playful.
RUMMY: Slang for strange. Also, a card game.
SAILOR: Any pet that loves water, especially a good swimmer.
SALADO: One of a kind.

SALINA: Good name for pet that enjoys a salt block.
SAMOO: Listener.
SAMRA: Listener.
SASHAY: To glide, to walk prissily.
SATCH: Short for satchel, like a sack.
SCARUM: From "harum-scarum," meaning wild, reckless.
SCARY: Frightening.
SCAT: To go away, usually associated with a cat.
SCHMOO: Lowly fellow. Misfortunate.
SCHREECHY: Noisy. High-pitched.
SCOOP: The name of a Beanie Baby pelican.
SCRATCHES: A pet that digs, claws.
SCREWBALL: Slang for unconventional one.
SCRIBBLE: Meaningless writing or marks.
SCUTTER: A pet that loves water but can't stay afloat for very long.
SCUTTLEBUTT: Slang for a drinking fountain on ship board. A thirsty pet.
SEAMORE: The name of a Beanie Baby seal.

SEAWEED: The name of a Beanie Baby otter.

SHADY: Clever.

SHALA: Short for shalamar.

SHANA: Lucky.

SHANDA: Glowing.

SHANDEL: Lucky.

SHANTE, SHANTI: Musical.

SHAPOO: Playful.

SHAY: Relaxing.

SHEESH: Playful.

SHELLA, SHELLEN: Of the water, ocean.

SHERBY: Cool.

SHIMP: Playful.

SHINA, SHYNNA: Bashful.

SHINE: Radiant, splendorous.

SHONA: Glowing.

SHONDA: Glowing.

SHONNIE: Glowing.

SHOTGUN: A smoothbore, shoulder-held gun for firing small shot at short range. A well-known name for dogs.

SHUFFLE: To barely move; to drag one's feet.

SIB: Short for sibling.

SIBLEY: A devoted sibling.

SIDONIE: Enchantress.

SIGH: Yearning.

SILLY: Playful.

SIMI: Akin.

SIMOLEON: Slang for a dollar.

SING SING: A name for a pet that sings such as a bird.

SIPPY: A pet who is often thirsty.

SIR WAGS-A-LOT: A pet that wags its tail all the time.

SIREN: A flirt.

SIS: Short for sister or sissy.

SISI: Daughter.

SISSY: Very feminine, prissy.

SKEEBO: Playful.

SKEEZO: Playful.

SLAPSTICK: Crude comedy, with lots of horseplay.

SLEEPER: A sleepyhead, a pet that likes to sleep most of the time.

SLEEPY: A sleepyhead.

SLOWPOKE: Moving very slowly.

SMUGGLER: A name for a pet that loves to hide food in unlikely places.

SNAP, SNAPPY: A pet that bites or tries to bite suddenly.

SNAPPER: A person or thing that snaps such as a snapping turtle.

SNARLA: Playful protector.

SNATCH, SNATCHER: To grab eagerly, hastily.

SNEAKER: A quiet, sneaky pet.

SNEAKERS: A term for tennis shoes. A pet that moves slowly, sneakily.

SNICKER: To seem to laugh, to find amusement.

SNIFFER: A pet that smells anything and everything.

SNIFFLES: A pet that breathes loudly.

SNITCH, SNITCHY: A tattletale, nosy.

SNITZER: Nosy.

SNOOZER: A pet that sleeps often and sometimes snores.

SNOOZY: A pet that spends its time sleeping.

SNUFFLES: A pet that often gets the sniffles.

SOAPY: Bubbly.

SOLEY: A loner.

SOLLY: Peaceful.

SOULI: Soulful.

SOUVENIR: Memorable.

SPIKEY: Tough.

SPOOF, SPOOFY: Tricky.

SPOONER: Noisy.

SPOONY: Sentimental.

SPRINKLE, SPRINKLES: A pet that wets.

SPRITE: A pixie, a fairy.

SPROCKET: A pet with bite. The teeth or points arranged to fit into the links of a chain.

SPY: Nosy, sneaky.

SQUEAK, SQUEAKS: High-pitched sound.

SQUEAKY: A pet that makes a high-pitched cry or sound.

SQUEALER: Noisy. A pet that makes a prolonged high-pitched sound.

SQUIGGLES: Wiggly.

SQUIGGY: Wiggly.

SQUIRRELY: Playful.

STARFIRE: Bright, heavenly.

STARGAZER: A dreamer.

STASH: A pet that constantly hides food or other items.

STEELE, STEELY: Strong.

STINKER: A mischievous pet.

ST. ELMO: From St. Elmo's fire, the patron saint of sailors.

STITCHES: A pet that is highly amusing as one that keeps you in stitches.

STOEY: Playful.

STOFFI: Good.

STOMPER: A noisy pet.

STOOGE: A compliant dupe.

STOOGIE: A stooge.

STOOLIE: A spy.

STRAGGLY: A stray.

STULLY: Silly.

STUMBO: Clumsy.

SUDIE: Bubbly.

SUDS, SUDSY: Bubbly.

SWAGGER: To walk with a bold stride; strut.

SWASHBUCKLER: A swaggering fighter.

SWEVEN: Archaic for dream, vision.

SWIG, SWIGGLES: Thirsty.

TABOO: Unconventional.

TALIA: (Hebrew) "Morning dew."

TALON: The claw of an animal or bird of prey.

TAPOO: Noisy.

TAPPY: A pet that often makes tapping noises.

TAROT: Intuitive.

TASH, TASHA: Festive.

TAY: Short for Taylor.

TAYLOR: Tasteful.

TAYREN: Tasteful.

TEAGUE: Creative.

TEASER: Playfully mischievous.

TEDDY: Short for Teddy Bear. A cuddly, lovable pet.

TEENSIE: From the saying "teensie weensie," meaning small, tiny.

TEEPEE: Home for an Indian.

TEETER: Short for teeter totter, a seesaw.

TENDERFOOT: Newcomer; inexperienced.

TETRA: Four.

TEWA: Moccasins.

THANKFUL: Appreciative.

THEO: A gift.

TICKER: Nervous. A device used to record stock quotations.

TICKLES: One who tickles or is ticklish; playful.

TIFF: Slang for an argument. Perhaps a name for a pet that is sometimes difficult.

TING-A-LING: Any pet that makes a high-pitched pet.

TING LEE: Tingly.

TINKER: A very playful pet.

TINKLER: A pet that wets.

TINSEL: Glistening; a pet with a "sparkling" personality.

TOBA: Full of goodness.

TOFF: British "swell, dandy."

TOKEN: Special, memorable.

TOMKINS: Male.

TOOBA: Tuba. Musical.

TOODLES: From toodle lu, a farewell. Any pet that frequently strays or just keeps out of sight.

TOOMEE: Playful.

TOOT: Noisy.

TOSHI: Playful.

TOY: Playful. Tiny.

TRAFFIC: A busy pet, always on the go.

TREASURE: Valuable.

TREAT: Pleasurable; entertaining.

TREKIE: A traveler. A nickname for a fan of "Star Trek."
TREY: Playful.
TREYLA: Playful.
TRICK, TRICKY: A playful pet that performs feats or tricks.
TRICKLE: Slow-moving.
TRICKS: A playful pet that performs feats or tricks.
TRICKSTER: A playful pet that performs feats or tricks. Often a sly, clever pet.
TRILBY: Echoic, noisy.
TRIPPER: Clumsy.
TRIPPY: Clumsy.
TRIX: A pet that loves to perform daring feats, stunts or tricks.
TROLLY: One who likes to be carried.
TROOPER: A pal.
TROPHY: Prized.
TRUE: Loyal as true-blue.
TRYKE: Slang for a child's tricycle.
TUSH: Rear.
TUSHI: Rear.
TUTTI: Musical.
TUTU: A dancer.
TWADDLES: Silly.
TWEEDLE, TWEEDLES: Musical spontaneous, careless.
TWEET: The chirping sound of a small bird.
TWINKLE: To sparkle with amusement or kindness as the eyes.
TWINKS: Shining.
TWITTY: Taunting.
TWIZ, TWIZZY: Playful.
TY: Worker.
TYRO: A beginner; learning.
TYROS: Learning.
U-BETCHA: Slang for certainly.
ULZANA: Zany.
UNI: One.
UNIQUE: Rare; one of a kind.
URI: Bright.
URSA: Fearless.
UZANA: Zany.
VAMPIRE: A pet that likes to bite.
VANIA: Vain.
VANITY: Vain.
VEX: Annoying.
VIBES: Easygoing as good vibes.
VICTORY: Winner.
VIKING: A pirate.
VILAS: Ill-mannered.
VITTLES: A pet with a hearty appetite.
VIXEN: The name of one of Santa's eight reindeers.
VOLARE: To fly.
VOLETTA, VOLETTE: Ex-

otic.

VONDA: Wanderer.

WACKY: Zany, silly.

WAGS-A-LOT: A pet that wags its tail all the time.

WAH-WAH: Repetitious.

WAKIZA: Wakeful.

WALKER: A pet that takes cautious steps.

WALLFLOWER: Shy.

WALLIS: Eccentric.

WANDERLUST: A traveling pet, a stray.

WARBLER: A bird that warbles, songbird.

WARLOCK: Wizard.

WATERBABY: A swimmer.

WAZOO: Playful.

WEEBLE, WEEBLES: For a child's toy that resembles small people or dolls with rounded bottoms that wobble.

WEEJI: Cooperative.

WEEPY: Tearful, often melancholy.

WEEZER, WEEZY: A pet that breathes loudly, wheezes.

WEIRDIE: Weird.

WELCOME: Friendly.

WHACKY: A clown, silly.

WHAMMY: Slang for a jinx.

WHIDDLES: To whiddle, a pet that loves to chew on wood.

WHIFFER: A pet that sniffs.

WHIFFLE: To blow or scatter as in a gust of wind.

WHIM: Caprice, fancy.

WHIMPER: A whiner.

WHIMSY: Idle notion; fanciful humor.

WHIPPERSNAPPER: Impertinent, presumptuous.

WHISPER: Quiet.

WHISTLE: Musical, shrill.

WILBERT: Bright wish.

WILBY: Wishful.

WILDFIRE: Fiery.

WILKIE: Wishful.

WIM: Whimsical.

WINGER: To take flight.

WINGS, WINGY: To take flight.

WINK, WINKS: To wink, twinkle.

WINKER, WINKY: To wink, twinkle.

WINNER: Champion.

WIRT: Worthy.

WISDOM: Wise, knowledgeable.

WISH, WISHY: Hopeful.

WISHBONE: Lucky.

WISHES: Hopes and dreams.

WISHFUL: A dreamer. A pet that seems thoughtful, hopeful, melancholy.

WIT, WITTY: Humorous.

WIZARD: Clever, skillful.
WONDERLY: Wonderful.
WONTON: A good name for an exotic pet from the Orient.
WOOFER: The term for the bass portion of a stereo speaker.
WORTH: Valued.
WOWSER: Upbeat.
WOZ, WOZZLE: Playful.
WUGGLES: Playful.
WUGGY: Playful.
WUZZLE: Playful.
XIMENA: Calm, carefree.
YANK: Slang for Yankee.
YAVAPAI: Smiling.
YAYA: Defiant.
YAZOO: Musical.
YIPPY: Noisy; cheerful.
YODI: A yodeler. A noisy, howling pet.
YOLI: Worthy.
YON: Yonder, distant.
YOWL: To utter a long, mournful cry, wail.
YO-YO: Repetitious.
YUKI: Playful.
ZADOCK: Comical.
ZANA: Zany.
ZANDIE, ZANDY: Fun-loving.
ZANDO: Playful.
ZANNA: Zany.
ZANY: Clownish.

ZAP, ZAPPER: Shocking.
ZED: The British name for the letter Z.
ZEE: A sleepyhead who likes to get his zzz's.
ZEEBO: Playful.
ZIMMIE: Playful.
ZINDEL: Delightful; insightful.
ZIPES: Clumsy.
ZIPPO: Slang for "zero."
ZITA: Persistent.
ZIZI: Playful.
ZOGA: Playful.
ZOGI: Playful.
ZOICKS: Zany.
ZOMBI: Tired.
ZOOG: Animal.
ZOWIE: Shocking.

Lolly, Ace and Brutus

Did You Know?

BILLY BUTTON: Ulysses S. Grant, the 18th President of the United States, had a pony with this name.

MONKEY: The son of Martin the Ape in the medieval beast epic Reynard the Fox. Any of the primates except man and the lemurs, specifically, any of the smaller, long-tailed primates. The real name of the monkey that starred as *Marcel* in the early episodes of the TV series "Friends" and also appeared in the Dustin Hoffman film *Outbreak*.

SCOUT: Slang for a fellow. Watchful. The name of Grammy-award winning singer Sheryl Crow's dog.

Babycake & Boodles

Billy and Nuzzy

Chapter 5

Affectionate and Endearing

There are pet lovers who flatly refuse to name their pet or pets "cutesy-poo" names like Sugar, Sweetums, Sweetpea, and assorted other terms of endearment. But the names offered in this chapter can often be the perfect name for that especially warm-hearted and loving pet. So, be brave, Dear Heart, and choose a sweet moniker for your warm, cuddly, sugar-sweet, new pet!

ADARA: Adoring; beautiful.
ADELPHE: Beloved.
ADONICA: Sweet.
ADORA: Beloved; adoring.
ADORE: To love greatly.
ADOREA, ADORI: To love greatly.
AFINA: Sweet.
ALVINA: Loved.
AMATA: Beloved.
AMESHA: Beloved.
AMOURELLE: Loving.
ANGEL BEAR: Heavenly beast.
ARLISS: Affectionate.
ARLISSA: Affectionate.
ASMUS: Loved.
BABY: Tiny, newborn. Term of endearment.

BABYCAKE, BABYCAKES: Tiny, sweet.
BABYDOLL: Cute.
BABY FACE: Cute; babyish.
BABYLOVE: Tender, loving.
BELOVED: Well-loved.
BETINA, BETTINA: Adoring.
BIG BOO: A term of endearment, meaning "my big man."
BOO: Scared. Also, a term of endearment, meaning "my man."
BOOBLES: Loving.
CANDI, CANDY: Sweet.
CARESS: Rub affectionately.
CARESSA: Lovable.
CASANOVA: A lover.
CHARIS: Loving.

CHARISSA: Loving.
CHARISSE: Loving.
CHARITA: Kind, caring.
CHARITY: Kind, caring.
CHENEY: Peace loving.
CHERELLE: Dear.
CHERISH: Dear. Highly valued.
CHI CHI: Affectionate, Also, frilly, elaborate.
CHUTNEY: Bittersweet.
CINTHIE: Sweet.
COOBY, KOOBY: Loving.
CUDDLE, CUDDLES: Affectionate.
CUDDLY: Affectionate.
DARLING: Beloved, dear.
DARSHA: Beloved.
DAVA: Beloved.
DAVEN: Beloved.
DAVIA: Beloved.
DAVIDA: Beloved.
DAVIE: Beloved.
DEAR, DEAREST: Beloved.
DEARBORN: Beloved.
DESIRE: Coveted, wanted.
DIMP: Short for dimples. Cute.
DIMPLES: A very cute pet.
ELMA: Amiable.
ELSPETH: Loving.
EMBRACE: Loving. Affectionate.
ERASMUS: Loved.

ERASTUS: Beloved.
FRANCHON: Loving.
GOOGIE, GOOGY: Babyish.
GOOGLE: Babyish.
GOO-GOO: Babyish.
HALLIE: Loving.
HALSEY: Affectionate.
HALSTON: Affectionate.
HART: Beloved.
HEART: Loved.
HEARTTHROB: Beloved.
HONEYBEAR: Sweet, cuddly.
HONEYBEE: Active, sweet.
HONEYCOMB: Sweet.
HONEYSWEET: Very sweet.
HUGGLES, HUGGY: Affectionate.
HUGGYBEAR: Affectionate.
HUGS: Affectionate.
JAMMY: Sweet.
KEEPER: Enduring.
KEEPSAKE: Precious.
KEEPSIE, KEEPSY: Precious.
KISS, KISSER: Affectionate.
KISSES: Loving smoocher.
KISSY: Affectionate.
LASS: Young female; a sweetheart.
LEMAN: A sweetheart. Dear man.
LIPS: Affectionate. The name of a fish Beanie Baby.

LITTLE BOO: A term of endearment, meaning "my little man."

LONELYHEART: Affectionate loner.

LOTHARIO: A lover.

LOVE: Affectionate.

LOVEJOY: Loving, joyful.

LOVELL, LOVELLA: Loving.

LUDMILLA: Loved.

LULLABY: Sleepy; babyish.

MABELLA: Lovable.

MABILIA: Amiable.

MAHONEY: Sweet.

MELI: Sweet.

MELIKA: Sweet.

MELITA: Sweet.

MELORA: Sweet.

MINNA: Love.

MISTY: (Old English: "covered with mist") Caring, tearful.

MOOSHI: Affectionate.

MOPPET: A small child, a term of affection.

MUZZY: Affectionate, cuddly, fuzzy.

NUZZLE: To rub with the nose. An affectionate pet.

NUZZY: Nuzzle.

OBELIA: Loving.

OLD SOFTY: Kindhearted.

PADDYCAKE: A child's game. Any playful, babyish pet.

PHEODORA: Adored.

PHILIPPA: Loving.

PHILOMENA: Loving.

POSSUM: Shortened for opossum. Often a term of endearment. Playful, as in playing possum.

PRINCE CHARMING: Perfect mate.

PUDDIN': Sweet. A term of endearment.

PUFF-A-LOVE: Lots of affection.

PUFFBABY: Sweet and fluffy.

PUNKIN: Pumpkin. A term of endearment.

RAPTURE: Carried away by joy, love.

ROMELLA: Loving.

SAMELLA: Affectionate.

SAPPY: Syrupy sweet as a sappy love story.

SATCHMO: Amiable.

SEAMUS: Precious.

SERAFINA: Loving.

SERGE: Loving, romantic.

SERGIO: Loving, romantic.

SHAJI: Playfully loving.

SHERENA: Beloved.

SHERENE: Beloved.

SHUG: Sugar. Sweet.

SMITTY: Loving.
SMOOCH, SMOOCHES: To kiss, affectionate.
SMOOCHI, SMOOCHY: To kiss, affectionate.
SNOOGLE, SNOOGLES: Affectionate.
SNOOKY: Loving.
SNUGGLE, SNUGGLES: Cuddly, affectionate.
SNUGGLEBEAR: Affectionate, bearlike, cute.
SNUGGY: Affectionate, cute.
SNUGGYBEAR: Affectionate, bearlike, cute.
SOFTY: Softhearted, kind.
SUGAR: A very sweet pet, lovable.
SUGAR BABE: Sweet baby.
SUGAR BABY: Sweet, little.
SUGARFOOT: A sweet busybody.
SUGARPLUM: Sweet.
SWEET: Loving.
SWEETHEART: Loved one.
SWEETIE: A darling, a sweet pet.
SWEETPEA: A sweet pet.
SWEETS: A pet that likes candies and cakes.
SWEETUMS: Loving.
TEELA: Loving.
TODDIE, TODDY: Sweet.
TOLLY: Affectionate.

TOOKIE, TOUKIE: Affectionate.
TOOTIE: Dear.
TOOTS: Dear. A playful form of address.
TOOTSIE: Sweet.
TRUELOVE: Loved one, beloved.
TRULY: Genuine as a true love or a true friend.
TURTLEDOVE: Sweet.
VALENTINA: Valorous. A sweetheart.
VALENTINE: (Latin: "strong") A sweetheart. For Saint Valentine, a Roman martyr-priest, who became known as a patron of lovers.
VALENTYNE: Valentine. A sweetheart.
VENA: Loving.
VENNA: Loving.
VIDAL: Beloved.

Taffy, Buxton and Minka

Did You Know?

BELLE: (French: "beautiful, lovely") A lady as in "Southern belle." Slash, guitarist for the rock band Guns N' Roses, has a golden retriever with this name.

LING LING: The name of the panda given to the United States by China.

SCANNON: A black Newfoundland that accompanied Lewis and Clark on the Pacific Expedition.

DIGGER

Chapter 6

ENERGETIC AND ADVENTURESOME

Sometimes a new pet is bounding with energy and getting into one adventure after another (and sometimes a little trouble along the way as well!) For the energetic, nonstop, always-on-the-go pet, try: **Bounder** or **Dango** or **Kiko** - or any of the names in this chapter!

AHLEAH: Agile.

ALLEY: A pet that strays.

ANNIHILATOR: Destroyer.

ARLON: Hunter.

ARLY: Hunter.

ARVID: Wanderer.

ATOR: Short for gladiator. Warrior.

AURA: Energy.

AURELINA: Aura.

AVI, AVIA: Flighty.

AVIS: Flighty.

AVIVA: Flighty.

AZAZEL: Spirited.

BANG: Noisy.

BANGAROO: Noisy; rowdy.

BANG BANG: Noisy.

BANGO: Noisy.

BARBAR: Short for barbarian.

BARBARIAN: A brute.

BARDO: Digger.

BASHER: Destructive.

BEAST: A brute.

BEASTIE, BEASTY: Active, frightful.

BIZZY: Busy.

BLIP: Fast.

BLITZ: Overwhelming. The name of a trained stunt dog performing at Dollywood, located in eastern Tennessee.

BLITZEN: Fast. The name of one of Santa's eight reindeer.

BLITZER: Overwhelming.

BLIX: Overwhelming.

BOAZ: Swift and strong.

BOBBLIN: A pet that bobbles about.

BOINGO: Springy.

BOLT: Fast as a lightning bolt.
BOMB: Noisy.
BOMBI: Noisy.
BOMBSHELL: Spontaneous.
BONG: Noisy.
BOOM BOOM: Noisy.
BOOMERANG: Repetitious; pesky.
BORG: Warrior.
BORK: Warrior.
BOSSY: A bully; fussy.
BOUNCE, BOUNCY: A noisy rush, to jump, spirited.
BOUNCER: Spirited, jumper.
BOUNDER: Calvin Coolidge, the 30th President of the United States, had a cat with this name.
BRAT: Mischievous pest.
BRAVE: Fearless.
BRAVESTAR: Fearless.
BRAWLER: Fighter.
BREE: Brisk.
BREEZE: Cool, flowing, graceful, or fast and destructive.
BREEZIE, BREEZY: Commotion, to move jauntily.
BRISBY: Energetic.
BRISCO: Self-assured; energetic.
BRISKER: Swift; energetic.
BRISKY: Swift; energetic.

BRUISER: A brawler.
BRUNHILDA: Active.
BRUT: A bully.
BRY: Short for Bryson.
BRYAN: Strong.
BRYANT: Strong.
BRYCE: Fast.
BRYNHILDE: Strong.
BRYNN: Strong.
BRYSON: Strong.
BUBBLES: Lively. The name of pop superstar Michael Jackson's pet chimp.
BUCCANEER: A hunter.
BUCKO: A bully.
BUCKSHOT: Fast as a shot. Any speedy pet.
BUCKY: Strong.
BUNGEE, BUNGEY: A daredevil.
BUZZER: Noisy, energetic.
BUZZY: Noisy, energetic.
CAMMY: Energetic.
CANNON: Noisy, fast.
CANNONBALL: Noisy, fast.
CAPRIOLE: Leap.
CASSIUS: Ruthless.
CHA CHA: Rhythmic.
CHANOOK: Agile.
CHASE, CHASER: A pet that chases its tail or another pet.
CISCO: Daredevil.
CISCO KID: Daredevil. From the song "Cisco Kid" by the

music group War.

COMMOTION: Disorderly.

CONQUEROR: Winner.

CORKY: Sprightly.

CRAZYLEGS: A very active and energetic pet.

CRUISER: Carefree.

CRUSHER: Ruthless.

CRUZ: Carefree.

CULVER: Flighty.

DANGER: Reckless.

DANGO: Reckless.

DAREDEVIL: Reckless.

DASH: Fast. Benjamin Harrison, the 23rd President of the United States, had a dog with this name.

DASHER: Spirited, fast. The name of one of Santa's eight reindeer.

DASHIELL: Fast.

DEAN, DEANE: A wanderer.

DEANA: A wanderer.

DEANIE: A wanderer.

DEIDRE: Spirited.

DEIRDRE: Spirited.

DEMETRIUS: Mighty.

DERRINGDO: Daring action, reckless courage.

DERRY: Daredevil.

DESPERADO: Dangerous, reckless outlaw.

DESTROYER: Destructive.

DETOUR: A pet that always takes a shortcut when called.

DEVIL: Mischievous.

DEVILLE: Devilish.

DICKIE: Strong.

DIEDRA: Spirited.

DIGBY: A digger.

DIGGER: Always digging.

DILLON: Strong.

DINTY: Energetic. A pet with a hearty appetite.

DIRK: Quick and strong.

DIVER: Any pet that loves to swim.

DONNYBROOK: A fight, ruckus.

DONOVAN: Ruler.

DONTE: Ruler.

DORSEY: Strong.

DOUBLE TROUBLE: Very naughty.

FIZZI: Noisy.

FIZZLE: Noisy.

FLETA: Fleeting, swift.

FLIP: Quick, active; a daredevil.

FLORETTA: Full of vigor.

FLURRY: Causing a commotion.

FOBIE: Mischievous.

FOOTLOOSE: Carefree.

FORTIS: Brave and daring.

FRANCHOT: Free.

FRANCI, FRANCIE: Free spirit.

DREW: Strong.
DRIFTER: A pet that often strays from home.
DRIFTY: A wanderer.
DRU: Strong. Short for Drucilla.
DRUCILLA: Strong.
DURAN: Strong. Tough.
DYNAMITE: Powerful, energetic.
DYNAMO: Powerful.
ELLAROO: She. Energetic.
ELORA: Conqueror.
ELSEN, ELSON: Powerful.
ELSU: Soaring.
ERROL: A wanderer.
ESCAPADE: Reckless, adventurous.
EUPHORIA: Vigorous.
EVERARD: Strong.
EVIE: Lively.
EWALD: Strong.
EXA: A wanderer.
EXO: Short for exodus. A wanderer.
EXODUS: A wanderer.
FABRICE: Worker.
FALCO: Swift, hunter.
FANDANGO: A lively dancer.
FANESTRA: Enthusiastic.
FARENA: Wanderer.
FARREL: Fearless.
FARREN: Strong.

FEARLESS: Brave.
FEISTY: Lively.
FERGUS: Strong; wild.
FERNANDO: Adventurous.
FEROCIOUS: Fierce.
FEROCITY: Ferocious.
FERRELL: Fearless.
FETCH: A good name for a dog that retrieves.
FETCHER: A pet that retrieves.
FIDGET, FIDGETY: Restless.
FINONA: A wanderer.
FIREBALL: Adventurous, hot-tempered.
FIREBRAND: Troublemaker.
FIZZ: Noisy.
FRANCINA: Free spirit.
FREEWAY: A pet that wanders.
FRENZY: Frantic, wildly excited.
FRISBEE: A toy that glides after it is thrown and caught. Any playful pet that loves to jump.
FRISKER, FRISKERS: Lively, frolicsome.
FRISKY: Lively, frolicsome.
FROLIC: Lively, merry.
GAMBLE: Playful; risk-taker.
GARETH: Swift.
GARREN: Swift.

GARMON: Warrior.
GARRICK: Warrior.
GATLING: Swift.
GILES: Warrior.
GIMLET: A digger.
GOFER: A pet that retrieves.
GRASSHOPPER: A pet that loves to jump.
GUS: Active.
GUSSIE: Active.
HADLEY: Brave warrior.
HADWICK: Brave warrior.
HADWIN: Brave warrior.
HAMP: Disruptive.
HARDEN: Swift.
HARVE: Warrior.
HARVEY: Warrior.
HASTINGS: Swift.
HASTY: Swift; hot-tempered.
HAVOC: Unruly.
HAZARD: Risky.
HEISHA: Spirited.
HEISHI: Spirited.
HELIX: Any pet that spins around or chases its tail.
HELMUTT: Strong.
HERNAN: Warrior.
HERNANDO: Warrior.
HERO: Having great strength and courage.
HERVE: Warrior.
HIJINKS: Mischief-maker.
HIKER: Active; wanderer.
HOBO: A wanderer.

HOHOKAM: Fleeting, swift.
HOOPI, HOOPIE: Excitable, active.
HOOPLA: Excitable, active.
HOP: Athletic. Any pet that hops.
HOPPO: A pet that hops.
HOPPY: Athletic. A pet that hops, especially a rabbit.
HOT FOOT: Full of energy; always in a hurry.
HUBBUB: Uproar.
HUGHES: Strong.
HUNTER: Fearless.
HUNTLEY: Hunter.
HUNTRESS: Lady hunter.
HURDLE: A pet that leaps over obstacles or races about.
HURLY, HURLEY: Hurly burly, meaning an uproar.
IGOR: Active. Russian form of Inger.
ILIA: Agile.
ISA: Strong, caring.
ISEA: Strong.
ISRA: A fighter.
JAEMEEL: Hunter.
JAMBOREE: Noisy.
JAMONA: Strong woman.
JAMU: Lively.
JANGLE, JANGLES: Noisy. For the popular song recorded by the Nitty Gritty Dirt Band, "Mr. Bo Jangles."

JAZZBONE: Lively.
JERANDA: Active.
JETTIE: Fast.
JIGGLES: Energetic.
JINKS: Short for hijinks. A playfully mischievous pet.
JITZI: Fidgety.
JONELLA, JONELLE: Flighty.
JUDD: Strong.
JUICY: Lively.
JUMBLE: Disorderly.
JUMPER, JUMPY: A pet that jumps or hops.
KABOOM: Noisy.
KAMESHA: Energetic.
KAMMY: Energetic.
KANGA: Short for Kangaroo. Jumpy.
KAOS: Chaos.
KAYO: A knockout. A rambunctious pet.
KAZAA: Active.
KEEJI: Mischievous.
KEELEE: Mischievous.
KEELER: Mischievous.
KEIFER: A wanderer.
KEIKO, KIKO: Energetic.
KELA: Brave.
KELBY: Warrior.
KEMPER: Eager.
KEMRA: Ruler.
KENRIC: Ruler.
KERSEY: Strong.

KERWIN: Strong.
KEV, KEVY: Short for Kevin.
KIERON: Strong.
KIKO: Lively, spirited.
KILLER: Aggressive, ferocious. Actor David Hasselhoff, the former star of the TV series "Knight Rider" and star of "Baywatch," has a Pomeranian with this name. Also, tennis great Martina Navratilova has a dog named Killer Dog.
KNUCKLES: Tough. The name of a Beanie Baby pig.
KOODOO: Swift. Kudu, meaning a grayish brown African antelope.
KYAN, KYEN: Active.
KYPER: Active.
LAIKA: A wanderer. A dog that reached orbit for the Russian space program in 1957.
LAMAR: Swift.
LAMIAS: Swift, fleeing.
LASSO: Active.
LAVITA: Lively.
LAWANDA: A wanderer.
LEATHER: Tough.
LEWEY: Warrior.
LEXINE: Kind.
LIAM: Protector.
LIDO: A fighter.
LISSA, LYSSA: Active.

LOOPY: Daredevil. A pet that performs physical feats.
LORI: Fast.
LORNA, LORNE: Energetic.
LOUISANNE: Warrior.
LUANN, LUANNA: Warrior.
LUDDIE: Loved.
LUGER: Strong.
LULA: Swift.
LULIE: Swift.
LUTWIDGE: A fighter.
MANETTE: Spirited.
MANGLER: Vicious.
MATADOR: Fearless, quick.
MESSENGER: Forerunner, runner of errands, bringer of news.
MILOS: Traveler.
MINX: Bold, lively.
MOBLEY: Mobile; always on the go.
MYLA: Traveler.
MYLEN: Traveler.
MYLES: Traveler.
MYLO: Traveler. The name of the dog that co-starred with comedian Jim Carey in the movie *The Mask.*
NIMBLE: Lively.
NINJA: A Japanese secret warrior.
NOMA: A wanderer.
NOMAD: A wanderer.
NOMIE: A wanderer.

OZELL: Lively.
OZELLA: Lively.
PEPPER: A zestful pet.
PEPPY: Brisk, energetic.
PERKY: Spirited, brisk.
PING PONG: An active, playful pet. A game similar to tennis, played on a table with a small, celluloid ball and small racket-shaped paddles. A pet that moves from side to side, to and fro.
PIPPA: Lively.
PISTOL: (Czech: "a whistling sound") A small firearm fired with one hand. A pet that whistles or is full of energy and quick like a shot.
POGI: Active.
POOBY: Rascally.
POOGIE, POOJIE: A rascally pet.
POPPIE: Spontaneous.
POPPO: Active.
POPSI, POPSY: Active.
POUNCER, POUNCY: A pet that leaps onto people or things. Playful and energetic.
POWER: Mighty, strong.
PRESTO: Quick.
PRESTON: Quick.
PUNCHY: Strong.
PYEWACKET: Causing a racket.

QUEST: Wandering; hunting.
QUICK: Fast.
QUIGLEY: Brisk.
RABBLE: From rabble rouser, one who is noisy and tries to stir up others by appealing to their emotions.
RACE: Speedy.
RACER: Speedy. A pet that is always trying to outrun you. A pet that races around the house.
RACINE: Fast.
RACKET: Noisy uproar.
RAIDER: Abrupt, unpredictable, fighter.
RAMBLER: A wanderer.
RANGER: A wanderer. Also, a U.S. warden who patrols government forests. George Bush, the 41st President of the United States, had a Springer spaniel with this name.
RAPSCALLION: A rascal.
RATHBONE: Quick.
RATTLES: Noisy.
RAVE: Wildly enthusiastic.
RAVON: Enthusiastic.
RAWHIDE: Tough.
REBEL: A warrior who resists authority.
RECKLESS: Careless.
REEVE: Rambler.
RENEGADE: One who aban-

dons. A pet that strays.
RESTLESS: Active. Uneasy.
RIPLEY: Rowdy.
RIPPLE: Small disturbance.
RISKIT: A daredevil.
RISKY: Hazardous.
ROAM: Wanderer. The name of a Beanie Baby buffalo.
ROAMER, ROAMY: A wanderer. A pet that strays.
ROAR, ROARY: A pet that roars.
ROLLIE, ROLLY: Short for Roland. A pet that likes to roll around on the floor or on the ground.
ROMEY: A wanderer.
ROMPER: One who engages in lively play.
ROO: Short for kangaroo. A pet that jumps, leaps or hops about.
ROUNDABOUT: Encircling, indirect.
ROUSER: A fighter.
ROVER: A wandering pet. A common name for a dog.
ROWDY: Rough, disorderly.
ROWSER: Rouser, a fighter.
RUCKUS: Noisy uproar.
RUFFY: Rough.
RUMBLE: A continuously noisy pet.
RUMBO: Powerful; noisy.

RUNNER: Fast, always on the run.

RUTHLESS: Vicious.

SABA: Active, healthy.

SAFARI: Hunting.

SAUCY: Lively.

SAVAGE: Wild.

SCALLI: Short for scalawag, meaning a scamp.

SCAMPER: A rascally, mischievous fellow.

SCHUYLER: (Pronounced "sky-lar") Free-spirited.

SCOUNDREL: A rascal.

SCRAMBLE: A fighter.

SCRAPPER: Slang for fond of fighting.

SCRATCH: Devilish.

SCREECHY: Noisy.

SCUFF, SCUFFY: Brawl.

SCURRY: To hurry hurriedly, scamper.

SEBERT: Warrior.

SHADRAC: Conqueror.

SHARKEY: Ferocious as a shark.

SHENANIGAN: Mischief; trickiness.

SHERIDAN: (Celtic-Gaelic) Wild.

SHINDIG: A commotion.

SHINDY: A commotion.

SHOO SHOO: Busybody.

SHORTCUT: A pet that usu-ally knows a shorter way to get to the same place.

SHOTSIE: Fast as a shot.

SHOW OFF: Vain.

SHREDDER: Destructive.

SHU-SHU: Busybody.

SIGWALD: Strong.

SKADOO: Speedy.

SKEDADDLE: A pet that scurries.

SKEETBOT: Active.

SKELTER: Short for helter-skelter, every which way.

SKID: Energetic.

SKIDBOOT: A pet that skids to a stop.

SKIDDER, SKIDDIE: A pet that skids or slides when coming to a stop after a brisk run.

SKIDDLES: A pet that skids to a stop.

SKIDDO: Energetic.

SKIPPER: One who skips.

SKITCH: Quick.

SKITTER: To dart about quickly, especially over water.

SKITTLE: A pet that glides or skips lightly or quickly.

SKITTY: Quick.

SKIZZY: Quick.

SKYE: Sky; free-spirited.

SKYLAR: Sky; free-spirited.

SLASH: Spirited.

SLINGSHOT: A forked stick

or other instrument with an elastic band attached for shooting small objects.

SLITHER: To slide; the motion a snake makes.

SLOOPY: To glide; a pet that swims well.

SMASH, SMASHER: A destructive pet.

SOCKO: Rowdy.

SOMER: Short for somerset, meaning a somersault. Any active pet that performs leaps or daredevil stunts.

SONIC: The name of the fast hedgehog in the game "Sonic the Hedgehog" from Sega.

SPARKLE, SPARKLES: Lively, glittering.

SPINNER: A pet that spins around, perhaps chasing after his tail.

SPIRIT: High-spirited, lively.

SPLASH, SPLASHY: Attention-getter, a pet that is prone to splashing in water or mud.

SPLASHER: A pet that splashes.

SPRIGHTLY: Lively, happy.

SPRING: Fresh, lively.

SPRITZ, SPRITZI: Lively.

SPRY: Full of life, active.

SPUNKY: Having spunk, a brave, spirited pet.

STARBLAZER: Bright; speedy.

STRAY: A wanderer.

STRAYKIT: Short for stray kitten, the name of one of author Mark Twain's pet cats.

STREAK: Fast.

STREAKER: Fast as a streak. John F. Kennedy, the 35th President of the United States, had a Welsh terrier with this name.

STREAKY: Fast.

STRIDER: To walk with long steps and in a vigorous or pompous manner.

STRIKER, STRYKER: Noisy, rough, rambunctious.

SUNDANCER: Lively.

SWIFTY: Fast.

SWOOSIE: Lively.

TAG: A playful pet; a pet that loves to run toward you and then quickly dash away.

TAILSPIN: A pet that chases its tail.

TAIR, TAIRON: Destructive.

TALLY: Short for tallyho, the cry of a hunter.

TARELL: Destructive.

TAREN, TARREN: Destructive.

TARGET: Defensive.

TELLY: Forceful; vocal.

TEMPEST: A strong wind; commotion.
TERMITE: Destructive.
TETCHY: Touchy, irritable.
THORA: Thunderous; loud.
THORTON: Thunderous; noisy.
THRASHER: Move about powerfully.
THUNDERBOLT: Loud.
THUNDERFOOT: Noisy; swift.
TIFFY: Argumentative.
TIGAR: Aggressive.
TIGE: Strong.
TIGUE: Strong.
TIKO: A bouncy, playful pet.
TILDA: Strong, brave.
TIZZY: Any pet often in a state of excited frenzy.
TNT: Explosive. Any pet that is extremely mischievous or temperamental.
TOAD, TOADY: A pet that jumps like a frog.
TOPHER: Strong.
TOPPER: Daring.
TOPPY: Daring.
TOPSY: From "topsy turvy," a fast, daring pet.
TOREN: A fighter.
TOUGHIE: Strong.
TRACKER: A hunter.
TRAP: Short for Trapper.

TRAPPER: A hunter.
TRAVELER: A pet that roams, strays.
TRAVEN: A traveler.
TRENDAN: (Anglo-Saxon: "to roll") A pet that rolls about or tumbles.
TRENDEL: (Anglo-Saxon: "a circle") A pet that sometimes moves in circles or chases its tail.
TRIGGER: Quick. The name of Roy Roger's horse.
TROT, TROTTER: A runner.
TROUBLE, TROUBLES: A pet that is always into something.
TROXEY: Active.
TRUNDEE: A pet that rolls about or tumbles.
TUCKER: Energetic.
TUG, TUGGER: Mischievous.
TUGGLES: Mischievous.
TUGGO: Mischievous.
TUMBELENA: A pet that tumbles, rolls.
TUMBLES: A pet that is active and energetic.
TUMBLEWEED: Gone like the wind, never in one place for long.
TUSSIE: From tussle meaning

to pull, struggle, wrestle.

TWEAKY: Abrupt, unpredictable.

TWIST, TWISTER: A pet that moves in circles or chases its tail.

TYCE: Explosive.

VAGABOND: A wanderer.

VALECIA: Strong.

VALEN: Strong.

VALENCIA: Strong.

VAMOOSE: To depart rapidly; run away.

VANDA: Wanderer.

VARMINT: Rascally.

VEGAS: A wanderer.

VERDA: Lively, unspoiled.

VICIOUS: A ferocious pet.

VIGOR: Energetic.

VINCENTIA: Conqueror.

VIVECA: Lively.

WAGGLES: A pet that wags its tail.

WALDEMAN: Strong, bold.

WALLOP: (Old French) Gallop.

WANDERER: A pet that strays.

WARNER: Protector.

WARRIOR: A fighter.

WAYFARER: Traveler.

WAYWARD: Willful, unpredictable.

WEN: Wanderer.

WENTWORTH: A roamer.

WHEELER: A pet that has excellent coordination.

WHIPLASH: Fast.

WHIRLY: A pet that travels in circles or chases its tail.

WHIZZ, WHIZZER: Swift.

WIGGLER: A wiggly, squirmy pet.

WIGGLES: A wiggly, squirmy pet.

WIGGLY: A pet that squirms. The name of a children's game, "Uncle Wiggly."

WINDY: Blowing in and out like the wind; a pet that keeps on the move.

WRANGLER: A fighter.

WYCLIFFE: A climber.

YORGI: Warrior.

YORI: Warrior.

ZIG-ZAG: A pet that zips in all directions.

ZING: Full of zest, fast.

ZINI: Vitality.

ZIP: A pet that zips here and there.

ZOLTAN: Strong.

ZONK, ZONKS: Lively.

ZONKY: Lively.

ZOOMER: Zooming, fast and sudden.

ZORGUS: Active.

Huxley

Did You Know?

DYLAN: Renee Zellweger, star of the movie *Bridget Jones's Diary*, has a Golden Retriever/collie mix with this name.

SEABISCUIT: For the thoroughbred racing horse that became a champion and then a legend and whose story became the basis for a bestselling book and movie.

TOM QUARTZ: Theodore Roosevelt, the 26th President of the United States, had a cat with this name.

Ed

Chapter 7

Favorite Televison Series and Movies

Favorite television series (as well commercials) and movies, past and present, can be wonderful sources of names for new pets: *Alf, Forest Gump, Morris, Good Boy!,* and others.

Kids can name their new pets after favorite characters in their favorite TV shows and movies: *Blue* (the clever dog in the children's TV series "Blue's Clues"), *Diesel* (one of the Siberian huskies in the Disney movie *Snow Dogs),* *Hubble* (the border terrier who is really an alien scout in the movie *Good Boy!),* *Tinky Winky* (the name of the purple character in the popular children's TV series "Teletubbies"), among others.

Naming a pet after a favorite character is a great way to help small kids remember a new pet's name.

ALF: Small like an elf. The furry, space creature from TV the series "Alf."

ALFALFA: Food for cows, goats, and other farm animals. The name of one the kids in the TV series "Our Gang," which later became better known as "The Little Rascals," and on which a movie was based.

ALLEGRA: Spirited. Energetic. The name of the preschooler in the children's TV series "Allegra's Window."

ANAKIN: Luke's father and creator of C-P30, a young pilot whose story was told in the

George Lucas film *Star Wars: Episode 1.*

ANGEL: (Greek: "a messenger of God") The name of one of the X-Men in the animated TV series and movie.

ANNE-MARIE: The name of the innocent young girl in the animated movie *All Dogs Go to Heaven.*

APPOLONIA: Musical goddess. For actress Appolonia, who starred with the pop star formerly known as Prince in the movie *Purple Rain.*

ARNOLD: (Old German: "strong as an eagle") The name of the highly intelligent pig in the 1960s TV series "Green Acres."

ASTA: Goddess. A dog in the movie series *The Thin Man.*

AVERY: Far-seeing, a ruler. The name of Murph's baby in the TV series "Murphy Brown."

BABY BOP: The name of the smallest dinosaur in the children's TV series "Barney & Friends."

BALKI: The name of a lovable but eccentric character in the TV series "Perfect Strangers."

BARBARA ANN: The white poodle in the movie *Good Boy!*

BARKLEY: A puppet, Barkley the Dog, on the PBS TV series "Sesame Street." Also, the name of the dog in the 1994 movie "Clean Slate" starring Dana Carvey.

BARKY: The name of the disgruntled dog mascot in the TV commercial for candy.

BARNABUS: Prophet. The vampire in the TV series "Dark Shadows."

BEA, BEE: Blessed, busy, droning. The name of Andy's Aunt Bee in the 1960s TV series "The Andy Griffith Show."

BEASTMASTER: Leader of animals. From the popular TV series "The Beastmaster."

BEAVER: Having large teeth, especially directly in front. The mischievous young son in the old TV series "Leave It to Beaver."

BEETHOVEN: For German composer Ludwig von Beethoven. The name of the mischievous Saint Bernard in the movie of the same name.

BEETLEJUICE: The name of the playful and sarcastic ghost in the movie and animated TV series "Beetlejuice."

BELVEDERE: For the English butler in the TV series "Mr. Belvedere." Also, the name of a cartoon dog in an oldie TV series.

BENJI: Loyal. The cute and clever dog in the Walt Disney movies.

BERFORD, BURRFORD: In the 1960s TV series "The Dick Van Dyke Show," the pet name Rob's brother called Rob and others when he was sleep-walking.

BERT, BURT: (Old English: "bright") The name of Ernie's friend in the long-running PBS series "Sesame Street."

BESSIE: Humble. The name of the cow in the old TV commercials for the Borden dairy products. The name of a brown and white Beanie Baby cow.

BETA: Second letter of the Greek alphabet. The name of the amorous young girl in the movie *My Girl.*

BETTY LOU: The name of a character in the PBS children's series "Sesame Street."

BIG BIRD: The large, yellow bird on the PBS TV series "Sesame Street."

BIONIC: A pet that does incredible stunts. The Bionic Dog was featured in the TV series "The Bionic Woman," starring Lindsay Wagner.

BIRCHUM: The name of the wacky outdoorsman in the TV series "Crank Yankers."

BLOSSOM: Colorful. The name of the teenage girl in the TV series "Blossom."

BODI: The real name of the dog featured in the movie *Steel Magnolias.*

BOND: For British novelist Ian Fleming's infamous Agent 007, James Bond, hero in the long-running movies series.

BONO: For lead singer of the Irish rock band U2.

BONZO: From *Bedtime for Bonzo,* a 1940s movie starring Ronald Reagan, who later became 40th President of the United States.

BOOMER: Loud. The name of a clever, lovable dog in the Disney TV series "Boomer."

BOZO: The name of Bozo the Clown in the children's TV series "The Bozo Super Sunday Show."

BRANDO: For actor Marlon

Brando who starred in many films including *A Streetcar Named Desire* and *Apocalypse Now.*

BRANDON: (Old English: "from the beacon hill") Energetic. The name of Punky's dog in the TV series "Punky Brewster."

BRADY: Repetitious. The name of the family in the TV series "The Brady Bunch."

BREATHLESS: Full of excitement. For the character portrayed by Madonna in the movie *Dick Tracy,* which was based on the comic strip.

BUCK: Strong. The name of the family dog, a briard, in the TV series "Married . . .With Children."

BUCKWHEAT: Dark. The name of one of the kids in the TV series "Our Gang," which later became better known as "The Little Rascals" and on which a movie was based.

BUD: The name of the dog in Ken Burns' *America's First Road Trip*, a filmed reconstruction of that historic first automobile trip.

BUDDY: Companion, friend. The name of the bull dog in the early episodes of the TV series "Veronica's Closet." Also, President Clinton, the 42nd President of the United States, had a chocolate Labrador retriever with this name.

BUFORD: The hound dog in the TV variety series "Hee Haw."

BULL: Powerful. Strong. The name of the lovable bald character on the TV series "Night Court."

BULLET: Fast. The name of the life-saving heroic dog in the 1950s TV series "The Roy Rogers Show."

C-3PO: The tall, worrisome android, made of spare and discarded parts, in George Lucas' movie "Star Wars."

CALISTA: Rhythmic, beautiful. The name of the actress, Calista Flockhart, who portrayed the lead character in the TV series "Ally McBeal."

CARABOO: From the true-life story and movie about Princess Caraboo, who charmed the English aristocrats.

CASABLANCA: The title of an enduring and romantic movie starring Ingrid Bergman and Humphrey Bogart.

CASEY: The name of the lovable baby, dinosaur-like creature in the movie "Gargantua."

CELESTE: Celestial. The name of the spotted cow in the children's TV series "Old MacDonald's Farm."

CHACHI: A spirited young man in the TV series "Happy Days."

CHANCE: Risk-taker. Lucky. For the bulldog puppy in the Disney movie *Homeward Bound.*

CHEECH: From Cheech Marin, one half of the '70s comedy team Cheech & Chong.

CHEWBACCA: A tall, furry creature in George Lucas's film *Star Wars.*

CHEWI, CHEWY: Always hungry. Nickname for Chewbacca, a tall, furry creature in George Lucas's film *Star Wars.*

CHRISTY: Anointed. The young schoolteacher and heroine of the novel *Christy* by Catherine Marshall and on which a TV series was based.

CHUCKLES: Mildly amused. The name of the clown who hosted a children's TV series in the "Mary Tyler Moore Show."

CINDEL: Bright. The name of the young girl in George Lucas's movie *The Ewok Adventure.*

CLARABELLE: Bright flower. The name of the clown in the 1950s children's TV series "Howdy Doody."

CLAUDE: Weak. The name of the poodle in early episodes of the TV series "The Beverly Hillbillies."

CLEO: Royalty. The dog in the vintage TV series "The People's Choice," starring Jackie Cooper.

CODY: Brave, strong. William Frederick Cody, an American scout and showman, who was known as Buffalo Bill. The name of the malamute in the TV series "Dr. Quinn, Medicine Woman."

COLUMBO: For the bumbling detective in the TV series "Columbo."

COMET: Swift. The name of the Tanner's pet golden retriever in the TV series "Full House." Also, the name of one of Santa's eight reindeer.

CONAN: Physically strong. For the comic book and motion picture series hero *Conan the Barbarian.*

COOKIE MONSTER: The name of the character who loves cookies in the children's TV series "Sesame Street." A good name for any pet that loves cookies.

COOPER: The name of the family dog in the movie *What Lies Beneath.*

CORRINA: Maiden. For the Whoopi Goldberg movie *Corrina, Corrina,* about a young girl who fixes her nanny up with her widowed father.

CORY: A flower. The name of the young son of "Julia" in the TV series starring Diahann Carroll.

COWBOY: The name of the Doberman in the movie *Nightkill.* President George W. Bush, the 43rd President of the Unites Stares, had a cat with this name.

CUJO: The ferocious Saint Bernard in the Stephen King novel of the same name, on which a movie was based.

DAPHNE: (Greek: "the bay tree") In Greek mythology, a nymph who escaped from Apollo by becoming a laurel tree. The name of the poodle in the movie *Look Who's Talking Too.*

DAR: The name of the hero in the TV series "Beast-master."

DARLA: Loving. The name of one of the kids in the TV series "Our Gang," which later became better known as "The Little Rascals" and on which a movie was based.

DARREN: Dear one. The name of Samantha's husband in the TV series "Bewitched."

DATA: Highly intelligent. The name of a character in the science fiction TV series "Star Trek: The Next Generation."

DAUBER: White. The name of a bumbling character in the TV series "Coach."

DEEJ: The name of a character in George Lucas's movie *The Ewok Adventure.*

DEMON: Devilish. The name of one of the Siberian huskies in the Disney movie *Snow Dogs.*

DIESEL: Known German engineer Rudolph Diesel who invented the diesel engine. The name of one of the Siberian huskies in the Disney movie *Snow Dogs.*

DIGIT: Intelligent. The name of a primate in the movie *Gorillas in the Mist,* which was based on anthropologist Dian Fossey's fight to save the gorillas from poachers.

DINK: Short for Dinky. Tiny. In wrestling (WWE), Doink the Clown's tiny sidekick. Also for the dinosaur in the cartoon TV series "Dink the Dinosaur." The name of the Chihuahua in the Taco Bell commercials.

DIPSY: The name of the green character in the popular children's series "Teletubbies."

D.J.: Short for disc jockey. The name of the oldest daughter on the TV series "Full House." A pet that craves attention.

DODGER: Tricky. Energetic. The name of the mischievous monkey in the movie *Monkey Trouble.*

DOINK: The name of a mischievous clown wrestler in the World Wrestling Entertainment (WWE). Doink's small sidekick is a tiny clown named Dink.

DOOGIE: The name of the teenage doctor in the TV series "Doogie Houser, MD."

DORF: Dwarf. The name of the short, stout character portrayed by comedian Tim Conway.

DOROTHY: Heavenly gift. The young girl swept away by a cyclone in L. Frank Baum's classic children's novel *The Wizard of Oz,* which became a movie starring Judy Garland.

DREYFUSS: The name of the family dog in the TV series "Empty Nest."

DROBNEY: Kingly. The name of a duck, said to be royalty, in the 1960s TV series "Green Acres."

DUCHESS: Noble. The name of one of the Siberian huskies in the Disney movie *Snow Dogs.*

DUDLEY: (Celtic: "fair field") The name of the bumbling dragon in the children's TV series "The Adventures of Dudley the Dragon." Also, the name of a dog in the children's TV series "The Bozo Super Sunday Show."

DUNCAN: (Gaelic: "brown

warrior") The name of Grover's family dog in the PBS children's series "Sesame Street."

DUNDEE: A seaport in Eastern Scotland. The name of the hero from "down under" in the movie series about Crocodile Dundee portrayed by Australian actor Paul Hogan.

EARNEST: The name of the dog featured in the TV series "Dave's World," Earnest was a rescue dog for eight years before she was added to this television series.

ED: Short for Edward. Guardian. The name of a hyena in the Disney animated movie *The Lion King.* Also, the name of the talking horse in the 1950s TV series "Mr. Ed."

EDDIE: A nickname for Edward. Valued guardian. The name of the Jack Russell terrier in the TV series "Fraiser."

ELIZA: Short for Elizabeth. For Eliza Doolittle, a character played by Barbara Streisand in the movie *My Fair Lady.* Also, the adventurous young girl in the animated movie *The Wild Thornberrys.*

ELSA: Elf. In the movie *Born Free,* the name given to the orphaned lion cub raised by a British game warden and his wife in Africa.

ELWOOD: The name of one of the Blues Brothers in the movie, which was based on a sketch from "Saturday Night Live."

ERIS: The moody Goddess of Chaos voiced by Michelle Pfeiffer in the animated movie *Sinbad: Legend of the Seven Seas.*

ERNEST: Resolute. From the comical character in the movies about a simple guy, as portrayed by actor Jim Varney.

ERNIE: (Old English: "earnest") The name of Bert's friend in the long-running children's series "Sesame Street." President George W. Bush, the 43rd President of the United States, has a cat with this name, a six-toed cat named after Ernest Hemingway.

E.T.: From the Steven Spielberg movie of the same name. Short for extra-terrestrial.

EUREKA, EUREEKA: Triumphant. The name of a character in the children's TV series "Eureeka's Castle."

EVER: Eternally. The name of actress Ever Caradine who starred in *My Boss's Daughter* and other movies and TV series.

EWOK: Small, furry creatures in George Lucas's *Star Wars* movie series.

FAIRCHILD: Elf. The name of the pet bear in the TV series "The Beverly Hillbillies."

FARFEL: The name of the dog in the vintage TV commercial for Nestle's chocolate.

FARLEY: Superior. The name of a character in the children's TV series "Sesame Street."

FERDIE: The name of Mickey Mouse's nephew in the Disney cartoons.

FESS: Truthful. For actor Fess Parker in starred in the TV series "Davy Crockett" and "Daniel Boone."

FESTER: From Uncle Fester, a character in the TV series "The Addams Family," on which a movie series was later based.

FESTUS: Warrior. Known as the name of the deputy on the TV western "Gunsmoke."

FIFE: Musical. A small, shrill-toned musical instrument resembling a flute. The last name of Barney in the TV series "The Andy Griffith Show."

FISH: The name of a character portrayed by Abe Vigoda in the 1970s TV series "Barney Miller."

FK: Short for Farrell Kid, a character in the *Mad Max* movie series.

FLASH: Swift. The hound dog in the TV series "The Dukes of Hazzard." Also from the comic book superhero Flash Gordon.

FLATNOSE: The name of a tree-climbing dog in South Carolina who was featured on the "Tonight" show with Johnny Carson and in a Japanese movie.

FLICKA: (Swedish: "little girl") From the mare in the old TV series and movie *My Friend Flicka.*

FLIPPER: The name of the pet dolphin in the 1960s TV series "Flipper."

FLOUNDER: Ariel's fish friend in the animated film and TV series *The Little Mermaid.*

FLUB-A-DUB: A character in the 1950s children's TV series "Howdy Dowdy."

FLUFFY: Soft and light. The name of the girl's cat in the 1970s TV series "The Brady Bunch." Also, more recently, the name of the three-headed dog in the book and movie *Harry Potter and the Sorcerer's Stone.*

FLUKE: The name of the extraordinary dog in the movie of the same name.

FONZ, FONZIE: Cool. From the character in the TV comedy series "Happy Days."

FOSTER: (Anglo-Saxon: "to nourish") Adopted. The name of the life-saving dog in the daytime TV series "General Hospital."

FOX: Slang for attractive. Sly one. The name of one of the FBI agents in the TV series "The X Files."

FOZZIE: The name of the bear in Jim Henson's TV series "Muppets."

FRAISER: Curly-haired. The name of the somewhat eccentric title character in the TV series "Fraiser."

FREMONT: The name of Mr. Wilson's dog in the 1960s TV series "Dennis the Menace."

FRENCHIE: Of France. The name of a character in the musical play and movie *Grease,* about teens in the 1950s.

FROGGY: A pet that resembles a frog or hops around like a frog. The name of one of the kids in the TV series "Our Gang," which later became better known as "The Little Rascals" and on which a movie was based.

FUDGE: The name of the mischievous younger brother in the children's TV series "Fudge."

FUZZHEAD: The name of the dog in the movie *Ollie Hopnoodles Haven of Bliss.*

GARNER: Thrifty. For actor James Garner, who starred in the TV western "Maverick" and the private-eye series "The Rockford Files."

GARTH: Serene. Wayne's comical sidekick, portrayed by comedian-actor Dana Carvey, in the movie *Wayne's World.*

GENTLE: Noble. Kind. Well-bred. From the 1960s TV series "Gentle Ben" about a boy and his pet bear.

GEOFRREY, JEFFREY: Peaceful. The name of the giraffe in the TV commercials for Toys R Us.

GIDGET: Tiny, perky. The name of a teenage girl in the 1960s TV series "Gidget."

GILBERT: Bright. The name of Beaver's friend in the 1950s TV series "Leave It to Beaver." Also, the name of Goofy's nephew in Disney cartoons.

GILLIGAN: Naive, clumsy. From the main character in the 1960s TV comedy series "Gilligan's Island."

GISMO, GIZMO: Slang term for mechanical gadget. Mischievous. The name of the cute, furry creature in the movie *Gremlins.*

GODZILLA: Large, vicious. From the series of Japanese movies about a lizard-like monster that attacks cities.

GOMER: The name of the bungling Marine in the 1960s TV series "Gomer Pyle, USMC."

GOMEZ: The name of the father in the 1960s TV series and movie series *The Addams Family.*

GONZO: The name of one of Jim Henson's Muppets.

GOOBER: (African:

"peanut") The name of Gomer's cousin in the 1960s TV series "The Andy Griffith Show."

GORDY: Considerate. The name of the lovable talking pig who becomes an executive in the movie *Gordy.*

GREMLIN: Small, furry. The mischievous creatures in the movie *Gremlins.*

GRIMACE: One who makes faces. The lovable purple creature in the MacDonald's TV ads.

GROVER: (Old English: "from the grove") The name of a puppet character in the long-running PBS children's TV series "Sesame Street." For Grover Cleveland, 22nd and 24th President of the United States.

GULLAH: Any of a group of Negroes living on the South Carolina and Georgia coast or nearby islands. Also from the children's TV series "Gullah Gullah Island."

HARRY: Home ruler. From *Harry and the Hendersons,* a movie and TV series about a bigfoot-like creature who befriends a family. For Harry S.

Truman, 33rd President of the United States. The name of the little dog with the white and black spots in the children's story "Harry the Dirty Dog" by Gene Zion. Also from the popular boy wizard in the series of Harry Potter books (which inspired a movie series) by author J. K. Rowling.

HAWKEYE: Having excellent eyesight. The nickname of the wise-cracking character in the TV series "M.A.S.H."

HENDERSON: Mr. Henderson, the name of Sally's cat in the 1960s TV series "The Dick Van Dyke Show."

HERBIE: Nickname for Herbert. Glorious soldier. The name of the lovable little car that comes to life in the Disney movie series *Herbie, the Love Bug.*

HERMAN: Godlike. The name of the father, Herman Munster, in the 1960s TV series "The Munsters." Also, the title character in the comic strip by Jim Unger.

HERRY: Herry Monster, a character in the children's TV series "Sesame Street."

HIGGINS: A highly intelli-

gent, aristocratic character in the TV detective series "Magnum P.I." Also, the name of the lovable dog in the 1960s TV series "Petticoat Junction."

HOOCH: The name of the bulldog in the Tom Hanks movie *Turner and Hooch.*

HOWDY: Greeting. Friendly. From Howdy Doody, a puppet character of the 1950s.

HUBBLE: The border terrier who is really an alien scout in the movie *Good Boy!*

HUGGY BEAR: Lovable. The name of a character in the 1970s TV series "Starsky & Hutch."

HULK: Huge. From the comic book, TV, and movie character *The Incredible Hulk* and for popular wrestling star Hulk Hogan.

HUXTABLE: From the Huxtable family, in Bill Cosby's 1980s TV series "The Cosby Show."

INDIANA JONES: Adventurous. From the hero in the series of Steven Spielberg movies about Indiana Jones' adventures.

ISAAC: Joyful. The real name of the basset hound who played

Quincy in the TV series "Coach."

JABBA: Enormous. From the large character Jabba the Hut from the *Star Wars* movie series.

JAKE: Just right. The name of one of the Blues Brothers in the movie, which was based on a sketch from "Saturday Night Live." Also, the name of a mallard duck Beanie Baby.

JALEEL: For actor Jaleel White, who portrayed the nerdy but lovable character of Steve Urkel on the TV series "Family Matters."

JAWS: Strong, ferocious. From the novel by Peter Benchley and the movie series about a killer shark.

JEANNIE: Gracious. From the 1960s TV series "I Dream of Jeannie," about a genie and her master.

JEB: Considerate. The name of the talking dog in the live-action children's TV series "V.R. Troopers."

JED: The name of the man from the hills who struck oil in the TV series and the movie "The Beverly Hillbillies."

JEDI: From the Jedi Knights in the movie *Return of the Jedi* and in George Lucas's series of *Star Wars* movies, books, and merchandise.

JEMIMA: (Hebrew: "dove") In the Bible, one of Job's daughters. The name of the daughter in the TV series "Daniel Boone."

JEN JEN: White. The name of a fesity little dog in an episode of the TV series "I Dream of Jeannie."

JETHREEN: Excellent. The name of Jethro's sister in the TV series "The Beverly Hillbillies," which provided the basis for the movie.

JETHRO: (Hebrew: "preeminence") The name of Jed's nitwit nephew on the TV comedy series and movie "The Beverly Hillbillies."

J.R.: Short for John Ross. A big shot; ruthless. From the wealthy, double-dealing oil tycoon in the TV series "Dallas."

JUDGE JUDY: For the outspoken judge who has her own TV series.

KATO: From a character in the oldie TV series "Green Hornet."

KERMIE: Respectful. Miss

Piggy's pet name for Kermit the Frog.

KERMIT: One of Jim Henson's Muppets, Kermit the Frog.

KIZZIE, KIZZY: One of the characters in Alex Haley's novel that became the TV mini-series "Roots."

KOJAK: In the TV crime drama of the same name, a New York City police detective whose most distinguishing feature was that he was bald.

KONG: Huge. From the enormous ape in the movie *King Kong.*

KUKLA: A puppet character from the old TV series "Kukla, Fran, and Ollie."

LAA LAA: The name of the yellow character in the popular children's TV series "Teletubbies."

LADADOG: The name of the family dog in the 1960s TV series "Please Don't Eat the Daisies."

LAMB CHOP: Shari Lewis's cute, lovable lamb and the star of the PBS children's series "Lamb Chop's Play-Along."

LASSIE: (Middle English: "young girl") The name of the lovable, brave collie in the TV series "Lassie."

LATKA: The name of an eccentric and foreign character in the 1970s TV series "Taxi."

LAVERNE: The name of one of the roommates in the TV series "Laverne and Shirley."

LEIA: (Hebrew) Weary. For Princess Leia Organa, a member of the royal family Alderaan, in the George Lucas movie *Star Wars.*

LEVAR: For actor Levar Burton, host of the children's TV series "Reading Rainbow."

LONE RANGER: The masked hero in the TV series "The Adventures of the Lone Ranger."

LOVEY: Loving. The name of a character in the 1960s TV series "Gilligan's Island."

LUCINDA: Bright, shining. The name of the small yellow bird in the children's TV series "Old MacDonald's Farm."

LUCY: (Latin: "light, light bringer") For American comedic actress and producer Lucille Ball, who starred in numerous movies and TV series including "I Love Lucy." Also for actress Lucy Lawless who played "Xena" in the popular TV series.

LUIGI: The name of Mario's younger brother in the movie *Super Mario Brothers,* which is based on the popular video game series.

LUKE: (Greek: "from Lucania") The name of Jedi Knight Luke Skywalker in the original "Star Wars" movie. Also, the name of a Beanie Baby dog, a black Labrador.

LURCH: The name of the Addams' butler in the TV series and the movie series based on "The Addams Family."

MACK: Huge, powerful. The name of one of the Siberian huskies in the Disney movie *Snow Dogs.*

MACY: The name of the scruffy little dog in the Disney TV series "Two of a Kind," starring twins Mary Kate and Ashley Olsen.

MADISON: The capital of the state of Wisconsin. For James Madison, 4th President of the United States. Also, the name of the mermaid in the Tom Hank's movie *Splash.* The name of a cartoon cat in the children's TV series "The

Bozo Super Sunday Show."

MAGYVER: Clever like the hero in the TV series starring Richard Dean Anderson.

MANTIS: Prophet. A carnivorous insect: the praying mantis. Also, the name of a super hero in the TV series "Mantis."

MARCEL: Short for Marcellus. Warrior. The pet monkey that appeared in early episodes of the TV series "Friends."

MARCIA, MARSHA: Warrior. The name of the eldest daughter in the TV series "The Brady Bunch," on which several movies were based.

MARGARET: The name of the cat in the movie *Ghost Cat.*

MARY ANN: The name of one of the castaways in the '60s TV series "Gilligan's Island."

MATISSE: For Henri Matisse, a French born modern artist. The name of the dog in the Nick Nolte movie *Down and Out in Beverly Hills.*

MAXWELL: A form of Maximillian. Greatest. From Maxwell Smart, a character portrayed by Don Adams in the 1970s TV series "Get Smart."

MAYNARD: Powerful, strong. The name of Dobie's beatnik friend in the TV series "The Many Loves of Dobie Gillis." Maynard was played by Bob Denver, who later became Gilligan of "Gilligan's Island."

McBEEVEE: Mr. McBeeVee, Opie's friend who "jingled" in an episode of "The Andy Griffith Show."

MEATHEAD: Archie Bunker's nickname for his son-in-law in the TV series "All in the Family."

MERA: The younger sister of Neri in the Disney TV series "Ocean Girl."

MILO: From the unlikely friends Milo (a cat) and Otis (a dog) in the movie *The Adventures of Milo and Otis.*

MIMI: (French: "faithful guard") A pet that follows your moves closely, mimics. The name of the clown-like character in the TV series "The Drew Carey Show."

MISS ELLIE: The name of the mother in the TV series "Dallas."

MISS KITTY: A good name for a female kitten or cat. The name of Marshal Matt Dillon's girlfriend in the TV western "Gunsmoke."

MISS PIGGY: One of Jim Henson's Muppets, a glamorous, self-centered pig.

MOONDOGGIE: The name of the teenage girl's boyfriend in the 1960s TV series "Gidget."

MORK: Mork from Ork, the character in the TV comedy series "Mork and Mindy," which was a spin-off from the long-running TV series "Happy Days."

MORRIS: An old English folk dance for which costumes were worn. The name of the finicky cat in the cat food commercials.

MR. BOOTS: The name of a cat in a pet food commercial.

MR. BOTTOMSLY: The name of a cat Fraiser was pet sitting for a friend in an episode of the TV series "Fraiser."

MR. SPOCK: The character in the TV series and movie series "Star Trek" with the prominent, pointed ears.

MUNCHIE: Tiny. From the movie *Munchie,* about a boy

befriended by a munchkin.

MUPPET: Puppet characters created by Jim Henson and appearing in various TV series and movies.

MURPHY: (Irish: slang for "potato") The name of the brash TV newswoman in the TV series "Murphy Brown."

MURRAY: (Welsh: "the sea") The name of the dog in the TV series "Mad About You."

MUTLEY: A mutt. The name of the dog in the TV series "Mac & Mutley."

NANA: (Spanish: "nursemaid; elder sister") The name of one of the Siberian huskies in the Disney movie *Snow Dogs.*

NATIONAL VELVET: From the movie *National Velvet* which starred Elizabeth Taylor and was the story of a girl who wins a classic English steeple chase disguised as a boy jockey, riding a horse named "The Py" that's been won in a lottery.

NEAL, NEIL: (Irish: "champion") The name of the dog in the 1950s TV series "Topper."

NELLIE: Bright. The name of the mischievous girl in the TV series "Little House on the Prairie."

NELLY: The Italian greyhound in the movie *Good Boy!*

NERI: The name of the girl in the Disney TV series "Ocean Girl."

NIGHT TRAIN: The name of Roosevelt Franklin's dog in the PBS children's series "Sesame Street."

NORTON: The name of the traveling cat whose adventures were chronicled in two books by author Peter Gethers. The name of the comically bumbling neighbor, played by the late Art Carney, in the old TV series "The Honeymooners."

NOSFERATU: Vampire in early black and white horror film. Any pet that bites, or tries to.

OBI-WAN-KENOBI: A dedicated Jedi Knight, who trained Luke Skywalker, in the George Lucas' *Star Wars* movie series.

OLD YELLER: The name of the mischievous dog in the classic Disney movie of the same name.

OPIE: The name of the young son in the 1960s TV series

"The Andy Griffith Show."

ORBIT: A pet that chases its tail or moves in circles. The family dog in the TV series "The Partridge Family."

OSCAR: (Scandinavian: "divine spearman") The name of a character in the movie and TV series *The Odd Couple.* Also, from Oscar the Grouch from the PBS children's series *"Sesame Street."*

OTIS: (Greek: "keen of hearing") From the unlikely friends Milo (a cat) and Otis (a dog), in the movie *The Adventures of Milo and Otis.*

OVERTON: Outgoing. The name of the comical and lovable handyman in the TV series "Living Single."

OZZIE, OZZY: Short for Osborn. For Ozzie Nelson of the TV series "Ozzie and Harriet." Also for outrageous British rock star Ozzy Osbourne, star of the TV series "The Osbournes."

PACEY: A character in the TV series "Dawson's Creek."

PEE WEE: Little, the runt. The name of a comical character actor who has starred in several movies, including *Pee Wee's Big Adventure.*

PETEY: A form of Peter. Sturdy. The name of the dog in the old TV series "Our Gang," which later became better known as "The Little Rascals," and on which a movie was based.

PICKLES: A mischievous pet, always in a pickle. The name of a character (often referred to, but rarely seen) in the 1960s TV series "The Dick Van Dyke Show." The title character in the comic strip by Brian Crane.

PIGGY: A pet with a ferocious appetite. From Miss Piggy, one of the most famous of Jim Henson's Muppets.

PINKIE, PINKY: Small as the pinkie finger. Also the name of a portrait of a young girl painted by Sir Thomas Laurence. The name of a flamboyant character in the TV series "Happy Days."

PITTY PAT: The name of Scarlet's aunt in Margaret Mitchell's novel *Gone With the Wind,* which became a popular movie starring Vivien Leigh and Clark Gable.

PO: The name of the red character in the popular children's TV series "Teletubbies."

PONCHO: An often colorful cloaklike blanket with a hole in the middle for the head. The name of one of the police officers on motorcycle in the TV series "CHiPS."

PONDER: Thoughtful. The name of a character in the TV series "Evening Shade."

POPPYCOCK: Zany. The name of the rooster in the children's TV series "Old Mac-Donald's Farm."

PORTER: Helper. The name of the father in the TV series "Flipper," about two young boys and their pet dolphin.

PRAIRIE DAWN: The name of a golden-haired character in the children's TV series "Sesame Street."

PRECIOUS: Of great value, beloved. Priceless. The name of the lovable baboon in the daytime drama "Passions."

PRETTY BABY: Attractive, young. The name of an early Brooke Shields movie.

PRINCESS LEIA: Princess Leia Organa, a member of the royal family Alderaan, in the George Lucas movie *Star*

Wars.

PUFNSTUF: From the children's TV series "HR Pufn-stuf."

PUGSLEY: The name of the Addams's son in the TV series and movie "The Addams Family."

PUNKY: Rowdy. The name of the free spirited young orphan in the TV series "Punky Brewster."

PY: The Py was the name of the horse in the movie *National Velvet*, starring Elizabeth Taylor.

QUEEN AMIDALA: The royal leader of Naboo in George Lucas' *Star Wars: Episode 1* and *Star Wars II: Attack of the Clones.*

QUINCY: (Old French: "from the fifth son's estate") The middle name of John Quincy Adams, 6th President of the United States and the son of the 2nd President, John Adams. Also, the name of the basset hound in the TV series *Coach.*

R2D2: The short, brave and intelligent android in George Lucas' movie *Star Wars.*

RADAR: An instrument that times the echo of radio waves

to detect objects they strike. A pet that is very sensitive to his surroundings. The name of a character on the TV series "M.A.S.H."

RAGS: The name of the shaggy dog in the 1946 western movie *Bad Bascomb.*

RAMBO: Strong warrior. A character played in a series of movies by Sylvester Stallone.

RED RYDER: For a cowboy of the 1950s.

RERUN: A pet that often repeats itself. The name of a comical, lovable character in the TV series "What's Happening!"

RHUBARB: Argumentative. The name of a dog in a cartoon segment of the children's TV series "Eureeka's Castle."

RIN TIN TIN: The German shepherd police dog in the TV series of the same name.

ROCK: Strong. The name of the mischievous dog in the movie *Look Who's Talking Too.*

RODAN: The name of the dinosaur-like creature in the Japanese movie of the same name.

ROGER: (Anglo-Saxon/Old German: "famous with the spear") The name of the cartoon bunny in the movie *Who Framed Roger Rabbit?*

ROWLF: A dog that likes to bark. The name of the dog in Jim Henson's TV series "The Muppet Show."

RUH: Sensitive. The name of Dar's tiger in the TV series "Beastmaster."

SALTY: From the folk song "Salty Dog." The name of Caroline's cat in the TV series "Caroline in the City."

SAM: The name of the dog in the Jim Carrey movie *Bruce Almighty.*

SASSY: The Himalayan cat in the movie Disney's *Homeward Bound.*

SCOOPER: Active. The name of one of the Siberian huskies in the Disney movie *Snow Dogs.*

SCOOTER: To scoot about, to scurry off, to go quickly. The name of one of Jim Henson's Muppet twins, Skeeter and Scooter.

SCOUT: The name of Tonto's horse in the movie and TV series "The Lone Ranger."

SCRAPS: The white and

brown dog in the Charlie Chaplin film *A Dog's Life.*

SCREECH: Noisy. High-pitched. The name of one of the kids in the TV series "Saved By the Bell."

SCRUFFY: Unkempt. The name of the family dog in the TV series "The Ghost and Mrs. Muir."

SCULLY: From scull, either of a pair of light oars used by a single person. A pet that enjoys playing in or around water. Also, the name of one of the FBI agents in the popular TV series "The X Files."

SCUTTLE: The cockeyed sea gull in the Disney animated movie and TV series "The Little Mermaid."

SHAG: The name of a dance made famous at Myrtle Beach, South Carolina, and on which the movie *The Shag* is based.

SHARAK: The name of the eagle in the TV series "Beastmaster."

SHEP: The large mountain dog in the movie *Good Boy!*

SILVER: A lustrous, grayish white color. The name of the Lone Ranger's horse in the old TV series.

SIMKA: The name of an eccentric character in the TV series "Taxi."

SINBAD: The heroic sailor of the seven seas in the series of Sinbad movies. Also, the name of a popular stand-up comedian.

SKEETER: Slang for mosquito. The name of one of Jim Henson's Muppet twins, Skeeter and Scooter.

SKIP: To leap, jump lightly. The name of the dog in the movie *My Dog Skip.*

SKIPPY: Playful, a skipper. The name of a kangaroo in a children's TV series.

SLIMEY: The name of Oscar's pet worm in the children's TV series "Sesame Street."

SMILEY: Good-natured, amusing. The name of the young son's dog in the TV series "Hazel."

SNIFF: Always smelling something. The name of one of the Siberian huskies in the Disney movie *Snow Dogs.*

SNOODLE: The name of a dog Phoebe accidentally injured in an episode of the TV series "Friends."

SNUFFLELUPAGUS: Big Bird's large friend in the PBS children's TV series "Sesame Street."

SOLITAIRE: A single gem, especially a diamond. Also, any of several card games, played by one person. The name of a lady villain, played by Jane Seymour, in the James Bond movie *Live and Let Die.*

SPANKY: Swift. The name of the leader in the TV series "Our Gang," better known as "The Little Rascals," on which a movie was based.

SPOCK: The character in the TV series and movie series "Star Trek" with the prominent pointed ears.

SPUDS: The name of the ultra cool dog Spuds Mackenzie in the TV commercials.

STARSKY: The name of one of the detectives in the TV series "Starsky and Hutch."

STORM: Moody. The name of one of the X-Men in the animated TV series and movie.

STRETCH: Flexible. The name of one of the California Raisins.

STYMIE: The name of one of the kids in the TV series "Our Gang," which later became better known as "The Little Rascals," on which a movie was based.

SUNDANCE: A ritual dance formed by Native Americans. Also, the name of a character in the western movie *Butch Cassidy and the Sundance Kid.*

TABATHA, TABITHA: (Aramaic: "gazelle") The name of Samantha and Darren's daughter in the TV series "Bewitched."

TALBOT: The name of Bert's goldfish in the PBS children's series "Sesame Street."

TAO: Harmony. The name of Dar's friend and companion in the TV series "Beastmaster."

TARA: (Irish Gaelic: "rocky pinnacle") The name of Scarlet's home in Margaret Mitchell's novel *Gone With the Wind.*

TATTOO: The name of the small man in the TV series "Fantasy Island."

TEEK: The name of the fast, furry creature in the movie *Ewoks: The Battle for Endor.*

THURSTON: Fast like lightning. The name of the millionaire in the TV series "Gilligan's Island."

TIMMY: A form of Timothy. The young boy who was master to the faithful (and often heroic) collie in the TV series "Timmy and Lassie."

TINKY: Tinky Winky, the name of the purple character in the popular children's TV series "Teletubbies."

TONTO: (Spanish: "silly") The name of the Lone Ranger's partner in the TV series and movies. Also, the name of the cat in the movie "Harry and Tonto," starring Art Carney as an aging widower traveling across country with his cat after being evicted from his apartment.

TOONCES: From the popular driving cat in the TV series "Saturday Night Live."

TOPANGA: An area in California. Also, the name of a girl in the TV series "Boy Meets World."

TOPPER: For the 1937 movie starring Cary Grant and Constance Bennett as a couple who must do a good deed to get into Heaven.

TRAPPER JOHN: A doctor in the long-running TV series

"M.A.S.H" and a later spin-off series "Trapper John, M.D."

TUDBALL: Mr. Tudball was Mrs. Wiggins's boss in the TV variety series starring Carol Burnette.

TUM TUM: The name of one of the kids in the *Three Ninjas* movies.

URKEL: From the nerdy but lovable character Steve Urkel in the TV series "Family Matters."

VADAR: From Darth Vadar, the villain in the *Star Wars* movie series.

VELVET: Soft, furry. From the movie *National Velvet* which starred Elizabeth Taylor and was the story of a girl who wins a classic English steeple chase disguised as a boy jockey, riding a horse named "The Py" that's been won in a lottery.

VINNIE: A conqueror. A lovable one-eared dog in the daytime talk show "Mike & Maddie."

WAGS: The name of the dog in the Australian children's singing group known as "The Wiggles."

WALDO: (Old German:

"ruler") The middle name of American essayist, philosopher and poet Ralph Waldo Emerson. The name of the family dog in the TV series "Nanny and The Professor." Also, known for the children's comics and books in the "Where's Waldo?" series.

WICKET: Small. The name of the furry, little Ewok in George Lucas's movies *Return of the Jedi* and *The Ewok Adventure.*

WIGGINS: Mr. Tudball's secretary, Miss Wiggins, a character played by Carol Burnette on her TV variety series.

WIGGLES: An Australian children's TV series about a singing group known as "The Wiggles."

WILLARD: Wishful. The name of the boy who befriended the rats in the movie *Willard.*

WILLIE, WILLY: From willy nilly, meaning willingly or unwillingly. The name of the whale in the movie *Free Willy,* the story of an orphan who befriends a neglected killer whale held in captivity at an aquatic show.

WILSON: Protector. The name of the elusive neighbor in the TV series "Home Improvement," starring comedian Tim Allen. In the movie Castaway, Tom Hanks has a soccer ball that he talks to and names Wilson. Also, the boxer in the movie *Good Boy!*

WINNIE: (Welsh: "fair") The name of the bear in A. A. Milne's classic children's story "Winnie the Pooh," on which the animated TV series is based.

WIZ: Short for Wizard. Clever, gifted. Also from the movie *The Wiz,* starring Michael Jackson.

WOJO: A character portrayed by actor-comedian Max Gail in the 1970s TV series "Barney Miller."

WONKA: From the children's movie *Willie Wonka and the Chocolate Factory.*

WOOF: Wolflike. The name of a movie in which a young British schoolboy keeps changing into a dog at the oddest times.

WOOKIEE: Furry creatures in George Lucas's *Star Wars* movie series.

XENA: The warrior princess in the popular TV series "Xena, Warrior Princess," starring Lucy Lawless.

XUXA: The name of the Swedish star of the popular kids' series of the same name.

YELLAR: Slang for cowardly. The name of the dog in the children's book and Disney movie *Old Yellar.*

YETTA: (Hebrew) Short for Henrietta. Fran's grandmother in the TV series "The Nanny."

YODA: Wise one. From the beloved character in the *Star Wars* movie series.

YODEL: Very vocal. A type of German singing that features abrupt alternating changes between the normal voice and the falsetto. Also spelled yodle. A pet that makes howls that sound like yodels The name of one of the Siberian huskies in the Disney movie *Snow Dogs.*

YOR: The name of a warrior in the movie *Yor, the Hunter from the Future.*

ZAK: The name of a character in the animated movie *Fern Gully.*

ZELDA: The young lady who loved Dobie in the TV comedy series "The Many Loves of Dobie Gillis."

ZEUS: The supreme deity of the ancient Greeks. The name of one of the pair of vicious Dobermans featured in the s TV series "Magnum, P.I.," which starred actor Tom Selleck.

ZOEY: Life. The name of a character in the long-running children's TV series "Sesame Street."

ZORRO: (Spanish: "foxy, crafty") The masked hero of Old California who carries a sword and rides a horse.

Noofy

Did You Know?

EGYPT: Ulysses S. Grant, the 18th President of the United States had a horse with this name.

LULU: A form of Louise. Renowned warrior. The name of Judge Judy's small dog.

MARMALADE: Actress Anne Bancroft and her husband, movie producer Mel Brooks, have a cat with this name.

Love and Kisses

The Adventures of Peanut Butter & Jelly!

Chapter 8

CARTOONS AND COMICS

Cartoons and comics appeal to pet lovers of all ages: *Astro* (the name of the family dog in the cartoon series "The Jetsons"), *Bart* (the name of the mischievous young boy in the animated TV series "The Simpsons"), *Butterbear* (a character, half butterfly and half bear, in the Disney animated TV series "The Wuzzles"), *Eeyore* (the name of the donkey in the animated TV series "Winnie the Pooh"), *Obelix* (Asterix's best friend in the "Asterix" comic book series), *Ziggy* (the lovable, rotund character in the comic strip by Tom Wilson), and others.

ABNER: The country mouse in the Disney cartoon short "The Country Cousin."

ABU: Aladdin's mischievous monkey friend in the Disney animated movie *Aladdin*.

AKELA: A wolf in the Disney animated movie *The Jungle Book*.

ALADDIN: The boy in *The Arabian Knights* who found a magic lamp and a magic ring, a story that formed the basis for the animated Disney movie.

ALVIN: (Old German: "beloved by all") Noble friend. The lead chipmunk in "Alvin and the Chipmunks."

AM: One of the two Siamese cats in the Disney animated movie *Lady and the Tramp*.

AMBROSE: A kitten that doesn't like to be bathed in Disney's *The Robber Kitten*.

ANASTASIA: One of the wicked stepsisters in the Disney animated movie classic *Cinderella*.

ANCHOR: The anchorhead shark voiced by Eric Bana in the Disney animated movie

Finding Nemo.

ANGELICA: Angelic. The name of the feisty young girl in the Nickelodeon TV series and animated movies *Rugrats.*

ANIMAL: Free-spirited. The name of the rowdy character in Jim Henson's TV series "The Muppet Show."

ARBUCKLE: The last name of Garfield's master Jon Arbuckle in the animated TV series "Garfield & Friends."

ARCHIE: Short for Archibald. From the teenager in the comic book and cartoon TV series "Archie."

ARIEL: The name of the mermaid in the animated Disney film and TV series *The Little Mermaid.* In astronomy the natural satellite of Uranus. Also spelled Arielle.

ARISTOCAT: From the Disney animated movie *The Aristocats,* about a group of feline friends.

ARLO: From the syndicated comic strip "Arlo & Janis" by Jimmy Johnson. Also for folk singer Arlo Gutherie, son of folk legend Woody Gutherie, who wrote the American classic "This Land Is Your Land."

ASTERIX: A comic book series set in Roman times under the rule of Caesar and about tiny warrior Asterix and his best friend, Obelix.

ASTRO: (Spanish: "star") The name of the family dog in the cartoon series "The Jetsons," Astro has the distinction of being TV's first dog in space.

ATTA: The name of the ant princess in the Disney animated movie *A Bug's Life.*

AUGIE: (Latin: "dignified, majestic") From the TV cartoon dog Augie Doggie.

AZTECA: The female ant, voiced by Jennifer Lopez, who works in the tunnels with Z in the animated movie *Antz.*

BABS: Unique. The name of a bunny in the animated TV series "Tiny Tune Adventures."

BABY HERMAN: The foul-mouthed, ill-tempered baby persona in the Disney animated movie *Who Framed Roger Rabbit?*

BAI BAI: Repetitious. The name of little blonde girl in the animated TV series "South Park."

BALA: The name of the cute female ant, Princess Bala, in the animated movie *Antz.*

BALOO: The big bear in the Disney animated TV series "TailSpin."

BAM BAM: Noisy. The name of the Rubbles' son in the 1960s animated TV series "The Flintstones."

BAMBI: (Italian: "baby") The name of the fawn in the Disney animated classic *Bambi.*

BANDIT: Mischievous, playful. The name of the pet dog in the animated TV series "Johnny Quest."

BANZAI: A Japanese greeting or shout, meaning "May you live ten thousand years!" The name of a hyena in the Disney animated movie *The Lion King.*

BARBATUS: The soldier ant voiced by Danny Glover who befriends Z and saves his life in the movie *Antz.*

BARKERVILLE: The name of one of the "Pound Puppies" in the animated TV series.

BARNEY: Bold like a bear; swift. The name of Fred's best friend and neighbor in the animated 1960s TV series "The Flintstones," which was the basis for a motion picture. The name of the hyper and often bumbling deputy in the long-running TV series "The Andy Griffith Show." Also, the name of the lovable purple dinosaur in the children's TV series "Barney & Friends."

BART: Short for Bartholomew. Earthy. The name of the mischievous young boy in the animated TV series "The Simpsons."

BASHFUL: Shy. The name of one of the dwarves in the Disney animated movie *Snow White and the Seven Dwarfs.*

BASIL: Sweet king. The name of the mouse in the animated movie *The Great Mouse Detective.*

BATMAN: From the comic book superhero and the movie series.

BAZOOKA: Musical; comical. From the comic strip character "Bazooka Joe."

BEAKER: The name of one of Jim Henson's Muppet characters.

BEAVIS: The name of Butthead's partner in the MTV cartoon series "Beavis and Butthead."

BEEBOP: Musical; lively.

The name of one of the California Raisins.

BEETLE: The name of the bungling soldier in the syndicated comic strip "Beetle Bailey" by Mort Walker.

BEHEMOTH: Any large animal. The name of a character in the animated movie *The Nightmare Before Christmas.*

BELLE: The beautiful heroine in the Disney animated movie *Beauty and the Beast.*

BENDER: The name of the robot in the animated TV series "Futurama."

BENT-TAIL: A coyote in the Disney cartoon "Sheep Dog."

BERLIOZ: One of the three kittens (along with Toulouse and Marie) in the Disney animated movie *The Aristocats.*

BERNARD: The handsome little brown mouse (voiced by veteran comedian Bob Newhart) in the Disney animated movie *The Rescuers* and the sequel *The Rescuers Down Under.*

BETTY BOOP: Old-time cartoon character, a woman with big dark eyes, dark hair, and a high-pitched voice.

BIG SLAMMU: One of the four crime fighting teen sharks in the animated TV series "Street Sharks."

BINKY: A beagle in the Disney animated TV series "DuckTales."

BLACK BART: A knight in the Disney animated movie *The Sword and the Stone.*

BLOAT: The name of the pufferfish voiced by Brad Garrett in the Disney animated movie *Finding Nemo.*

BLONDIE: Blonde-colored, golden. The name of a character in the syndicated comic strip of the same name.

BLUE: The loyal Fluppy in the animated TV special "Disney's Fluppy Dogs." Also, the name of the clever dog in the children's TV series "Blue's Clues."

BLUTO: Strong. A character in the cartoon TV series "Popeye."

BLYKEN: A cute little boy in the Disney cartoon about three tots called "Wyken, Blyken and Nod," also, the names Opie gave three orphaned baby birds in an episode of the 1960s TV series "The Andy Griffith Show."

BOBO: The elephant who befriends a mouse in the Disney cartoon short "Mickey's Elephant."

BOLIVAR: The name of Donald Duck's Saint Bernard.

BONGO: Rhythmic. The little performing bear who wants a new life in the Disney animated movie *Bongo*.

BOO BOO: Rambunctious. The name of Yogi Bear's pal in the animated TV series.

BOOMHAUER: An eccentric character in the animated TV series "King of the Hill."

BORIS: One of the singing dogs in the Disney animated movie *Lady and the Tramp*.

BOUNCER: A beagle in the Disney animated TV series "DuckTales."

BOWSER: A cartoon dog in the Disney cartoon "Man's Best Friend."

BRAIN: Intelligent. The name of the dog in the animated TV series "Inspector Gadget."

BRAINY: Highly intelligent. The name of one of the Smurfs in the cartoon TV series.

BRUCE: (Old French: "from the brush-wood thicket") The name of a shark voiced by Barry Humphries in the Disney animated movie *Finding Nemo*.

BRUM: The name of the superhero car in the British animated series "Brum."

BRUNO: The dog in the animated Disney movie classic *Cinderella*.

BUBBA: From Bubba Duck, a country bumpkin in the Disney animated TV series "DuckTales."

BUCKY: The neurotic cat in the comic strip "Get Fuzzy" by Darby Conley.

BUDDERS: A buddy. The name of a young boy in the animated series "South Park."

BUGLER: The name of an elephant in the Disney animated movie *The Jungle Book*.

BUGS: A prankster. Zany. Any pet that eats bugs. From the cartoon rabbit Bugs Bunny.

BULLSEYE: A direct hit. The name of Woody's trusty horse in the Disney animated movie *Toy Story II*.

BULLWINKLE: The name of the moose in the cartoon TV series "Rocky and Bullwinkle."

BUMBLELION: A character, half bumblebee and half lion, in the Disney animated TV series "The Wuzzles."

BUSTER: Close friend. The name of a bunny on the cartoon TV series "Tiny Toon Adventures."

BUTCH: The tough, macho bulldog in several Disney cartoons.

BUTTERBEAR: A character, half butterfly and half bear, in the Disney animated TV series "The Wuzzles."

BUZZ: From astronaut Buzz Lightyear in the Disney animated movie *Toy Story.*

BUZZ-BUZZ: The name of a bumblebee that tests Donald Duck's patience in the Disney cartoon "Bee On Guard." In later cartoons, the bee was called Spike.

CADPIG: The runt of the litter. The name of the runt in the Disney animated movie *101 Dalmatians.*

CALVIN: (Latin: "bald") For Calvin Coolidge, 30th President of the United States. The name of the boy in the comic strip "Calvin and Hobbes" about a boy and his cat, Hobbes.

CAPP, CAPPY: From the comic strip character Andy Capp.

CASPAR, CASPER: (Persian: "treasurer") The name of the friendly ghost in the cartoon TV series "Casper."

CATTY: An elephant in the Disney animated movie "Dumbo."

CAVIN: The first human ever to enter Gummi Glen (the land of Gummi Bears) in the Disney animated TV series "Gummi Bears."

CHARLOTTE: (French: "little and womanly") The name of the spider who befriends Wilbur in E. B. White's classic children's story and animated movie *Charlotte's Web.*

CHEDDARHEAD CHARLIE: A rogue mouse in the animated Disney TV series "Chip 'n Dale Rescue Rangers."

CHEETARA: A character, half-human and half cheetah, in the 1980s cartoon series "Thundercats."

CHIP: Small. The name of one of the playful chipmunks in the

Disney TV series "Chip 'n Dale Rescue Rangers." Also, the name of a male wasp in the animated movie *Antz*.

CHUMLEY: A walrus in the cartoon series "Tennessee Tuxedo."

CLARA: (Greek: "clear and bright") An older Disney character, a hen named Clara Cluck.

CLARICE: The gorgeous, curvy nightclub singer who stole Chip and Dale's hearts in the Disney cartoon "Two Chips and a Miss."

CLEO: The cute little goldfish in the Disney animated movie *Pinocchio*.

CLIFFORD: The name of the huge dog in the children's animated TV series "Clifford, the Big Red Dog."

COLLOSSUS: Any great thing, large. The name of one of the X-Men in the animated TV series and movie.

COOLER: One of the "Pound Puppies."

COPPER: Reddish brown. The name of a young hound pup in the Disney animated movie *The Fox and the Hound*.

CORAL: Of the water. A clownfish, Nemo's mother, voiced by Elizabeth Perkins in the Disney animated movie *Finding Nemo*.

CREEPER: A comic bad creature in the Disney animated movie *The Black Cauldron*.

CRUSH: The mellow sea turtle in the Disney animated movie *Finding Nemo*.

CRYSTA: The name of a character in the animated movie *Fern Gully*.

CUBBI: The youngest of the Gummi Bears and the most prone to getting into trouble in the Disney animated TV series.

CUTTER: From the ant Colonel Cutter , voiced by Christopher Walken, who is the general's main henchman in the animated movie *Antz*.

CYRIL PROUDBOTTOM: Mr. Toad's tuneful horse in the Disney animated anthology *The Adventures of Ichabod and Mr. Toad*.

DACHSIE: A dachshund in the dog pound in the Disney animated movie *Lady and the Tramp*.

DAFFY: Silly. From Daffy Duck, the TV cartoon character.

DAGWOOD: Absentminded. Blondie's husband in the syndicated comic strip.

DAISY: From Daisy Duck, Donald's love interest in Disney cartoons including "Mr. Duck Steps Out."

DALBEN: A wizard in the Disney animated movie *The Black Cauldron.*

DALE: Small. The name of one of the playful chipmunks in the animated TV series "Chip 'n Dale Rescue Rangers."

DAVID: (Hebrew: "beloved") The name of a gnome in the animated TV series "The World of David the Gnome."

DAWSON: A city in Yukon Territory, Canada, on the Yukon River. The name of a character in the Disney animated movie *The Great Mouse Detective.*

DENVER: The name of the dinosaur in the animated TV series "Denver, the Last Dinosaur." Also, the capital of Colorado.

DeSOTO: A menacing Doberman in the Disney animated movie *Oliver & Company.*

DEWEY: (Welsh: "prized") Refreshing. The name of one of Donald Duck's nephews.

DICK: A nickname for Richard. Strong king. From the syndicated comic strip "Dick Tracy," on which a movie starring Warren Beatty and Madonna was based.

DIEGO: Wanderer. The name of the saber-toothed tiger in the animated movie *Ice Age.*

DILBERT: Worker. The name of a character in the syndicated comic strip by Scott Adams.

DIM: The lovable rhino beetle in the Disney animated movie *A Bug's Life.*

DIM-WITTY: Disney's Moby Duck has a ship hand, a duck, with this name.

DINAH: The second love of Pluto's life, an enticing dachshund, in several Disney cartoons. Also, the name of Alice's little kitten in the Disney animated movie *Alice In Wonderland.*

DINKY: The comical little yellow sparrow in the Disney animated movie *The Fox and the Hound.*

DINO: Short for dinosaur. The pet dinosaur in the cartoon TV series "The Flintstones."

DITHERS: From Mr. Dithers, the name of Dagwood's boss in the syndicated comic strip "Blondie."

DOC: The name of one of the dwarves in the Disney animated movie *Snow White and the Seven Dwarfs.*

DOCTOR: The sadistic mouse in the Disney animated movie *The Rescuers Down Under.*

DODGER: The daring yet lovable dog (voiced by singer/songwriter Billy Joel) in the Disney animated movie *Oliver & Company.*

DOGBERT: The name of Dilbert's dog in the comic strip "Dilbert."

DOGMATIX: The cute and brave dog in the "Asterix" comic book series set in Roman times under the rule of Caesar and about tiny warrior Asterix and his best friend, Obelix. Matix for short.

DOLI: A tiny, elflike creature in the Disney animated movie *The Black Cauldron.*

DOLORES: The elephant who outsmarts Goofy in the Disney cartoon "The Big Wash."

DONALD: Ruler. From the Walt Disney cartoon character Donald Duck.

DONATELLO: Ruler. The name of one of the "Teenage Mutant Ninja Turtles."

DOPEY: The name of one of the dwarves in the Disney animated movie *Snow White and the Seven Dwarfs.*

DORA: A gift. The adventurous girl in the children's animated series "Dora the Explorer."

DOT: Having dots or spots. The name of the sister in the Warner Bros.' cartoon TV series "Animaniacs." Also, the name of a tiny ant in the movie *A Bug's Life.*

DOUBLE-O: Secretive. The name of a Disney character, Double-O Duck.

DOUG: Short for Douglas. Dark gray. The name of a boy in the popular children's cartoon series "Doug."

DOWAGER: A minor character in the Disney animated movie *The Rescuers Down Under.*

DRIZELLA: One of the wicked step-sisters in the Disney animated movie classic

Cinderella.

DROOPY: Loose folds of fur or skin. From the cartoon dog who has very loose skin and is a bit of a slowpoke.

DUCHESS: The beautiful, slim, slinky white cat modeled after Eva Gabor (who provided the voice) in the animated Disney movie *The Aristocats.*

DUMBO: Having large ears. The elephant with the huge ears in the Disney animated movie *Dumbo.*

EEYORE: The name of the donkey in the animated TV series "Winnie the Pooh," which is based on A. A. Milne's classic children's story.

EGON: Self-centered. The name of a character in the movie series and animated TV series *Ghostbusters.*

EIDILLEG: The tiny, plump King Eidilleg in the Disney animated movie *The Black Cauldron.*

EILONWY: The strong heroine in the Disney animated movie *The Black Cauldron.*

ELEROO: A character, half elephant and have kangaroo, in the Disney animated TV series "The Wuzzles."

ELLSWORTH: Glowing. The name of Goofy's pet raven in Disney cartoons.

ELMER: Noble. From cartoon character Elmer Fudd, a hunter who is always chasing Bugs Bunny. Also, the name of the cute little elephant in the Disney cartoon "Elmer Elephant."

ELMO: Amiable. A lovable red-furred character in the children's TV series "Sesame Street." Also, from St. Elmo's fire, the patron saint of sailors.

ELROY: Regal. The name of the son in the cartoon TV series "The Jetsons."

ERNEST: One of the friends in the comic strip "Frank and Ernest" by Bob Thaves.

EUBIE, EUBY: Good. The name of the male penguin in the animated movie *The Pebble and the Penguin.*

EVINRUDE: The striped dragonfly in the Disney animated movie *The Rescuers.*

FADOOZLE: The name of a character, Inspector Fadoozle, in the 1950s children's TV series "Howdy Dowdy."

FAGIN: A villian in the Disney animated movie *Oliver & Company.*

FALINE: A friend of Bambi's, a doe, in the Disney animated movie classic *Bambi*.

FALOO: The name of a kangaroo in the Disney animated movie *The Rescuers Down Under*.

FANTASIA: Fantasy, musical. From the animated Disney movie classic *Fantasia*.

FELIX: (Latin: "happy") The name of the feline who tries to rescue a princess from an evil inventor in the animated movie *Felix the Cat*. Actor Mickey Rooney has a cat named General Felix.

FENTON CRACKSHELL: Scrooge's accountant in the animated Disney TV series "DuckTales."

FETHRY DUCK: Donald Duck's weird cousin.

FIDGET: The dim-witted, bumbling bat in the Disney animated movie *The Great Mouse Detective*.

FIEVEL: The name of the lovable mouse in the animated feature film *Fievel Goes West*.

FIFI: A mischievous, little brown dog who was Pluto's first love in early Disney cartoons.

FIGARO: A cute and cuddly kitten in Disney's *Pinocchio* and several other cartoons.

FLANNERY: The no-nonsense station manager in the Disney cartoon "Pigs Is Pigs."

FLICK: Fast. The name of a bug in the movie *A Bug's Life*.

FLINTSTONE: Grayish or brown. From the animated TV series "The Flintstones."

FLOWER: A skunk named when Bambi mistakenly thinks he is a flower in the Disney animated movie classic *Bambi*.

FLUFFY: The name of one of the kittens in the Disney cartoon "The Three Orphans."

FLUPPY: From the colorful pups in the animated TV special "Disney's Fluppy Dogs."

FLUTTER FOOT: The big-footed, snow-shoed rabbit in the Disney cartoon "Mail Dog."

FOXWORTHY: Sly. The name of a cartoon fox in old TV commercials.

FRANCES: Spirited. The name of a bug in the movie *A Bug's Life*.

FRANCIS: Free spirit. The name of a male ladybug in the

Disney animated movie *A Bug's Life*. Also, the somewhat cultured bulldog in the Disney animated movie *Oliver & Company*.

FRANK: One of the friends in the comic strip "Frank and Ernest" by Bob Thaves.

FRANKIE: Minnie Mouse's little yellow bird in the Disney cartoon "Figaro and Frankie."

FRECKLES: One of the best known of the pups in the Disney animated movie classic *101 Dalmatians.*

FRITZ: Peaceful ruler. German nickname for Frederick. From the "Fritz the Cat" cartoon series.

FROSTIE, FROSTY: Chilly, cool. The name of the lovable snowman in the animated Christmas special "Frosty the Snowman."

FROU-FROU: The horse in the Disney animated movie *The Aristocats.*

FUDD: Old-fashioned as in "fuddy duddy." Fussy. From the cartoon character Elmer Fudd, who's always chasing Bugs Bunny.

GAMBIT: Clumsy, daring. The name of one of the X-Men in the animated TV series and movies.

GARFIELD: The name of the lovable but mischievous cat in the comic strip and animated TV series created by Jim Davis.

GARGOYLE: Odd, extravagant. From the animated TV series "Gargoyles."

GAZOO: Small. The name of the tiny spaceman in the animated 1960s TV series "The Flintstones."

GEECH: The name of a popular syndicated comic strip.

GENERAL SNOZZIE: The Official Hound of the Junior Woodchucks, a Disney character.

GEORGETTE: The dainty poodle in the Disney animated movie *Oliver & Company.*

GERMANIA: Large blonde valkyrie in "Education for Death," the Disney animated parody of *Sleeping Beauty.*

GHOULIE: Spooky. Elusive. From the animated TV series "The Groovie Ghoulies."

GIBBER: The canine air pirate in the Disney animated TV series "TailSpin."

GIDEON: The comical cat in

the animated Disney movie *Pinocchio*.

GIGGLES: An elephant in the Disney animated movie *Dumbo*.

GIL: A fish in the short-lived animated TV series "Fish Police."

GILL: The Moorish idol named Gill, voiced by Willem Dafoe in the fish tank in the Disney animated movie *Finding Nemo*

GLEEP: One of the friendly blobs in the 1980s animated TV series "Herculoids."

GLOOP: One of the friendly blobs in the 1980s animated TV series "Herculoids."

GODDARD: The name of Jimmy Neutron's robotic dog in the cartoon series about a boy genius and inventor in the Nickelodeon TV series "Jimmy Neutron: Boy Genius."

GO-GO: A dancer. The name of the pet goat in the TV series "The Rudy and Go-Go Cartoon Show."

GOLDFEATHER: Described as the "poutingly sensual" duck in the animated Disney TV series "DuckTales."

GOO: Messy. The name of

one of Gumby's friends in the children's TV series.

GOOFY: Silly. The name of a popular Walt Disney cartoon dog.

GRAMMI: The motherly figure of the Gummi bear family in the Disney animated TV series "Gummi Bears."

GREEN: The cool Fluppy in the animated TV special "Disney's Fluppy Dogs."

GRIMSBY: A wise character in the Disney animated movie *The Little Memaid*.

GRINCH: From Dr. Seuss's classic children's story and animated TV special "How the Grinch Stole Christmas."

GRUFFI: The grumpy Gummi bear in the Disney animated TV series "Gummi Bears."

GRUMPY: The name of one of the dwarves in the Disney animated movie *Snow White and the Seven Dwarfs*.

GUMBY: A child's rubber toy. The name of a claylike green character in the children's animated TV series "Gumby."

GURGI: A furry little creature in the Disney animated movie *The Black Cauldron*.

GUS: From Gus Goose in the Disney cartoon "Donald's Cousin Gus."

GYPSY: Colorful, sly. The name of the moth in the Disney animated movie *A Bug's Life.*

GYRO: A Disney character, a brilliant yet somewhat absent-minded inventor.

HAGAR: From the syndicated comic strip "Hagar the Horrible" by Dik Browne.

HAMTON: The name of the pig in the animated TV series "Tiny Toon Adventures."

HAPPY: The name of one of the dwarves in the Disney animated movie *Snow White and the Seven Dwarfs.*

HAPPY JACK: A circus owner in the animated Disney TV series "DuckTales."

HEATHCLIFF: From the cat in the cartoon TV series "Heathcliff."

HECKLE: From the cartoon TV series about two magpies named Heckle and Jeckle.

HEIMLICH: From the Heimlich maneuver, the manual application of sudden upward pressure on the upper abdomen of a choking victim to force a foreign object from the wind-pipe, named for American surgeon Henry J. Heimlich. Also the name of a caterpillar in the movie *A Bug's Life.*

HEKA: The cobra in the cartoon "Mummies Alive."

HE-MAN: Manly. From the superhero in the animated TV series "He-Man and the Masters of the Universe."

HI: A character from the syndicated comic strip "Hi and Lois" by Mort Walker and Dik Browne.

HOBBES: From the syndicated comic strip "Calvin and Hobbes" about a boy and his cat, Hobbes.

HOMER: (Greek: "promise") A Greek epic poet of the 8th century B.C. and, according to legend, the author of the *Illiad* and the *Odyssey.* The name of the dad in the TV cartoon series "The Simpsons."

HONKER: From Honker Muddlefoot, a tiny boy duck in the Disney animated TV series "Darkwing Duck."

HOPPER: The name of the leader of the grasshoppers in the Disney animated movie *A Bug's Life.*

HOPPOPOTAMUS: A character who is half hippopotamus and half rabbit, in the Disney animated TV series "The Wuzzles."

HOPPY: The name of a kangaroo in the animated TV series "The Flintstones."

HOT DOG: The name of the kids' dog in the cartoon series "The Archies."

HUEY: A form of Hugh. Intelligent. The name of the duck in the animated TV series "Baby Huey." Also, the name of one of Donald Duck's nephews.

HUMAN: The name of a dog in the cartoon TV series "Stunt Dawgs."

IAGO: The villainous parrot in the Disney animated movie *Aladdin.*

IDGIT: Idgit the Midget, a dwarf bad guy in Disney cartoons.

IGOO: The rock-ape in the animated TV series "Herculoids."

ITCHY: The mouse in the cartoon series "Itchy and Scratchy," featured in the TV series "The Simpsons."

JAB: One of the four crime fighting teen sharks in the animated TV series "Street Sharks."

JAFAR: Ill-mannered. The villain in the Disney animated movie *Aladdin.*

JASMINE: Colorful. A tropical and subtropical shrub of the olive family, with fragrant flowers of yellow, red, or white. The name of the princess in the Disney animated movie *Aladdin.*

JECKLE: From the cartoon TV series about two magpies named Heckle and Jeckle.

JEEPERS: Old-fashioned expression similar to "Oh, my gosh." A favorite saying of the mischievous kid in the comic strip and TV series "Dennis the Menace."

JEREMY: Short for Jeremiah. Appointed. From Jeremy Crow in the animated movie *The Secret of NIHM.*

JERRY: (Latin: "holy name") The name of the mischievous mouse in the animated TV series "Tom and Jerry."

JESSICA RABBIT: The curvy rabbit in the Disney animated movie *Who Framed Roger Rabbit?* She's considered most sensual animated character ever to heat up the big screen.

JESSIE: The name of the cowgirl who co-starred with Woody in his old TV series in the animated movie *Toy Story II.*

JETSON: Fast. The name of the space-age family in the cartoon TV series "The Jetsons."

JIM DANDY: A crow in the Disney animated movie *Dumbo.*

JIMINY: Schemer. From the cartoon character Jiminy Cricket in the Disney animated movie *Pinocchio.*

JOCK: The plucky little terrier in the Disney animated movie *Lady and the Tramp.*

JOSE: From Jose Carioca, a Brazillian parrot in the Disney animated movie *The Three Caballeros.*

JOSIE: Prosperous. The name of the leader of a rock band in the cartoon TV series and movie *Josie and the Pussycats.*

J. THADDEUS TOAD: The tuneful frog in the Disney animated anthology "The Adventures of Ichabod and Mr. Toad."

JUGHEAD: Bumbling. The name of one of Archie's teenage pals in the comic book and cartoon TV series "Archie."

JUMBA: The name of the alien scientist in the Disney animated movie *Lilo and Stitch.*

JUNIOR: Pluto's son Pluto, Junior in Disney cartoons.

KABOOBIE: The name of a camel in the 1960s cartoon series "Shazzan."

KAOLAKEET: A character, half koala bear and half parakeet, in the Disney animated TV series "The Wuzzles."

KING GREGOR: The honorable king in the Disney animated TV series "Gummi Bears."

KING HUBERT: The small, tubby king in the Disney animated movie *Sleeping Beauty.*

KING STEFAN: The tall, distinguished king in the Disney animated movie *Sleeping Beauty.*

KIT: A bear cub in the Disney animated TV series "Tail-Spin." James Garfield, the 20th President of the United States, had a horse with this name.

KOOKIE: A brightly colored

bird in the Disney animated movie *The Rescuers Down Under.*

KREBBS: A large, plump Kaola bear in the Disney animated movie *The Rescuers Down Under.*

KRUSTY: From Krusty the Clown in the animated TV series "The Simpsons."

KRYPTON: A rare chemical gas, an inert gas present in very small quantities. The name of the planet on which Superman was born.

KRYPTONITE: The mineral that gave Superman his heroic powers.

LADY: A female of good breeding. The name of a dog in the animated Walt Disney movie *Lady and the Tramp.* When Donny Osmond and his brothers were kids, they had a dog with this name.

LAMBERT: The tiny lion cub in the Disney cartoon "Lambert, the Sheepish Lion."

LAMPWICK: The boy who befriends Pinocchio on Pleasure Island in the Disney animated movie *Pinocchio.*

LAUNCHPAD: From Launchpad McQuack,

Scrooge's pilot in the Disney animated TV series "DuckTales."

LAVENDER: The loving Fluppy dog in the animated TV special "Disney's Fluppy Dogs."

LILO: The name of the spirited little girl in the Disney animated movie *Lilo and Stitch.*

LINUS: (Greek: "flaxen-haired") The name of a character in Charles Schulz's syndicated comic strip "Peanuts."

LIPPY: The name of one of the Three Little Pigs in the Disney animated musical.

LITTLE HELPER: The name of Gyro's mechanical helper in an old Disney cartoon.

LITTLE HIAWATHA: The cute Indian lad who wants to be a great hunter in the Disney cartoon of the same name.

LITTLE TOOT: The name of a small tugboat in Disney cartoons.

LOAFY: The cartoon dog in the commercial breaks for the Fox TV network.

LOIS: A character from the syndicated comic strip "Hi and Lois" by Mort Walker and Dik Browne.

LOUIE: Nickname for Louis. Warrior. The name of one of Donald Duck's nephews. The name of the dog in the comic strip "Overboard" by Chip Dunham. Actress Loni Anderson, who starred in the TV series "WKRP In Cincinnati," has an Abyssian cat named Louie.

LUCIFER: Devilish. The name of a cat in the Disney animated classic *Cinderella*.

LUCKY: Fortunate. One of the best known of the pups, the pup who's addicted to watching television, in the Disney animated movie classic *101 Dalmatians*. Ronald Reagan, the 40th President of the United States, had a Bouvier des Flandres sheepdog named this.

LUMPY: Shapeless, plump. The name of one of the Three Little Pigs in the Disney animated musical.

MAGGIE: The name of the youngest Simpson, the baby Maggie, in the long-running animated TV series "The Simpsons."

MAGILLA: The name of the cartoon gorilla in the cartoon TV series "Magilla Gorilla."

MAGOO: From the cartoon TV series "Mr. Magoo," who was nearsighted and had a companion, his dog McBarker.

MAJOR: The horse in the animated Disney movie classic *Cinderella*.

MANDIBLE: From the ant General Mandible, voiced by Gene Hackman, an ambitious military leader who plans to rebuild the colony in his own image in the animated movie *Antz*.

MANNY: Strong. The name of the woolly mammoth in the animated movie *Ice Age*. Also, the name of the praying mantis in the Disney animated movie *A Bug's Life*.

MARAHUTE: A huge golden eagle in the Disney animated movie *The Rescuers Down Under*.

MARIE: One of the three kittens (along with Berlioz and Toulouse) in the animated Disney movie *The Aristocats*.

MARINA: Of the sea. The name of the female penguin in the animated movie *The Pebble and the Penguin*.

MARLIN: A large, slender deep-sea fish related to the

sailfish. The name of the clownfish, Nemo's dad, voiced by Albert Brooks in the Disney animated movie *Finding Nemo.*

MARMADUKE: The Great Dane in the comic strip "Marmaduke" by Brad Anderson.

MARVIN: (Old English: "lover of the sea") The cartoon alien in the animated TV series "Marvin the Martian."

MAX: The name of the Grinch's dog in Dr. Seuss's "How the Grinch Stole Christmas." Also, the name of Prince Eric's sheepdog in the animated movie and TV series *The Little Mermaid.* Bestselling author Sidney Sheldon had a German Shepherd with this name.

MARBLEHEAD: A pelican trying Donald's patience in the Disney cartoon "Lighthouse Keeping."

MARCIE: Warrior. The name of Peppermint Patty's best friend in the comic strip and animated series "Peanuts," created by Charles M. Schulz.

MARGE: A pearl. The name of the mother with the tall blue hair in the animated TV series "The Simpsons."

McBARKER: The name of Mr. Magoo's dog in the animated TV series.

McBOO: From Dangerous Dan McBoo, a large thief and companion to Idgit the Midget.

McGRUFF: The name of the cartoon dog that takes "a bite out of crime" in the TV commercials for the National Crime Prevention Council.

MEEKO: The name of the raccoon in the Disney animated movie *Pocahontas.*

MEGAVOLT: A living power-battery and adversary of Darkwing Duck in the Disney animated TV series "Darkwing Duck."

MERRYWEATHER: One of the good fairies in the Disney animated movie *Sleeping Beauty.*

MICHAELANGELO: For Italian painter, sculptor, architect, and poet Michaelangelo. Also, the name of one of the "Teenage Mutant Ninja Turtles" in the TV and movie series.

MICKEY: A form of Michael. From the world's most famous

cartoon mouse, Walt Disney's Mickey Mouse.

MIGHTY MOUSE: The name of a cartoon mouse who has superpowers.

MILKTOAST: A minor character in the Disney animated movie *The Rescuers Down Under*.

MILLHOUS: The middle name of Richard Nixon, 37th President of the United States. Also, the name of Bart's best friend in the animated TV series "The Simpsons."

MILTON: The fluffy cat in the Disney cartoon *Cold Turkey*.

MINNIE: Tiny. Love. The name of Mickey's friend Minnie Mouse in the Walt Disney cartoon series.

MISS BIANCA: The beautiful white mouse (voiced by Eva Gabor) in the Disney animated movie *The Rescuers* and the sequel *The Rescuers Down Under*.

MISSIS: Female. A dog in the Disney animated movie *101 Dalmations*.

MODO: A mouse in the cartoon "Biker Mice from Mars."

MOLT: The name of a grasshopper in the Disney animated movie *A Bug's Life*.

MONCHICHI: A 1980s cartoon series. "The Monchichis," based on dolls that resemble monkeys.

MOOSEL: A character, half moose and half seal, in the Disney animated TV series "The Wuzzles."

MORTIMER: Sea warrior. Walt Disney had a pet mouse with this name which may have been the inspiration for one of Disney's most famous and popular characters, Mickey Mouse.

MORTY: Short for Mortimer. Sea warrior. The name of Mickey Mouse's nephew in the Disney cartoons.

MUFASA: The name of a lion in the Disney animated movie *The Lion King*.

MUFFY: The name of a female wasp in the animated movie *Antz*. Also, the name of one of the kittens in the Disney cartoon "The Three Orphans."

MULDOON: The tough cop character in the Disney cartoon "How to be a Detective."

MUMBLY: Noisy. From the cartoon dog *Detective*

Mumbly.

MUNCEY: A huge English sheepdog in the Disney cartoon "The New Neighbor."

MUSCLES: Strong. From Muscles McGurk, a not-so-nice neighbor of Mickey Mouse.

NALA: The name of a lion in the Disney animated movie *The Lion King.*

NANA: In *Peter Pan*, the loving and very capable nurse for the Darling children, Nana just happens to be a dog.

NANI: The name of Lilo's older sister in the Disney animated movie *Lilo and Stitch.*

NATASHA: A Russian form of Natalie. From the villainess, a Russian spy, in the cartoon TV series "Rocky and Bullwinkle."

NEMO: Sea captain. From the animated movie *Little Nemo: Adventures in Slumberland.* Also, the name of the clown fish voiced by Alexander Gould in the Disney animated movie *Finding Nemo.*

NERMAL: The name of Garfield's niece in the comic strip "Garfield."

NICODEMUS: Victory. The name of a mouse in the animated movie *The Secret of NIMH.*

NIGEL: Champion. The wise pelican voiced by Barry Humphries in the Disney animated movie *Finding Nemo.*

NOD: A cute little boy in the Disney cartoon about three tots called "Wyken, Blyken and Nod," also, the names Opie gave three orphaned baby birds in an episode of the 1960s TV series "The Andy Griffith Show."

NOSE: The Nose, one of the "Pound Puppies."

NUTSY: The not-so-smart vulture in the animated Disney movie *Robin Hood.*

OBELIX: Asterix's best friend in the "Asterix" comic book series set in Roman times under the rule of Caesar and about tiny warriors resisting Roman rule in a Gaul village.

ODIE: The name of the dog in the comic strip and animated TV series "Garfield."

OLIVE: Popeye's girlfriend Olive Oyl in the animated TV series "Popeye."

OLIVER: Cute but feisty little cat in the Disney animated movie *Oliver & Company,* based on Charles Dicken's classic novel *Oliver Twist.*

O'MALLEY: From Thomas O'Malley, the heroic cat in the Disney animated movie *The Aristocats.*

OPUS: (Latin: "magnum opus," meaning great work) The penguin character in the comic strip "Bloom County."

ORVILLE: A baby bird in the Disney cartoon "Pluto's Fledgling."

OSWALD: The lovable blue whale in the animated Nickelodeon TV series "Oswald."

OTTO: From Otto the Baby Bird in the Disney cartoon "Birds in the Spring."

PABLO: Distinguished. From Pablo the Penguin in the Disney animated movie *Three Caballeros.*

PADDINGTON: The name of the small brown bear in the animated children's series of the same name.

PANCHITO: The reddish colored bird of Mexican origin in the Disney animated movie *The Three Caballeros.*

PANDEAVER: A character, half panda and half beaver, in the Disney animated TV series "The Wuzzles."

PARANNO: A character in the cartoon series "Street Sharks."

PATCH: One of the best known of the pups in the Disney animated movie classic *101 Dalmatians.*

PEABODY: From the highly intelligent dog Mr. Peabody in the cartoon TV series "Rocky and Bullwinkle."

PEACH: The shy Fluppy in the animated TV special "Disney's Fluppy Dogs."

PEANUTS: The name of a comic strip created by Charles M. Schulz.

PEARL: The octopus voiced by Erica Beck in the Disney animated movie *Finding Nemo.*

PEBBLES: Fred and Wilma's daughter in the TV cartoon series "The Flintstones."

PECO, PECOS: Large like a city. From the Disney movie *Tall Tale: The Unbelievable Adventures of Pecos Bill.*

PEDRO: One of the singing dogs, the Chihuahua, in the Disney animated movie *Lady and the Tramp.*

PENNY: One the pups in the Disney animated movie classic *101 Dalmatians.*

PEPE: Spanish form of Joseph, meaning "he shall increase." From the cartoon skunk Pepe Le Pew.

PEPPER: One of the best known of the pups in the Disney animated movie classic *101 Dalmatians.*

PEPPERMINT: A plant of the mint family with lance-shaped leaves and pink flowers. For the character Peppermint Patti from Charles Schulz's "Peanuts."

PERCY: The horse who tested Goofy's patience in the Disney cartoon "How to Ride a Horse."

PERDITA: (Latin: "lost") The name of the mother dog in the Disney animated movie *101 Dalmatians*

PERI: (Greek) "Lives in the Mountains." The tabby cat in the children's TV series "Blue's Clues."

PHILLIPPE: An intelligent, steadfast horse in the Disney animated movie *Beauty and the Beast.*

PIGGYPINE: A character,

half sow and half porcupine, in the Disney animated TV series "The Wuzzles."

PIGPEN: Unkempt. The name of the untidy kid in the syndicated comic strip and animated TV series "Peanuts."

PINK: The pretty Fluppy in the animated TV special "Disney's Fluppy Dogs."

PLUCKY: From the cartoon character Plucky Duck in Steven Spielberg's "Tiny Toon Adventures."

POGO: A pet that is always jumping. The name of a crocodile in the syndicated comic strip "Walt Kelly's Pogo."

POKEY: Slow moving as a slowpoke. The name of Gumby's horse in the children's TV series "Gumby."

PONCHITO: Poncho. The name of a character in the Disney animated movie *Saludos Amigos.*

PONGO: The name of the father dog in the Disney animated movie *101 Dalmatians.*

POOKY: The name of Garfield's bedtime companion, a teddy bear.

POPEYE: The spinach-eating

character, a sailor, from the cartoon TV series "Popeye, the Sailor Man."

PORKY: Plump. From the cartoon TV pig named Porky.

PORPY: The name of a Disney character, Moby Duck's pet porpoise.

PRICKLES: Prickly. The name of one of Gumby's friends in the children's TV series. The name of a Beanie Baby hedgehog.

PRIMO: A little wolf in the Disney cartoon "Primitive Pluto."

PRINCE ERIC: The name of Ariel's prince charming in the animated movie and TV series The *Little Mermaid.*

PRINCESS CALLA: A beautiful, petite, and delicate young lady in the Disney animated TV series "Gummi Bears."

PRINCE VALIANT: Handsome, brave. From the long-running comic strip of the same name.

PRISSY: An elephant in the Disney animated movie *Dumbo.*

PRUNELLA: From Prunella Pullet, a love-smitten chicken in the Disney cartoon "Cock o'

the Walk."

PUMBAA: The name of a warthog in the Disney animated movie *The Lion King.*

PUMYRA: A character, half-human and half puma, in the 1980s cartoon series "Thundercats."

QUACKERJACK: An offbeat toymaker in the Disney animated TV series "Darkwing Duck."

QUACKMORE: The name of Donald Duck's father, Quackmore Duck.

RAFIKI: The name of a baboon in the Disney animated movie *The Lion King.*

RAJA: The crafty tiger in the Disney cartoon "Goliath II."

RAJAH: A friendly tiger in the Disney animated movie *Aladdin.*

RAPHAEL: (Hebrew: "God hath healed") The name of one of the Teenage Mutant Ninja Turtles.

RATIGAN: Rat-like. The name of a character in the Disney animated movie *The Great Mouse Detective.*

RED: Red or reddish colored. The name of one of the Claymation animated characters known as the California Raisins.

REN: The name of the Chihuahua in the animated TV series "Ren and Stimpy."

RHINOKEY: A character, half rhinoceros and half monkey, in the Disney animated TV series "The Wuzzles."

RICHIE: Short for Richard. The name of the wealthiest young boy in the world in the comic book and cartoon TV series "Richie Rich," which was the basis for a movie.

RICOCHET: Fast, a pet that jumps from place to place. The name of a cartoon bunny, "Ricochet Rabbit."

RIPSTER: One of the four crime fighting teen sharks in the animated TV series "Street Sharks."

RITA: The Afghan hound with the heart of gold in the Disney animated movie *Oliver & Company*.

ROCKO: Strong. The name of the streetwise penguin in the animated movie *The Pebble and the Penguin*. Also, the name of the little Australian wallaby in Nickelodeon's cartoon series "Rocko's Modern Life."

ROCKY: A form of Rochester. The character played by Sylvester Stallone in the series of *Rocky* movies. Also, the name of the flying squirrel in the cartoon TV series "Rocky and Bullwinkle."

ROGER RABBIT: The zany, wobble-eared rabbit in the Disney animated movie *Who Framed Roger Rabbit?*

ROGUEFORT: The tiny brown mouse who befriended the felines in the Disney animated movie *The Aristocats*.

ROLL: The name of a Hungarian pill bug in the Disney animated movie *A Bug's Life*.

ROLLY: One of the best known of the pups in the Disney animated movie classic *101 Dalmatians*.

RONNIE: A cuddly little Saint Bernard in the Disney cartoon "The Purloined Pup."

RONNO: A male deer (a buck) in the Disney animated movie classic *Bambi*.

ROSIE: The name of the spider in the Disney animated movie *A Bug's Life*.

RUBBLE: Rough. From Barney Rubble, Fred's best friend

and neighbor, in the animated TV series "The Flintstones," on which a movie is based.

RUDOLPH: (Old German: "famed wolf") The name of the red-nosed reindeer in the animated TV Christmas special "Rudolph, the Red-Nosed Reindeer." Also spelled Rudolf.

RUDY: Wolflike. The name of the puppet who co-hosts the children's series "The Rudy and Go Go Cartoon Show."

RUFF: Rough. The name of Dennis the Menace's dog in the comic strip and movie.

RUMPUS: Noisy. The name of Donald Duck's destructively lazy and gluttonous relative in Disney cartoons.

RUPERT: Bright. The name of a boy in an animated music video, "Rupert and the Frog Song," by pop star Paul McCartney.

SAD SACK: Slang for a one who means well but is clumsy, incompetent. The character in the comic strip of the same name.

SALLY: A form of Sarah. A princess; witty. The name of Charlie Brown's little sister in the syndicated comic strip "Peanuts."

SANCHO: A character from Miguel de Cervantes's *Don Quixote*. Also, the name of the cartoon character Sancho Panda.

SANTA'S LITTLE HELPER: The name of the family dog, a greyhound rescued after being retired from dog racing, in the animated TV series "The Simpsons."

SATCHEL: For Satchel Pooch, the cranky dog in the comic strip "Get Fuzzy" by Darby Conley.

SAVOIR FAIRE: French for "to do and say the right thing in a social situation." The name of a rat in the cartoon series "Tennessee Tuxedo."

SCAMP: The name of Lady and Tramp's puppy in the Disney animated classic *Lady the Tramp*.

SCAR: The name of a lion in the Disney animated film *The Lion King*.

SCHNOZZES: Characters in the animated movie *Monster in My Pocket* with the Schnozzes, characters with large noses.

SCHRODER: Musical. The

name of one of Charles Schulz's "Peanuts" characters.

SCOOBY DOO: The cowardly great dane in the cartoon series of the same name. Scooby is the longest-running cartoon dog in history.

SCOUNGER: One of the "Pound Puppies" in the animated TV series.

SCRAPPY: Slang for fond of fighting. The name of Scooby Doo's nephew Scrappy Doo.

SCRATCHY: The cat in the cartoon series "Itchy and Scratchy," featured in the TV series "The Simpsons."

SCUTTLE: A shifty character in the Disney animated movie *The Little Memaid.*

SERENDIPITY: Intuitively talented. From the children's animated movie *Serendipity, the Pink Dragon.*

SHADOW: Dark; a pet that is always close-by as your shadow. From a golden retriever in the Disney movie *Homeward Bound.*

SHAGGY: Scooby's master in the cartoon series "Scooby Doo."

SHAZAM: From the comic book superhero Captain Marvel, who is a young orphan until he utters the word "Shazam!" and is transformed into a superpowered adult.

SHAZZAN: The name of a genie in a popular 1960s cartoon series of the same name.

SHELDON: (Anglo-Saxon: "valley") The name of the sea horse voiced by Erik Per Sullivan in the Disney animated movie *Finding Nemo.*

SHENZI: The name of a hyena in the Disney animated movie *The Lion King.*

SHE-RA: Princess. The name of a popular children's cartoon character.

SHERMAN: (Old English: "shearer") The name of Mr. Peabody's young student in the cartoon TV series "Rocky and Bullwinkle."

SHIRLEY: (English: "one who came from Shirley," in England) One of the zany roommates in the TV series "Laverne and Shirley." The name of the loon in the cartoon TV series "Tiny Tune Adventures."

SHOE: The name of the bird in the popular syndicated comic strip "Shoe" by Jeff

MacNelly. A good name for any pet that loves to chew on your shoe.

SHTINKY: The name of the small tabby cat in the comic strip "Mutts" by Patricia Mc-Donnell.

SI: One of the two Siamese cats in the Disney animated movie *Lady and the Tramp.*

SID: Short for Sidney. The name of the sloth in the animated movie *Ice Age.*

SIMBA: Leader. The name of the lion in the Disney animated movie *The Lion King.*

SIRI: The name a leopard, voiced by Chrissie Hynde of the rock band The Pretenders, in the animated movie *Rugrats Go Wild.*

SKOWL: A character, half skunk and half owl, in the Disney animated TV series "The Wuzzles."

SLADE: The vicious old hunter, Amos Slade, in the Disney animated movie *The Fox and the Hound.*

SLEEPY: The name of one of the dwarves in the Disney animated movie *Snow White and the Seven Dwarfs.*

SLIM: Thin lean. The name of a walking stick in the Disney animated movie *A Bug's Life.*

SLIMER: Slimy at times, such as a snail, snake, or other pet. The name of the friendly ghost in the cartoon series "The Real Ghostbusters."

SLINKY: Slithery. The name of the dog in the animated movie *Toy Story.*

SLUE FOOT SUE: The red-haired cowgirl that Pecos Bill falls for in the Disney cartoon "Pecos Bill."

SLUGGO: Nancy's friend in the Nancy comic strip and comic books.

SMOKEY: A smoke-colored, gray, or blackish colored pet. From "Smokey Bear" - the U.S. Forest Service's animated bear that warns people to prevent forest fires.

SMURF: From the tiny, blue-colored creatures in the cartoon TV series "The Smurfs."

SMURFETTE: The name of the female Smurf in the cartoon TV series.

SNAFU: Military slang for "situation normal all fouled up," meaning a characteristic disorder or confusion. Also, the name of a syndicated comic strip.

SNAGGLEPUSS: The name of a cartoon cat.

SNEEZY: A pet who sneezes. The name of one of the dwarves in the Disney movie *Snow white and the Seven Dwarfs.*

SNOOPY: Charlie Brown's beagle in Charles Schulz's "Peanuts" comic strip and the animated TV series based on the comic strip.

SNOW WHITE: White as snow, pure. The name of the fair maiden in the Disney animated classic *Snow White and the Seven Dwarfs.*

SNOWY: TinTin's dog in the comic book series.

SNUFFLES: The dog in the cartoon series "Quick Draw McGraw."

SNUFFY: Short for Snuffelupagus, the large friend of Big Bird's on the PBS TV children's series "Sesame Street." Also, the name of a comic strip, "Snuffy Smith" by John Rose.

SPARKY: Lively, glittering. The name of Stan's dog in the animated TV series "South Park."

SPAZ, SPAZZ: The lion in the animated movie *Monster in My Pocket* with the Schnozzes, characters with large noses.

SPEEDY: Swift. The name of the cartoon mouse Speedy Gonzales, who is always outwitting Daffy Duck.

SPIDEY: Like a spider; having many legs or other characteristics of a spider. Nickname for the comic book superhero "Spiderman."

SPIKE: The name of the dog voiced by Bruce Willis in the animated movie *Rugrats Go Wild.*

SPUNKY: The name of the dog in the Nickelodeon cartoon series "Rocko's Modern Life."

SQUEEKS: The caterpillar that became a beautiful butterfly in the Disney animated movie *The Fox and the Hound.*

SQUEEKY: The talking Chihuahua in the comic strip "Bizzaro" by Dan Piraro.

STIMPY: The name of the cat in the animated TV series "Ren and Stimpy."

STITCH: The name of the lovable alien in the Disney animated movie *Lilo and Stitch.*

STORM: The name of a sea-horse in the cartoon series "Aquaman."

STREEX: One of the four crime fighting teen sharks in the animated TV series "Street Sharks."

STROMBOLI: A large and moody character in the Disney animated movie *Snow White and the Seven Dwarfs.*

SULLIVAN: From the John Goodman character James P. Sullivan, a large blue monster with purple spots, in the Disney animated movie *Monsters, Inc.* Sullivan's nickname in the movie is Sully.

SUNNI: The next to youngest Gummi Bear, like the youngest bear, she also gets into mischief in the Disney animated TV series.

SUPERMAN: Heroic. From the comic book superhero.

SYKES: A villian in the Disney animated movie *Oliver & Company.* Also for popular comic Wanda Sykes, star of the TV series "Wanda at Large."

SYLVESTER: (Latin: "from the wood") The name of the cat that chases Tweety in the cartoon TV series "Sylvester and Tweety."

TALBOT: A hound dog in the Disney animated movie *The Sword and the Stone.*

TARAN: The boy who wants to become a great warrior in the Disney animated movie *The Black Cauldron.*

TAZ: Short for the popular cartoon character the Tasmanian Devil.

TEMPLETON: Reformed. The rat with the huge appetite in the animated movie *Charlotte's Web,* which is based on the classic children's book by E. B. White.

TESS: The name of Dick Tracey's wife, Tess Trueheart, in the long-running comic strip.

THEODORE: Gift. The name of one of the chipmunks from the cartoon TV series "Alvin and the Chipmunks." For Theodore Roosevelt, 26th President of the United States.

THROTTLE: One of the mice in the cartoon "Biker Mice from Mars."

THUMBELINA: Small dancer. From the children's book and the animated Disney movie *Thumbelina,* based on the children's tale by Hans Christian Andersen.

THUMPER: The rabbit in the classic Disney cartoon movie *Bambi.*

THUNDERBOLT: The dog in the parody of Lassie in the Disney animated movie classic *101 Dalmatians.*

THUNDERTHUD: A character, Chief Thunderthud, in the 1950s children's TV series "Howdy Dowdy."

TIGER LILY: The little Indian girl in the Disney animated movie *Peter Pan.*

TILLIE: From Tillie Tiger, a cute little tiger cub in the Disney cartoon "Elmer Elephant."

TIMON: The name of a meerkat in the Disney animated movie *The Lion King.*

TIMOTHY: (Greek: "honoring God") The name of the mouse that befriends the flying elephant in the Disney animated movie *Dumbo.*

TINTIN: Little bell. From the children's TV series "Adventures of Tintin," an animated series about a boy reporter.

TITO: The excited little chihuahua (voiced by Cheech Marin, of Cheech and Chong fame) in the Disney animated movie *Oliver & Company.*

TOBY: From Toby Tortoise in the Disney cartoon *The Tortoise and the Hare.*

TOD: The name of a young fox that befriends a hound pup in the Disney animated movie *The Fox and the Hound.*

TOLIVER: The Saint Bernard that befriends the kittens Fluffy, Muffy, and Tuffy in the Disney cartoon "More Kittens."

TOOTSIE: A cute penguin in the Disney cartoon "Donald's Penguin."

TOUCHÉ: Used to indicate a hit in fencing or an appropriate point in a discussion or argument. The turtle in the 1960s cartoon series "Touche Turtle and Dum Dum."

TOUGHY: One of the singing dogs in the Disney animated movie *Lady and the Tramp.*

TOULOUSE: One of the three kittens (along with Berlioz and Marie) in the animated Disney movie *The Aristocats.*

TOWSER: A hound dog in the Disney animated movie

classic *101 Dalmatians.*

TRAMP: A hobo. From the dog in the Disney animated movie *Lady and the Tramp.*

TRUSTY: The bloodhound in the Disney animated movie *Lady and the Tramp.*

TUCK: The name of a Hungarian pill bug in the Disney animated movie *A Bug's Life.*

TUFFY: One of the kittens in the Disney cartoon "The Three Orphans."

TUMMI: The largest of the Gummi Bears, a kindly, loyal fellow in the Disney animated

TUNDRO: The rhinoceros in the 1980s animated TV series "Herculoids."

TUSKERNINNI: A shapely walrus in the animated TV series "Darkwing Duck."

TWEETY: The small yellow bird pursued by Sylvester the cat in the cartoon TV series.

TYCOON: A character, half tiger and half racoon, in the Disney animated TV series "The Wuzzles."

VALIANT: Courageous. From the long-running comic strip "Prince Valiant."

VIXEY: The beautiful fox that befriended Tod and saved his life in the Disney animated movie *The Fox and the Hound.*

WART: A small creature changed into a fish, squirrel, and a sparrow in the Disney animated movie *The Sword and the Stone.*

WEAVER: The name of Z's buddy, a soldier ant, in the animated movie *Antz.*

WEBBIGAIL: Webbigail Vanderquack in the Disney animated TV series "DuckTales."

WEBBY: Nickname for Webbigail Vanderquack in the Disney animated TV series "DuckTales."

WENDY: Short for Gwendolyn. White. The name of the nurturing girl in the Disney animated movie *Peter Pan.*

WHIMPY: Dependent. The little man who eats the hamburgers in the cartoon TV series "Popeye."

WHITEY: A seagull in the Disney cartoon "The Whale Who Wanted to Sing at the Met."

WILBER, WILBUR: (Anglo-Saxon: "willow town") The name of the pig in E. B. White's classic children's book and animated movie *Char-*

lotte's Web. Also, the name of the enterprising albatross in the Disney animated movie *The Rescuers Down Under.*

WILLIE: The whale in the Disney cartoon "The Whale Who Wanted to Sing at the Met."

WILMA: Wishful protector. The name of Fred's wife in the 1960s animated TV "The Flintstones."

WILYKAT: A character in the 1980s cartoon series "Thundercats."

WILYKIT: A character in the 1980s cartoon series "Thundercats."

WIMPER: One of the two hound dog detectives in the 1970s cartoon series "Woofer and Wimper Dog Detectives."

WINDWAGON: From the blond, bold, muscular guy in the Disney cartoon "The Saga of Windwagon Smith."

WINIFRED: An elephant in the Disney animated movie *The Jungle Book.*

WINTHROP: Friendly. From the dog of this name in the syndicated comic strip by Dick Cavalli.

WOLVERINE: The name of one of the X-Men in the animated TV series and movie.

WOODSTOCK: The small yellow bird in the Charles Schulz comic strip "Peanuts." Also, the site of a 1960s rock music festival and the recent revival.

WOODSY: The name of the cartoon owl in the TV commercial promoting a clean environment.

WOODY: Of the woodland. The name of the bird in the cartoon TV series "Woody Woodpecker." Also, the name of the cowboy in the Disney animated movie *Toy Story.* The name of the bird in the cartoon TV series "Woody Woodpecker." Also, the name of the cowboy in the Disney animated movie *Toy Story.*

WOOFER: One of the two hound dog detectives in the 1970s cartoon series "Woofer and Wimper Dog Detectives."

WOOLRUS: A character, half lamb and half walrus, in the Disney animated TV series "The Wuzzles."

WUZZLE: From the Disney animated TV series "The Wuzzles."

WYKEN: A cute little boy in the Disney cartoon about three tots called "Wyken, Blyken and Nod" also, the names Opie gave three orphanded baby birds in an episode of the 1960s TV series "The Andy Griffith Show."

WYLIE: Clever. From the cartoon character Wylie Coyote, who chases the Roadrunner in the animated TV series.

WZOWSKI: From the Billy Crystal character Mike Wazowski, a green, opinionated, feisty little one-eyed monster in the Disney animated movie *Monsters, Inc.*

YELLOW: The playful Fluppy in the animated TV special "Disney's Fluppy Dogs."

YOGI: A philosopher. The name of the clever, playful cartoon bear "Yogi Bear." Also for baseball great Yogi Berra.

YOSEMITE: Ill-mannered. From Yosemite National Park in east central California, containing high waterfalls, cliffs, and redwood trees. Also from the cartoon character Yosemite Sam.

YUKON: Territory of Northwest Canada. The name of the character Yukon Cornelius in the animated holiday favorite "Rudolph the Red-Nosed Reindeer."

Z: The ant who is the main character in the animated movie *Antz.*

ZANDOR: The king in the 1980s animated TV series "Herculoids."

ZAZU: The name of a hornbill in the Disney animated movie *The Lion King.*

ZIGGY: The lovable, rotund character in the comic strip by Tom Wilson.

ZINNY: The monkey in Disney's animated movie "Dinosaur."

ZIPPER: A cartoon fly in the Disney animated TV series "Chip 'n Dale Rescue Rangers."

ZIPPY: Energetic. The name of the comic book series about a clown named Zippy.

ZOBOO: The little lemur in the PBS children's TV series "Zoboomafoo."

ZOK: The laser dragon in the 1980s animated TV series "Herculoids."

ZONKER: A character in the

popular syndicated comic strip
"Doonesbury" by Gary
Trudeau.
ZUMMIE: Described as the
most sophisticated of the
Gummi Bears in the animated
Disney TV series.

Seaweed

Did You Know?

ALGONQUIN: Theodore Roosevelt, the 26th President
of the United States, had a pony with this name.

BUTTERFLY: John F. Kennedy, the 35th President
of the United States, had a Welsh terrier with named this.

LE BEAU: John Tyler, the 10th President of the United
States, had a greyhound with this name.

Matisse & Monet

Tanga

Jack and Andre

Chapter 9

Children's Literature

Children may sometimes name a new pet after a character from a favorite book or story: *Corduroy* (the bear who lost a button in the children's story by Don Freeman), *Ping* (the lost duckling in the popular children's book), *Harry Potter* (the young wizard in the series of books by J. K. Rowling).

ANDRE: Manly. The cute and smart seal who adopts a human family in the movie *Andre*, which is based on the book *A Seal Called Andre* by Harry Goodridge and Lew Dietz.

BA-BA: From the children's nursery rhyme, "Ba-Ba Black Sheep."

BABAJI: The small boy in the children's book *The Story of Little Babaji* by Helen Bannerman.

BABAR: From the elephant in the children's book *The Story of Babar* by Jean de Brunhoff, which inspired the animated TV series "Babar."

BEDELIA: Blessed, solitary. The name of the princess in the children's story *The Practical Princess* by Jay Williams.

BINGO: The name of a dog in a children's song. Also, the name of a dog in the best-selling book *The Hidden Life of Dogs* by Elizabeth Marshall Thomas.

BLACK BEAUTY: The enduring horse in Anna Sewell's classic children's novel *Black Beauty.*

BO-PEEP: Young. From the children's rhyme "Little Bo-peep."

BUNNICULA: A bucktooth bunny. The vampire rabbit in the contemporary children's book *Bunnicula.*

CLAIRE: Bright. The name of

the bunny in the children's picture book *First Tomato* by Rosemary Wells.

COTTONTAIL: A bunny in Beatrix Potter's classic children's book *The Tale of Peter Rabbit.*

CORDUROY: (French: "cord of the king") The bear who lost a button in the children's story by Don Freeman.

DOOLITTLE: Lazy. The doctor who talks to the animals in the children's book *Dr. Doolittle.*

DR. SUESS: Pen name of Theodore Suess, American writer and illustrator of children's books including such classics as "How the Grinch Stole Christmas."

ELLEN: Glowing. The girl in the children's story *Ellen's Lion* by Crockett Johnson.

FERDINAND: (Old German: "world-daring") A bull in a children's story *Ferdinand* by Munro Leaf.

FLOPSY: Having long ears. The name of a bunny in Beatrix Potter's classic children's book *The Tale of Peter Rabbit.*

GEORGIE, GEORGY: Down to earth. Also from the children's rhyme "Georgy Porgy," who kissed the girls and made them cry.

GINGER: Spicy, spirited. The name of a mare in Anna Sewell's classic children's novel *Black Beauty.*

GLENDA, GLINDA: Magical, beautiful. The name of the good witch in the classic children's novel *The Wizard of Oz* by L. Frank Baum.

GOLDILOCKS: Golden-haired. The name of the young girl in the classic children's story "The Three Bears."

GORF: Temperamental. From Mrs. Gorf, the teacher, in the children's book *Sideways Stories from Wayside School* by Louis Sachar.

GRUFF, GRUFFY: Rude. From children's story "The Three Billy Goat's Gruff."

HANS: (Hebrew: "Lord is gracious") For Danish writer Hans Christian Andersen, author of "The Ugly Duckling" and other fairy tales. Also from the classic children's book *Hans Brinker, or the Silver Skates* by Mary Mapes Dodge.

HARRY POTTER: The young wizard in the series of

novels by author J. K. Rowling.

HEIDI: Humble. The charming orphan girl in a children's novel by Johanna Spyri. Dwight D. Eisenhower, the 34th President of the United States, had a Weimaraner with this name.

HENNY: From Henny Penny, a chicken in the children's story "Chicken Little."

HORTON: Outdoorsy. From the elephant in the children's story *Horton Hears a Who* by Dr. Suess.

HUMPTY: From the children's rhyme "Humpty Dumpty."

INGLE: Fiery. For Laura Ingles Wilder, the author of books about her family's life in the wilderness, on which the TV series "Little House on the Prairie" is based.

JACK: (Hebrew: "seizing by the heel, a supplanter") The name of the boy who slays the giant in the classic children's story "Jack and the Beanstalk." From Jack the Pumpkin King in the animated movie *The Nightmare Before Christmas.* Abraham Lincoln, the 16th President of the United States, had a turkey named Jack. Also, the name of the dog that co-hosts the "Pet Department" series on the FX cable channel.

JILL: A girl or young lady, a sweetheart. The name of the girl who went up the hill with Jack in the children's nursery Rhyme "Jack and Jill."

KING COLE: From the children's nursery rhyme about "Ole King Cole who was a merry ole soul." Calvin Coolidge, the 30th President of the United States, had a shepherd with this name.

MADELINE: (Greek: "woman from Magdala") The French school girl in the children's book by Ludwig Bemelmans.

MAISIE, MAYZIE: A form of Margaret. The name of a girl who sprouted a flower from her head in Dr. Seuss's TV special "Daisy-Head Mayzie," based on a 20-year-old manuscript found after the death of the author of numerous popular children's books.

McGUFFEY: For William Holmes McGuffey, an American educator and editor of

McGuffey's Reader.

MERRYLEGS: The name of a horse in Anna Sewell's classic children's novel *Black Beauty.*

MOPSEY: A bunny in Beatrix Potter's classic children's book *The Tale of Peter Rabbit.*

MUFFIT: From the children's rhyme about "Little Miss Muffit" who was scared by a spider who sat down beside her.

MUGGLES: In the Harry Potter book series by author J.K. Rowling, Muggles are non-magical beings.

MUNCHKIN: One of the little people in the classic motion picture *The Wizard of Oz,* based on L. Frank Baum's classic children's novel.

NANA: In *Peter Pan*, the loving and very capable nurse for the Darling children, Nana just happens to be a dog.

NANCY: Graceful. The name of the young sleuth in the Nancy Drew Mysteries.

NARNIA: The land where the stories take place in the Chronicles of Narnia by C. S. Lewis.

NICHOLAS: (Greek: "victory of the people") The name of the bunny in the children's story *I Am a Bunny* by Ole Risom.

NUTKIN: From *Squirrel Nutkin,* a book by Beatrix Potter.

OWEN: Well-born. The name of the little mouse in the children's picture book of the same name by Kevin Henkes.

OZ: Dorothy was swept away by a cyclone and landed in the kingdom of Oz in L. Frank Baum's classic children's novel *The Wizard of Oz.*

PETER: (Greek: "rock") The name of a rabbit in the classic children's book *The Tale of Peter Rabbit* by English author and illustrator Beatrix Potter. Also the name of the naive country cat from Sweden who gets tricked into traveling to the United States in the movie *Peter No-Tail In America.*

PETER PAN: From Sir James Barrie's play (and later children's books) about a little boy who never grows up. Calvin Coolidge, the 30th President of the United States, had a terrier with this name.

PETUNIA: A plant of the nightshade family, with variously colored, funnel-shaped flowers. The name of the silly goose in the children's picture book of the same name by Roger Duvoisin.

PIERRE: (French: "Peter") The boy who didn't care in the children's story *Pierre: A Cautionary Tale in Five Chapters and a Prologue* by Maurice Sendak.

PIGLET: Pooh Bear's friend, a small, pink pig, in the children's classic *The Adventures of Winnie the Pooh.*

PING: Fast. The name of a duckling that gets lost in the children's book of the same name.

PINOCCHIO: The name of the wooden boy, in the classic children's story *The Adventures of Pinocchio,* whose nose grew each time he told a fib.

PIPER: A person who plays a bagpipe. A howlingly musical pet. The kitten in the children's story *No Kiss for Mother* by Tomi Ungerer.

POOH: An exclamation of disbelief, impatience. The name of the bear that loves honey in A. A. Milne's *Winnie the Pooh.*

PORGIE, PORGY: From the children's nursery rhyme "Georgie Porgie" about a lad who kissed the girls and made them cry.

PUFF: From the song by Peter, Paul and Mary, "Puff, the Magic Dragon."

PUNCH: The hero of the puppet show "Punch and Judy." Pleasing, as in the phrase "pleased as punch."

PUSS: A term that refers to a cat. From the bold, fearless, and enterprising cat in the children's story *Puss in Boots.*

RAGGEDY ANDY: The boy rag doll in the children's book *The Raggedy Ann Stories* by Johnny Gruelle.

RAGGEDY ANN: The beloved rag doll in the children's book The Raggedy Ann Stories by Johnny Gruelle.

ROLAND: (French-Old German: "famous land") The name of the maiden's beloved in the children's story *Sweetheart Roland.*

SKIDMORE: An energetic pet. The name of a mouse in the children's book *She Was Nice to Mice* by Alexandra Sheely.

SONIA, SONYA: Wise. The

name of a character in the children's book *No One Is Going to Nashville* by Mavis Jukes.
STELLALUNA: The heroic fruit bat in the children's book of the same name by Janell Cannon.
STEVIE: A crown. The name of the African-American boy in the children's book *Stevie* by John Steptoe.
SWIMMY: The name of the fish who swam faster than his brothers and sisters in the children's book by Leo Lionni.
TAILYPOO: From the children's book of the same name.
TIGGER: A tiger in the children's classic story *Winnie the Pooh* by A. A. Milne.
TINKERBELL: The fairy in the children's story *Peter Pan.*
TITCH: The little girl in the children's book by Pat Hutchins.
TOM: Short for Thomas. A common name for male cats. The name of the young boy in Mark Twain's class children's novel *The Adventures of Tom Sawyer.* Also, the name of the mischievous cat in the animated TV series "Tom and Jerry."

TOMTEN: A small creature resembling a little man in the children's book *Tomten* by Astrid Lindgren.
TOOTLES: In *Peter Pan*, one of the lost boys who fell out of his perambulator when a baby, he now lives in Neverland.
TOTO: Dorothy's small, black dog in L. Frank Baum's classic children's story "The Wizard of Oz." Actor David Hasselhoff, the former star of the TV series "Knight Rider" and star of "Baywatch," has a gray Cairn terrier, which he says looks just like the dog from "The Wizard of Oz," with this name.
TREEHORN: The young boy in the children's picture book *The Shrinking of Treehorn* by Florence Parry Heide.
VELVETEEN: Soft. From the children's book *The Velveteen Rabbit* by Margery Williams.
VIRGIE: A form of Virgil or Virginia. The name of a town in Kentucky. Also, the name of the little African-American girl who wanted to go to school in the children's book *Virgie Goes to School With the Boys* by Elizabeth Fitzgerald

Howard.

WELLINGTON: The name of the beloved Cavalier King Charles spaniel in the book *Wellington's Windows* by Marilyn Mae Randall.

WHITE SHADOW: The young girl's dog in the children's story "Corky and the White Shadow."

WILDER: Wild. For Laura Ingles Wilder, the author of books about her family's life in the wilderness on which the TV series "Little House on the Prairie" was based.

WILLABY: From the children's song "Willably Wallaby."

WINKIE: From the nursery rhyme "Wee Willie Winkie," about the lad who runs through town making sure all the children are in their beds.

YEARLING: An animal one year old or in its second year. *The Yearling* is the title of a popular children's book by Marjorie Kinnan Rawlings.

Did You Know?

BERTHA BLUE: Actor David Boreanaz (star of the TV series "Angel") has a dog named Bertha Blue.

CHARLIE: Strong, manly. A character in Charles Schulz's comic strip "Peanuts." Comedian Bea Arthur, the former star of the TV series "Maude" and "The Golden Girls," had a German Shepherd with this name. Also, actor David Hasselhoff, the former star of the TV series "Knight Rider" and star of "Baywatch," has a gray African parrot with this name.

EAGLE FEATHERS: When he was a young boy, Michael Jackson had two Indian friends, brother and sister, who had a kitten with this name.

Rembrandt

Picasso

Chapter 10

LITERATURE AND THE ARTS

Literature and the arts can inspire creative names that reflect a pet lover's knowledge and interests: **Artists (*Picasso, Matisse, Rembrandt*), Authors (*Doyle, Namby Pamby, Zola*), Composers (*Basie, Mozart, Ludwig*), Musical (*Disco, Mambo, Sonata*), Books (*Moby Dick, Scarlett, White-Fang*).**

ACHILLES: In Homer's *The Iliad*, the Greek hero of the Trojan War.

AESOP: A Greek fable writer who lived c. 620-560 B.C.

AHAB: A sea captain in Herman Melville's *Moby Dick*.

AJAX: Powerful. In Homer's *The Iliad*, a Greek hero in the Trojan War.

AKELA: The gray wolf in Rudyard Kipling's *The Jungle Book*.

ALI: Ali Baba, a poor woodcutter, who, in *The Arabian Knights*, found the treasure of forty thieves in a cave.

ANDANTE: Softly musical.

ANDANTINO: Lively musical.

ANGELOU: Angelic. For African-American poet Maya Angelou.

ARIA: A melody. Also, a striking solo performance.

ARTFUL: Clever. From the character Artful Dodger, the crafty waif, created by English novelist Charles Dickens in *Oliver Twist*.

BAGHEERA: A cunning black panther in Rudyard Kipling's *The Jungle Book*.

BALOO: A sleepy brown bear in British author Rudyard Kipling's children's classic *The Jungle Book*.

BANJO: Plucky. Musical instrument with strings and a round body.

BARCLAY: Scottish Quaker author Robert Barclay.

BASIE: William Basie, better known as Count Basie, American bandleader and composer.

BEARDSLEY: English illustrator Audrey Vincent Beardsley.

BEATRIX: Happy. For English author and illustrator Beatrix Potter, who created the children's classic *The Tale of Peter Rabbit.*

BEOWULF: The oldest English epic poem, probably composed in the early 8th century.

BLUE BOY: *The Blue Boy* is the name of a portrait of a young boy painted by Sir Thomas Gainsborough.

BOFFO: An opera singer who plays a comic role.

BOUFEE: A comic opera.

BOZ: The pen name of 19th century English author Charles Dickens.

BRIAR: Thorny, fussy. Wild rose. From *Briar Rose* (also known as *Sleeping Beauty*) the beautiful princess who is awakened by a kiss from a handsome prince in a Grimm's fairy tale.

BRONTE: For English novelist Charlotte Brontë, who wrote the classic novel *Jane Eyre.*

BRUNNEHILDE: In German composer Richard Wagner's *Die Walkure,* a Valkyrie whom Siegfried releases from a spell.

BULDEO: The village hunter in Rudyard Kipling's *The Jungle Book.*

BURGESS: American humorist and illustrator Gelett Burgess.

CALYPSO: Musical.

CAMUS: French novelist, essayist and dramatist, Albert Camus.

CANOE: Ron Stob's book *A Cat Named Canoe* tells how he and his wife planned to buy a canoe and ended up with a cat - which they named *Canoe.*

CAPRICCO: Musical. Lively.

CARROLL: Grown. For Lewis Carroll, the English writer who wrote *Alice's Adventures in Wonderland.*

CATLIN: Known for American artist George Catlin.

CELLINI: Italian goldsmith and sculptor, Benvenuto Cellini.

CHANT: A song; to sing.

CHANTÉ: (Pronounced

"shawn-tay") A song; melody.

CHANTEY: Musical. A tune sung, especially by sailors, to set the rhythm of their physical labor.

CHAUCER: English poet Geoffrey Chaucer.

CHESHIRE: The proverbial grinning cat of Cheshire, England, especially as described in Lewis Carroll's *Alice's Adventures in Wonderland.*

CHICKADEE: Musical. Also, a small bird.

CHIL: The name of the bird in Rudyard Kipling's *The Jungle Book.*

CHOPIN: For Franco-Polish composer Frederic François Chopin (1810–1849), who brought romantic piano music to unprecedented heights of expressiveness.

CHUCHUNDRA: A muskrat in Rudyard Kipling's *The Jungle Book.*

CINDERELLA: The young lady in a fairy tale who marries a prince.

CIRCE: In Homer's *Odyssey,* an enchantress of men.

CODA: Musical. In music, a final passage, closing a composition or movement.

CONBRIO: In music, with spirit; lively.

CONGA: A dancer. From the Latin American dance in which the dancers form a winding line.

COPLEY: American portrait painter John Singleton Copley.

CREB: The name of a male character in Jean M. Auel's prehistoric novel *The Clan of the Cave Bear.*

CRUSOE: The hero of Daniel Defoe's novel *Robinson Crusoe.*

CYRANO: A French author of satire; the name is associated with a big nose.

DADA: Child's cry. A movement (1916–22) in art and literature characterized by formless, sub-conscious expression.

DALLAS: A character in S.E. Hinton's coming of age novel *The Outsiders.*

DANTE: For Italian poet Alighieri Dante, who wrote *The Divine Comedy.*

DARROW: American lawyer and author, Clarence Seward Darrow.

DARRY: A character in S.E.

Hinton's coming of age novel *The Outsiders*.

DARZEE: A tailorbird in Rudyard Kipling's *The Jungle Book.*

DAUMIER: For French caricaturist and painter, Honore Daumier.

DEFOE: For English Novelist Daniel Defoe, author of Robinson Crusoe.

DEGAS: For Edgar Degas, French Impressionist painter and sculptor.

DICKENS: The little dickens, meaning mischievous. From Shakespeare, meaning devil. Also for Charles Dickens, 19th century English novelist.

DIDGERIDOO: A large bamboo or wooden trumpet of the Australian Aborgines.

DISCO: A pet that dances to or likes music. Also, the name of a dog, a Border Collie, in Purina Dog Chow Incredible Dog Team, precision-trained dogs that travel the country performing at halftime shows, on television programs and a variety of other public events.

DITTY: A short, simple song.

DOBIE: James Frank Dobie, American folklorist.

DOBSON: English poet and essayist, Austin Dobson.

DON: Chivalrous, unrealistic hero *Don Quixote* of a satirical romance by Miguel de Cervantes. Also, in Spanish legend, Don Juan was a dissolute nobleman and lady's man.

DORRIT: Little Dorrit, the title character in one of English author Charles Dickens's novels.

DOYLE: Reserved. From English author Sir Arthur Conan Doyle creator of Sherlock Holmes, the best known of all fictional detectives.

DRACULA: A pet that bites. From the vampire Count Dracula, the title character in a novel written by English novelist Bram Stoker.

DR. SPOCK: Benjamin McLane Spock, American physician and author of well-known books on childcare.

DULCIE: The female of the pair crime-solving cats in the novel *Cat to the Dogs* by Shirley Rousseau Murphy.

EBENEZER: (Hebrew: "stone of help") From Ebenezer Scrooge, an old miser in

Charles Dickens's *A Christmas Carol.*

EDGE: For "The Edge," guitarist for the Irish rock band U2.

EL GRECO: A Spanish painter.

ELIOT: Reverent. For English poet and essayist T. S. Eliot, one of the most influential literary figures of the 20th century and winner of the 1948 Noble Prize for literature.

EMERSON: For American essayist, philosopher, and poet Ralph Waldo Emerson.

EMILY: Excellent. For Emily Dickinson, one of the greatest poets in American history; her subsequent fame came after her death and her work has had great influence on 20th-century poetry.

ESTIENNE: A French family of painters and book-sellers.

EZRA: American poet Ezra Loomis Pound.

FENIMORE: For James Fenimore Cooper, the first major American novelist and author of *The Last of Mohicans, The Deerslayer,* and other books.

FIDDLE: Musical, especially a pet that loves bluegrass or country and western music.

FRANKENSTEIN: A fictional character in Mary Shelley's novel, Dr. Frankenstein created a creature that later destroyed him. Often, mistakenly, the creature is referred to as Frankenstein, but the creature is actually Frankenstein's monster.

FRIDAY: The day of the goddess. The sixth day of the week. The name of Crusoe's devoted servant in the classic novel *The Life and Adventures of Robinson Crusoe* by Daniel Defoe. John F. Kennedy, Jr. had a dog with this name.

FRODO: The name of a Hobbit created by English novelist and scholar J. R. R. Tolkien.

GARGANTUA: Enormous. A giant with prodigious appetites in *Gargantua and Pantagruel,* a satire by Rabelais.

GARP: Sharp-witted. From *The World According to Garp,* a novel that made American author John Irving an overnight success.

GATSBY: From the title character in American author F. Scott Fitzgerald's *The Great*

Gatsby.

GOYA: For Spanish painter and graphic artist Francisco Jose de Goya, the greatest painter of his era.

GRETEL: A pearl. The name of the young girl in the Grimm's fairy tale "Hansel and Gretel."

GRIMM: For the Brothers Grimm, Jakob and Wilhelm, who collected fairy tales.

GULLIVER: The character in Jonathan Swift's satire *Gulliver's Travels,* who voyages to the imaginary land of the Lilliputians and others.

HADLEY: American composer Henry Kimball Hadley.

HAMLET: The hero in William Shakespeare's tragic play of the same name.

HANSEL: The name of the young boy in the Grimm's fairy tale "Hansel and Gretel."

HARLEQUIN: A clown in early Italian comedy and pantomime.

HATHI: An elephant in Rudyard Kipling's *The Jungle Book.*

HAWTHORNE: (Anglo-Saxon: "hedge thorn") Prickly. Known for American writer Nathaniel Hawthorne, author of stories and novels, including his most famous novel *The Scarlet Letter.*

HIAWATHA: The hero of a long epic poem by American poet Henry Wordsworth Longfellow.

HOBBIT: Goblin. Tiny. From *The Hobbit,* written by English author J.R.R. Tolkien.

HOGARTH: William Hogarth, English painter and engraver.

HOLMES: For English author Sir Arthur Conan Doyle's fictitious detective Sherlock Holmes.

HUBBARD: American writer Elbert Greer Hubbard.

HUCKLEBERRY: The name of the young boy in Mark Twain's novel *Huckleberry Finn.* Also for the dog Huckleberry Hound, in the 1950s cartoon series. The show was one of the first animated series to win an Emmy Award for Best Children's Program, in 1959.

HUXLEY: English novelist and critic Leonard Huxley.

HYDE: Moody. From Scottish writer Robert Louis Stevenson's *The Strange Case of Dr.*

Jekyll and Mr. Hyde, a science fiction novel with moral overtones.

IAGO: Temperamental. The name of the villain in William Shakespeare's play *Othello.*

ICHABOD: Studious. From the character of the awkward, timid schoolteacher Ichabod Crane, in "The Legend of Sleepy Hollow," a short story by American author Washington Irving.

IZA: The name of a female character in Jean M. Auel's prehistoric novel *The Clan of the Cave Bear.*

JABBERWOCKY: Idle chatter. From the book *Alice in Wonderland* by English author Lewis Carroll.

JANE: (Hebrew: "the Lord is gracious") For English novelist Jane Austen, author of *Pride and Prejudice* and other novels.

JAZZ, JAZZY: Lively. A form of improvisational music that originated in the United States.

KEATS: English poet John Keats.

KEBEL: English clergyman and poet John Kebel.

JEKYLL: Moody. From Robert Louis Stevenson's *The Strange Case of Dr. Jekyll and Mr. Hyde,* a science fiction thriller with moral overtones.

JIP: The small black spaniel who walked on the dinner table in Charles Dickens' David Copperfield.

JOE GREY: The male of the pair of crime-solving cats in the novel Cat to the Dogs by Shirley Rousseau Murphy.

JORINDA: The name of the beautiful maiden in Grimm's fairy tale "Jorinda and Joringel."

JORINGEL: The name of the handsome youth, Jorinda's beloved, in Grimm's fairy tale "Jorinda and Joringel."

JUAN: Devout. For Don Juan, a legendary tale, widely told by the Spanish, about a reckless young man.

JULIET: Youthful. The name of the young heroine in William Shakespeare's romantic tragedy *Romeo and Juliet.*

KAA: The friendly python in Rudyard Kipling's *The Jungle Book.*

KACHINA: A Native American dancer.

KANO: Creative. A family or school of Japanese painters.

KEATS: For John Keats, considered one of the greatest English poets.

KICHE: A she-wolf in Jack London's book *White-Fang*.

KIPLING: For Rudyard Kipling, British poet, short story writer and novelist, author of the beloved classic *The Jungle Book*.

KITHARA: An ancient Greek musical instrument.

KLEE: For Paul Klee, a Swiss painter.

KOKO: The siamese cat who investigates crime in the series of novels by Lillian Jackson Braun.

KOTICH: The baby seal in Rudyard Kipling's *The Jungle Book*.

LARGO: In music, slow and stately.

LEAR: A king. From William Shakespeare's play *King Lear*.

LEMUEL: (Hebrew: "belonging to God") The first name of the hero of Jonathan Swift's classic novel *Gulliver's Travels*.

LILLIPUT: In Jonathan Swift's *Gulliver's Travels*, a land inhabited by tiny people.

LIP-LIP: The pup who turns all the dogs against White-Fang in Jack London's book.

LITTLE DORRIT: The title character in a book by Charles Dickens.

LOLLAPALOOZA: Excellent. The name of a popular music festival held annually.

LONDON: For Jack London, American author whose books include *The Call of the Wind, The Sea-Wolf,* and *White-Fang*. Also, a county and city in southeastern England.

LONGFELLOW: For American poet Henry Wadsworth Longfellow, one of the most popular poets of all time and author of "The Song of Hiawatha" and "Paul Revere's Ride."

LOUISA: Renowned warrior. For Louisa May Alcott, an American novelist whose best-known book is *Little Women*.

LUCIAN: A Greek writer best For his vigorous and witty satire.

LUDWIG: German version of Louis. For German composer Ludwig von Beethoven. Also, from the duck in Disney's "Ludwig von Drake."

LYRE: A small stringed instrument of the harp family, played by the ancient Greeks.

MACBETH: King of Scotland and subject of William Shakespeare's play *Macbeth.*

MAESTRO: Master of any art.

MAMBO: A rhythmic ballroom dance to music of Cuban Negro origin.

MANCHA: (Spanish: "speckle, spot") From *Don Quixote de la Mancha,* a novel by Spanish writer Miguel Cervantes.

MANG: The bat in Rudyard Kipling's *The Jungle Book.*

MARIA: Rebellious. The name of a dog in the best-selling book *The Hidden Life of Dogs* by Elizabeth Marshall Thomas.

MATISSE: French artist Henri-Emille-Benoit Matisse.

MATKAH: A seal in Rudyard Kipling's *The Jungle Book.*

MEDLEY: Musical.

MELVILLE: For American author Herman Melville, author of the masterpiece *Moby Dick.*

MISERY: Always ailing. The title character in a novel by modern horror novelist Stephen King.

MOBY: From the novel about a captain's search for a white whale, *Moby Dick* by Herman Melville. Also, the name of a Disney character, Moby Duck, Captain of the seven seas.

MOLIERE: The pseudonym of Jean Baptiste Poquelin, a French dramatist.

MONA LISA: From Leonardo da Vinci's portrait of a lady, often said to be the most beautiful woman ever.

MONET: For French impressionist painter Claude Monet.

MOR: The loud peacock in Rudyard Kipling's *The Jungle Book.*

MOWGLI: Man-cub. A boy raised by wolves in Rudyard Kipling's *The Jungle Book.*

MUSKETEER: Soldier. From French author Alexandre Dumas's book *The Three Musketeers,* about three swashbuckling companions.

NAG: A snake in Rudyard Kipling's *The Jungle Book.*

NAGAINA: A snake in Rudyard Kipling's *The Jungle*

Book.

NAMBY PAMBY: Sentimental, insipidly pretty. Nickname of English poet Ambrose Phillips.

NANKI POO: A character in the opera *Madame Butterfly.*

NICKLEBY: A character created by English novelist Charles Dickens, in his work *Nicholas Nickleby.*

ODYSSEUS: The hero of the Greek epic poem *Odyssey.*

O. HENRY: Surprising. The pen name of William Sydney Porter, an American short story writer whose stories are noted for their careful plotting, ironic coincidences, and, of course, surprise endings.

OTHELLO: A tragic play by William Shakespeare.

OUIDA: The pen name of English novelist Louise de la Ramee, who wrote the children's book *A Dog of Flanders.*

PAZ: A Mexican author.

PHIDIAS: Greek sculptor.

PICASSO: From Spanish painter and sculptor Pablo Picasso.

PICCOLO: A small flute, pitched an octave above the ordinary flute. A noisy pet.

PICO: Short for piccolo. A musical pet or a pet that likes music.

PIPPY: The name of an adventurous girl in a series of children's books and movies called *Pippy Longstocking.*

POE: For Edgar Allan Poe (1809–1849), an American poet, critic, and fiction writer, who is considered to have been one of the most brilliant and original writers. Among Poe's best known short stories are "The Masque of the Red Death," "The Fall of the House of Usher," and "The Murders in the Rue Morgue." Poe's best known poems include "The Raven" and "Annabel Lee."

POLLYANNA: The persistently optimistic heroine of the stories by Eleanor H. Porter.

PONY BOY: The name of a character in the coming of age novel *The Outsiders* by S. E. Hinton.

PRIMA: Short for prima donna, a vain person or the principal female lead singer, as in an opera.

PRIMA DONNA: A vain person or the principal female lead

singer as in an opera.

PUCCINI: Giacomo Puccini, Italian operatic composer.

PUCK: A mischievous sprite; goblin, elf. From the mischievous sprite in William Shakespeare's *Midsummer Night's Dream.*

QUIXOTE: Extravagantly chivalrous, as in the satirical romance *Don Quixote,* by Miguel de Cervantes.

RAMFUS: A character in the opera *Madame Butterfly.*

RAPUNZEL: The beautiful maiden, in the Grimm's fairy tale, whose hair was so long it was used as a ladder.

REGGAE: (Jamaican: "ragged") From a popular music of Jamaican origin.

REMBRANDT: For the Dutch painter, etcher, and draftsman who was the greatest master of the Dutch school.

RENOIR: French Impressionist painter Pierre-Auguste Renoir.

REYNARD: Clever. The fox in the medieval beast epic *Reynard the Fox.*

RHAPSODY: Musically spontaneous.

RHETT: The hero in Margaret Mitchell's Civil War novel *Gone With the Wind.*

RIKKI: From Rikki-Tikki-Tavi, the name of the heroic mongoose in Rudyard Kipling's *The Jungle Book.*

RIP: Sleepy. From the long-sleeping character of *Rip Van Winkle,* a story by American author Washington Irving.

RIZZIO: Italian musician Riccio Rizzio, favored by Mary, Queen of Scots.

ROBINSON: From Robinson Crusoe, the hero of Daniel Defoe's novel about a sailor who is shipwrecked on a tropical island.

ROMEO: (Italian: "pilgrim to Rome") The name of Juliet's beloved in William Shakespeare's tragic play about the ill-fated lovers titled *Romeo and Juliet.*

RONDO: Musical.

ROSE RED: The name of Snow White's beautiful sister in the Grimm's fairy tale *Snow White and Rose Red.*

ROUNDELAY: Simply musical.

RUMPELSTILTSKIN: The name of the little man who grants wishes to a maiden in the Grimm's fairy tale.

RUM TUM TUGGER: A character in the Broadway musical *Cats*.

SABIAN: Maker of music instruments: percussion.

SAH: The name of a porcupine in Rudyard Kipling's *The Jungle Book*.

SAKI: The pen name of English author Hector Hugh Munro, who wrote witty and often bizarre stories and novels.

SALVADORE: Friendly. For Spanish painter Salvador Dali, who became a leader of Surrealism.

SAMBA: A Brazilian dance of African origin.

SAWYER: Smart, clever. From *Tom Sawyer* a classic novel by Mark Twain.

SAX: Short for saxophone. Musical like the brass wind instrument.

SCARLETT: Red-colored. The heroine in Margaret Mitchell's Civil War novel Gone With the Wind.

SCHERZANDO: In music, playful, playfully sportive.

SCROOGE: The miserable old man in Charles Dickens' story *A Christmas Carol*.

SEA CATCH: The name of the gray seal in Rudyard Kipling's *The Jungle Book*.

SHAKESPEARE: For William Shakespeare, an English poet and dramatist referred to as the Bard of Avon.

SHANDY: From English author Laurence Sterne's masterpiece *Tristram Shandy*.

SHANGRI LA: The scene of J. Hilton's novel *Lost Horizon*. Imaginary utopia or hidden paradise.

SHERE: Shere Khan, the ruthless jackal in Rudyard Kipling's *The Jungle Book*.

SHERLOCK: (Old English: "fair-haired") The detective in Sherlock Holmes series of novels by Sir Arthur Conan Doyle.

SHYLOCK: The relentless moneylender in William Shakespeare's *Merchant of Venice*.

SODA: A character in S.E. Hinton's coming of age novel *The Outsiders*.

SOFTSHOE: Quiet. A form of tap dancing done without taps on the shoes.

SONATA: Musical.

SPOCK: Benjamin McLane

Spock, American physician and author of well-known books on childcare. Also, known for Mr. Spock, a character in the original "Star Trek" series.

STENTOR: Loud. A Greek herald in Homer's *The Illiad* who had a loud voice.

SWIFT: English satirist Jonathan Swift, author of *Gulliver's Travels.*

TABAQUI: A jackal in Rudyard Kipling's *The Jungle Book.*

TABOR: Soft; noisy. The name of a small musical drum instrument.

TAMA: Maker of music instruments: percussion.

TANGO: A pet that loves to dance.

TARANTELLA: A fast, whirling, southern Italian dance for couples.

TARZAN: From the novel *Tarzan of the Apes* by American writer Edgar Rice Burroughs.

TASSO: Italian poet.

TAVI: Elusive. From Rikki Tikki Tavi, the heroic mongoose in Rudyard Kipling's *The Jungle Book.*

THELONIOUS: For Jazz musician Thelonious Monk.

THOREAU: For American naturalist, philosopher and writer Henry David Thoreau, one of the most influential figures in American thought and literature and author of the legendary Walden.

THORNTON: For Pulitzer Prize–winning American author Thornton Wilder, whose novels maintain that meaning and beauty are found in ordinary experience.

THURBER: For James Thurber, an American humorist, who wrote for the New Yorker magazine. Thurber's cartoons and stories were also published in collections including *Thurber Country.*

TIKI, TIKKI: Elusive. From Rikki Tikki Tavi, the heroic mongoose in Rudyard Kipling's *The Jungle Book.*

TOLKIEN: English author John Ronald Reuel Tolkien, who wrote *The Hobbit* and *The Lord of the Rings.*

TOLSTOY: Russian novelist Count Lev Nikolayevich.

TOM JONES: The name of the cat in the May Sarton's

book *The Fur Person*, a fictionalized account of her cat's life and adventures prior to coming into the author's life.

TOM-TOM: Any of various primitive drums played by hand or sticks. Any noisy pet that loves to bang things around.

TOOMAI: Big Toomai and Little Toomai, elephants in Rudyard Kipling's *The Jungle Book*.

TRISTRAM: In medieval legend, a knight who is involved in a tragic romance with Prince Isolde. From English author Laurence Sterne's masterpiece *Tristram Shandy*.

TROUBADOUR: Romantic, affectionate. Any of a class of lyric poets who lived in southern France and northern Italy from the 11th to the 13th centuries and wrote poems of love and chivalry.

TRUMBALL: American painter John Trumball.

TUBA: Noisy; musical. A large brass-wind instrument of the saxhorn group.

TUNE, TUNES: Musical melody. Harmony.

TUSCHE: Pronouned "toosh."

A technique used by screen-printers and other graphic artists.

TWAIN: For author Mark Twain, whose real name was Samuel L. Clemens, one of the masters of American literature and author of books including *The Adventures of Tom Sawyer* and *The Adventures of Huckleberry Finn*.

TWEEDLEDEE, TWEEDLEDUM: The obnoxious identical twin brothers in Lewis Carroll's classic book *Alice In Wonderland*.

VAN GOGH: Artist Vincent Willem van Gogh, one of the Dutch masters.

VIVACA: In music, lively, spirited.

WADSWORTH: For American poet Henry Wadsworth Longfellow who created a body of romantic American legends in such long narrative poems as *Evangeline, The Song of Hiawatha, The Courtship of Miles Stanish,* and *Paul Revere's Ride*.

WALT: Short for Walter. For poet Walt Whitman, considered one of the greatest American poets. Also, for Walter Elias Disney, better known as Walt Disney, creator of Disney empire.

WATSON: From Dr. Watson, Sherlock Holmes's companion in the detective novels by Sir Arthur Conan Doyle.

WHISTLER: For James Abbot McNeil Whistler, an American painter best known for *Arrangement in Gray and Black,* a painting commonly referred to as Whistler's Mother.

WHITE-FANG: The name of the dog in a story by American writer Jack London.

WILLA: Willowly. For American author Willa Sibert Cather, who wrote *O Pioneers!, My Antonia,* and the book considered her masterpiece, *Shadows on the Rock.*

WINKY: The name of the heroine's cat in the mystery novel *Stabbing Stephanie* by Evan Marshall.

WOLFGANG: (Old German: "advancing wolf") For Austrian composer Wolfgang Amadeus Mozart.

XEUXIS: Greek painter.

YEATS: Irish poet and dramatist William Butler Yeats.

ZANE: For American writer Zane Grey, who wrote popular tales of the American West, most notably *Riders of the Purple Sage.*

ZOLA: For French novelist and critic Emile Zola.

ZWEIG: For German author Arnold Zweig.

Truffles

Did You Know?

BUNS: Sweet. Very fit; in great physical shape. Victoria Principal, actress and former star of the TV series "Dallas," has a Burmese cat with this name.

NIPPER: A pet that sometimes tries to bite. Also, the name of the dog pictured on early RCA Recordings.

TRUXTON: Andrew Jackson, the 7th President of the United States, had a horse with this name.

Poco

Kirby

Chapter 11

Human Names: Female and Male

Human names have long been among the most popular (and the most common) for pets of all kinds and remain so to this today.

ABIGAIL: (Hebrew) "Father is rejoicing."

ABRA: (Hebrew) "Mother of the multitude."

ADA, ADAH: (Hebrew: "beauty") Happy.

ADABELLE: Joyous and fair.

ADALIA: Noble one.

ADALINE: Noble.

ADDELAIDE: (Old German) Noble, kind.

ADELICIA: (Old German) Noble quality.

AGATHA: (Greek: "good, kind") For Agatha Christie, renowned English mystery writer.

AGGIE: Sacred, pure.

AGNES: Pure, revered.

AILEEN: Lighthearted.

ALBERTA: Bright through nobility.

ALBERTINA, ALBER-TINE: Honorable.

ALESSA, ALISSA, ALYSSA: Helper; noble. Short for Alessandra.

ALESSANDRA: Helper.

ALEXA: Cooperative.

ALEXANDRA: Considerate, helpful.

ALEXIA: Resourceful.

ALEXINA, ALEXINE: Resourceful.

ALEXIS: Companionable.

ALFREDA: Far-seeing, wise.

ALICE: (Greek: "truth"; also Old German: "noble") Cheerful.

ALICIA: Noble, good-natured.

ALISON, ALLISON: Fiery. Temperamental.

ALTHEA: Healthy, wholesome.

ALVERNA: White; beloved.

AMABEL, AMABELLE: Lovable; kind.

AMANDA: (Latin) Worthy to be loved.

ANDRA: Womanlike.

ANDREA: (Latin: "womanlike") Sporty.

ANDRENA: Womanly.

ANETTE, ANNETTE: Graceful.

ANGE: Angelic.

ANGELA: (Latin) Angelic.

ANGELEAH: Angelic.

ANGELINA, ANGELINE: Saintly messenger.

ANGELIQUE: Angelic.

ANGELLE: Angelic.

ANGIE: Angelic; happy.

ANITA: Full of grace.

ANITRA: Graceful.

ANJANETTE: Valuable.

ANN, ANNE: (Hebrew: "having grace") Saintly.

ANNA: (Hebrew: "having grace") Saintly.

ANNABEL, ANNABELLE: Joyful.

ANNALEE: Graceful.

ANNA MARIA, ANNE MARIE: Graceful; rebellious.

ANNETTE: Gracious.

ANNIS: (Middle English: "Agnes") Pure.

ANTOINETTE: Of great value.

ANTONIA: Of great value.

ARLENA, ARLENE: Beaming.

ASHLEY: (Old English: "from the ash tree meadow") Gray, white-gray.

ASTRID: Spontaneous. Divine strength.

AUDA: (Old English) Rich.

AUDREY: (Old French) Noble might.

AVA: (Latin) Birdlike.

BARB: Short for Barbara. Unique.

BARBRA, BARBARA: (Greek: "foreign, strange") Unique.

BEAH: Blessed.

BEATRICE: (Latin) "She who makes happy."

BECCA: Old-fashioned.

BECKY: (Hebrew: "bound") Old-fashioned.

BELINDA: (Latin) Graceful.

BENITA: Glorify.

BERENICE: (Greek) "Bringer of victory."

BERNADETTE: Favored.

BERNADINE: Well-mannered.

BERNETTE: Steadfast.

BERNICE: (Greek) "Bringer of victory."

BERNITA: Steadfast.
BERTA: Bright.
BERTHA: (Old English) Bright, shining.
BERTICE: Bright.
BERTRICE: Bright.
BERYL: Precious jewel.
BESS: Humble.
BETH: (Hebrew) "House of God."
BETTY: (Hebrew: "oath of God") Purity.
BEULAH: (Hebrew) Married.
BEV: Short for Beverly. Trendy.
BEVERLY: (Anglo-Saxon: "beaver meadow") Trendy. From Beverly Hills, California, as in the TV series *Beverly Hills 90210.*
BIANCA: Italian form of Blanche. White, fair.
BONNIE, BONNY: (Scottish English: "pretty") Good.
BRENDA: (Old English: "firebrand") A sword.
BRIDGET: (Irish Gaelic) Resolute strength.
BROOK, BROOKE: (Old English) "From the brook."
CAITLIN: Pure.
CARLOTTA: Regal.
CAROL: A song of joy.
CAROLEE: Full of joy.

CAROLINE: Feminine.
CAROLYN: Feminine.
CARRIE: Feminine.
CASAUNDRA: A form of Cassandra. Disbelieved.
CASEY: (Irish-Gaelic) Brave.
CASSIE: (Greek) Pure.
CATERINA, CATERINE: Purity.
CATHA: Pure.
CATHLEEN: Pure.
CATHY: Short for Catherine or Cathleen.
CECE: Short for Cecelia.
CECELIA, CECILIA: Hazy.
CECILE: Hazy.
CECILY: Hazy.
CHELSEA: (Old English) A port of ships.
CHERYL: Dear.
CHESSA: (Slavic) Peaceful.
CHRIS: Short for Christina, Christine. Blessed.
CHRISSA, CHRISSY: Nicknames for Christina and Christine.
CHRISTIANA: Blessed.
CHRISTINA: Anointed.
CHRISTINE: Anointed.
CORDELIA: (Celtic) "Daughter of the sea."
COTILDA: Busybody.
COURTNEY: (Old English) "From the court."

CINDY: Short for Cynthia, the goddess of the moon.
CLARE, CLAIR: Illustrious.
CLARISSA: Bright.
CLAUDENE: Frail.
CLAUDETTE: Frail.
CLAUDIA: Frail.
COLLEEN: (Irish Gaelic: "girl") Ladylike.
CONNIE: Faithful.
CORA: Maiden.
CORABETH: Maiden.
CORALEE: Maiden.
CORINNE, CORRINE: Maiden.
DANA: (Scandinavian) "From Denmark."
DANELLA: Judged.
DANETTE: Judged.
DANIELLE: (Italian) Feminine form of Daniel. "God is my judge."
DANIELLIA: A form of Danielle. Judged.
DANNI: Judged. Nickname for Danielle.
DARLENA, DARLENE: Loving.
DEBBIE, DEBBY: (Hebrew) Bee.
DEBBRAH, DEBRA, DEBRAH: (Hebrew) Bee.
DELIA: (Latin) "Island of the Cyclades."

DENA, DINA: Pleasant, colorful.
DENISE: Mellow.
DEVON: (Old English) "Of Devonshire."
DEVONY: Of Devonshire.
DIANE: Divine.
DIONNE: Noble.
DONNA: A lady.
DORALEE: A gift.
DORAN, DOREN: A gift.
DOREA, DORIA: A gift.
DOREEN: A gift.
DOREL: Noisy, vocal.
DORENA: A gift.
DORIA: Generous gift.
DORIAN: (Greek) "From the sea."
DORINDA: Generous gift.
DOROTHEA: (Greek) "A gift of God."
DORTHY, DOROTHY: Gift.
EDDA: Poetic.
EDIE: Of value.
EDITH: Riches.
EDWINA: Valued friend.
EFFIE, EFFY: Well-known.
EILEEN: Bright.
ELAINE: Warm.
ELEANOR, ELINOR: Glowing.
ELEANORA: Glowing.
ELIA: The highest.
ELISE: Solemn.

ELISHA: (Hebrew) "God is salvation."

ELIZABETH: Respectful, loving.

ELOISE: Renowned warrior.

ELON: (African) "God loves me."

ELSIE: Truthful.

ELVERNA: Fresh. Spring-like.

EMELINE: Excellent.

EMIL, EMILLE: Excellent.

EMILIA: Excellent.

EMMA: (Old German) "Universal nurse."

EMMELINE: Excellent.

EMMIE, EMMY: (Old German) "Universal nurse."

EMOGENE: Innocent.

ERIN: (Irish Gaelic) Peace.

ERMA: Distinguished.

ERMINA: Delightful.

ERNESTINA, ERNESTINE: Resolute.

ESME: Short for Esmeralda.

ESMERALDA: A precious jewel.

ESTHER: (Perisan) Star.

ETHEL: (Anglo-Saxon) Noble.

ETHELBERT: Bright, noble.

ETHELENE: Noble.

EUDORA: Good gift.

EUGENIA, EUGENIE: Genius.

EVA: Life.

EVANGELINE: Reverent.

EVELINA: Pleasant.

EVELINE: (Celtic) Pleasant.

EVELYN: (Celtic) Pleasant.

FANNIE, FANNY: Spirited.

FAY, FAYE: (Old French) Fairy, elf.

FELICIA: (Latin) Happy.

FLO: Short for Florence. Blooming.

FLORENCE: Blooming.

FLORENE: Blooming.

FRAN: Short for Frances and Francine. Free spirit.

FRANCESCA: Free spirit.

FRANCHETTA: Free spirit.

FRANCHETTE: Self-efficient.

FRANCINE: Free spirit.

FRANNY: Free spirit.

FREDA, FRIEDA: Peace.

FREDERICA: Peaceful ruler.

GABRIELLA, GABRIELLE: Devoted, strong.

GAIL: Happy.

GENELE: Wellborn.

GEORGIANA: Down to earth.

GEORGINA: Down to earth.

GERALDINE: Ruler.

GERTIE: Short for Gertrude.

Dear, beloved.

GERTRUDE: (Old German: "warrior woman") Dear, beloved.

GIGI: (Old German: "brilliant pledge") The name of a Beanie Baby poodle.

GILDA: (Old German: "covered with gold") Golden-haired.

GILLIAN: Young.

GINA, GENA: Short for Angelina. Angelic.

GINNY: Maidenly.

GLAD: Short for Gladys. Cheerful.

GLADYS: Cheerful.

GLENNA: A hermit.

GLENNIE: A hermit.

GLORIA: Glory.

GLYNIS, GLYNNIS: A hermit.

GRACE, GRACIE: (Latin) Graceful.

GRETA: A form of Margaret. A pearl.

GRETCHEN: German form of Margaret. A pearl.

GWENDOLYN: (Celtic) White.

HANNA, HANNAH: (Hebrew) Grace.

HARRIET: Home ruler.

HAZEL: (Old English: "hazel nut tree") Commanding authority.

HELGA: Reverent.

HENRIETTA: Home ruler.

HESSIE: Love goddess.

HESTER: Love goddess.

HILARY, HILLARY: (Greek) Cheerful, merry.

HILDA, HILDY: Warrior.

HILDEGARDE: Protector.

HILDERETH: Helper.

HOLLY: (Old English) Holly tree.

HORTENSE: Of the garden. Outdoorsy.

INGRID: Goddess.

IRENA, IRENE: Peaceful.

JACKEE, JACKIE: A schemer.

JACQUELINE: A supplanter.

JACQUELYN: A supplanter.

JAIME, JAMIE: Schemer.

JAN, JANET: Gracious.

JANETTA, JANETTE: Gracious.

JANICE: Gracious.

JANIE: Gracious.

JANINE: Gracious.

JEAN, JEANNE: Pretty.

JEANNETTE: Gracious.

JENNIFER: (Welsh: "white, fair") Bestselling author Sidney Sheldon has a German Shepherd with this name.

JESS: Wealthy.
JESSE: Wealthy.
JESSICA: (Hebrew) Wealthy.
JILLIAN: A girl or young lady.
JO: Short for Josephine.
JOANNA, JOANNIE: A supplanter.
JOCELNE, JOCELYN: (Latin) Jester.
JODY: Careful.
JOHANNA: Gracious.
JOSEPHINE: (Hebrew: "he shall increase") The late Jacqueline Susann, bestselling author, had a poodle with this name, and she wrote about her friendship with her pet in the book, *Everynight, Josephine.*
JOSETTA, JOSETTE: Prosperous.
JOYCE: (Latin) Merry.
JUDITH: (Hebrew) Praised.
JUDY: Short Judith.
JULAI: A Form of Julia. Youthful.
JULIA, JULIE: Youthful.
JULIANA: Youthful.
KAREE: Blessed.
KAREN: Pure.
KARENA, KARENE: Pure.
KATE: Pure. Fashion designer Bill Blass has a golden retriever with this name.

KATELYN, KATELYNN: Purity.
KATERINA, KATERINA: Purity.
KATHARINA, KATHERINE: (Greek) Pure.
KATHLENA, KATHLEEN: Pure.
KATHRYN: Pure.
KATIA: Pure.
KATIE, KATEY: Pure. When actress Susan Dey, who starred in the TV series "The Partridge Family" and "L.A. Law," was a girl, her family had a Brittany spaniel named Katie.
KATRICE: Pure.
KATRINA: Pure.
KATRINE: Pure.
KAY: Pure.
KAYA: Pure.
KAYLA: Pure.
KAYLI: Pure.
KAYRA: Pure.
KAYRON: Pure.
KELLY: (Irish Gaelic) Warrior.
KELSEY: (Scandinavian) From the ship-island.
KENDAL, KENDALL: Fiery.
KERRY: Adult-like.
KIM: (Old English) Chief, ruler.

KIMBERLY: Ruler.
KIRBY: (Old English) "From the church town."
The name of a dog, a Australian Shepherd, in Purina Dog Chow Incredible Dog Team, precision-trained dogs that travel the country performing at halftime shows, on television programs and a variety of other public events.
KIRSTEN, KIRSTIN: Blessed.
KIRSTON: Blessed.
KIRSTY: Blessed.
KRISTA: Blessed.
KRISTIN: Blessed.
KRISTY: Blessed.
LARA: (Latin) Shining, famous. James Buchanan, the 15th President of the United States, had a Newfoundland with this name.
LAURA, LAURIE: A winner, conqueror.
LAURALEE: A winner, conqueror.
LAUREN: Honorable.
LAURINDA: A winner, conqueror.
LEAH: (Hebrew) Gazelle.
LEIGH: (Anglo-Saxon) Meadow.
LENORA: Lighthearted.

LENORE: Lighthearted.
LEONA: A feminine form of Leo. A lioness.
LEONARDA: A lioness, strong.
LEONE: Strong as a lion.
LEONIE: Strong as a lion.
LEONORA: Fiery.
LEONORE: Fiery.
LEONTYNE: Blessed lioness.
LEORA: Lioness.
LETITIA: (Latin) Gladness.
LIB: Short for Libby. Truthful.
LIBBY: A form of Elizabeth. Truthful.
LILA, LYLA: Short for Delilah.
LILLIAN: (Latin) Lily flower.
LILY, LIILIE: (Latin) Short for Lillian.
LINDSAY, LINDSEY: (Old English) "From the linden tree island."
LISA: A form of Elizabeth. Honest.
LISBETH: A form of Elizabeth. Honest.
LIV: (Latin: "olive tree") Short for Olivia.
LIVIA: (Latin: "olive tree") A form of Olivia.
LIVIE, LIVY: (Latin: "olive tree") Short for Olivia.
LIZ, LIZZIE: Short for Eliza-

beth. Respectful, loving.
LIZA: Short for Elizabeth. Honest.
LIZABETH: A form of Elizabeth. Honest.
LIZETTE: A form of Elizabeth. Honest.
LOIS: Golden. Proud.
LORETTA: A winner.
LORETTE: A winner.
LORRAINE: Fearless.
LOTTA: Short for Charlotta. Strong.
LOTTIE: Short for Charlotte. Strong.
LOUELLA: Warrior.
LOUISE: (Old German) "Renowned warrior."
LYDIA: Majestic.
LYLA: Strong.
LYNELLE: Flowing.
LYNETTE: Flowing.
LYNN, LYNNE: (Welsh) Lake.
MABEL: (Latin) "Lovable."
MADDIE: Short for Madeline.
MADELENA: A form of Madeline.
MADELYN: (Greek) "Woman from Magdala."
MADGA: A pearl.
MADGE: A pearl.
MAE: (Hebrew) Rebellious.
MAEVE: Rebellious.

MAGDA: Short for Magdalene.
MAGDALEN, MAGDALENE: (Greek) "A town on the Sea of Galilee."
MAGGIE: A form of Margaret. A pearl. Pop star Rod Stewart made the name famous in his 1970s classic "Maggie May."
MANDY: A form of Amanda. Worthy of love.
MARGARET: (Greek) Pearl.
MARGERY, MARJORIE: A pearl.
MARGIE: A pearl.
MARGO, MARGOT: A pearl.
MARGUERITA, MARGUERITE: A pearl.
MARIAN, MARION: Rebellious.
MARIANNA, MARIANNE: Rebellious.
MARIBELLE: Rebellious; pretty.
MARIEL: Rebellious.
MARIELLE: Rebellious.
MARILEE: Rebellious.
MARIS: Short for Marissa. Bright, easily understood.
MARJABELLE: Bright; beautiful.
MARJORIE, MARJORY:

Rebellious.

MARLA: Calm, carefree.

MARLENA, MARLENE: Respectful.

MARLEY: From the march meadow.

MARSHELLA, MARSHELLE: Warrior. In charge.

MARYBELLE: Beautiful rebel. John F. Kennedy, the 35th President of the United President of the United States, had a parakeet with this name.

MATILDA: (Middle English) "Powerful in battle."

MATTIE: A nickname for Martha or Madelyn. A gift.

MAUDE: Powerful battler.

MAUDEY: A form of Maude.

MAUREEN: Rebellious.

MAVIS: Songbird.

MAXINE: Greatest.

MAYBELLE: (Latin) "Beautiful great one."

MAYBELLINE: Beautiful.

MEG: Short for Megan and Margaret. Great; pearl.

MEGAN: (Greek) "Great."

MEGGIE: Great. Franklin Delano Roosevelt, the 32nd President of the United States, had a Scottish terrier with this name.

MEL: (Latin: "honey") Short for Melvin.

MELANIE: (Greek) "Dark-clothed."

MELINDA: "Gentle one."

MELISSA: (Greek) "Bee."

MELLIE, MELLY: Short for Melanie.

MELODY: (Greek) "Song."

MEREDITH: (Welsh) "Sea protector."

MICHELLE: (Hebrew) "Who is like God."

MILDRED: (Anglo-Saxon) "Mild, powerful."

MILLICENT: (Old German) "Strong."

MILLIE: Short for Camille. Elegant. Pure. George Bush, the 41st President of the United States, had an English springer spaniel with this name.

MINDY: A form of Melinda. Gentle one.

MIRANDA: (Latin) "Wonderful."

MIRIAM: Rebellious.

MISSY: Short for Melissa.

MOLLIE, MOLLY: (Irish) A form of Mary. Rebellious.

MONICA, MONIKA: (Latin) "To warn."

MONIQUE: (Latin) "advisor."

MOREEN, MOREENA: Rebellious.
MORGAN: (Scottish Gaelic) "From the edge of the sea."
MURIEL: Bright one.
MYRA: A form of Mary. Rebellious.
MYRNA: Obedient.
NADINE: (French) "Hope."
NAJWA: (Arabic) "Passionate."
NAN: Short for Nancy.
NANCE: Grace.
NANETTE: Graceful.
NAOMI: (Hebrew) "My delight."
NATALIA: A form of Natalie.
NATALIE: (Latin: "born on Christmas day") Christmas.
NATTIE: Short for Natalie.
NICKIE, NIKKI: Victory.
NICOLE: (Greek) "Victory of the people."
NICOLETTE: Victory.
NOELA: A form of Noel and Noelle. Joyful.
NOELENE: Joyful.
NOELLE: (Latin: "born on Christmas day") Joyful.
NOLA: A form of Noelle. Joyful.
NORA: Bright.
NOREEN: Obedient.
NORMA: (Latin) "Carpenter's square."
OBADIAH: (Hebrew) "Servant of the Lord."
OCTAVIA: (Latin) Eighth.
OLEA: (Latin) Olive tree.
OLIVIA: (Latin) Olive tree.
OPHELIA: (Greek) Helper.
PAIGE: Servant.
PAM: Short for Pamela.
PAMELA: Sweet.
PAMMY: A form of Pamela. Sweet.
PAT: Noble.
PATRICIA: (Latin) "Of the nobility."
PATSY: Gullible.
PATTI, PATTY: Short for Patricia. Noble.
PAULA: (Latin) Small.
PAULETTE: Petite.
PAULINE: Small.
PEG: Short for Peggy.
PEGGY: A pearl.
PEARLIE, PEARLY: A pearl.
PENELOPE: (Greek) Weaver.
PENNY: Short for Penelope. Brown or copper-colored.
PHOEBE: (Greek) Shining.
PHYLLIS: (Latin/Greek) Green leaf.
POLLY: Rebellious. A common name for parrots. Geo-

rge Washington, the First President of the United States, had a pet parrot with this name.

PORTIA: (Latin) Offering.

PRISCILLA: (Latin) "From ancient times."

PRUDENCE: (Latin) Discretion.

REGINA: (Latin) Queen.

RENA, RINA: Maiden.

RENE: Reborn.

RENEE: A French name. Reborn.

RENI, RENNIE: Reborn.

RETA, RITA: A pearl.

REVA, RIVA: A dreamer.

RHODA: A rose.

RHODY: A rose.

RHONDA: A rose.

ROBERTA: (Old English) "Bright fame."

ROLANDA: (Old German) "Famed land."

RONA: Strong ruler.

RONDA: (Spanish) "Night patrol; night watcher."

RONEE, RONIE: Short for Veronica. Truthful.

RONETTA, RONETTE: Strong ruler.

ROSALIND: Pretty rose.

ROSALYN: Graceful rose.

ROSEANNA: Graceful rose.

ROSE MARIE: Divine rose.

ROSITA, ROSLYN: A rose.

ROXANNA, ROXANNE: (Persian) Dawn.

ROXETTE: A form of Roxanne.

ROXY: Short for Roxanna or Roxanne.

RUTH: (Hebrew) Companion.

RUTHANN: Gracious companion.

RUTHIE: Companion.

SADIE: Princess.

SAM: Short for Samantha. When singer/actor David Cassidy, who starred in the TV series "The Partridge Family," was a kid, he had a dog with this name.

SAMANTHA: (Aramaic) Listener.

SANDRA: Defender.

SARA, SARAH: (Hebrew) Princess.

SELENA: Moonstruck.

SELMA: (Greek) Ship.

SERENA: Serene.

SHANNON: (Irish Gaelic) Small, wise.

SHANNY: Short for Shannon.

SHEA: (Irish Gaelic) "From the fairy fort."

SHELLIE, SHELLY: (Old English) "From the meadow on the edge."

SHERRY: Little, womanly.
SHIRL: One who comes from Shirley, England.
SIMONE: Listener.
SOLANA: (Latin) Wind from the East.
SOPHIA, SOPHIE: (Greek) "Wisdom."
STACY, STACEY: Quiet, calm.
STEFF, STEFFI: Short for Stephanie.
STELLA: (Latin) Star.
STELLITA: (Latin) Little star.
STEPHANA: A form of Stephanie. A crown.
STEPHANIE: (Greek) Crown.
SUE: Short for Susan. Lily.
SUEANN: Gracious lily.
SUSAN: (Hebrew: "lily") Pretty.
SUSANNA, SUSANNE: (Hebrew) Lily
SUSIE: A nickname for Susan. Pretty.
SYBIL: (Greek) Prophetess.
SYBILLA: A form of Sybil. Prophetess.
SYL: Short for Sylvia.
SYLVIA: (Latin) "From the wood."
SYLVIE: A form of Sylvia.

TAMARA: Regal.
TAMARRA: Regal.
TAMMY: (Hebrew) Perfection.
TANYA: A name of slavic origins. Tan.
TAVIA: (Latin: "eighth) Short for Octavia.
TERESA, THERESA: (Greek) "To reap."
TERRI, TERRY: Short for Teresa, Theresa.
TESSA, TESSIE: (Greek) "To reap." Short for Teresa.
THERESE: A form of Teresa, Theresa.
THOMASINA: (Greek/Latin) "Little twin."
TIFFANY: (Greek) "Appearance of God."
TILLIE, TILLY: A form of Matilda. Powerful warrior.
TINA: A nickname for names ending with "Tina," such as Christina, LaTina.
TRACY, TRACEY: Distant.
TRENA, TRINA: Pure.
TRICIA: A form of Patricia.
TRUDY: Short for Gertrude. Beloved.
UNA: (Latin) One.
URSULA: (Latin) She-bear.
VAL: Short for Valerie and

Valene. Strong.
VALARA: Strong.
VALERIA: (Latin) "To be strong."
VALERIE: (Latin) "To be strong."
VANESSA: For Venus, the goddess of love.
VELDA: Wise.
VELEKA: Wise.
VELMA: Wise.
VERA: True.
VERNA, VERNIE: Like spring, fresh.
VERNETTA, VERNETTE: Like spring, fresh.
VERONICA: True image.
VICKIE, VICKY: Short for Victoria. Victorious.
VICTORIA: (Latin: "victory") Richard M. Nixon, the 37th President of the United States, had a dog named this during his White House years.
VIRGILLIA: Pure.
VIRGINIA: (Latin) Maidenly.
VIVACA: Lively, spirited.
VIVIAN, VIVIEN: Alive, lively.
VONCILLE: Praise worthy.
VONETTA: Praise worthy.
VONNA: Nickname for Yvonne. Praise worthy.
VONNIE: Nickname for

Yvonne. Praise worthy.
WANDA: Roamer, a wanderer.
WENDELIN, WENDOLYN: A stray, meander.
WILHELMINA: Wishful, protector.
WINONA: First born daughter.
YOLANDA, YOLANDE: Worthy.
YVETTE: Impulsive.
YVONNE: Praise worthy.
ZAN: Short for Zandra, Zandrah.
ZANDRA, ZANDRAH: Dutiful.
ZOE: (Greek) "Life."
ZORA: Life.

Male:

AARON: Noble.
ABBA: Father.
ABBOTT: Father.
ABDUL, ABDULLAH: Servant of the Lord.
ABE: (Hebrew) Short for Abraham. Father.
ABNER: (Hebrew) "The father is a light."
ABRAHAM: (Hebrew: "father of the multitude") For Abraham Lincoln, 16th Presi-

dent the United States.

ABRAM: (Hebrew) "father of many." Middle name of James Garfield, 20th President of the United States.

ADAM: (Hebrew) "Man of the red earth."

AL: Short for Albert. Bright, noble.

ALBERT: Bright through nobility.

ALDO: (Old German: "old and wise") Shortened form of Aldous.

ALDOUS: (Old German) "Old and wise."

ALESSANDRO: Helper.

ALEX: Considerate.

ALEXANDER: (Greek) "Helper of mankind."

ALEXI: Companionable.

ALFIE: (Old English: "small, wise") Loyal.

ALFONSE, ALFONSO: Eager, ready.

ALFRED: Psychic, wise counselor.

ALFREDO: Wise.

ALLISTER: Helpful.

ALONSO, ALONZO: Warrior.

ALOYSE, ALOYSIA: Instigator.

ALOYSIUS: Known warrior.

ALSTON: (Old English) "From the manor."

ALTON: (Old English) "Our town."

ALVA, ALVAH: White.

ALVAN: White.

AMBROSE: Immortal.

AMOS: (Hebrew) "Burden-bearer."

ANATOLE: (Greek) "From the east."

ANDREAS: (Greek) Manly.

ANDY: Short for Andrew. Strong, manly.

ANGELI: Saintly messenger.

ANGELO: Angelic.

ANTHONY: Of great value.

ANTON: Great.

ANTONIO: Of great value.

ANTONIUS: Valuable.

ANTONY: (Latin) Priceless.

ARCHIBALD: (Old German: "nobly bold") A prince.

ARN: Strong. Short for Arnold.

ARNIE: (Old German) Strong.

ART: Noble, valorous.

ARTHUR: (Celtic) Noble.

ARTIE: Noble, valorous.

ARVE: From the eagle tree.

ASA: (Hebrew) Healer.

ASHBY: (Old English) "From the ash tree meadow."

AUSTIN: (Latin: "majestic

dignitary") Exalted.

AXEL: (Old German) "Father of peace."

BAILEY: (Old French) "one who bakes." Also (Latin) "bear a burden."

BANARD: Bold bear.

BARLEY: (Old English) "From the bare hill."

BARLOW: Companion.

BARNABY: (Greek) "Son of prophesy."

BARRY: (Irish) Spear-like, pointed.

BARTH: Short for Bartholomew. Earthy.

BARTHOLOMEW: (Hebrew: "son of Talmai") Earthy.

BASTIAN: Short for Sebastian. Majestic.

BAXTER: (Old English) Baker.

BEAU: (French) Beautiful, handsome.

BECK: (Old Norse) A brook.

BEN: Short for Benjamin. Loyal.

BENEDICT: Blessed.

BENET, BENNETT: Blessed.

BENJAMIN: (Hebrew: "son of the right hand") Loyal. For Benjamin Harrison, 23rd President of the United States and grandson of the 9th President, William Henry Harrison.

BENNY: Loyal.

BENSON: (Hebrew English) "Son of Benjamin."

BENTLEY: (Old English: "from the moor") Classy.

BERNARD: (Old German) "Brave bear."

BERTIS: Bright.

BERTON, BURTON: Glorious raven.

BERTRAM: Bright raven.

BERTRAND: Bright.

BILLY: Guardian.

BING: (Old English) Kettle-shaped.

BLAKE: (Old English) Fair-haired, fair-complected.

BOB: Short for Robert. Bright fame.

BOBBY: Bright.

BOSLEY: An aristocratic name, of English origin.

BRAD: Lean.

BRADLEY: (Old English: "from the broad meadow") Lean.

BRENDAN: (Irish Gaelic) Little raven.

BRENT: Worthy of trust.

BRENTON: (Old English) Steep hill.

BRETT: Strong.

BREWSTER: (Old English) Brewer.

BRIAN: (Irish Gaelic: "virtue, strength") Strong.

BROCK: (Old English) Badger.

BRUNO: (Old German) Brown.

BURKE: (French) "From the fortress."

BURL: (Old English) "Cup bearer."

BURR: (Anglo-Saxon) "Of the town."

BURTON: (Old English) "From the fortress."

CALEB: (Hebrew) Faithful.

CALVERT: (Old English) Herdsman.

CAM: In motion; energetic. Short for Cameron.

CAMERON: Energetic.

CARL: Manly.

CARLISLE: (Old English) "From the fortified town."

CARLTON: (Old English) "Farmer's town."

CARMICHAEL: Immortal.

CASEY: (Irish Gaelic) Brave.

CECIL: Unseeing.

CHAD: (Old English) Warlike.

CHANCELLOR: (Latin) "Keeper of the barrier."

CHARLES: (Old German) Strong, manly.

CHAUNCY: (Middle English: "chancellor") Well-behaved.

CHRIS: Short for Christopher. Blessed.

CHUCKIE: Strong. A nickname for Charles.

CLARENCE: Illustrious.

CLAY: Earthy.

CLAYBORN: Born of the earth.

CLEAVON: Faithful.

CLEM: (Latin) Merciful.

CLEOTUS: Royalty.

CLETUS: Royalty.

CLIFF: Short for Clifford.

CLIFFORD: (Old English) Steep rock, cliff.

CLIFTON: Town at a cliff.

CLINT: (Old English) "From the headland form."

CLYDE: (Scottish Gaelic) Rocky eminence.

COLIN, COLLIN: (Latin) "dove."

CONNOR: Conning, playful.

CONSTANTINE: Forthright.

COREY, CORY: (Irish Gaelic) "From the hollow."

CORNELIUS: Noble.

CRAIG: Rugged.

CURT: Short for Curtis.

CURTIS: Courteous.

CYRIL: Lordly.

DAN: Judged.

DANIEL: (Hebrew) "Judged by God."

DANNY: Judged. Nickname for Daniel.

DARRELL, DARRYL: Dear one.

DAVE: Beloved.

DENNIS: Mellow.

DEREK, DERRICK: Leader.

DION: Noble.

DONNIE, DONNY: Ruler.

DUANE, DWAYNE: Unselfish.

EARL: (Anglo-Saxon) Warrior.

EDGAR: (Old English) "Successful spearman."

EDMOND, EDMUND: Protector.

EDWIN: Valued friend.

ELI, ELY: The highest.

ELIAS: The highest.

ELIJAH: (Hebrew) "Jehovah is God."

ELMORE: Amiable.

EMERY, EMORY: (Old German) "Work ruler."

EMILIO: Excellent.

EMMET: A hard worker. Also spelled Emmett.

ERIC: (Scandinavian) "Ever-ruler, ever-powerful."

ETHAN: Strength.

EUGENE: Well-born. Genius.

EUSTACE, EUSTUS: Fruitful.

EVAN: (Celtic) Young man.

EVERETT: Strong.

EZ: Short for Ezra. Helpful.

EZRA: (Hebrew) Help.

FLOYD: Gray.

FRANCO: Of France. Free spirit.

FRANK: From Francis, Latin meaning "Frenchman."

FRANKIE: From Francis, Latin meaning "Frenchman."

FRED: Short for Frederick, (Old German) meaning "ruler in peace." Author William F. Buckley, Jr. has a spaniel with this name.

FREDDIE, FREDDY: Peaceful ruler.

FREDERICK: (Old German) "Ruler in peace."

FREDO: Peaceful warrior.

GARRET: (Anglo-Saxon: "swift spear") Watchful.

GENE: Short for Eugene.

GENO, GINO: (Italian) Short for Ambrogino and Luigino. Genius.

GERALD: Speared ruler. For Gerald Rudolph Ford, 38th

President of the United States.

GARY: Swift.

GEOFFREY: Serene.

GERARD, GERRAD: Speared ruler.

GLEN: (Celtic) Valley. Herbert Hoover, the 31st President of the United States, had a collie with this name.

GODFREY: Peaceful.

GRAHAM: Natural.

GRANT: Promise.

GREG: Short for Gregory. Watchful.

GREGORY: (Latin) Watchful.

HAL: Bright, strong.

HAROLD: Leader.

HECTOR: (Greek) Steadfast.

HERB: Warrior.

HOLDEN: Kind.

HOWARD: (Old English: "watchman") Middle name of William Taft, 27th President of the United States.

HOWIE: Short for Howard. Protector, watcher.

HUBERT: (Old German) Bright spirit.

HUGH: (Old English) Intelligence.

IAN: Gracious.

IDAN: Noble.

IKE: Cheerful.

IRA: (French: "to go") A good name for a pet that is always on the go.

IRVIN: Beautiful.

IRVING: (Irish Gaelic) Beautiful.

IRWIN: Friend.

JACOB: (Hebrew) "Seizing by the heel, a supplanter."

JACQUES: French form of James or Jacob. Schemer.

JAMIE, JAMEY: Schemer.

JAQUES: A supplanter.

JARED: (Hebrew) "descent."

JASPER: (Persian: "Lord of the treasure." Colorful.

JAY: (Old French) Bluejay.

JEFF: Short for Jeffrey. Peaceful.

JEFFREY: Peaceful.

JEREMIAH: (Hebrew) "Appointed by Jehovah."

JEROME: Reverent.

JIM: Short for James. A schemer.

JODY: Careful.

JOE: Short for Joseph.

JOEL: Reverent.

JOEY: Short for Joseph. A term for a young kangaroo in Australia.

JONAS: A form of Jonah.

JONATHAN: (Hebrew) "The Lord has given."

JOSH, JOSHY: Short for Joshua.

JOSHUA: (Hebrew) "Helper of Jehovah."

JOSIAH: (Hebrew) "The Lord supports."

JOSIAS: A form of Josiah.

JUDAH: (Hebrew) "Praised."

JULE, JULES: Youthful.

JULIAN: A form of Julius. Youthful.

JULIO: Youthful.

JUSTIN: (Latin) "Righteous, proper."

KARL: Manly.

KEITH: (Gaelic) "The wind."

KEN: Handsome.

KENNETH: (Gaelic) Handsome.

KENNY: Handsome.

KENT: (Welsh) "Border country."

KEVIN: (Old Irish) "Comely birth."

KIRBY: (Old English) "From the church town."

KIRK: Reverent.

KIRKLAND: Reverent.

KYLE: (Irish Gaelic) Handsome.

LAIRD: (Scottish) Lord.

LANCE: (Old English) Land.

LARS: A Scandinavian form of Laurence, Lawrence. Laurel.

LAURENCE, LAWRENCE: (Latin) Laurel.

LEE: (Anglo-Saxon) Meadow.

LELAND: Meadow land.

LEN, LENNY: Short for Leonard, strong as a lion.

LEON: A form of Leonard; strong as a lion.

LEONARD: Strong as a lion.

LESTER: Loyal.

LIONEL: A lion.

LLEWELLYN: (Welsh) Lion-like.

LLOYD: (Welsh) Gray.

LORENZO: A form of Laurence, Lawrence. Laurel.

LOU: Warrior.

LOUIS: (Old German) "Renowned warrior."

LOWELL: Loved.

LUCAS: Bright.

LUCIUS: (Latin) Light.

LUIGI: (Italian) Warrior.

LUTHER: (Old German) "Famous fighter."

LYLE: Strong.

MAC: (Scottish Gaelic: "son of") The name of a Beanie Baby bird, a cardinal.

MARCUS: (Latin) Mars, god of war.

MARICE: Ill-tempered.

MARIO: Italian form of Mark. God of war. From the popular

Nintendo game *Super Mario*.

MARLEY: From the march meadow.

MARSHALL: (Old French: "steward, horse keeper") In charge.

MARTY: A miracle.

MARV: Miracle.

MATT: Short for Matthew. A gift.

MATTHEW: (Hebrew) "Gift of God."

MAURICE: (Latin) "A moor."

MAURY: Short for Maurice.

MAXIMILLIAN: (Latin) Greatest.

MELVIN, MELVYN: A friend.

MERLE: (Latin) Blackbird.

MERT: Short for Merton.

MERTON: (Anglo-Saxon) "Town by a lake."

MEYER: Helper.

MICAH: (Hebrew) "Who is like God."

MICHAEL: (Hebrew) "Who is like God."

MIKE, MIKEY: Short for Michael.

MILES, MYLES: Traveler.

MILTON: (Anglo-Saxon) Mill town.

MITCH: Short for Mitchell. A

gift.

MITCHELL: A form of Michael. A gift.

MONTI, MONTY: Short for Montgomery.

MORGAN: (Scottish Gaelic) "From the edge of the sea."

MORT: Short for Mortimer and Morton. Sea warrior.

MORTON: (Anglo-Saxon) "Moor, town."

MURDOCK: (Scottish Gaelic) "Wealthy sailor."

MURPH: Short for Murphy.

MURPHY: (Irish) Slang for potato.

NATE: Short for Nathaniel or Nathan.

NED: Protector.

NELS: Short for Nelson. Champion.

NELSON: Champion.

NEV: Short for Neville.

NEVIL, NEVILLE: Accommodating.

NICK: Short for Nicholas.

NICO: Victory.

NICOS: Victory.

NOEL: (Latin: "born on Christmas day") Joyful.

NOLAN, NOLAND: Well-known.

NORM: Short for Norman.

NORMAN: (Old French)

Norseman.

NORMIE: A form of Norman.

NORRIS, NORRY: From the north.

NOWELL: Born on Christmas Day.

OCTAVIUS: (Latin) Eighth.

OMAR: (Arabic) "First son, follower of the prophet."

PARKER: (Middle English) "Guardian of the park."

PATRICK: (Latin) Nobleman.

PAUL: (Latin: "small") A Beanie Baby walrus named after Paul McCartney for the Beatle's song "I Am the Walrus," which contains the line "The walrus was Paul."

PAYTON, PEYTON: Noble.

PERCIVAL: (Old French) "Pierce valley."

PERCY: Short for Percival.

PERRY: (Middle English) Pear tree.

PETE: Sturdy.

PHIL: Short for Phillip.

PHILLIP: Loving.

PRESCOTT: (Old English) "From the priests' cottage."

QUENT: Short for Quentin. Also spelled Quint.

QUENTIN, QUINTIN: The fifth born.

RAD: Short for Radcliffe.

RADCLIFFE: Red cliff.

RAFFERTY: (Irish Gaelic) "Rich and prosperous."

RAFFI: Short for Rafferty.

RALPH: (Old English) "Wolf-counselor."

RAND: (Anglo-Saxon) A shield.

RANDALL: (Anglo-Saxon) "Shield-wolf."

RANDOLPH: (Old English) "Shield-wolf."

RANDY: Short for Randolph.

RAY: Short for Raymond.

RAYMOND: Wise protector.

REG: Short for Reginald.

REGINALD: (Medieval Latin Old German) Strong ruler.

REUBEN: (Hebrew) "Behold, a son."

REYNOLD, REYNOLDS: Strong ruler.

RICHARD: (Old French Old German) Strong king.

RICK: Short for Richard.

ROB: Short for Robert or Robbie.

ROBBIE, ROBBY: Bright fame.

ROBERT: (Old English) Bright fame.

ROD, RODDY: Nicknames for Rodney or Roderick.

RODERICK: (Medieval Latin

Old German) A king.

RODNEY: (Old English) "From the island clearing."

RODOLPH: Famed wolf.

RON, RONNY: Strong ruler.

ROSCO, ROSCOE: (Scandinavian) "From the deer forest."

ROSS, ROSSY: (Welsh) Hill, moor.

ROWLAND: (French-Old German) "Famous land."

ROY: A king; reddish colored.

RUSS: Short for Russell.

RUSSELL: (French) Red.

RYAN: Bright.

SAM: Short for Samuel. When singer/actor David Cassidy, who starred in the TV series "The Partridge Family," was a kid, he had a dog with this name. Andrew Jackson, the 7th President of the Unites States, had a horse named Sam Patches.

SAMMY: A form of Samantha or Samuel.

SANFORD: (English) Sandy ford.

SCOTT: (Old English) Scotsman.

SCOTTIE, SCOTTY: (Old English: "Scotsman") Scottie, the name of a Beanie Baby ter-

rier.

SEAN, SHAWN: An Irish form of John. Gracious.

SEBASTIAN: (Latin) Venerated, majestic.

SEDGE: Short for Sedgewick.

SEDGEWICK: Conqueror.

SEYMOUR: (Anglo-Saxon) "sea, lake" or "mor, a hill."

SHAMUS: An Irish form of James.

SHANE: An Irish form of John. Gracious.

SIDNEY: (Old French) "From St. Denis."

SILAS: From the Greek.

SILVA: (Latin) "The wood."

SILVAN, SYLVAN: (Latin) "The wood."

SILVANO, SILVANOS: (Latin) "From the woods."

SINCLAIR: Distinguished.

SMITH: (Anglo-Saxon) "One who repairs." Often used as an alias.

SMITHY: A variation of Smith.

SPENCE: A form of Spencer.

STAN: Short for Stanley.

STANLEY: (Old English) "From the rocky meadow." The flat boy in the children's story "Flat Stanley" by Jeff Brown.

STEFAN, STEPHAN: A form of Stephen.

STEFANO: A form of Stephen.

STEPHEN, STEVEN: (Greek) A crown.

STERLING: (Anglo-Saxon) Small star.

STEVE: Short for Stephen, Steven.

STU: Short for Stuart, Stewart.

STUART, STEWART: (Anglo-Saxon) Chamberlain.

SYD: Short for Sydney.

SYDNEY: (Old French) "From St. Denis."

TAVIUS: (Latin: "eighth") Short for Octavius.

TED: A gift.

TERENCE: Jovial.

TIM: Honorable.

TODD: Clever. Brad Pitt and Jennifer Aniston had a dog named Todd Potter.

TOMMY: Tiny twin.

TRAVIS: A traveler. Bandleader Doc Severinsen has a cat with this name.

UPTON: (Old English) "From the upper town."

URIAH: (Hebrew) "God is light."

URSUS: (Latin) Bear.

VAUGHAN, VAUGHN: Small.

VERN: Fresh.

VIC: Short for Victor. Conqueror.

VICTOR: (Latin) Conqueror.

VINCE: Short for Vincent. Conquering.

VINCENT: (Latin) Conquering.

WADE: Full of energy.

WAINWRIGHT: (Anglo-Saxon) "Builder or repairer of wagons."

WALLACE: (Welsh) Foreign.

WALLY: A warrior.

WALTER: (Old German) Powerful warrior.

WARD: (Anglo-Saxon: "to watch") Protector, guardian.

WARREN: (Old German) Defender.

WARRICK, WARWICK: Ruler.

WAYNE: Unselfish.

WEBSTER: (Middle English) Weaver.

WENDALL: (Old German) Wanderer.

WES: Short for Wesley.

WESLEY: (Old English) "From the western meadow."

WESTLY: A form of Wesley.

WESTON: From the west.

WEXLEY: A form of Wesley.

WILFRED, WILFRID: (Anglo-Saxon) Wishful, peaceful.

WILHELM: German form of William.

WILL: Short for William.

WINIFRED: (Welsh) White wave.

WINSOM: (Anglo-Saxon) Pleasant.

WYNN: (Welsh) Fair.

ZACCHEUS: Loyal.

ZACH, ZACHY: Short for Zachary.

ZACHARIAH: (Hebrew) "Jehovah hath remembered."

ZACHARIAS: Memorable.

ZACHARY: (Hebrew: "Jehovah hath remembered") For Zachary Taylor, 12th President of the United States.

ZANDER: Dutiful.

ZEB: A gift.

ZECHARIAH: Memorable.

ZEKE: Short for Zachary, Zechariah. Memorable.

Did You Know?

BIZKIT: Fred Durst, the leader of the hard rocking band Limp Bizkit has a bulldog with this name.

CUBA: The name of one of author Ernest Hemingway's forty cats.

SPIKE: Tough. Comedian Joan Rivers has a tiny dog named Spike who appeared frequently with Joan in her syndicated TV talk show.

Dusty

Oscar

Cleveland

Chapter 12

HISTORICAL FIGURES

Philosophers, scientists, politicians, frontiersmen and other historical figures can provide inspiration for pet names: *Aristotle*, *Copernicus*, *Euclid*, *Rasputin*, *Einstein*, and others. In fact, for any pet lover who has a strong interest in history, it can seem a natural to name a new pet after a favorite historical figure.

ABENAKI: A group of North American Indians living in northern New England and parts of Quebec, Canada.

AINU: A member of a primitive race of Japan.

AKBAR: Emperor of India (1556–1605).

AMADEUS: For classical composer Wolfgang Amadeus Mozart.

AMELIA: (Old German: "a hard worker") For American aviator Amelia Earhart, 1897–1937, who was the first woman to fly across the Atlantic (1928) and the first to fly it alone (1932). She was the first person to fly alone from Hawaii to California. Also from the somewhat backward maid in the humorous children's book *Amelia Bedelia* by Peggy Parish.

AMERIGO: Explorer. For Italian navigator Amerigo Vespucci, who explored the New World after Columbus and for whom America was named.

ANDREW: (Greek: "manly") For Andrew Jackson, 7th President of the United States. Also for Andrew Johnson, 17th President of the United States.

ARISTIDES: An Athenian statesman and general, (530?–468? B.C.)

ARISTOTLE: Greek philosopher, pupil of Plato.

ARIUS: Greek theologian of Alexandria.

ATILLA: For the Mongolian conqueror Atilla the Hun.

AUDUBON: For John James Audubon (1785–1851), an American ornithologist, painter, and naturalist.

AZTEC: Tan, brownish. A member of a people who lived in Mexico and had an advanced civilization before the conquest of Mexico by Cortes in 1519.

BANTU: A member of a group of tribes in central and southern Africa.

BARACK: Blessed. For Barack Obama, the 44th President of the U.S. The first Africa-American President and also the first President from Hawaii.

BARNUM: For Phineas Taylor Barnum of Barnum and Bailey Circus.

BARRETT: Bear-like. For English poet Elizabeth Barrett Browning, wife of poet Robert Browning.

BELLOWS: For American painter George Wesley Benton.

BENTON: For American poet Thomas Hart Benton.

BETSY: Pure. For Betsy Ross, the American woman who made the first American flag.

BILL: (Old German: "determined guardian") For U.S. plainsman and circus manager Buffalo Bill, whose full name was William Frederick Cody.

BIRCHARD: For Rutherford Birchard Hayes, 19th President of the United States.

BONAPARTE: For French general and emperor Napoleon Bonaparte.

BOOKER: Smart. For African-American educator and author Booker T. Washington.

BOONE: Good. For American frontiersman Daniel Boone.

BRADFORD: Known for Pilgrim father William Bradford.

BRECKENRIDGE: American politician and Vice-President of the US (1857-61), John Cabell Breckenridge.

BUCEPHALAS: Alexander the Great's horse.

CAESAR: (Latin: "emperor") For Roman statesman and general Julius Caesar.

CAJUN: Native of Louisiana. Spicy. Hot-tempered.

CALAMITY JANE: Calamity means "trouble." For Calamity Jane, a legendary heroine of the Old West. Calvin Coolidge, the 30th President of the United States, had a sheepdog with this name.

CALHOUN: American politician and Vice-President of the US (1852-32), John Caldwell Calhoun.

CAPONE: For 1930s gangster Al Capone.

CHADWICK: English physicist, Sir James Chadwick.

CHARLEMAGNE: Leader. Ruler. For Charles Charlemagne, emperor of the West, Carolingian king of the Franks.

CHEROKEE: Native American tribe in North Carolina and Georgia.

CHESTER: (Old English: "from the fortified camp") For Chester Alan Arthur, who was the 21st President of the United States.

CHEYENNE: Native American tribe that lived in Minnesota and North and South Dakota.

CHIPPENDALE: Pertaining to furniture designed by, or in the graceful rococo style of English cabinetmaker Thomas Chippendale.

CHIPPEWA: A Native American people of Lake Superior area and westward; the tribe is also called Ojibwa.

CICERO: Marcus Tullius Cicero, Roman statesman, orator, and Stoic philosopher, 106–43 B.C.

CLEVELAND: For Grover Cleveland, 22nd and 24th President of the United States.

COLBERT: French statesman Jean-Baptiste Colbert.

COMANCHE: Native American tribe that originated in the Western Plains. Also, the name of a horse, a survivor of Little Big Horn, depicted in the movie *Tonka*.

CONFUCIOUS: For the Chinese philosopher and teacher (551–479? B.C.)

COPERNICUS: For Polish astronomer Nicholas Copernicus.

CORTES: Explorer. For Spanish soldier and explorer Hernando Cortes, conqueror of Mexico.

CRAZY HORSE: Sioux Indian Chief.

CREE: A member of a tribe of

Alogonquian Indians who lived in central Canada.

CROCKETT: Known for David Crockett, better known as Davy, American frontiersman and politician.

CUSTER: For U.S. Army officer George Armstrong Custer, who along with his entire detachment of over men were killed by Indians on Little Big Horn, often referred to as "Custer's last stand."

DAKIN: English chemist Henry Drysdale Dakin.

DALI: For Spanish painter Salvador Dali, who became a leader of Surrealism.

DANTON: French revolutionary, George-Jacques Danton.

DARLAN: French admiral, Jean-Louis-Xavier-Francois Darlan.

DARNLEY: Henry Stewart Darnley, husband of Mary, Queen of Scots.

DARUIS: The name of three Kings of Persia.

DARWIN: For English naturalist Charles Robert Darwin, who pioneered the theory of evolution. Also, the name of the dolphin in the TV series "SeaQuest DSV."

DAVIS: For Jefferson Davis, American statesman and President of the Confederate states. Ulysses S. Grant, the 18th President of the United States, had a horse named Jeff Davis.

DAVY: Beloved. For American frontiersman David "Davy" Crockett, who had a reputation as a great hunter and eventually won a seat on the Tennessee legislature, and later Congress. Also, "Davy Jones," a humorous name given by sailors to the spirit of the sea.

DAWSON: Sir John William Dawson, Canadian geologist.

DIZZY: Silly. Also refers to jazz great Dizzy Gillespie (born John Birks Gillespie), a South Carolina native, who led the bop movement of the 1940s with Charlie Parker.

DRACO: Athenian lawgiver.

DRAPER: American astronomer Henry Draper.

DRYDEN: English poet and dramatist John Dryden.

DWIGHT: Wise. For Dwight David Eisenhower, a general who became 34th President of the United States.

EDISON: Brilliant. For American inventor Thomas Alva Edison, whose inventions include the record player, motion pictures, and the incandescent lamp.

EINSTEIN: For American theoretical physicist Albert Einstein, famous for his theory of relativity.

ESKIMO: A member of a race living in Greenland, the Arctic coasts of North America, the Labrador coast, Alaska, and northeastern tip of Asia. Also, Eskimo dog, a strong breed of dog with grayish, shaggy fur, used by Eskimos to pull sleds.

EVITA: For Argentine actress Evita Duarte, who climbed from poverty to stardom and eventually married her country's President, Juan Peron.

FABRE: A worker. For French entomologist Jean Henri Fabre.

FARNSWORTH: For the inventor of the first electric television Philo Farnsworth.

FERRIS: Amusing. For George W. G. Ferris, who invented the Ferris wheel.

FILLMORE: A pet with a voracious appetite. Also, for Millard Fillmore, 13th President of the United States.

FITZGERALD: For John Fitzgerald Kennedy, 35th President of the United States. Also for American author F. Scott Fitzgerald, one of the great American writers of the 20th century.

FRANKLIN: Free. For American statesman, scientist, printer, and writer, Benjamin Franklin, who helped draft the Declaration of Independence, which he signed. Also for Franklin Pierce, 14th President of the United States; and for Franklin Delano Roosevelt, 32nd President of the United States.

GALEN: A Greek physician, writer of the 2nd century A.D.

GALILEO: For the Italian astronomer and physicist (1564–1642).

GAMALIEL: (Hebrew: "reward of God") Middle name of Warren Gamaliel Harding, 29th President of the United States.

GANDHI: For Mahatma Gandhi, the Hindu leader of India until 1948.

GERONIMO: Strong. For the leader of the Chiricahua

Apaches.

GINSBERG: American poet, Allen Ginsberg.

GODFREY: Known for Godefroy de Rouillon, French crusader.

GOLDA: Golden. For Golda Meir who was premier of Israel.

HANCOCK: For John Hancock, the American statesman who was the first to sign the Declaration of Independence.

HANNIBAL: A Carthaginian general who crossed the Alps to invade Italy.

HENRY: (Old German: "ruler of an estate") Home ruler. Middle name of William Henry Harrison, 9th President of the United States and grandfather of the 23rd President, Benjamin Harrison. Also, the name of the boy in the children's picture book *Cloudy with a Chance of Meatballs* by Judi and Ron Barrett.

HERBERT: (Old German: "glorious soldier)" For Herbert Clark Hoover, 31st President of the United States.

HOFFA: For American labor leader Jimmy Hoffa.

HOOVER: Herbert Clark Hoover, 31st President of the United States. The name of pop music legend Carole Bayer Sager's Lhasa apso.

HOPI: Serene. A member of a Pueblo tribe of Indians in northeastern Arizona.

HORACE: Serious. A Roman poet of 65–8 B.C.

HOUDINI: For Harry Houdini, an American magician and escape artist.

HUBBLE: Known for American astronomer Edwin Powell Hubble.

HUDSON: English navigator and explorer, Henry Hudson.

HUXLEY: For English biologist and writer Thomas Henry Huxley.

INCA: Any member of a group of Indian tribes that dominated ancient Peru until the Spanish conquest. The Incas had a highly developed civilization.

ISAIAH: A Hebrew prophet of the 8th century B.C.

IXION: In Greek legend, a Thessalian king who was bound to a constantly revolving wheel in Tartarus for seeking the love of Hera.

JAMES: A supplanter. For James Knox Polk, 11th President of the United States. Also for James Buchanan, 15th President of the United States.

JEFFERSON: For American Revolutionary leader Thomas Jefferson, who drew up the Declaration of Independence and was 3rd President of the United States.

JERONIMO: Strong. Alternate spelling for Geronimo, the leader of the Chiricahua Apaches.

JIMMY: A form of James. A schemer. For Jimmy Carter, 39th President of the United States.

JOAN: Martyr. For Joan of Arc, French heroine and saint.

JULIUS: (Latin: "youthful") For Julius Caesar, Roman emperor.

JUVENAL: Youthful. For a Roman poet.

KAHN: From Genghis Kahn, the Mongol conqueror of central Asia.

KENYON: For American phonetician John Samuel Kenyon.

KIDD: For Captain Kidd, a Scottish pirate.

KIERAN: For American journalist John Francis Kieran.

KING TIMAHOE: While in office, Richard M. Nixon, 37th President of the United States, had a dog with this name.

KING TUT: The most famous mummy found and the most famous of all the kings found in the Valley of the Kings was Tutankhamun. Herbert Hoover, the 31st President of the United States, had a shepherd with this name.

KIOWA: A Native American people.

KIT: For U.S. frontiersman Kit Carson.

LADYBIRD: Good-natured. Nickname of Claudia Alta Taylor Johnson, wife of Lyndon Baines Johnson, 36th President of the United States.

LAFAYETTE: Noble. The name of a French statesman and general Marquis de Lafayette.

LANGLEY: American astronomer and airplane pioneer Samual Pierpont Langley.

LEONARDO: For Italian painter, sculptor, architect, musician, engineer, and scientist Leonardo da Vinci.

LEWIS: Warrior. For English

writer Lewis Carroll, author of the classic children's book *Alice's Adventures in Wonderland.*

LINCOLN: For Abraham Lincoln, 16th President of the United States.

LUCRETIUS: A Roman poet and philosopher (95?–55 B.C.).

LYNDON: For Lyndon Baines Johnson, 36th President of the United States.

MacARTHUR: For American five-star General Douglas MacArthur.

MAHALIA: For African-American gospel singer Mahalia Jackson.

MALAY: Any of a group of brown-skinned peoples living in the Malay Peninsula, the Malay Archipelago, and nearby islands.

MALCOLM: Servant. For civil rights leader Malcolm X.

MANCHU: A member of the Mongolian people of Manchuria. Theodore Roosevelt, the 26th President of the United States, had a Pekingese with this name.

MANDINGO: A member of a people of western Africa.

MANDINKA: A widespread tribe in western Africa.

MARCO: Warrior. For Marco Polo, the Venetian traveler in Asia.

MARIE: Rebellious. For the queen of France Marie Antoinette, the wife of Louis XVI.

MARTIN: (Latin: "warlike") For Martin Van Buren, 8th President of the United States.

MATA HARA: A Dutch dancer and spy for Germany in World War I.

MAYA: The highly civilized race of Indians who lived in southeastern New Mexico and Central America. Also for distinguished poet Maya Angelou.

McINTOSH: Healthy. A late-maturing variety of red apple named for the man who first cultivated it, J. McIntosh, of Canada.

MERIWETHER: For American explorer Meriwether Lewis, who lead the Lewis and Clark Expedition.

MILLARD: For Millard Fillmore, 13th President of the United States.

MONROE: For James Monroe, 5th President of the United States, who issued the Monroe Doctrine.

MONTEZUMA: Warlike. For the Aztec emperor of Mexico, who was conquered by Cortes.

MOZART: A pet that enjoys music. For Austrian composer Wolfgang Amadeus Mozart, whose oeuvre marks one of the great peaks of musical history.

NAPOLEON: Emperor of France.

NAVAHO: A member of a tribe of Athapascan Indians now living on a reservation in Arizona, New Mexico, and Utah.

NEWTON: (Anglo-Saxon: "new town") For Sir Isaac Newton, English mathematician and natural philosopher (physicist), considered by many the greatest scientist of all time.

NIGHTINGALE: Nurturing. For Florence Nightingale, the English pioneer of modern nursing.

NIKOLA: For Serbian-American physicist Nikola Tesla, a pioneer in high-tension electricity.

OTTAWA: A member of the tribe of Algonquian Indians who lived in southeastern Ontario and southwestern Quebec, Canada. Also, the name of the capital of Canada.

OVID: A Latin poet who was a major source of inspiration for the Renaissance.

PANCHO: For Pancho Barnes, a free-spirited female barnstormer (stunt pilot) of the 1920s and '30s who later trained pilots for World War II combat.

PAWNEE: A member of a Native American tribe formerly living in Nebraska, and now in northern Oklahoma.

PLATO: (Greek: "broad-shouldered") A Greek philosopher.

PLINY: A Roman naturalist and writer.

POCAHONTAS: American Indian princess who saved Captain John Smith, an English colonist in Virginia, from execution; her story has been the basis for many books and a Disney animated movie.

POMPEY: For Pompey the Great, a Roman general and statesman.

PONCE: For Spanish explorer Juan Ponce de Leon, who discovered Florida.

PRIAM: The last king of

Troy, who reigned during the Trojan war.

QUASIMODO: For Italian poet and translator Salvatore Quasimodo, who won the Nobel Prize for literature in 1959.

RALEIGH: For English explorer, courtier, historian, and poet Sir Walter Raleigh. Also, the capital of North Carolina.

RED CLOUD: For the well-known Sioux Indian Chief.

REVERE: To regard with deep love, respect, and awe. For American Revolutionary leader Paul Revere.

RIPLEY: For Robert Ripley founder of *Ripley's Believe It! or Not!*

ROCKEFELLER: Prosperous. For the family of American industrialists, bankers, and philanthropists.

RONALD: Strong ruler. For Ronald Wilson Reagan, who was an actor before becoming governor of California and later 40th President of the United States.

ROOSEVELT: The name of a character in the children's TV series "Sesame Street." For Franklin Delano Roosevelt,

32nd President of the United States.

SACAJAWEA: The name of the gentle, courageous Shoshone (Native American) woman who guided Meriwether Lewis and William Clark in their two-year expedition.

SAINT SIMON: From Louis de Rouvroy, a French soldier, statesman and writer.

SAXON: Ancient people who lived in northern Germany. Also, Anglo-Saxon.

SCHUBERT: For Austrian composer Peter Franz Schubert, one of the foremost exponents of romanticism.

SENECA: A Roman philosopher, dramatist, and statesman.

SEQUOYAH: For the Cherokee Indian leader who created a written language for the Cherokee.

SHAWNEE: A member of a tribe of Algonquin Indians that migrated from South Carolina and Tennessee into Ohio and now live in Oklahoma.

SHOSHONE: A Native American tribe in the Southwest United States.

SIGMUND: For Austrian psychiatrist Sigmund Freud, the founder of psychoanalysis.

SIOUX: A member of a confederation of Siouan Indian tribes living in the northern U.S.

SOCRATES: For the Greek philosopher and teacher, generally regarded as one of the wisest men of all time.

SOONER: The settlers who came to the early West before the homesteaders. Also, the name of the mascot for the University of Oklahoma.

SPARTACUS: For a Roman gladiator who led a slave revolt that was the last and most important of the Serville wars. The name of Finch's (the character portrayed by David Spade of "Saturday Night Live" and movies) cat in the TV series "Just Shoot Me."

SWAZI: A member of the Bantu people of southeastern Africa.

TESLA: For Serbian-American inventor and electrician Nikola Tesla, a pioneer in high-tension electricity.

THAYER: American army officer and educator Sylvanus Thayer.

THOMAS: (Hebrew: "twin") For Thomas Jefferson, the American Revolutionary leader who drew up the Declaration of Independence, and became the 3rd President of the United States.

THURGOOD: For Thurgood Marshall, the first black Supreme Court justice.

TILDEN: American politician Samuel Jones Tilden.

TOBIN: American economist James Tobin.

TROGG: Short for troglodyte. A cave man; a hermit. One who lives a primitive or crude lifestyle.

TROJAN: Energetic, determined. Of ancient Troy, its people.

TRUDEAU: Pierre Elliot Trudeau, Canadian prime minister.

TULLY: For Marcus Tullius Cicero, Roman statesman, orator, and Stoic philosopher (106–43 B.C.).

TUPI: A member of a group of South American Indian tribes living chiefly in the lower Amazon.

TUSCARORA: A member of a tribe of Iroquoian Indians at

one time living in North Carolina, but later in New York and Ontario.

TUT: Short for Tutankhamem. Egyptian king of the 14th century B.C.

TYLER: (Old English: "maker of tiles") For John Tyler, 10th President of the United States. Former U.S. Secretary of State, Henry Kissinger had a yellow retriever with this name.

ULYSSES: (Latin: "Odysseus") For Ulysses Simpson Grant, 18th President of the United States.

VESPUCCI: Italian navigator and explorer Amerigo Vespucci.

VIRGIL: Flourishing. For the Roman poet, author of *The Aeneid.*

WELLINGTON: The British general and statesman who defeated Napoleon at Waterloo.

WILKIE: For American politician Wendell L. Wilkie.

WILLIAM: Protector. For William McKinley, 25th President of the United States.

WINNEBAGO: A tribe of North American Indians who lived in Wisconsin and had an Eastern Woodlands culture with some plain traits, observing many elaborate ceremonies such as the winter feast and the buffalo dance.

WINSLOW: For Winslow Homer, an American artist who first won acclaim as a magazine illustrator, most notably for his Civil War reportage.

WOODROW: Forest lover. For Woodrow Wilson, 28th President of the United States.

WYATT: For English poet, statesman Sir Thomas Wyatt.

XENOPHON: Greek general and historian (434?–355? B.C.)

XERXES: (Persian: "ruler") For Xerxes the Great King of Persia (486–465 B.C.)

YANKEE: A native of the Northeastern states.

ZENGER: For German-born journalist and painter John Peter Zenger.

ZENO: A Greek philosopher, founder of Stoicism.

ZEPHANIAH: A Hebrew prophet of the 7th century B.C.

ZIEGFELD: For theatrical producer Florenz Ziegfeld.

ZULU: A member of the great Bantu nation of Southeastern Africa.

Pongo

Did You Know?

BIG BEN: Herbert Hoover, the 31st President of the United States, had a fox terrier with this name. Nickname for the bell in the clock tower of the Houses of Parliament in London, England.

CHRISSY SNOW: Actress Suzanne Somers has a cat named *Chrissy Snow* after her character in the TV series "Three's Company"; Chrissy is short for Christmas and the name means "Christmas Snow."

GEORGE: (Greek: "farmer") Nature lover. Known for George Washington who was the First President of the United States and who was commander in chief of the colonial armies in the American Revolution. Also, known for George Bush, who was the 41st President of the United States and father of George Walker Bush, the 43rd President. Actress Valerie Bertinelli, the former star of the TV series "One Day at a Time" and wife of Eddie Van Halen, the leader of the rock band Van Halen, has a Burmese cat named George.

Noah

Chapter 13

Biblical and Religious

Biblical and religious names can inspire pet names. Names have been taken from Christianity, Judaism, Hindu, and other religious contexts and sources.

AARON: From the Hebrew name Aharon. Aaron was the older brother of Moses and the first high priest of the Israelites in the Old Testament.

ABADDON: (Hebrew: "ruin, destruction"; pronounced "ah-BAD-un") The name of an angel of the abyss in Revelation in the New Testament.

ABBOT: The superior of a monastery for men.

ABEDNEGO: (Pronounced "ah-BED-ne-go") Servant of Nebo, the Babylonian god of wisdom. The name given to Azariah, one of the three men cast into a flaming inferno but saved by God in the Old Testament.

ABEL: Vain. In the Bible, Abel was slain by his elder brother, Cain. Cheryl Ladd, actress and former star of the TV series "Charlie's Angels," has a malamute with this name.

ABIEL: (Hebrew: "God is my father"; pronounced "AY-bee-el") The grandfather of Saul in the Old Testament.

ABIJAH: (Hebrew: "My father is Yahweh"; pronounced "a-BIE-ja") A character both male and female, including the king of Judah.

ABILENE: (Hebrew: "grass"; pronounced "a-bi-LEE-ne") A biblical place.

ABISHAG: (Hebrew: "my father strays") In the Old testament, Abishag was a young woman who took care of King David in his old age.

ABISHAI: (Hebrew: "my father is a gift") Pronounced "a-BISHie," in the Old Testament, one of King David's heroes.

ABNER: (Hebrew: "my father is a light") In the Bible, Abner was the cousin of Saul and the commander of his army.

ADAH: (Hebrew: "adornment") In the Old Testament, the name of the wives of both Lamech and Esau.

ADALIA: (Hebrew: "Yahweh") In the Old testament, the son of Haman.

ADAM: (Hebrew: "man") In Genesis in the Old Testament, Adam was the first human being created by God.

ADINA: (Hebrew: "slender, delicate") The name of a soldier in the Old Testament.

ADINO: (Hebrew) Ornament.

AGRIPPA: (Pronounced "a-GRI-pa") In the New Testament, Herod Agrippa, a grandson of Herod the Great, the king of Israel who had Apostle James put to death.

AHAB: (Hebrew: "uncle"; pronounced "AY-hab") In the Old Testament, a king of Israel and the husband of Jezebel.

ALLON: (Hebrew) Oak.

ALVAH: (Hebrew) His high-ness.

AMARIAH: (Hebrew: "Yahweh has said") The name of several characters in the Old Testament.

AMITTAI: (Hebrew: "my truth"; pronounced "a-MI-tie") The father of the prophet Jonah in the Old Testament.

AMMIEL: (Hebrew: "God is my kinsman") In the Old Testament, one of the spies sent out by Moses.

AMOS: (Hebrew: "to carry") In the Old Testament, one of the minor prophets, author of one of the oldest prophetic books, the Book of Amos.

ANAN: (Hebrew) Cloud.

ANANI: (Hebrew) My cloud.

ANANIAS: (Pronounced "an-a-NIE-as") A Greek form of Hananiah. In the New Testament, the name of several characters, including a disciple in Damascus.

ANATH: (Hebrew: "answer") The father of Shamgar in the Old Testament.

ANNAS: (Pronounced "AN-as") Short for Ananias. The name of a high priest of the Jews in the New Testament.

APPHIA (Hebrew: "increasing"; pronounced AY-fee-a) Name mentioned in Paul's epistle to Philemon in the New Testament.

ARELI: (Hebrew: "lion of God") In the Old Testament, the son of Gad.

ARI: Lion of God.

ASA: (Hebrew: "doctor"; pronouced "AY-sa") King of Judah in the Old Testament.

ASAPH: (Hebrew) Collector.

ASHER: (Hebrew: "happy"; pronounced "A-shur") In the Old Testament, Asher was the son of Jacob and Leah's handmaid.

ATARAH: (Hebrew: "crown") The wife of Jerahmeel in the Old Testament.

ATHELIA: The Lord is mighty.

AZAREL: (Hebrew) "God has helped."

AZARIAH: (Hebrew: "Yahweh has helped") The name of several characters in the Old Testament.

AZUBAH: (Hebrew: "forsaken") The name of Caleb's wife in the Old Testament.

BALAAM: In the Bible, a prophet who was rebuked by his donkey.

BARAK: Lightning. A military commander in the Old Testament. Also Barack. The given name of the 44th U.S. President: Barack Obama.

BARTHOLOMEW: (Greek: "son of Tamai"; Talmai means "furrowed" in Hebrew) An apostle in the New Testament.

BARUCH: (Hebrew: "blessed"; pronounced "be-ROOK, BER-ook") Companion to prophet Jeremiah in the Old Testament.

BATHSHEBA: (Hebrew: "daughter of oath"; pronounced "bath-SHEE-ba") In the Old Testament, the woman who married King David after she had her husband killed in battle.

BEATA: Divine.

BEATO: Blessed.

BEELZEBUB: (Hebrew: "lord of flies"; pronounced "bee-EL-zu-bub, BEEL-zu-bub") A pagan god worshiped by the Philistines.

BETHANY: (Hebrew: "house of figs") The town where Lazarus lived, in the New Testament.

BETHEL: (Hebrew: "house of

God" pronounced "BETH-el") A town north of Jerusalem, where Jacob saw his vision of the stairway.

BEULAH: (Hebrew: "married"; pronounced "BYOO-la") Refers to the land of Israel in the Old Testament.

BOAZ: (Hebrew: "swiftness"; pronounced "BO-az") Ruth's husband in the Old Testament.

BODAN: Given by God.

BOSCO: Saint.

BUZ: (Hebrew: "contempt") In the Old Testament, a son of Nahor.

CAEL: Heaven.

CAIN: (Hebrew: "acquired") To create a commotion. In Genesis in the Old Testament, Adam and Eve's oldest son, who killed his brother Abel.

CALEB: (Hebrew: "dog") In the Old Testament, one of twelve spies sent into Israel by Moses.

CARMEL: (Hebrew: "garden"; pronounced "KAR-mel") A mountain in Israel mentioned in the Old Testament.

CARMI: (Hebrew: "vine") One of Reuben's sons in the Old Testament.

CARPUS: (Latin: "fruit, profits," from the Greek name "Karpos"; pronounced "KAR-pus") The second epistle of Timothy in the New Testament.

CEPHAS: (Arabic: "rock"; pronounced "SEE-fas") Apostle Simon was called Cephas because he was to be the rock upon which the Christian church was to be built.

CHRISTIAN: Blessed.

CHRISTMAS: A holiday that celebrates the birth of Jesus Christ.

CHRISTOPHER: Anointed. For St. Christopher, the patron saint of travelers, whose medallion is said to be a good luck charm.

CORNELIUS: (Latin: *cornus,* "horn"; pronounced "kor-NEE-lee-us") Roman family name.

CRISTALYN: Anointed.

CRISTO: Blessed.

CYRUS: (Pronounced: "SIE-rus") The name of several kings of Persia, including Cyrus the Great, who captured Babylon.

DAGON: The main god of the ancient Philistines.

DAMARIS: (Greek: "calf";

pronounced "DAM-ar-is") In the Bible, a woman converted to Christianity by Saint Paul.

DAN: (Hebrew: "he judged") In the Old Testament, the name of the twelve sons of Jacob and the founder of one of the twelve tribes of Israel.

DEBORAH: (Hebrew: "bee") The nurse who cared for Rebecca in the Old Testament.

DELILAH: (Hebrew: "delicate") In the Old Testament, Delilah was Samson's lover, who betrayed him to the Philistines by cutting his hair, which was the source of his power.

DEO: (Latin) God.

DEUS: (Latin) A god.

DIANTHA: Supreme one.

DIMANDA: Divine and beloved.

DIMITRI: Godly.

DINAH: (Hebrew: "judged") In the Old Testament, the daughter of Jacob and Leah.

DIO: Godly.

DIVINE: (Latin: "a god") Supreme being.

DORCAS: From the Greek word *dorkas* meaning "gazelle."

DRUSILLA: A female pet in a Roman family. The name of Felix's wife in the New Testament.

EASTER: A holiday that celebrates Jesus' resurrection.

EDEN: (Hebrew: "place of pleasure") In the Old Testament, the place where Adam and Eve lived before they were cast out.

EDNA: (Hebrew: "pleasure") A name appearing in the Old Testament Apocrypha, the Book of Tibit.

EDOM: (Hebrew: "red") In the Old Testament, Esau was given the name Edom because he traded his birthright for a serving of a red broth.

ELI: (Hebrew: "height, ascension"; pronounced "EE-lie") In the Old Testament, the teacher of Samuel and high priest of Israel.

ELIEZER: (Hebrew: "God is my helper"; pronounced "el-ie-EE-zur") In the Old Testament, the name of one of the sons of Moses.

ELIHU: (Hebrew) "Yahweh is God." (Pronounced "ee-LIE-hyoo.")

ELIJAH: (Hebrew: "my God is Yahweh"; pronounced "ee-

LIE-zha") A Hebrew prophet of the 9th century B.C., during the reign of King Ahab and his queen, Jezebel.

ELISHA: (Hebrew: "God is my helper"; pronounced "ee-LIE-sha") In the Old Testament, Elisha was a prophet and the successor of Elijah.

ELIUD: (Hebrew: "God is grandeur"; pronounced "ee-LIE-ud") An ancestor of Jesus.

ELKANAH: (Hebrew: "God has created"; pronounced "el-KAYN-a") The father of Samuel in the Old Testament.

EMANUEL, EMMANUEL: (Hebrew: "God is with us;" pronounced "e-MAN-yoo-el") Foretold as the name of the Messiah in the Old Testament.

ENOCH: (Hebrew: "dedicated"; pronounced "EE-nawk") The son of Cain in the Old Testament.

ENOSH: (Hebrew: "human being"; pronounced "EE-nawsh") The son of Seth and a grandson of Adam in the genealogies in the Old Testament.

EPAPHRAS: (Pronounced "EP-a-fras") In the New Testament, the name of one of Paul's co-workers.

EPHRAIM: In the Bible, the younger son of Joseph.

ERAN: (Hebrew: "watchful, vigilant") The grandson of Ephraim in the Old Testament.

ERASTUS: (Greek: "lovely"; pronounced "ee-RAS-tus") Paul's assistant in Acts and in the New Testament.

ESAU: In the Bible, the son of Isaac and Rebekah, who sold his birthright to his younger twin brother. He was named Edom after partaking of the red broth.

EUNICE: (Greek: "good victory") In the New Testament, the mother of Timothy.

EVE: (Hebrew: "life") In the Book of Genesis of the Old Testament Adam and Eve were the first humans. Eve gave Adam the forbidden fruit, and as a result, they were cast out of the Garden of Eden.

EZEKIEL: (Hebrew: "God stregthens"; pronounced "e-ZEE-kee-ul") A major prophet in the Old Testament and author of the Book of Ezekiel.

EZRA: (Hebrew: "help" pronounced "EZ-ra") A prophet in the Old Testament, author of the Book of Ezra. Also for American poet Ezra Pound.

GABRIEL: Devoted, strong. An angel who announces births; he announced the birth of Jesus to Mary in the New Testament.

GOLIATH: In the Bible, the giant killed by David with a sling.

HOSANNA: Reverent. Praise.

HOSEA: (Hebrew; pronounced "ho-ZAY-a.") Salvation.

HOSS, HOSSIE: Praise.

ICON: Supreme image.

IDOL: Image of a god.

IRA: (Hebrew: "watchful"; pronounced "IE-ra") In the Old Testament, the name of King David's priest.

ISAAC: (Hebrew: "he laughs"; pronounced "IE-zak") In the Old Testament, Isaac was the son of Abraham and the father of Esau and Jacob.

ISAIAH: (Hebrew: "Yahweh is salvation"; pronounced "ie-ZAY-a, ie-ZIE-a") In the Old Testament, Isaiah was a major prophet.

ISHMAEL: (Hebrew: "God will hear"; pronounced "ISHmay-el") In the Old Testament, one of Abraham's sons.

ISRAEL: (Hebrew: "he who wrestles with God"; pronounced "IZ-ray-el") In the Old Testament, Israel wrestled with an angel.

JABEZ: (Hebrew: "sorrow") In the Old Testament, the name of a man blessed by God.

JABIN: (Hebrew: "perceptive") The kings of Hazor in the Old testament.

JADON: (Hebrew; pronounced "JAY-dun") Thankful.

JAHLEEL: (Hebrew) "God waits."

JAHZEEL: (Hebrew: "God apportions") The son of Naphtali in the Old Testament.

JAIR: (Hebrew) "He shines."

JAMES: In the New Testament, one of the apostles, the brother of the apostle John.

JAMIN: (Hebrew: "right hand") In the Old Testament, a son of Simeon.

JAPHETH: The youngest of Noah's three sons. (Pronounced: "JAY-feth.")

JAVAN: (Hebrew: "Greece"

pronounced "JAY-van") In the Old Testament, a grandson of Noah.

JEDIDAH: (Hebrew: "beloved"; pronounced "jee-DIE-da") In the Old Testament, the wife of King Amon of Judah and the mother of Josiah.

JEHOASH: (Pronounced "jee-HO-ash") In the Old Testament, the name of a king of Israel.

JEHOSHAPHAT: (Hebrew: "Yahweh has judged"; pronounced "jee-HAWSH-a-fat") A king of Judah in the Old Testament.

JEHU: (Hebrew: "Yahweh is he"; pronounced "JEE-hyoo") In the Old Testament, a king of Israel.

JEREMIAH: (Hebrew: "uplifting"; pronounced "jer-e-MIE-a") A major prophet in the Old Testament, author of the Book of Jeremiah.

JEREMIEL: (Hebrew: "God uplifts") An archangel in the apocryphal books of Esdras and Enoch in the Old Testament.

JERUSHA: (Hebrew: "possession"; pronounced "je-ROO-sha") The wife of King Uzziah of Judah and the mother of Jotham in the Old Testament.

JEZEBEL: (Hebrew "not exalted," derived from Iyzebel) In the Old Testament, the sinful wife of Ahab, the king of Israel.

JOAB: (Hebrew: "Yahweh is the father"; pronounced "JO-ab") The commander of King David's army in the Old Testament.

JOACHIM: (Hebrew: "established by Yahweh"; pronounced "JO-a-kim") In the Old Testament, Joachim is a king of Judah.

JOB: (Hebrew: "persecuted") In the Book of Job in the Old Testament, a patient man who is mistreated by God in order to be tested.

JONAH: (Hebrew: "a dove") In the Bible, a Hebrew prophet who was swallowed by a whale, but later was cast up unharmed.

JOSEPH: (Hebrew: "he will add," derived from Yoseph) In the New Testament, he is the husband of Mary, mother of Jesus.

JOSES: (Pronounced: "JO-seez") Greek form of Joseph.

JOSIAH: (Hebrew: "Yahweh supports"; pronounced "jo-SIE-a") In the Old Testament, a king of Judah famous for his religious reforms.

JOTHAM: (Hebrew: "Yahweh is right"; pronounced "JO-tham") In the Old Testament, the name of a son of Gideon.

JUBAL: (Hebrew: "small stream") The first musician mentioned in the Old testament.

JUDAH: (Hebrew: "praised"; pronounced "JOO-da") The name of one of the twelve sons of Jacob and the ancestor of the tribe of Judah in the Old Testament.

JUDAS: (Pronounced "JOO-das") Greek form of Judah. In the New Testament, Judas Iscariot was the apostle who betrayed Jesus.

JUDE: Variation of Judas.

KETURAH: (Hebrew: "incense"; pronounced "ki-TOOR-a") In the Old Testament, the wife of Abraham after Sarah's death.

KEZIAH: (Hebrew: "cassia"; pronounced "ke-ZIE-a") In the Old Testament, Keziah was one of Job's daughters.

LABAN: (Pronounced "LAY-ban") White. In the Old Testament, the name of the father of Rachel and Leah.

LAMECH: (Hebrew: "to make low"; pronounced "LAY-mek") In the Old Testament, the father of Noah.

LAZARUS: (Pronounced "LAZ-ur-us") Humble. In the New Testament, Lazarus was a man from Bethany who was restored to life by Jesus.

LEHI: (Hebrew) Jawbone.

LEVIATHAN: Huge. In the Bible, a sea monster.

MADAI: (Hebrew: "medes") In the Old Testament, a son of Japheth.

MAGDALENE: (Pronounced "MAG-da-leen") A woman who was cleaned of evil spirits by Jesus.

MAHLAH: (Pronounced "MAY-la") Possibly means "weak" in Hebrew. A masculine and feminine name in the Old Testament.

MALACHI: (Hebrew: "messenger"; pronounced "MAL-a-kie") A Hebrew prophet of the 5th century B.C.

MANASSEH: (Hebrew: "causing to forget"; pronounced "ma-NA-se") In the Old Testament, the oldest son of Joseph.

MANUEL: Reverent.

MANUELA: (Hebrew) "God with us."

MARTHA: (Greek) "lady." The name of sister of Lazarus and Mary in the New Testament.

MARY: (Hebrew) "rebellious." In the New Testament, the name of Jesus' mother, the virgin Mary, wife of Joseph.

MATTHIAS: (Pronounced "ma-THIE-as") In the New Testament, the apostle chosen to replace the traitor Judas Iscariot.

MENAHEM: (Hebrew: "comforter") The name of a king of Israel in the Old Testament.

MESHACH: (Pronounced "MEE-shak") The Babylonian god of the moon. In the Old Testament, Meshach was the Babylonian name of Mishael, one of the three men saved by God after being cast into a flaming furnace.

MICAH: (Hebrew: "who is like Yahweh"; pronounced MIE-ka) In the Old Testament, a minor prophet who predicted the destruction of Jerusalem.

MICAIAH: (Hebrew) "Who is like Yahweh." (Pronounced "mie-KAY-a")

MICHELENE: Divine.

MICHELLA: Divine.

MONK: (Greek: "alone") Solitary. Also a man who joins a religious order living in retirement according to a rule and under vows of poverty, obedience, and chastity.

MORDECAI: (Persian: "servant of Marduk"; pronounced "mor-de-KIE") The chief Babylonian god. In the Old Testament, Mordecai was the cousin of Esther.

MORIAH: (Hebrew: "seen by Yahweh"; pronounced "mo-RIE-a") A place in the Old Testament, the mountain upon which Solomon built the temple.

MOSES: In the Bible, the leader and lawgiver who brought the Israelites out of slavery in Egypt and into the

Promised Land, and who received the Ten Commandments.

NAAMAH: (Hebrew: "sweetness") In the Old Testament, the wife of Solomon.

NAHOR: (Hebrew: "snorting"; pronounced "NAY-hor") The brother of Abraham in the Old Testament.

NAHUM: (Hebrew: "comforter"; pronounced "NAY-um") One of the minor prophets in the Old Testament.

NAPHTALI: (Hebrew: "struggling"; pronounced "NAF-ta-lie") In the Old Testament, the son of Jacob by Rachel's servant Bilhah.

NATHAN: (Hebrew: "giver") In the Old Testament, the son of King David.

NATHANIEL: (Hebrew) "Gift of God."

NEBO: The Babylonian god of wisdom.

NEHEMIAH: (Hebrew: "comforted by Yahweh"; pronounced "nee-he-MIE-a") In the Old Testament, the leader of the Jews who helped the rebuilding of Jerusalem.

NEKODA: (Hebrew: "marked") In the Old Testament, the head of a family of temple servants.

NERIAH: (Hebrew: "lamp of Yahweh") The father of Baruch in the Old Testament.

NICODEMUS: (Pronounced ni-ko-DEE-mus") Victory. In the New Testament, a man who helped Joseph of Arimathea entomb Jesus.

NIMROD: In the Bible, a mighty hunter.

NOAH: (Hebrew: "rest, comfort") In the Bible, the patriarch commanded by God to build the ark on which he, his family, and two of every kind of creature survived the great flood.

OPHRAH: (Hebrew) "Fawn." (Pronounced "OF-ra")

ORPAH: In the Old Testament, she was Naomi's second daughter-in-law in the Book of Ruth.

OSIRIS: A legendary Egyptian ruler and god who symbolized the creative forces of nature.

OTHNIEL: (Hebrew: "lion of God") The nephew of Caleb in the Old Testament.

PARADISE: Heavenly.

PENINNAH: (Hebrew:

"precious stone") In the Old Testament, one of the wives of Elkanah.

PERSIS: (Greek: "Persian woman") A woman mentioned in Paul's epistle to the Romans in the New Testament.

PHILEMON: (Greek: "affectionate"; pronounced "fi-LEE-mun") One of the recipient of one of Paul's epistles in the New Testament.

PHINEHAS: (Pronounced "FIN-ee-as") Nubian. In the Old Testament, the grandson of Aaron who killed an Israelite because he married a Midianite woman, which in turn stopped a plague sent by God.

PONTIUS: (Derived from Greek *pontos:* "sea"; pronounced "PAWN-tee-us") For Pontius Pilate, who was Roman governor of Judea in the New Testament.

PRISCA: (Pronounced "PRIS-ka") A name used in the epistles in the New Testament, referring to Aquila's wife, Priscilla.

RACHEL: (Hebrew: "ewe") In the Old Testament, the wife of Jacob and the mother of Joseph and Benjamin.

RAHAB: (Hebrew: "spacious"; pronounced "RAY-hab") In the Old Testament, a prostitute of Jericho who aided the Israelites.

RASPUTIN: Russian monk Grigory Yefi Rasputin who served during the reign of the last Russian czars.

REBECCA: (Hebrew: "noose") In the Old Testament, the wife of Isaac and the mother of Esau and Jacob.

REUBEN: (Hebrew: "behold a son"; pronounced "ROO-ben") In the Old Testament, the eldest son of Jacob and Leah.

REUEL: (Hebrew) "Friend of God." (Pronounced "ROO-el")

RHODA: (Derived from Greek *rhondn:* "rose"; pronounced "RO-da") In the New Testament, a maid in the house of Mary, the mother of John Mark.

RUTH: Friend. In the Old Testament, the central character, an ancestor of King David, in the Book of Ruth.

SAINT: Reverent. One officially recognized through canonization as worthy of holiness. A good name for a Saint Bernard.

SALOME: (Pronounced "sa-LO-mee") In the Bible, the stepdaughter of Herod Antipas whose dancing pleased Herod very much.

SAMSON: (Hebrew: "sun") From the Bible; Samson had a mistress named Delilah.

SAMUEL: (Hebrew: "to hear") The last of the ruling judges in the Old Testament who anointed Saul to be the first king of Israel.

SAPPHIRA: (Pronounced "sa-FIE-ra") Sapphire. In the New Testament, a character killed by God for lying.

SARAH: (Hebrew: "princess, lady") At the age of 90, she gave birth to Isaac.

SARAI: (Hebrew: "contentious"; pronounced "SER-ie") The name of Sarah in the Old Testament before God changed it.

SARAMA: (Hindu) God Indra's watchdog.

SARASWATI: (Hindu) Goddess of Speech.

SAUL: (Hebrew: "of God") The first king of Israel who ruled just before King David.

SCHEHERAZADE: Queenly.

SELA: (Hebrew: "rock") A city, the capital of Edom, in the Old Testament.

SETH: (Hebrew: "appointed") In the Old Testament, the third son of Adam and Eve, and forefather of the human race.

SHADRACH: (Pronounced "SHAD-rak") Commander. The name of the Babylonian god of the moon.

SHAMGAR: (Hebrew: "sword") A judge in the Old Testament.

SHEBA: (Hebrew: "oath") In the Bible, a name for a region of the Arabian peninsula.

SHEM: In the Bible, Noah's oldest son.

SHERAH: (Hebrew: "kinswoman") In the Old Testament, the name of a daughter of Ephraim.

SHILOH: (Hebrew) "of the Messiah."

SHIPHRAH: (Hebrew: "beautiful"). In the Old Testament, one of the midwives who disobeyed the Pharaoh's order to kill any Hebrew boys delivered.

SHIVA: (Hindu) The God with a third eye.

SILAS: (Pronounced "SIE-las") A companion of Saint

Paul in Acts in the New Testament.

SIMEON: (Hebrew: "heard"; pronounced "SIM-ee-un") In the Bible, a son of Jacob.

SOLOMON: (Hebrew: "peaceful") The son of David and king of Israel in the 10th century B.C., noted for his wisdom.

SUSANNA: In the New Testament, a woman who ministered to Christ.

SYNTYCHE: (Ancient Greek: "common fate"; pronounced SIN-ti-kee) In the New Testament, a woman mentioned in Paul's epistle to the Philippians.

TALITHA: (Arabic) "little girl." (Pronounced "TAL-i-tha")

TAMAR: (Hebrew: "date palm"; pronounced "TAY-mar") In the Old Testament, the daughter-in-law of Judah.

TEMAN: (Hebrew: "right hand") In the Old Testament, a place name.

TERAH: (Hebrew: "wild goat"; pronounced "TEE-ra") In the Old Testament, the father of Abraham.

THADDEUS: (Arabic: "heart"; pronounced "THAD-ee-us") In the New Testament, one of the apostles.

THEOPHILUS: (Greek: "friend of God"; pronounced "thee-AWF-i-lus") In the New Testament, the evangelist Luke addresses the Book of Acts to Theophilus.

TIMOTHY: (Derived from *Timon:* "honoring God") Timothy was a companion of Saint Paul on his missionary journeys.

TIRAS: (Hebrew: "desire") A grandson of Noah in the Old Testament.

TIRZAH: (Hebrew: "favorable") In the Old Testament, one of the daughters of Zelophehad.

TITUS: (Pronounced "TIE-tus") Honorable. In the New Testament, a companion of Saint Paul.

TOBIAH: (Derived from Hebrew *Tobiyah:* "Yahwel is good"; pronounced "to-BIE-a") In the Old Testament, an Ammonite in the Book of Nehemiah.

TOBIAS: (Pronounced "to-BIE-as") A Greek form of Tobiah. In the Old Testament, a hero in Book of Tobit.

TOBIT: The father of Tobias.

TRYPHENA: (Derived from Greek *tryphe:* "softness, delicacy") In the New Testament, a companion to Tryphosa.

TRYPHOSA: (Derived from Greek *tryphe:* "softness, delicacy") In the New Testament, a companion to Tryphena.

URI: (Hebrew: "light") In the Old Testament, the father of Bezalel.

URIAH: (Hebrew: "Yahweh is my light"; pronounced "yoo-RIE-a") In the Old Testament, a Hittite warrior in King David's army, the first husband of Bathsheba.

URIEL: (Hebrew) "God is my light." (Pronounced: "YUWR-ee-el")

UZI: (Hebrew) "Power."

UZZIAH: (Hebrew: "my power is Yahweh"; pronounced "u-ZIE-a") A king of Judah in the Old Testament.

UZZIEL: (Hebrew) "My power is God." (Pronounced "u-ZIE-el, UZ-ee-el").

VARUNA: (Hindu) God of Waters.

VASHTI: (Hebrew: "thread"; pronounced "VASH-tee") In the Old Testament, the first wife of King Ahasuerus of Persia.

VAYU: (Hindu) God of Wind.

YOCHANAN: A Hebrew form of John.

ZACCHAEUS: (Pronounced "za-KEE-us") Pure. In the New Testament, a tax collector of Jericho who donated half of his possessions to charity.

ZACHARIAS: (Pronounced "zak-a-RIE-as") A Greek form of Zechariah.

ZEBADIAH: (Hebrew) "Yahweh has bestowed." (Pronounced ze-ba-DIE-a)

ZEBEDEE: (Pronounced "ZEB-e-dee") A Greek form of Zebadiah. In the New Testament, the father of Apostles James and John.

ZEBULON: A variation of Zebulun.

ZEBULUN: (Hebrew: "exaltation"; pronounced "ZEB-yoo-lun") A plain in Israel.

ZECHARIAH: A minor prophet in the Old Testament. Pronounced: "ze-ka-RIE-a."

ZEDEKIAH: (Hebrew: "justice of Yahweh"; pronounced "ze-de-KIE-a") The last king of Judah in the Old Testament.

ZEPHANIAH: (Pronounced "ze-fa-NIE-a") A minor prophet in the Old Testament.

ZILLAH: (Hebrew: "shade"; pronounced "ZIL-a") In the Old Testament, the second wife of Lamech.

ZILPAH: (Hebrew: "frailty"; pronounced "ZIL-pa)" In the Old Testament, the slave girl who was given to Jacob by Leah.

ZIMRI: (Hebrew: "praise my music"; pronounced "ZIM-rie") A king of Israel who ruled for only seven days.

ZION: Heaven. A hill in Jerusalem designated as holy.

ZIPPORAH: (Pronounced "zi-POR-a," "ZIP-or-a") Bird. In the Old Testament, the wife of Moses.

Did You Know?

ALFRED: Far-seeing. When she was a young girl, actress Susan Dey, the star of the TV series "The Partridge Family" and "L.A. Law," had a pet worm with this name. Also, the name of the pig in the children's TV series "Old Mac-Donald's Farm."

BOSWELL: An aristocratic name, English origin. Well known mystery writers, husband and wife, Hillary Waugh and Shannon OCork have a cat named Mr. Boswell.

LADY NASHVILLE: Andrew Jackson, the 7th President of the Unites States, had a horse with this name.

Fedora and Pez

Asta, Celesta, Jove, Karma
and Evermore

Chapter 14

Celestial and Ethereale

Names that relate to the cosmos and the spiritual realm can inspire unique names for new pets. This chapter offers up: *Ara, Celia, Equinox, Infinity*, and other uplifting names!

AQUARIUS: In astronomy, a large central constellation, supposedly outlining a man pouring water from a pitcher. In astrology, the eleventh sign of the Zodiac, the waterbearer.

ARA: Aura.

ARIES: In astronomy, a northern constellation, supposedly outlining a ram. In astrology, the first sign of the Zodiac, the ram.

ASTRA: A star.

AUGUST: Majestic, inspiring. The eighth month of the Gregorian calendar year.

BIG DIPPER: In astronomy, a dipper-shaped group of stars in the constellation Ursa Major (the Great Bear).

BISHOP: Spiritual. High-ranking.

CAPRICORN: Heavenly. In astronomy, a southern constellation resembling a goat in outline. In astrology, the tenth sign of the Zodiac, the goat.

CARMA: Fate.

CELESTA: Celestial.

CELESTIAL: Heavenly.

CELESTINA: Heavenly.

CELESTINE: Heavenly.

CELIA: Celestial.

CELINDA: Celestial; pretty.

CENTAUR: The astrological sign for Sagittarius, the ninth sign of the Zodiac.

CHERON: One of the satellites (moons) of the planet Pluto.

COSMIC: Order, balanced.

COSMO: Order, balanced.

COSMOS: Of the universe, cosmic.

DAVENA, DAVINA: Divine.
DAWN: (Anglo-Saxon) Early to rise in the morning.
DAWNA: Dawn.
DAWNELLE: Dawn.
DECEMBER: The twelfth and last month of the year. Full of cheer because Christmas is near!
DESTINA, DESTINE: Fateful.
DESTINY: Fortunate.
DESTYNE: Fateful, destiny.
DOMINIC: Saint.
DOMINIQUE: Heavenly.
ECTO: Outside. Spiritual.
ENDURA: Lasting; forever.
EQUINOX: (Latin: "equal night") The time when the sun crosses the equator, making night and day of equal lengths in all parts of the earth. A moody pet.
ESSENCE: Entity.
ESTELITA: A star.
ETERNIA: Eternal. Forever.
ETERNITY: Endless, lasting, eternal as love lasts forever.
EVERMORE: Forever.
FEBRUARY: The second month of the Gregorian calendar year. Brisk, honorable.
FOREVER: Eternal.
FRIDAY: The day of the goddess. The sixth day of the week. An old children's rhyme says "Friday's child is loving and giving." The name of Crusoe's devoted servant in the classic novel The Life and Adventures of Robinson Crusoe by Daniel Defoe.
FUTURE: What is to be or come.
GALAXY: (Greek: "milk," hence our galaxy's name Milky Way) A light-colored pet or any pet that seems to travel in its own space, galaxy.
GEMINI: In astronomy, a constellation in the Northern Hemisphere. In astrology, the third sign of the Zodiac, the twins. Also, a series of space flights under the United States space program.
GREAT BEAR: Large, ferocious. In astronomy, the constellation Ursa Major.
INFINITY: Endless.
JANUARY: Chilly. The first month of the Gregorian calendar year, named for the Roman god Janus.
JOVE: Another name for the planet Jupiter.
JULY: The seventh month of the Gregorian calendar year.

JUNE: Warm. The sixth month of the Gregorian calendar year. The name of one of the nieces of Donald Duck's girlfriend, Daisy, in Disney cartoons.

KARMA: Fate, destiny.

KARMALEA, KARMALEE: Destiny.

KARMALENA: Destiny.

KARMALYNE: Destiny.

LEO: (Latin: "lion") In astronomy, a northern constellation supposedly outlining a lion. In astrology, the fifth sign of the zodiac, the lion.

LIBRA: In astronomy, a southern constellation supposedly resembling a pair of scales in shape. In astrology, the seventh sign of the Zodiac, the scales of balance.

LITTLE BEAR: Small but strong. In astronomy, the constellation Ursa Minor.

LITTLE DIPPER: In astronomy, a dipper-shaped group of stars in the constellation Ursa Minor (the little bear).

LYRA: In astronomy, a northern constellation supposedly outlining a lyre.

MARCH: The third month of the Gregorian calendar year. Named for the god Mars, the Roman god of war.

MARS: The Roman god of war. The fourth planet from the sun in our solar system.

MAY: (Hebrew: "rebellious") The fifth month of the calendar year. The springtime of life; youth. The name of one of the nieces of Donald Duck's girlfriend, Daisy, in the Disney cartoon.

MERIDIAN: Of or passing through the highest point or course of any heavenly body.

MILLENNIUM: A thousand years. The name of a Beanie Baby bear.

MONDAY: (Anglo-Saxon: "moon's day") The second day of the week. An old children's rhyme says "Monday's child is fair of face."

MOON: The satellite of the earth that evolves around the earth once every 29 ½ days and shines at night by reflecting the sun's light. Also, for actress Moon Unit Zappa, daughter of the late rock star Frank Zappa.

MYSTIC: Perceptive. Mysterious.

NEPTUNE: The Roman god of the sea. The eighth planet

from the sun and the third largest planet in our solar system.

NOVA: A star that suddenly increases in brightness.

NOVEMBER: The 11th month of the Gregorian calendar.

OCTOBER: The 10th month of the Gregorian calendar.

ORBIT: To travel in circles like the planets and moons.

ORION: In Greek mythology, a giant hunter. In astronomy, an equatorial constellation near Taurus, supposedly outlining a hunter with a belt and sword.

PISCES: A constellation south of Andromeda, supposedly resembling a fish in shape. In astrology, the twelfth sign of the Zodiac, the fish.

PLUTO: The smallest planet in our solar system and most distant planet from the sun. Any pet that is small and distant. Also, the name of Goofy's dog in Disney cartoons.

POLARIS: Polar star, the North Star.

QUASAR: A bright, distant celestial object whose power output is several thousand times greater than our galaxy.

RION: Short for Orion.

SAGITTARIUS: A southern constellation said to resemble a centaur shooting an arrow. In astrology, the ninth sign of the Zodiac, the centaur.

SATURDAY: Saturn's day. The seventh and last day of the week. An old children's rhyme says "Saturday's child works hard for a living."

SATURN: In Roman mythology, the god of harvests. The name of the second largest planet in our solar system. Saturn, the sixth planet from the sun, has a remarkable ring system composed of billions of water-ice particles orbiting around the planet.

SCORPIO: A southern constellation said to resemble a scorpion in shape. In astrology, the eighth sign of the Zodiac, the scorpion.

SEPTEMBER: From Latin meaning seven, September was originally the seventh month, now September is the ninth month of the Gregorian calendar year.

SIRIUS: In astronomy, the Dog Star.

STAR: A heavenly body seen as small, fixed points of light in a night sky. A small, bright pet or any pet that aspires to be a star!

STARGAZER: A dreamer.

SUNDAY: (Anglo-Saxon: "the day of the sun") The first day of the week. An old children's rhyme says "But the child born on the Sabbath day is bonny and blithe, and good and gay."

SUNDOG: A small halo or rainbow near the sun.

TAURUS: In astronomy, a northern constellation, supposedly resembling the forequarters of a bull. In astrology, the second sign of the Zodiac, the bull.

THURSDAY: The 5th day of the week. An old children's rhyme says "Thursday's child has far to go."

TUESDAY: The third day of the week. An old children's rhyme says "Tuesday's child is full of grace." Also, known for actress Tuesday Weld.

URANUS: In Greek mythology, Heaven personified, a god regarded as the father of Titans, Furies, and Cyclops; he was overthrown by his son Cronus (Saturn). The seventh planet from the sun in the solar system.

VEGA: (Spanish: "rich lowland area, water meadow") A blue-white star of the first magnitude in the constellation Lyra.

VIRGO: In astronomy, a constellation between Leo and Libra, supposedly outlining a woman. In astronomy, the sixth sign of Zodiac.

WEDNESDAY: The fourth day of the calendar week. An old children's rhyme says "Wednesday's child is full of woe." Also, the name of the daughter in the 1960s TV series "The Addams Family," on which a movie series was based.

ZODIAC: An imaginary belt in the heavens extending on either side of the apparent path of the sun and including the paths of the moon and the principal planets. In astrology, twelve constellations represent the signs of the Zodiac.

Beans & Baxter

Did You Know?

BARK: Comedian Bill Murray, former "Saturday Night Live" star and the star of popular movies including *Ghost busters*, has a golden retriever who has this name.

CATCHER: Any pet that catches. Kate Jackson, actress and former star of the TV series "Charlie's Angels," has a Siberian husky with this name.

PURTY: When they were a couple, Brad Pitt and Jennifer Aniston had a Weimaraner with this name.

Butterbear

Nikko

Chapter 15

Nature and Science

From a favorite flower or plant (*Abelia, Bluebell, Rose*) to precious to semiprecious stones (*Emerald, Jade, Topaz*) to weather (*Rainbow, Lightning, Thunder*), nature and science can inspire many imaginative names like those in this chapter.

AARDVARK: An anteater. Nocturnal mammal of southern and eastern Africa that feeds on insects, mainly termites.

ABALONE: Edible rock-clinging mollusks that have a flattened shell lined with mother-of-pearl.

ABELIA: Any of a group of shrubs of Asian or Mexican origin with opposite leaves and flowers of white, red, or pink.

ABNAKI: Outdoorsy.

ABYSS: Of the ocean, the primeval great deep. Anything too deep for measurement.

ACACIA: Thorny. A tree or shrub of the mimosa family.

AGATE: A fine-grained variety of mineral with colored bands or irregular clouding.

AJUGA: A plant in the mint family.

ALABASTER: A fine textured white and translucent gypsum used for carving vases and other items.

ALFRESCO: In the open air, outdoors.

ALGA: Any of a number of plants that grow in sea and fresh water. A good name for a water pet, such as a fish or turtle.

AMARYLLIS: Delicate. A South African flowering bulb with deep red to white flowers.

AMETHYST: A gem. Violet.

ASTER: Colorful.

ATOM: (Greek: "uncut") A tiny particle. In chemistry and physics, any of the smallest particles of an element that combine with similar particles of other elements to produce compounds; atoms consist of complex arrangements of electrons, protons, and neutrons.

AZALEA: Bright, colorful.

BAMBOO: Springy. Slim.

BANYAN: An East Indian fig tree whose branches take root and become new trunks. Exotic, of the tropics.

BARTLEY: Earthy.

BAT: A nocturnal flying mammal. Any pet that has these characteristics.

BEGONIA: Pretty. A plant with showy white, pink, or red flowers and ornamental leaves.

BLUEBELL: A plant with blue bell-shaped flowers.

BOB CAT: A North American Lynx that has a reddish fur with dark markings. Betty White, star of "The Golden Girls" and other TV series and movies, has a male Himalayan with this name.

BONFIRE: Having a fiery passion for the outdoors.

BOSKY: Of the forest.

BRINI: Of th sea.

BRONTO: Short for brontosaurus.

BRONTOSAURUS: (Greek: "thunder lizard") Huge, extinct American dinosaur of the Jurassic period.

BUDGIE: Short for budgerigar, a small Australian parrot, usually light green with black and yellow markings.

CACTUS: Prickly.

CALLA: White or tan-colored. A plant of the arum family, with a large, white leaf surrounding a yellow flower spike.

CAMELLIA: An evergreen plant bearing red or white flowers.

CAMPER: Liking the outdoors.

CARNELIAN: Reddish; a semiprecious stone.

CARAWAY: White-flowered aromatic herb.

CEDAR: Strong, reddish brown. Any of the tall, fragrant evergreen trees in the pine family.

CEREBUS: Cloudlike.

CHAMELEON: Changeable. Any of various lizards that can change the color of their skin.

CHEETAH: Wild, fast. A leopard-like animal, with a small head and a black-spotted, tawny coat, of Africa and Asia.

CHAMELEON: Changeable. Fickle. Any of various lizards that can change the color of their skin. Any pet with changeable moods.

CHEROKEE ROSE: A Chinese climbing rose with a fragrant white flower.

CHESCA: Outdoorsy.

CHIMP: Intelligent. Short for chimpanzee, an anthropoid ape of Africa, with black hair and large ears. The chimpanzee is smaller than a gorilla and noted for its intelligence.

CHINQUAPIN: The dwarf chestnut tree. Lucy Johnson, daughter of the 36th President of the United States Lyndon Baines Johnson, had a dog named Chinquapin during her father's years in the White House.

CHIPMUNK: A small, striped North American squirrel.

CIRO, CIRRO: Short for cirrocumulus, small, white, fleecy clouds in rows.

CLEMATIS: One who clings. Vining plants in the buttercup family and having white, red, pink or purple flowers.

CLOUD: Fluffy, white.

CLOVER: Lucky. Low-growing herbs having trifoliolate leaves and flowers in dense heads and valuable for foliage and attracting bees.

COLUMBINE: Pretty flower. Any of a group of plants in the buttercup family with showy, spurred flowers. Also, the saucy sweetheart of Harlequin in comedy and pantomime.

COSGROVE: Vast forest.

COUGAR: A tawny-brown animal of the cat family, with a long, slender body.

COVEY: A mature bird.

CROCUS: Spring flower. Any of a large group of herbs in the iris family that have long-tubed flowers appearing in early spring.

CRYSTAL: (Latin: "rock crystal") Clear.

DAFFODIL: Yellow-colored. A plant with flowers that have a long corona shaped like a trumpet.

DAHLIA: Pretty flower. A perennial plant of the composite family, with tuberous roots and large, striking flowers.

DAISY: Yellow-colored.

Golden. A flower of the composite family, bearing flowers with white or pink rays around a yellow disk.

DAMASK ROSE: A large fragrant pink rose widely introduced from Asia Minor.

DANDELION: Golden lion. A great name for a yellow tabby cat. Yellow-colored wildflowers also considered a weed.

DELANCY: Of the land.

DELMA: Woodland goddess.

DELMAR: Woodland dweller.

DELMUS: Woodland dweller.

DELON: Woodland dweller.

DELORA: Woodland goddess.

DIAMOND: Valuable, sparkling.

DRAKE: A male duck.

EAGLE: Graceful, strong. A large, predatory bird of prey.

EARTH: Our home planet. The fifth largest planet in our solar system, third from the sun.

EON: Aeon, indefinitely long period of time.

EUCALYPTUS: Fragrant. Eucalyptus is an evergreen tree native to Australia and a favorite food of koala bears. The name of a koala bear Beanie Baby.

EUDELL: Nature lover.

FALCON: Swift, a hunter. A hawk used for falconing.

FAWN: (Old French: "young deer") Pale yellowish brown. Affectionate.

FEATHER, FEATHERS: Soft, light. Protective coat that covers the body of birds.

FERN: Soft, fluffy. Flowerless spore-producing plants.

FIELDING: Nature lover.

FIRE: Red-colored.

FIREFLY: Warm, bright. Nocturnal beetles that produce a bright soft light for courtship.

FORDY: Shallow water.

FORREST: A nature lover, outdoorsman.

FORSYTHIA: Golden. A shrub with yellow bell-shaped flowers, which appear in early spring before the leaves.

FROG: Resembling a frog; any pet that hops around like a frog.

GARCIA: Nature lover.

GARDENIA: Golden. A white or yellowish flowering shrub with fragrant, waxy petals.

GATOR: Short for alligator. A

pet that bites.

GARNET: A gem, a reddish, usually clear, mineral.

GAZELLE: Any the small, swift, graceful antelopes of Africa, the Near East, and Asia, with spirally twisted horns and large, lustrous eyes.

GECKO: A soft-skinned, insect-eating lizard with suction pads on its feet.

GERANIUM: A plant with strong-smelling flowers of pink, red, and purple and leaves with many lobes.

GILA: Gila monster, a stout, poisonous lizard covered with bead-like scales in alternating rings of black and orange.

GNAT: Tiny. Any of a number of small, two-winged insects that bite or sting.

GOLDENROD: Golden. A North American plant of the composite family, typically with long, branching stalks bearing clusters of small, yellow flowers through the later summer and autumn.

GOPHER: A pet that digs. For the small, burrowing rodent, with wide cheeks.

GORILLA: Huge. The largest and most powerful of the man-like apes, native to the jungles of equatorial Africa.

GRANGER: Land lover.

GRANITE: Grayish. Stubborn. A very hard natural rock.

GRIZZLY: Streaked with gray. A species of bear that is large and ferocious, found in western North America.

GUPPY: Small. Colorful. A tiny, brilliantly colored freshwater fish of the West Indies and other areas.

HAGOOD: Nature lover.

HALLEY: From Halley's comet, last seen in 1910 and whose periodic reappearance was predicted by English astronomer Edmund Halley (1656–1742).

HARTEBEEST: Beast. A large, swift South African antelope having long horns curved backward at the tips.

HAWK: Strong. A bird of prey.

HAYDEN: Nature lover.

HEATH: Heather.

HEATHER: (Middle English: "flowering heather") A wildflower native to the northeastern US with pinkish purple flowers.

HERMIONE: Earthy.

HICKORY: Tough, strong tree, brown-colored. Any of the North American hardwood trees of the walnut family that produce sweet edible nuts.

HOLLYHOCK: Pretty. A tall, perennial of the mallow family with spikes of showy flowers.

HONEYDEW: Sweet. A pale smooth-skinned winter melon with sweet greenish flesh.

HONEYSUCKLE: Sweet. From the climbing, twining vines with small, fragrant flowers of red, yellow, or white.

HOOSIER: Nature lover. A nickname for the state of Indiana.

HORNET: Noisy. A large wasp.

HUGO: A form of Hugh. Well-known as the name of the hurricane that swept through South Carolina in 1989.

HURRICANE: Noisy. A tropical cyclone with winds of 74 miles per hour or greater.

HYACINTH: Fragrant flowering bulb. Blue gem; blue or blue-eyed.

ICE: Frozen liquid, usually water.

IVY: Clinging. An ornamental climbing vine of the ginseng family with evergreen leaves, small yellowish flowers, and black berries.

JACINTH: A reddish orange precious stone.

JACKAL: Yellowish gray, wild dog of Asia and North Africa, smaller than a wolf.

JADE: Green-colored or green-eyed. A tough gemstone, usually green but also other colors, that can be highly polished to a glossy finish.

JAGUAR: Wild. An animal, like a huge leopard, yellowish with black spots, found in Central and South America.

JARO: Earthy.

JAROBI: Earthy.

JARON: Earthy.

JONQUILL: A variety of narcissus with yellow or white flowers and long slender leaves.

JOREL, JORG, JORN: Earthy.

JUNCO: A small American finch, with a pink bill, ashy gray head and back, and white lateral tail feathers.

JUNIPER: Tiny. A small evergreen shrub or tree of the

pine family, with scalelike foliage and berrylike cones.

KALMIA: Colorful. Any of a group of North American evergreen shrubs of the heath family, with flower clusters of white, rose, or purple.

KOALA: An Australian tree-dwelling animal with thick, gray fur.

KODIAC: A large brown bear found on Kodiac island.

KUMQUAT: A small, orange-colored, round fruit, with a sour pulp and a sweet rind, used in preserves. Golden-colored.

LADYBUG: A small flying beetle. Lucky.

LADYHAWK: Female bird.

LADY SLIPPER: A wild orchid whose flowers somewhat resemble a slipper. Also called Lady's Slipper.

LAIR, LAIRA: Wild.

LAKEN: Of the lake, stream.

LAMB: Gentle. Innocent. Woolly. A baby sheep less than a year old.

LASSEN: The name of one of the two active volcanoes in the continental United States, located in the Cascade range of Northern California.

LAVA: Gray. Ash-colored. The melted rock that erupts from a volcano that is solidified by cooling.

LAVENDER: A fragrant European plant of the mint family, having spikes of a pale purplish flowers and yielding an aromatic oil.

LEMMING: A mouselike rodent of arctic or northern regions and inhabiting tundra or open meadows. Also, from the popular video game "Lemmings."

LEMUR: Nocturnal animal with large eyes and soft fur.

LIANA: Clinging. A luxuriantly growing, woody, tropical vine that roots in the ground and climbs, as around tree trunks.

LICORICE: Candy flavored with the licorice plant, a European plant of the pea family.

LIGHTNING: Fast. A flash of light produced by a discharge of atmospheric electricity.

LIGHTNING BOLT: Fast.

LILAC: Bushy. A shrub with clusters of tiny, fragrant flowers.

LIMPET: A shellfish which clings to rocks and timbers by means of a thick, fleshy foot.

LINDEN: Golden. A tree with heart-shaped leaves and fragrant, yellowish flowers.

LION: Brave. Large wildcat with tawny-colored body and dark mane (in the male).

LIONESS: A female lion.

LITCHI: A Chinese evergreen tree.

LOBELIA: A flower. Any of the large plants with long clusters of blue, red or white flowers.

LOTUS: Dreamy. Any of several varieties of water lillies.

LYNX: Wildcat.

MAGNOLIA: Any of a group of trees or shrubs with large, fragrant flowers of white, pink, or purple. Magnolia is often associated with the South, as in the movie *Steel Magnolias.*

MAGPIE: A noisy bird of the crow family, with black-and-white coloring and a long tail.

MAIZE: Indian corn.

MALTESE: A variety of domestic cat with bluish gray fur.

MANDARIN: A small orange tree of southeastern Asia.

MANDRAKE: May apple.

MANGO: (Spanish: "good-looking lad") Golden. A yellow-red, somewhat acidic tropical fruit with a thick rind and juicy pulp.

MARIGOLD: Golden-colored. A flower with yellow to gold-colored flower heads.

MARJORAM: Any of the various plants of the mint family.

MESA: A small, high plateau with steep sides and, often, a layer of rock covering it.

MIRAGE: Elusive. A pet that is, perhaps, fleeting as a dessert mirage, an optical illusion by which distant objects can be seen.

MISTRAL: Master. A cold, dry, north wind that blows over the Mediterranean coast of France and nearby regions.

MOLE: A pet that often digs in the dirt. From the small, burrowing, insect-eating mammal with very small eyes and ears and soft fur. Moles live mainly underground.

MOONFLOWER: A pet that is up at all hours of the night. From a night-blooming plant.

MOOSE: The largest animal of the deer family, native to the northern U.S. and Canada. The name of the Jack Russell terrier that portrays Eddie in the TV series "Fraiser."

MORIAH: The wind. Rebellious.

MOSQUITO: Small; sometimes prone to bite. Insect that bites and sucks blood from its victims.

MOSS, MOSSY: Green. A plant that loves damp places. Any pet that is content or stays put.

MOUSE: Small rodents found throughout the world, especially the house mouse which infests human dwellings. Any pet that resembles a mouse.

MUDPUPPY: A puppy or dog that frequents mud puddles. From a North American salamander that lives in mud under water.

MUM: Quiet, motherly. Shortened name for the flower chrysanthemum.

MYRTLE: Pretty. A shrub with evergreen leaves, white or pink flowers, and dark berries.

NANOOK: Wild dog of the north.

NEBULA: Any of the cloud-like patches seen in the night sky. A pet that seems distant.

NESTLING: A baby bird.

NEWT: Any of the small amphibious salamanders. Also, short for Newton.

NIGHTHAWK: A night owl. Any pet that stays up nights.

NIKKO: The name of a variety of hydrangea.

NUTMEG: The hard, aromatic kernel of the seed of an East Indian tree from which a spice is made. A pet that is spicy-tempered or brown-colored.

OASIS: Sanctuary. A fertile place in the desert, due to the presence of water.

OCEANA: Of the ocean.

ONYX: Black-colored. A type of agate with alternate layers of color.

OPAL: A glassy, translucent silica of various colors that can refract light and then reflect it in a play of colors; some types are semiprecious stones. A precious pet.

ORCA: A killer whale. A good name for a pet fish.

ORCHID: Any of several related plants having flowers with three petals, one of which is enlarged and irregularly shaped.

ORRIS: A plant of the iris

family, having fragrant roots.

OZONE: Pure ozone is an unstable faintly bluish gas with a characteristic fresh, penetrating odor. The most chemically active form of oxygen, ozone is formed in the ozone layer of the stratosphere. A name for a pet that loves the outdoors.

PANDA: A white-and-black, bearlike animal of Asia.

PANSY: (Greek: "fragrant") An early spring flowering garden plant.

PANTHER: A black leopard.

PASSION FLOWER: Heart's delight. A plant with variously colored flowers and yellow egglike fruit, passion fruit.

PEACH: Slang for any person or thing that is well liked. Also, a small tree with pink blossoms that produces fruit with a fuzzy skin. From the starfish voiced by Allison Janney in the Disney animated movie *Finding Nemo*.

PEARL: A gem. A smooth, hard, usually white or bluish gray, roundish growth, formed around a foreign body within the shell of some oysters and other mollusks.

PEBBLE: A small, smooth stone.

PECAN: An olive shaped, brown-colored nut with a thin shell. A pet that is tan or brown. The name of a golden-colored Beanie Baby bear.

PENGUIN: Any of various short-legged, flightless aquatic birds. A pet that wobbles when walking.

PEONY: Greek name for Apollo, the god of medicine. Also, any of a group of plants with large pink, white red, or yellow, showy flowers.

PERIWINKLE: Slow-moving. A creeping plant with evergreen leaves and white or blue flowers.

PINEAPPLE: A juicy, edible tropical fruit somewhat resembling a pine cone. Also, slang for a small explosive such as a hand grenade.

PINON: Tall as a pine. Any of certain pine trees with large, edible seeds.

PIRANAH: A pet that bites. Small South American fish that has very sharp teeth.

PLUM: Small. Any of several trees having smooth-skinned fruit with a smooth pit.

POINCIANA: Colorful. Any

of various related tropical trees with beautiful red, orange, or yellow flowers.

POINSETTIA: A plant with large scarlet or pink leaves often displayed at Christmas.

POPPY: Spirited. Any of certain related plants with deeply cut leaves, milky or colored juice, and variously colored flowers. A very active, playful pet.

PORCUPINE: Prickly. A gnawing animal having coarse hair mixed with long, stiff, sharp spines.

POTAMUS: Short for hippopotamus, a large plant-eating mammal of the hog family.

PRIMROSE: Any of a number of related plants having variously, tubelike flowers. A yellowish color. Golden.

PUFFIN: Puffy. A sea bird with a short neck and deep grooved multicolored bill.

PUMA: A tawny-brown cat animal of the cat family, with a long, slender body.

PUMPKIN: A large, round, orange-yellow, edible gourd-like fruit with many seeds. A large pet.

QUICKSILVER: Mercury.

RACCOON: A small, flesh-eating, tree-climbing mammal of North America, active at night and having long yellow-black fur and a long, black-ringed tail. A pet that resembles a raccoon.

RAINBOW: Beautifully colored. The arc containing the colors of the spectrum in consecutive bands, formed in the sky by the refraction, reflection, and dispersion of the sun's rays in falling rain or mist.

RAM: A male sheep.

RASPBERRY: Dark. Any of a group of prickly shrubs of the rose family.

RAVEN: Dark. A large bird of the crow family, with lustrous black feathers and a sharp peak, and said to have a voracious appetite.

RAVENA: Earthy, somber.

REDBUD: A tree with small, pink, budlike flowers. A tiny pet.

RHINO: Nose. Short for rhinoceros, a large thick-skinned, plant-eating mammal of Africa and Asia, with one or two upright horns on the snout.

RIPTIDE: Rough. A strong

current flowing out from the shore.

RODENT: A pet that gnaws. Rodents are any of several small animals including rats, mice, rabbits, squirrels, etc.

ROOSTER: The male of the domestic chicken. A pet that wakes you up every morning promptly at the break of dawn.

ROSE: A thorny shrub bearing flowers in various colors.

ROSEMARY: A fragrant evergreen shrub.

ROWAN: The mountain ash, a tree with white flowers and reddish berries.

RUBY: (Old French) A deep red, valued precious stone. Tennis great Martina Navratilova has a dog with this name.

SAGO: A small palm tree. An exotic pet.

SALMON: A game and food fish of the North Atlantic, with silver scales. Any pet that loves to eat fish or other seafood.

SAMARA: A dry, hard, winged fruit as of the elm or ash. A protective pet.

SAPPHIRE: Deep-blue. A brilliant blue precious stone.

SARSAPARILLA: (Spanish: "bramble vine") A tropical American plant with fragrant roots used as a flavoring.

SASSAFRAS: A slender tree with yellow flowers and bluish fruit. The roots of the tree are used in medicine and as a flavoring.

SEASON: Nature lover. A time of year characterized by change of temperature and other circumstances.

SEGO: Flower. A perennial bulb plant with trumpet-shaped flowers.

SERPENT: A snake.

SHAD: Short for Shadrac. Any of several saltwater fishes related to the herring but spawning in rivers.

SHAMMY: Chamois, a small goatlike antelope of the mountains of Europe and southwestern Asia. Fawn colored, soft.

SHAMROCK: The national emblem of Ireland. Any of certain clovers with leaflets in threes. The four-leaf clover is considered to be lucky. Also, the name of Mickey Mouse's detective friend, Shamrock Bones, in Disney cartoons.

SHARK: Vicious. Any of several large fishes, mostly marine, with a tough, slate-gray skin.

SHARON: From rose of Sharon, the althea, a tall shrub of the mallow family with beautiful flowers.

SHELL: Of the water, ocean.

SHORA: Water lover.

SILK: The fine, soft and shiny fiber produced by silkworms and woven into a fabric. A pet with fine, soft hair that glistens.

SILVANA: From the forest.

SILVIO: Lover of nature, the forest.

SKYLARK: The Old World lark, famous for the song it utters as it soars toward the sky. A pet that plays boisterously, frolics.

SNAIL: Slow-moving or lazy. From the gastropod mollusk living on land or in water and having a short, thick, worm-like body and a protective, usually spiral shell.

SNAPDRAGON: Colorful. Any of various plants with white, yellow, red, or purplish, two-lipped flowers.

SNOOK: A prized food and sport fish.

SOCKEYE: A red salmon of the north Pacific.

SONGBIRD: Any bird that chirps a tune.

SPARROW: Any of several small finches, especially the common small bird the house sparrow.

SPIDER: Any of various small arachnids with a body composed of a cephalothorax bearing four pairs of legs and an abdomen bearing spinnerets used to spin the silk threads for webs to trap insects. A pet that seems to be all legs. From the comic book hero Spiderman, who has characteristics of a spider.

SPINDRIFT: A spray blown from a rough sea or surf.

STEPPENWOLF: Prairie wolf.

STING RAY: A large ray having a whiplike tail with sharp spines capable of inflicting severe wounds.

SUNBEAM: A beam of sunlight, golden.

SUNFLOWER: Any of the tall plants having yellow, daisy-like flowers with disks that contain edible seeds. A golden-colored pet with long legs. Happy, carefree.

SWEET PEA: A popular plant with slender climbing steams and large fragrant flowers.

SYEEDA: Forest maiden.

SYLER: Forest lover.

SYLVIO: Forest lover.

SYRINGA: Pleasant. Any of the lilacs.

TADPOLE: Tiny. The larva of certain amphibians, such as frogs and toads, having gills and a tail and living in water.

TANGERINE: Reddish yellow color. A citrus fruit with a deep orange skin.

TARO: A tropical plant of the arum family, with a starchy, tuberous root that is edible.

TEQUILA: A plant of Mexico.

TERRANCE: Earthy.

TERRELL: Earthy.

TERRELLE: Earthy.

TERREN: Earthy.

THUNDER: The sound that follows a flash of lightning, caused by the sudden disturbance of air by electrical discharge. A very noisy pet.

THUNDERCLAP: The sound of thunder. Sudden noise.

TIGER: A large carnivorous animal of the cat family with a striped, irregular pattern.

TIGRESS: A female tiger.

TITI: (Prounced "tee tee") A tree of the southeastern United States with leathery leaves and white, fragrant flowers.

TOPAZ: A gem. Golden-colored.

TORNADO: A whirlwind; a disruptive, rambunctious pet.

TORPEDO: Temperamental; disruptive. An electric ray (fish). Any of various explosive devices used as underwater mines, in oil-well drilling, and the like.

TORTOISE: Slow-moving. A turtle, especially one that lives on land.

TOURMALINE: Rare, precious. A mineral that is a gem when transparent.

T-REX: Short for the dinosaur Tyrannosaurus Rex.

TROGON: A brightly colored tropical bird.

TULIP: A flower that blooms in the spring, named for its turban-shaped flower.

TUNDRA: Distant. Any of the vast, nearly level, treeless plains of the arctic.

TUPELO: Little. Any of various trees with small, greenish flowers and blue or purple fruit.

TURTLE: Like or resembling a turtle. Any of various land and water reptiles having a toothless beak and a soft body encased in a hard shell.

TYPHOON: A cyclone; a pet that is disruptive, rambunctious.

VALLEE: Of the valley. A pet that loves the outdoors.

VERBENA: Any of various plants with spikes or clusters of red, white, or purplish flowers.

VIOLA: A violet. A plant with white, yellow or purple flowers that resemble small pansies.

VIOLET: (Latin: "violet flower") Early spring blooming plant with light blue to deep purple flowers.

VIPER: Malicious. A snake belonging to either of two groups of venomous snakes: true vipers or pit vipers.

WALAPAI: Forest lover.

WALDEN: From Henry David Thoreau's Walden Wood, immortalized in his book *Walden*.

WALLABY: A small kanga-

roo, sometimes as small as a rabbit.

WALRUS: A massive sea animal, having two tusks protruding from the upper jaw, a thick mustache, a thick hide, and a heavy layer of blubber.

WATER LILY: Any of various plants having large, flat, floating leaves and beautiful flowers in many colors. A good name for a fish or other water pet.

WEASEL: Cunning. An agile mammal, with a long, slender body, short legs, and a long, bushy tail.

WHALE: A large, warm-blooded fishlike sea mammal that breathes air and bears live young.

WHITE BEAR: White and large as a polar bear.

WILDFLOWER: Beautifully wild. Any of a large number of native species of flowering plants.

WILDWOOD: Forest dweller; nature lover.

WILLOW: Sorrowful. Any of various trees with narrow leaves and tassel-like spikes of flowers.

WINKLE: Short for periwinkle, any of the small salt water snails.

WINTER: A distance, moody pet. The season that follows autumn. Winter is the coldest season.

WISTERIA: Beautiful flower. A twining shrub of the pea family, with clusters of bluish, white, or purplish flowers.

WOLF: A wild, doglike mammal. Slang for to eat ravenously.

YAK: A long-haired Asiatic ox.

YARROW: An herb with a strong scent and white flowers.

YUCCA: A plant of the lily family, with stiff, sword-shaped leaves and white flowers. A pet that is white or lightly colored.

YURI: Land-lover.

ZEPHYR: The western wind; a gentle, soft breeze. A calm, serene pet.

ZINNIA: A colorful pet. A show-off. The zinnia is a plant having showy yellow or red flowers.

Did You Know?

PISTON: (Latin: "to pound") A rough, pounding pet. The name of ice skater/Gold Medalist Kristi Yamaguchi's Rat Toy Fox Terrier.

MISTE: Mist. Pop superstar Whitney Houston has a cat with this name.

MARLOW, MARLOWE: Known for the tough, honorable detective Phillip Marlowe in the brutally realistic novels by American writer Raymond Chandler, whose books include *The Big Sleep*. The master of horror and suspense novels, Stephen King, has a Pembroke Welsh Corgi with this name.

Dandelion & LuLu

Dido & Calliope

Chapter 16

Mythology and Tall Tales

Myths, legends and tall tales can inspire interesting pet names that have a larger-than-life appeal when you think of the stories and history attached to the names - like *Phoenix*, a beautiful bird that rose from the ashes and *Sir Galahad*, a knight in Arthurian legend, who was so pure and noble he was successful in his quest for the Holy Grail, among many others.

ADONIS: Handsome. In Greek mythology, a young man loved by Aphrodite.

AEGIR: In Norse mythology, the god of the sea.

AENEAS: In Greek and Roman legend, a Trojan warrior who escaped from ruined Troy and wandered for years before coming to Latium.

AEOLUS: In Greek mythology, the god of the winds.

AESCULAPIUS: In Roman mythology, the god of medicine and healing.

ALPHRODITE: In Greek mythology, the goddess of love and beauty.

AMARANTH: In poetic terms, an imaginary flower that never fades or dies.

AMAZON: Large, strong. In Greek mythology, a female warrior of a race supposed to have lived in Scythia, near the Black Sea. Also, a river in South America, flowing from the Andes in Peru, across northern Brazil into the Atlantic.

AMBROSIA: Immortal. In Greek and Roman mythology, the food of the gods.

ANDROMEDA: In Greek mythology, an Ethiopian princess whom Perseus rescued from a sea monster and then married. Also, in astronomy, a northern constellation south of Cassiopeia.

APOLLO: In Greek and Roman mythology, the god of music, poetry, prophecy, and medicine, later identified with Helios, a sun god. Also, a series of space missions launched during the years from 1968 to 1973 in the U.S. Also, the name of one of the pair of vicious Dobermans featured in the TV series "Magnum, P.I.," which starred actor Tom Selleck.

ARES: In Greek mythology, the Olympian god of war.

ARGO: In Greek legend, the ship which Jason sailed on to find the Golden Fleece. Also a large southern constellation.

ARGUS: In Greek mythology, a giant with a hundred eyes, who was killed by Hermes. An alert watcher.

ARIADNE: In Greek legend King Minos' daughter, the princess who gave Theseus the thread by which he found his way out of the Minotaur's labyrinth.

ARTEMIS: In Greek mythology, goddess of the moon and hunting.

ASGARD: In Norse mythology, the home of the gods and slain heroes.

ASHTORETH: The Phoenician goddess of love, war and fertility.

ASHUR: God of war and empire.

ASTARTE: The Phoenician goddess of fertility and love.

ATALANTA: In Greek legend, a beautiful, swift-footed maiden who offered to marry any man able to defeat her in a race.

ATHENA: In Greek myth, the goddess of wisdom, skills, and warfare.

ATLANTIS: A legendary island or continent in the Atlantic Ocean west of Gibraltar, supposed to have sunk into the ocean.

ATLAS: In Greek legend, a giant who supported the heavens on his shoulders.

ATROPOS: In Greek mythology, that one of the three Fates who cuts the thread of life.

AUGEAS: In Greek legend, a king whose stables Hercules cleaned in one day.

AURORA: In Greek and Roman mythology, the goddess of

dawn.

BALDER: Beautiful and gracious Norse god of light.

BAST: The Egyptian Goddess of Matrimony and Feminine Sensuality.

BIGFOOT: Large, furry. The legendary, humanlike creature supposedly sighted in the Pacific Northwest. This creature was called Sasquatch by Native Americans.

BLUEBEARD: A legendary character in a folk tale.

BOREAS: In Greek, mythology the god of the north wind.

BUNYAN: For Paul Bunyan, the legendary American lumberjack of fantastic size and strength, hero of of many "tall tales" in the Western timber country. His prized possession was the huge Babe the Blue Ox, whose horns were 42 ax handles apart.

CADMUS: In Greek legend, a Phoenician prince who killed a dragon and sowed its teeth.

CALLIOPE: In Greek mythology, the Muse of eloquence and epic poetry.

CASSANDRA: (Greek: "helper of men, disbelieved by men") In Greek legend, Priam's prophetic daughter, whose prophecies, Apollo decreed, should never be believed.

CASSIOPEIA: In Greek legend, the mother of Andromeda.

CERES: In Greek and Roman mythology, the goddess of agriculture.

CHLOE: (Greek: "blooming") The goddess of green grain in Greek mythology.

CORYBANT: In Greek mythology, an attendant of the goddess Cybele.

CRONUS: In Greek mythology, the youngest Titan; son of Uranus and Gaea.

CUPID: The Roman god of love and son of Venus. Also, the name of one of Santa's eight reindeer.

CYBELE: Showy. In Greek mythology, the goddess of nature.

CYCLOPS: In Greek mythology, one of a race of giants living in Sicily, who had a single eye, centered in the forehead. The name of one of the "X-Men" in the animated TV and movie series.

CYNTHIA: The goddess of the moon.

CYNTHIE: A form of Cynthia: The goddess of the moon.

DAEDALUS: In Greek legend, the skillful artist and inventor who built the labyrinth in Crete.

DAEMON: In Greek mythology, any of the secondary divinities ranking below the gods.

DAMOCLES: In Greek legend, a courtier of ancient Syracuse to whom the king, Dionysius, demonstrated the dangers of a ruler's life by seating him at a banquet just below a sword hanging by a hair.

DAMON: In Roman legend, friends Damon and Pythias were so devoted to each other that when Pythias was condemned to death and wanted time to arrange his affairs, Damon pledged his life that his friend would return; Pythias did return.

DANAUS: In Greek legend, a king of Argos.

DEMETER: In Greek mythology, goddess of the harvest and fertility.

DIANA: (Latin: "divine") In Roman mythology, the goddess of the moon and the hunt. Also, for Diana, the late Princess of Wales.

DIDO: In Roman legend, the founder and queen of Carthage.

DIONYSUS: The Greek god of vegetation.

DRAGON: A mythical creature, usually represented as a large reptile with wings and claws, breathing out fire and smoke. The name of a character in the animated movie *The Secret of NIMH.*

ECHO: Any pet that seems to mimic sounds when spoken to. In Greek mythology, a mountain nymph.

ELECTRA: Bright. In Greek mythology, the daughter of Agamemnon and Clytemnestra. The name of Cathy's small dog in the syndicated comic strip by Cathy Guisewite.

ELF: In folklore, a small fairy, supposedly exercising magic powers and inhabiting woods and hills.

ENDYMION: In Greek legend, a beautiful young shepherd loved by Selene.

EOS: The Greek goddess of dawn.

ERATO: In Greek mythology,

the Muse of lyric and love poetry.

ERIS: In Greek mythology, the goddess of strife and discord.

EROS: In Greek mythology, the god of love.

EUCLID: Greek mathematician who lived in the third century B.C.

EUROPA: In Greek mythology, a Phoenician princess loved by Zeus who, taking on the form of a white bull, carried her off to Crete.

EXCALIBUR: In Arthurian legend, King Arthur's sword.

FAUNA: Goddess. The sister of Faunus, the Roman god of animals. The animal life of a given region, time, or environment.

FAUNUS: The Roman god of animals.

FLORA: Colorful. In Roman mythology, the goddess of flowers.

GAEA: In Greek mythology, the earth personified as a goddess.

GALAHAD: In Arthurian legend, a knight, referred to as Sir Galahad, who was successful in his quest for the Holy Grail

because of his purity, nobility.

GALATEA: In Greek legend, the statue of a maiden with whom the sculptor, Pygmalion, fell in love.

GANYMEADE: In Greek mythology, a beautiful youth who was a cupbearer to the gods.

GAWAIN: In Arthurian legend, a knight of the Round Table, nephew of King Arthur.

GENIE: Mythical spirit with magical powers.

GNOME: (Greek: "thought") In folklore, a dwarf said to dwell in the earth and guard its treasures. From the characters in books by author J.R.R. Tolkien. Also from the animated TV series "David the Gnome."

GOBLIN: In folklore, a mischievous elf.

GORGON: In Greek mythology, any of three sisters who turned onlookers to stone.

GRIFFIN: Fabulous. In Greek mythology, an animal with the head and wings of an eagle and the body of a lion.

GRISELDA: Resolute. In medieval romance, a heroine famous for her patience.

GRYPHON: A griffin: in Greek mythology, an animal with the head and wings of an eagle and the body of a lion.

GUINEVERE: In Arthurian legend, the wife of King Arthur.

GUNNAR, GUNNER: In Norse mythology, the husband of Brynhild. Warrior.

HELEN: Bright. In Greek mythology, the most beautiful of women.

HELIOS: In Greek mythology, the sun god.

HERA: In Greek mythology, the wife of Zeus, queen of the gods, and the goddess of marriage.

HERCULES: (Greek: "glorious gift") In Greek and Roman mythology, a hero renowned for feats of strength; the most popular of Greek heroes, famous for strength and courage.

HERMES: In Greek mythology, a god who served as a messenger to the other gods.

HESTIA: In Greek mythology, the goddess of the hearth.

ICARUS: In Greek legend, the son of Daedalus: escaping from Crete by flying with wings made by Daedalus, Icarus flew so high that the sun's heat melted the wax by which his wings were fastened, and he fell to the sea.

IO: In Greek mythology, a maiden loved by Zeus.

IPHIGENIA: In Greek mythology, a daughter of Agamemnon, offered by him to Artemis but saved by a goddess.

IRIS: (Greek: "a rainbow") In Greek mythology, the goddess of the rainbow and a messenger to the gods.

ISHTAR: Babylonia and Assyrian goddess of love and fertility.

ISIS: The Egyptian goddess of fertility.

JANUS: In Roman mythology, the god who was guardian of portals and patron of beginnings and endings.

JASON: (Greek: "healer") In Greek legend, a prince who lead the Argonauts and got the Golden Fleece.

JOHN: Gracious. For John Adams, 2nd President of the United States. Also for the legendary black American famous for his strength and who is celebrated in ballads and tales. In one version of the story, John Henry tries to outwork a steam drill and succeeds, but he dies from the strain. The legend may have some historical basis.

JOHNNY: Nickname for John. Gracious. For American pioneer John Chapman, popularly known as Johnny Appleseed. He wandered for 40 years through Ohio, Indiana, and western Pennsylvania, sowing apple seeds, and inspired many legends.

JOSS: A god. The figure of a Chinese god.

JOTUNN, JOTUN: In Norse mythology, a giant.

JUNO: In Roman mythology, the goddess of marriage, Jupiter's wife and queen of the gods.

JUPITER: In Roman mythology, the supreme god. Also, the name of the fifth planet and largest in our solar system.

LADY GODIVA: Independent minded.

LADY GUINEVERE: In Arthurian legend, the wife of King Arthur.

LANCELOT: (Old German:

"land") In Arthurian legend, the most celebrated of the Knights of the Round Table: Sir Lancelot.

LAR: A god or spirit associated with Lares and Penates, the guardians of the house or household gods.

LARES: From "Lares and Penates," the guardians of the house or household gods of the ancient Romans. The treasured belongings of a family or household.

LEDA: Slow-moving. In Greek mythology, the wife of Tyndareus, King of Sparta.

LEPRECHAUN: In Irish folklore, a fairy in the form of a little old man who can reveal hidden treasure to anyone who catches him. John F. Kennedy, the 35th President of the United States, had a pony with this name.

LOHENGRIN: In German legend, a knight of the Holy Grail. Also, the title character in an opera by Richard Wagner.

LOKI: In Norse mythology, the god who constantly created discord and mischief.

LORELEI: Beautiful. In German legend, a siren whose singing on a rock in the Rhine lured sailors to shipwreck on the reefs. Also, the name of the family dog who witnesses the death of her mistress in the novel *The Dogs of Babel* by Carolyn Parkhurst.

MATIN: Goddess of dawn.

MEDEA: In Greek legend a sorceress who helped Jason get the Golden Fleece.

MEDUSSA: In Greek mythology, one of the three Gorgons.

MELEAGER: Hero of Greek mythology.

MENELAUS: In Greek legend, a king of Sparta.

MERCURY: In Roman mythology, the god of commerce and messenger of the gods. The planet in our solar system that is closest to the sun.

MERLIN: In medieval legend, a magician, seer, and helper of King Arthur in the land of Camelot. The name of a dog, a Queensland Heeler (Australian Cattle Dog), in Purina Dog Chow Incredible Dog Team, precision-trained dogs that travel the country performing at halftime shows, on televi-sion programs and a variety of other public events.

MERMAID: Sea maiden. A legendary sea creature with the head and trunk of a beautiful woman and the tail of a fish. Also, a reference to a young girl or lady who swims well.

MIDAS: In Greek legend, the king of Phrygia to whom Dionysus granted the power of turning everything he touched into gold.

MINERVA: The ancient Roman goddess of wisdom, technical skill, and invention.

MINOS: In Greek mythology, King Minos.

MINOTAUR: In Greek mythology a beast shaped half like a man and half like a bull.

MORPHEUS: In Greek mythology, the god of dreams, son of the god of sleep.

MUSE: In Greek mythology, any of nine goddesses who presided over literature and the arts and sciences.

NAIAD: A water maiden of springs and streams.

NARSISSUS: In Greek mythology, a beautiful youth who pined away for love of his own reflection.

NEMESIS: In Greek mythology, the goddess of retribution.
NEREID: In Greek mythology, a sea maiden, one of the fifty daughters of Nereus.
NEREUS: In Greek mythology, a sea god.
NESTOR: In Greek legend, a wise old counselor who fought with the Greeks at Troy.
NIKE: In Greek mythology, the winged goddess of victory.
NIX, NIXIE: In German folklore, a water sprite.
NYX: In Greek mythology, the goddess of night.
OBERON: In early folklore, the king of fairyland and husband of Titania.
OCEANUS: A Titan who rules over a great river encircling the earth in Greek mythology.
ODIN: In Norse mythology, the supreme god.
OEDIPUS: In Greek legend, a king of Thebes.
OLYMPIA: A plain in ancient Greece, site of the Olympic games. An athletic pet.
OLYMPUS: Heavenly. In Greek mythology, the home of the Olympian gods.
ORESTES: In Greek legend,

brother of Electra.
ORPHEUS: In Greek mythology, a musician with magic ability on the lyre.
OURANOS: A male god, in Greek mythology, who symbolized "heaven."
PALLAS: In Greek mythology, Athena, the goddess of wisdom.
PANDORA: (Greek: "all-gifted") In Greek mythology, the first mortal woman. The fictitious name (*Pandora Spocks*) used by actress Elizabeth Montgomery in the series' credits when she played the character *Serena* in her TV series " Bewitched." Actor Clayton Moore, best known as the "Lone Ranger," had a Persian cat with this name.
PEGASUS: In Greek mythology, a winged horse, a symbol of poetic inspiration. Also, a northern constellation. A pet that is inspiring, poetic in behavior or movements.
PELE: The Hawaiian goddess of fire.
PENATES: Of "Lares and Penates," the household gods of the ancient Romans. The treasured belongings of a family or

household.

PERSEUS: In Greek mythology, the son of Zeus.

PHAEDRA: In Greek legend, the wife of Theseus.

PHAETHON: In Greek and Roman mythology, the son of Helios.

PHOEBUS: In Greek mythology, Apollo, god of the sun.

PHOENIX: In Egyptian mythology, a beautiful bird that lived for 500 years and was consumed by fire, then rose from the ashes. A symbol of immortality.

POSEIDON: In Greek religion, god of the sea, protector of all waters.

PROCRUSTES: In Greek mythology, a giant.

PSYCHE: Soulful. In Greek mythology, a maiden who becomes the wife of Cupid and is made immortal; she personifies the soul.

PYGMALION: In Greek legend, a sculptor who fell in love with his stature of a maiden, Galatea, later brought to life by Aphrodite.

PYTHIAS: In Roman legend, friends Pythias and Damon were so devoted to each other that when Pythias was condemned to death and wanted time to arrange his affairs, Damon pledged his life that his friend would return: Pythias returned.

RA: The sun god, principal god of the ancient Egyptians.

REMUS: In Roman mythology, the brother of Romulus the King who with his brother was raised by a wolf.

RHADAMANTHUS: In Greek mythology, a son of Zeus.

RHEA: Mother of the gods. In Greek mythology, the daughter of Uranus and Gaea.

ROBIN: Bright fame. From Robin Hood who, in English legend, was an outlaw who lived with his followers in the Sherwood Forest and robbed the rich to help the poor. For Robin Goodfellow, a mischievous elf in English folklore. Also the name of superhero Batman's sidekick.

ROMULUS: In Roman mythology, the founder and first king of Rome. He and his brother were raised by a wolf.

SASQUATCH: Large, furry. The legendary, human-like

creature, called Sasquatch by Native Americans, and supposedly sighted in the Pacific Northwest.

SELENE: The Greek goddess of the moon.

SIEGFRIED: The hero of several German legends. In the Nibelungenlied, he wins a treasure, kills a dragon, and rescues Brunhild.

SIGURD: In Norse legend, a hero identified with Siegfried.

SIR GALAHAD: In Arthurian legend, a knight who was successful in the quest for the Holy Grail because of his purity and nobility.

SIR LANCELOT: In Arthurian legend, the most celebrated of the Knights of the Round Table.

SISYPHUS: In Greek mythology, a greedy king.

SPHINX: An Egyptian statue having a lion's body and the head of a man, ram, or hawk. In Greek mythology, a winged beast.

TANTALUS: In Greek mythology, a king whose punishment was to stand in water that always receded when he tried to drink it and under

branches of fruit that rose when he reached for them.

TATIANA: Mythical.

THALIA: Spirited, lively. In Greek mythology, the muse of comedy and pastoral poetry.

THESEUS: In Greek legend, the principal hero of Attica, king of Athens.

THETIS: In Greek mythology, Achilles' mother.

TITAN: In Greek mythology, any of a race of giants, who were overthrown and succeeded by the Olympian gods.

TITANIA: In early folklore, the queen of fairyland.

TOM THUMB: The tiny hero of many English folk tales.

TRITON: God of water. In Greek mythology, a sea god. The name of Ariel's father, a sea king, in the animated movie and TV series *The Little Mermaid.*

TROILUS: In Greek legend, a son of King Priam. In Shakespeare and Chaucer, Troilus was the lover of the faithless Cressida.

TROLL: (Old Norse: "a wanderer") In Scandinavian folklore, any of a rare of supernatural beings, such as giants and dwarfs living underground in caves.

TYR: In Norse mythology, the god of war.

URANIA: In Greek mythology, the Muse of astronomy.

VENUS: The Roman goddess of love. The second largest planet in our solar system.

VESTA: In Roman mythology, the goddess of the hearth and the hearth fire.

VULCAN: In Roman mythology, the god of fire and of metalworking.

WEREWOLF: Wolflike. In folklore a person changed into a wolf or one who can assume the form of a wolf at will.

WODAN, WODEN: The chief Germanic god.

XANADU: Mythical kingdom.

YETI: The name of the unconfirmed species to which the abominable snowman, a long-haired, manlike creature, is supposed to belong.

Did You Know?

HARRY: Billy Bob Thornton bought Angelina Jolie (star of the *Lara Croft* movie series) a pet rat as a gift; they named the rat *Harry* - even though the rat is a girl!

MISHA: Russian form of Michael, meaning "God-like." The name of a dog in the bestselling book *The Hidden Life of Dogs* by Elizabeth Marshall Thomas. Melissa Joan Hart (the star of Sabrina, the Teenage Witch) has a dog, a husky, with this name.

WEEJIE: Herbert Hoover, the 31st President of the United States, had an elkhound with this name.

Brisby

Darius

Chapter 17

Royalty and Military

Names for new pets can be inspired by **Royalty** (*Cleopatra, Fergie, Princess Diana*) **Titles** (*King, Queen, Duke, Duchess*), and the **Military** (*Digsby, El Cid, Patton*).

ADAR: Prince, ruler.
ADMIRAL: Commander.
AMEER, AMIR: King or prince.
ANTONY: Roman general who, with Cleopatra, was a part of one of the most romantic couples of all-time.
ARMAND: Soldier, fighter.
ARMANDO: Soldier, fighter.
ARMON: Fighter.
AVERIL: Ruler. Warrior.
AWOL: Absent without permission.
BALLAN: Mighty soldier.
BARON: A nobleman on the continent of Europe of varying rank.
BARONESS: Of nobility. The wife of a baron.
BASIA: Royal.
BRIGADIER: Brigadier General, a commissioned officer in the army, marine corps or air force who ranks above a colonel and whose insignia is one star.
BUSHIDO: A Japanese military code of behavior.
CADET: Behaved. One in training for a military or naval commission.
CANUTE: A king.
CAPTAIN: Commander.
CHEOPS: King.
CHIEF: Leader.
CHUCK: Strong. Often a reference of jest to England's Prince Charles. A nickname for Charles.
CLEONY: Royalty.
CLEOPATRA: Egyptian queen who is often referred to as the "queen of the Nile," one

of the great romantic heroines of history.

COLONEL: Leader.

COMMANDER: Leader.

COMMANDO: A warrior.

COMMISSAR: Russian leader.

COMRAD: Fellow soldier.

CONTESSA: Noble.

CORONA: (Latin) Crown.

COUNT: Noble. A man holding the title of earl or count.

COUNTESS: Noble. A woman who holds rank as an earl or count or is married to or widowed by an earl or count.

COUNTESSA: Noble.

CYRUS: Cyrus the Great, a Persian king.

CZAR: Commander; emperor.

DARIEL: Royalty.

DARIEN: Royalty.

DARIUS: Royalty; a Persian king.

DAUPHINE: Royalty.

DIGSBY: English naval commander, diplomat and author Sir Kenelim Digsby.

DUCHESS: The wife or widow of duke.

DUKE: A nobleman of the highest hereditary rank.

EL CID: Spanish soldier and hero.

EMPEROR: The sovereign or supreme male monarch of an empire.

EMPRESS: A woman who is the sovereign or supreme monarch of an empire.

EXCELSIOR: The highest of excellence.

FABIOLA: Queen of King Baudouin I of Belgium.

FERGIE: Nickname for the Duchess of York, Sarah Fergusen, the ex-wife of England's Prince Andrew.

GENERAL: A commissioned officer in the military who ranks above a lieutenant general and whose insignia is four stars.

GILROY: Knight.

GLADIATOR: Warrior.

HARTLEY: Royal.

HEZEKIAH: King.

HIGHNESS: A title for a person of rank as a king or queen.

HYDER: Indian ruler and soldier, Ali Hyder.

IVAN: Russian form of John. For Ivan the Terrible, a grand duke of Moscow, who had himself crowned a czar and engaged Russia in several unsuccessful wars.

JACOBEAN: Name for James

I of England.
JEHOSAPHAT: Righteous
of the great romantic heroines
of history.
JUDGE: A public official who
rules on questions brought before a court.
KAISER: (Latin) King.
KAISHA: Royalty.
KEPI: A cap with a flat, round
top and stiff visor, worn by
French soldiers.
KING: Supreme. A male
monarch of a major territory.
KINGSLEY: Kinglike.
KING TUT: For the famous
Egyptian boy king, whose
mummy was discovered with
many treasures.
KNIGHT: (Anglo-Saxon:
"boy") In the Middle Ages, a
military attendant of the king
or other feudal superior. Later
a man of high birth and chivalrous conduct. A lady's devoted
companion or attendant.
KUMA: Prince.
KUMAR: (Indian) "prince."
LADY DI: Short for Lady Diana, the late Princess of Wales.
LANCER: A soldier.
LEADER: Commander in
charge, whether a king, other
dignitary or a military supe-

rior. Elizabeth Dole, North
Carolina senator, had a miniature schnauzer with this name.
LERDY: (Old French) "king."
LEROY: A king.
LIEUTENANT: A commis-
sioned officer in the army,
marines, air force or coast
guard ranking above a lieu-
tenant junior grade and below a
lieutenant commander.
MADAME: A title for a mar-
ried woman not of English-
speaking nationality.
MADEMOISELLE: An un-
married French girl or woman.
MAHARAJA: Great king.
MAHARANI: Great queen.
MAJESTY: Sovereign power,
authority, or dignity.
MAJOR: Of great importance.
A military officer in the United
States Army, Air Force, or
Marines. Franklin Delano Roo-
sevelt, the 32nd President of the
United States, had a German
Shepherd with this name.
MAJORDOMO: Male in
charge, especially in a royal
household.
MASTER: Ruler.
MIGHTY MO: Known as the
nickname of the U.S.S. Mis-
souri, one of the United States

Navy's battleships.

MIKADO: Japanese emperor, but also used as a title for non-Japanese.

MING: Ruler.

MISS: A title for an unmarried woman or girl.

MISTER: A title for a married or unmarried man or boy.

MONARCH: Noble ruler; royalty as a king, queen, emperor.

PASHA: A man of high rank or office.

PATTON: American General George Smith Patton.

PHARAOH: A ruler of ancient Egypt.

PRESIDENT: Leader; commander-in-chief. Franklin Delano Roosevelt, the 32nd President of the United States, had a Great Dane with this name.

PRINCE: (Latin: "chief") Royal. A classic name for dogs. The former name of a popular singer and actor who starred in and recorded a soundtrack for the movie *Purple Rain.* Also for England's Prince Charles, among others.

PRINCELING: A small, young prince.

PRINCESS: Royal miss. For England's late Princess Diana, among others.

PRINCESSA: Royal.

QUEEN: The wife or widow of a king.

QUEENIE: Regal.

QUENBY: Regal.

RAINIER: For Prince Rainier of Monaco.

RAJ: Ruler.

RAJA, RAJAH: Authoritative. A prince or ruler in India.

RANI: In India, a reigning queen or princess.

REGAL: (Latin) "kingly."

REGAN: Royal.

REGANNA: Royal.

REGIA: Kingly.

REGIME: A pet that rules.

REXFORD: Kingly.

REXI, REXY: Kingly.

RICARDO: Strong king.

ROYA: Royal.

ROYAL: A king or a queen.

SADA: Princess.

SAL: Prince.

SAMURAI: A Japanese warrior practicing the code and conduct of the Bushido.

SARELLE: Princess.

SARGE: Short for sergeant.

SARITA, SERITA: A princess.

SENTINEL: One who guards a group against attack.
SERGEANT: A noncommissioned officer in the army, marines, or air force.
SHAH: A king. The title of the ruler of certain Eastern lands, especially Iran.
SHEIK: (Arabic: "old man") The chief of an Arab family.
SHOGUN: Leader of an army. Any military governors of Japan.
SIR: A title for a man or boy.
SIRE: Poetic for "father." A king.
SOLDIER: A fighter.
SPENCER: Princess Diana's maiden name.
SQUIRE: A shield-bearer or armor bearer of a knight.
SULTAN: A king.
SULTANA: Wife, mother, daughter, or sister of a sultan.
TOGO: Japanese admiral Marquis Togo.
TOJO: Japanese general Hideki Tojo.
TORA, TORRA: Royal, from the castle.
VICEROY: A king, ruler.
VLAD: Short for Vladimir. Prince.
VLADIMIR: A prince.

ZADA: Queenly.
ZADIE, ZADY: Princess.
ZARA: Princess.
ZENOBIA: Queen of Palmyra.

Roland

Did You Know?

SALE GOSSE: The name of TV anchorwoman
Barbara Walter's poodle.

SENIOR: Elder. Actress Stephanie Powers, star
of the TV series "Hart to Hart," has a cat
with this name.

VETO: James Garfield, the 20th President of the
United States, had a pet dog fish with this name.

Corky

Aruba

Chapter 18

Geography and Landmarks

A special place or a well-known landmark can inspire a unique name for a new pet. In fact, the name can take on an added meaning when the place or landmark is one that you have visited, one that has special memories for you. Every time you call your pet's name, you can be reminded of that wonderful time in your life!

Of course, you don't have to visit a place to name a pet after a favorite city or other location. You can name a pet after a favorite place because it's beautiful, because you like the way it sounds - or for any reason. Imagine a sleek, sophisticated cat named *Paris*, a chattering, colorful parrot named *Tonga*, or a beautiful, graceful horse named *Mandalay*.

AKITA: A Japanese coastal city and port.

ALEXANDRIA: A city in Egypt, on the Mediterranean.

ANDALUSIA: A region on the Mediterranean Sea in southwestern Spain.

ANDORRA: A republic in the Pyrenees Mountains, between Spain and France.

ANTIGUA: An island in the West Indies.

ANTILLES: A group of islands in the West Indies.

ARCADIA: Spiritual. A place of peace and simplicity. A region of Greece whose inhabitants, the Arcadians, lived a pastoral life.

ARIZONA: A southwestern state of the U.S. Also, the name of Goofy's archeologist cousin, Arizona Goof.

ARUBA: An island in the Netherlands Antilles, in the West Indies, off the coast of Venezuela.

ASIA: The largest Continent,

situated in the Eastern Hemisphere and separated from Northern Europe by the Ural Mountains.

ATLANTA: Of, relating to, or resembling Atlas, the giant in Greek mythology. Strong. The name of the capital of Georgia.

ATTICUS: Derived from Attica, a state of ancient Greece.

BALI: An island in Indonesia.

BAUHAUS: Pronounced "ba-ha." A German school of art and architecture closed by the Nazis in 1933.

BEAUJOLAIS: A district in France.

BEAUMONT: Handsome. A city in southeastern Texas.

BEDFORD: A county in England.

BELIZE: A former British crown colony that gained independence 1981.

BERINGER: The name of a winery in Napa Valley, California.

BIG BEN: The great bell in the Parliament clock in the tower in London.

BISMARK: A group of islands northeast of New Guinea. Also, the name of the capital city of North Dakota.

BOLIVIA: A country in South America. Andrew Jackson, the 7th President of the United States, had a horse with this name.

BOTSWANA: A country in south-central Africa.

BRISBANE: Energetic. The name of a seaport on the East coast of Australia.

BRITTANY: (Latin: "from England") A province on the northwest coast of France.

BROMLEY: A borough of London, England.

CAMELOT: The legendary English town where King Arthur had his court.

CHESNEE: A city in South Carolina.

CHILLIWACK: A municipality of Canada.

COLUMBIA: The capital of South Carolina.

CONGO: A great river of Africa that flows generally north and west through Zaire to the Atlantic Ocean in northwestern Angola.

DAKOTA: For the U.S. states North and South Dakota.

DALLAS: Large. A city in northeastern Texas.

DANZIG: A seaport in

Poland.

DELPHI: A city in ancient Greece.

DENALI: (Algonquin: name for "the Great One") Another name for Mount McKinley, a mountain in south central Alaska with the highest peak in North America.

DIJON: A city in eastern France. Yellow-colored like Dijon mustard.

DIXIE: From the South, the Land of Dixie.

DOMINICA: Ruler. For the island nation of Dominica.

DONEGAL: A county in Ireland.

DONNER: Swift. The name of a mountain in the Sierra Nevada mountains of California. Also, the name of one of Santa's eight reindeer.

DORIS: An ancient region of Greece.

DRAPER: The name of a city in Utah.

DUBLIN: A seaport and the capital of the Republic of Ireland.

EDESSA: Ancient city of Mesopotamia (modern Urfa, Turkey).

EGYPT: A country in north-eastern Africa, on the Mediterranean and Red seas.

ELLIS: Reverent. For Ellis Island, a small island in New York harbor where immigrants were once examined before being allowed into the United States.

ETNA: Explosive. A volcanic mountain in Sicily. Also spelled Aetna.

EVEREST: For Mount Everest, a peak of the Himalayas, between Tibet and Nepal. At 29,002 feet, Mount Everest is the highest mountain in the world.

FARGO: A city in North Dakota.

FEZ: The name of a city in Morocco.

FIJI: A group of islands in the South Pacific.

FLORIDA: Sunny, warm. A state on a peninsula in the southeastern United States.

FRISCO: Short for San Francisco, a city on the coast of central California.

FUJI: Known for Mount Fuji, a volcano and the highest point on Honshu, Japan. When Donny Osmond was a kid, he had a Japanese Akita named

Fuji.

GALATIA: An ancient kingdom and later a Roman providence, in central Asia Minor.

GENEVA: A city in Switzerland, on Lake Geneva.

GENOA: A seaport in northwestern Italy where Christopher Columbus lived.

GEORGIA: Down to earth. The name of a southern state.

GETHESMANE: A garden outside of Jerusalem.

GIBRALTAR: Strong. From the Rock of Gibraltar, a large rock forming a peninsula in southern Spain, at the Straight of Gibraltar.

GILEAD: A region in ancient Palestine, east of the Jordan.

GOBI: A large desert in Asia, chiefly in Mongolia.

GORKY: A city in eastern European Russia, on the Volga and Oka rivers. Also for Armenian-born painter Arshile Gorky, who was influenced by Surrealism and later influenced Abstract Expressionism.

GOTHAM: According to legend, an English village near Nottingham whose inhabitants were said to be very foolish. Also, known for Gotham City, the hometown of comic book superhero *Batman*.

GRACELAND: The name of Elvis Presley's home in Memphis, Tennessee.

HAMPTON: A city in southeastern Virginia.

HILO: The name of a dormant volcano on the island of Hawaii.

HIMALA: Short for Himalayas, a mountain system between India and Tibet.

HOLLYWOOD: For Hollywood, California, known as the movie capital. A pet that thinks he or she is a star.

HOUSTON: A city in southeastern Texas.

INDIA: A large peninsula of Asia, between the bay of Bengal and the Arabian Sea. President George W. Bush, the 43rd President of the United States, has a cat with this name. India is a black, short-haired cat nicknamed Willie.

ITHACA: An island off the west coast of Greece: legendary home of Odysseus.

JAFFA: The name of a seaport in Israel.

JERICHO: A town in Israel, mentioned in the Bible. Pronounced: "JER-i-ko."

JORDAN: The name of a river in the Near East, flowing into the Dead Sea.

JUNEAU: The capital of Alaska.

KASHMIR: A state of northern India.

KATMANDU: A city in and the capital of Nepal.

KENYA: From the Republic of Kenya in east central Africa.

KIEL: Keel. Strong. A seaport in northern Germany, on the Kiel Canal.

KLONDIKE: A region in eastern Alaska and Western Yukon Territory, Canada, and celebrated for its gold fields.

KOKOMO: A city in India.

KONA: A city on the island of Hawaii.

LAOS: A country, formerly part of French Indochina, in Asia.

LINDISFARNE: Reverent. An island off the coast of Northumberland, northeastern England.

LOGAN: A mountain in the Yukon, in northwestern Canada. From the character in the science fiction movie and TV series "Logan's Run."

LOUSIANNA: A state in the southern United States.

MACEDONIA: An ancient kingdom north of Greece.

MADRID: The capital of Spain.

MALTA: An island in the Mediterranean between Sicily and Africa.

MANDALAY: A city in central Burma, on the Irrawaddy River.

MARIETTA: Rebellious. The name of a town in Georgia.

MARLBORO: A county in South Carolina.

MARRAKESH: A city in Morocco.

MARTINQUE: A French island of the Windward group, in the West Indies.

MAUI: An island in central Hawaii.The second largest of the Hawaiian islands. Also, the name of the dog who played *Murray* in the TV series "Mad About You."

MEDINA: A city in western Saudi Arabia.

MEMPHIS: A port in Tennessee, on the Mississippi.

MOAB: A town in Utah.

MOHAVE, MOJAVE: A member of a tribe of Indians

that lived around the Colorado River.

MONACO: A principality on the Mediterranean, geographically in southeastern France, widely known for its royal family and for the city of Monte Carlo, a gambling resort.

MONTANA: One of the western states of the U.S.

MONTEGO: From Montego Bay, a port and commercial center in Jamaica.

MOROCCO: Soft; tan-colored. A country of northwestern Africa.

NAPA: A county in California known for vineyards.

NAVARRE: A former kingdom of northern Spain and southwestern France.

NEPAL: A country the size of Arkansas, located between India and the Tibetan Autonomous Region of China.

NEVADA: A state in the western United States.

NILE: A river in eastern Africa, flowing through Egypt into the Mediterranean.

ODESSA: A town in Texas.

OGDEN: Persistent. A city in northern Utah.

ORINOCO: Large. A river in Venezuela flowing south from Mt. Delgado Chalbaud, in the Guiana Highlands, to a vast, marshy delta in the northeast.

ORLANDO: Famed. A city in central Florida.

OSAKA: A city in Japan.

OSLO: The capital of Norway.

OZARK: A pet that loves to climb, especially when outdoors. A low mountain range in southwestern Missouri, northwestern Arkansas, and northeastern Oklahoma.

PAGO: The main seaport of American Samoa, on Tutuila Island.

PANAMA: A republic in South Central America.

PARIS: In Greek legend, a son of Priam, king of Troy. The capital of France, said to be the city of lovers.

PECOS: A town in western Texas, near the Pecos River.

PEKING: The capital of China. Short for Pekingese, a small dog with long, silky hair, short legs, and a pug nose.

PERSIA: The Persian Empire. A good name for a Persian cat.

PERU: A republic in South America.

PHENICIA, PHOENICIA:
An ancient kingdom on the
Mediterranean in modern Syria
and Palestine.
PHILLY: A nickname for the
city of Philadelphia, Pennsyl-
vania.
PHOENIX: The name of the
capital of Arizona.
PISA: A city in northwestern
Italy known for its Leaning
Tower.
POMPEII: An ancient city in
Italy, on the Bay of Naples.
Pompeii was buried by an
eruption of Mount Vesuvius.
RALEIGH: A city in North
Carolina. The name of Clay
Aiken's (of "American Idol")
tiny dog, named after his
hometown.
RENO: A city in Nevada.
RUBICON: Decisive. A small
river in northern Italy crossed
by Caesar on his return from
Gaul to seize power in Rome.
RUMNEY: A city in New
Hampshire.
SAHARA: A vast desert ex-
tending over northern Africa.
SALEM: A city on the coast
of northern Massachusetts.
SAVANNAH: Feminine. A
seaport town in eastern Geor-
gia.
SHASTA: A daisy. Also, the
name of a volcanic mountain in
northern California and the
name of a lake.
SHASTINA: "Little Shasta"
the smaller lake north of Lake
Shasta in California.
SHENAN: Short for Shenan-
doah.
SHENANDOAH: A river in
Virginia that flows into the Po-
tomac River.
SHERWOOD: A forest near
Nottingham, England, famous
for the Robin Hood legends.
SIAM: The former name of
Thailand.
SIERRA: A range of moun-
tains with a saw-toothed ap-
pearance.
SOLEDAD: (Spanish)
"solitary." For news anchor
Soledad O'Brien. Also, a city
in California.
SORBONNE: Creative. The
liberal arts college of the Uni-
versity of Paris.
SPAIN: A country in Europe.
ST. LOUIS: A city in Mis-
souri. Ulysses S. Grant, the 18th
President of the United States,
had a horse with this name.
STROMBOLI: One of the

Aeolian Islands of Italy.

TAHITI: An island in the South Pacific.

TASMAN, TASMIN: Short for Tasmania, an island off southeastern Australia.

TETON: A range of the Rocky Mountains. A large pet.

TIBET: An administrative part of China.

TIMBUKTU: A town in central Mali.

TOBAGO: An island in the West Indies.

TONGA: A group of British islands in the South Pacific, east of the Fiji Islands. A good name for a tropical bird or other pet.

TORRANCE: A city in southwestern California.

TRENT: The name of a city in Italy.

TRENTON: The capital of New Jersey, on the Delaware River.

TRINIDAD: An island in the West Indies.

TRIPOLI: A former Barbary State, now a part of Libya.

TROY: A city in New York.

TULSA: A city located in the oil-rich region of Oklahoma.

TUSCANY: A region of Italy known for its vineyards.

UTAH: A state in the western United States.

VEGAS: For Las Vegas, a city in Nevada best known for legalized gambling.

VENICE: Graceful. A seaport in northeastern Italy, built on more than a hundred small islands in an inlet of the Gulf of Venice.

VERNON: Like spring. The name of a town in France.

VERONA: True image. A city in northeastern Italy.

WABASH: A river flowing through Ohio, Indiana, and Illinois. Also, from a song "The Wabash Cannonball."

WACO: A city in central Texas.

WAIKIKI: A famous resort in Hawaii.

WATERLOO: The name of a river in Belgium, the scene of Napoleon's final defeat.

WINCHESTER: A city in Hampshire, England.

WYOMING: A western state of the United States.

YONKERS: A city in southeastern New York, on the Hudson.

YUKON: A territory in

Canada. Herbert Hoover, the 31st President of the United States, had a malamute with this name.

ZAIRE: A republic in central Africa.

ZAMBIA: A republic in south-central Africa.

ZANZIBAR: An island off the Eastern coast of Africa.

Did You Know?

CHOCOLATE CHIP: Brown with dark flecks or spots. When he was a boy, Donny Osmond and his brothers had a cat named Chocolate Chip.

EAGLEHURST GILLETTE: Herbert Hoover, the 31st President of the United States, had a setter with this name.

JENNIE, JENNY: Female. Comedian Bea Arthur, the former star of the TV series "Maude" and "The Golden Girls," had a Doberman pinscher with the name Jennie.

Wiener Dog

Chapter 19

Food and Beverages

Food for Thought – and Names! Foods and beverages can often inspire just the perfect name for a new pet who has a ferocious appetite or a favorite food or drink (like *Spam* the cat, *Cocoa* the gerbil, *Popcorn* the dog, among others!) This chapter offers an abundance of food-friendly names – from *Alpo* to *Zotz*! Bon appetit!

ALPO: A brand of pet food.

AMARETTO: Macaroons made with almonds.

ANCHOVY: A species of small fishes resembling herrings.

APPLE: Firm, healthy. Rounded red, yellow and green fruit.

APPLEBEE: From Applebee's restaurants.

APRICOT: Tasteful. Orange-colored fruit that resembles a peach.

ARBY: From Arby's, the restaurant chain known for its roast beef sandwiches.

ASPARAGUS: Old World plant with edible shoots cultivated when young and tender.

AVOCADO: A green or purple nutty-flavored edible fruit.

BACON: A thin, sliced meat.

BAGEL: Rounded, plump. A hard donut-shaped roll.

BALONEY: A pet who enjoys eating bologna.

BANANA: Golden, yellowish. Zany. A long, tropical fruit with a yellow skin.

BARBATO: From the restaurant chain Barbato's.

BASKIN: For Baskin-Robbins, the chain of ice cream shops.

BEEF O'GRADY: Restaurant chain Beef O'Grady's.

BISCUIT: Light brown,

baked bread, often shaped like a large cookie.

BLACKBERRY: Black or dark purple juicy, seedy fruits. Calvin Coolidge, the 30th President of the United States, had a chow with this name.

BLIMPIE: A submarine sandwich shop.

BLUEBERRY: Any of a species of plants bearing blue, bell-shaped flowers.

BONBON: A rich, chocolate-covered candy.

BORDEAUX: White or red wine of the Bordeaux region of France.

BRAMLEY: A type of apple for cooking.

BRANDY: Mellow. A beverage distilled from wine or fruit juice.

BRIE: A cheese with a whitish exterior, a pale yellow interior.

BUGABOO: From Bugaboo Creek Steakhouse.

BURGERS: A pet that likes to eat hamburger.

BURRITO: Spicy. Hot-tempered. A flour tortilla rolled or folded, and filled with meat, beans, cheese, etc.

BUTTER: A creamy food for spreading and cooking. A tan or golden-colored pet.

BUTTERFINGER: A crunchy peanut butter and chocolate candy bar.

BUTTERMILK: The liquid left after butter has been churned from milk or cream.

BUTTERWORTH: For Mrs. Butterworth, a brand of syrup.

CADBURY: From Cadbury, the famous English chocolate manufacturer.

CAPPUCHINO: Dark brown. A beverage made with strong coffee and milk.

CARAMEL: Sweet, tan. Brown substance created by heating sugar and used as a flavoring and coloring in foods, especially desserts and candies.

CARROT: The edible orange root of the carrot plant. A good name for a rabbit or other pet that loves eating carrots.

CASHEW: A tropical American tree with an edible nut.

CAVIAR: Living a life of leisure. Processed fish roe (eggs), a delicacy.

CHABLIS: A dry sharp white California wine.

CHARDONNAY: A dry white table wine of Chablis type.

CHEDDAR: Yellow-colored. A type of cheese.

CHEESECAKE: Attractive. A dessert with a pastry or crumb shell and a cheese filling.

CHEETO: For Cheetos snack products.

CHEESTOS: A brand of snack foods.

CHERRY: (Old French: "cherrylike") Sweet. Any of a variety of trees or shrubs, in the rose family, producing deep-red or blackish fruit.

CHESTNUT: Reddish brown. Any of a variety of trees or schrubs in the beech family and producing edible nuts.

CHIANTI: A red wine from the Tuscany region of Italy.

CHI CHI: From the restaurant chain Chi Chi's.

CHICORY: Tasteful. A plant whose roots are ground for mixing with coffee or as a coffee substitute.

CHILI: Spicy. Hot-tempered. A thick sauce that contains chili peppers.

CHOCOLATE: Brown, black, or reddish brown. A food prepared from roasted cocoa beans.

CICI: From CiCi's Pizza, the restaurant chain.

CINNAMON: Reddish brown. An aromatic spice derived from the inner bark of the cinnamon tree.

CLARET: A red Bordeaux wine.

COCOA: Dark. A beverage made by heating cocoa with milk.

COCONUT: Sweet. Light colored. The fruit of the coconut palm.

COFFEE: Tan, brown, or black. A beverage made from roasted and ground seeds of a coffee plant.

COGNAC: A brandy distilled from white wine.

COTTON CANDY: Fluffy, sweet, attractive. A candy made of spun sugar.

COUSCOUS: A North African dish of steamed semolina, usually served with meat or vegetables.

COZYMEL: For Cozymel's Mexican Grill.

CRACKERJACK: A brand of toffee-covered popcorn.

CRACKERS: A cookie or biscuit, often refers to the unsweetened variety.

CRUMPET: Sweet. A small, unsweetened bread cooked on a griddle.

DAIQUIRI: A cocktail made of rum, fruit juice and sugar.

DAMON: From Damon's restaurants.

DANNON: A brand of yogurt.

DENNY: From Denny's, the restaurant chain.

DOMINO: For the Dominos's pizza chain.

DONATO: From Donato's Pizza.

DONUT: Sweet. A ring-shaped cake.

DUCCHESS: From Ducchess Sweet Potato Pie.

ELANA: From Elana Honey Almond, a chocolate candy with mild almond flavor.

EVIAN: A brand of bottled water.

FARLEY: From Farley's Co-conut Stacks.

FIDDLE FADDLE: A brand of toffee-covered popcorn.

FLAPJACK: Large. Breakfast food, a pancake.

FRANKFURTER: A pet that loves to eat hot dogs or sausage.

FRENCH FRY: Strips of potato deep-fried.

FRITO: Short for Fritos.

FRITOS: A brand of snack foods.

FRITTER: A fried dough often filled with fruit or meat.

GINGERBREAD: Spicy sweet. A cake whose ingredients include ginger and sugar.

GINGERSNAP: Spicy, tiny. A thin, brittle cookie sweetened with molasses and flavored with ginger.

GOULASH: (Hungarian: "shepherd") A hearty meat and vegetable stew.

GRAVY: A pet that loves to eat. A sauce thickened and seasoned with the juices of cooked meat.

GRIDDLE: A flat metal surface for cooking food.

GRITS: Hearty. Coarsely ground grain boiled and served as a breakfast food in the southern United States. Jimmy Carter, the 39th President of the United States, had a pet with this name.

GUACAMOLE: Pureed or mashed avocado with seasonings.

GUAVA: Golden. A tropical American tree or shrub bearing a yellowish, pear-shaped, edible fruit.

GUMBALL: Bubblegum.

GUMBO: Sticky. A soup thickened with unripe okra pods, a part of the Creole cooking of New Orleans.

GUMBY: From Gumby's Pizza.

GUMDROP: A small, firm, jellylike piece of candy.

GUMMI BEARS: Gelatin candies of various colors. Also, the name of a Disney animated TV series about a clan of bears who live in Gummi Glen.

HAM: Salt cured meat. In 1961, months before the first human went into space, Ham the chimpanzee survived a test run into space.

HAPPY JOE: From Happy Joe's restaurants.

HERSHEY: Dark. A brand name for candy, especially chocolate.

HOBEE: The restaurant chain Hobee's.

HOECAKE: Yellow-colored. A small cake made of cornmeal.

HOMINY: Grits.

HONEY: A sweet liquid substance made of nectar from flowers by bees.

HOPS: A restaurant chain.

HOT DOG: A pet that enjoys eating hot dogs and is especially daring! Also the name of the kids' dog in the cartoon series "The Archies." A good name for a dachshund, a wiener dog (excuse the pun!)

HOT TAMALE: Ill-tempered. A hot ground meat seasoned with chilli, wrapped in cornmeal dough, wrapped in corn husks and steamed.

HUNGRY HOWIE: From Hungry Howie's restaurants.

JAM: Sweet. Food made by boiling fruit and sugar.

JAMBALAYA: A stew made with rice, shrimp, meats, and seasonings.

JAVA: Coffee.

JEEPER: For Jeeper's Restaurant chain.

JELLO: A brand of flavored gelatin.

JELLY: A fruit-flavored gelatin food substance.

JELLYBEAN, JELLY-BEANS: Sweet. A sugar-glazed bean shaped candy.

JELLYROLL: Plump. A thin sheet of sponge cake spread with jelly and rolled up.

JOHNNY ROCKET: For the 1950s-inspired Johnny Rocket restaurant chain.

JUICE: Lively. Beverage made from fruits or vegetables.

JUJUBE: Sweet. A fruit-flavored gumdrop.

JULEP: Spicy. Fresh. A drink consisting of liquor, sugar, crushed ice and mint.

KIBBLES: A brand of pet food.

KIT KAT: From the chocolate covered crispy wafers.

KIWI: Down to earth. Fruit of a Chinese gooseberry. The name of a Beanie Baby bird, a toucan.

KOO KOO ROO: For the restaurant chain.

KRISPY: From Krispy Kreme, the donut chain.

KRYSTAL: From Krystal's, best known for their tiny hamburgers.

KUCHEN: A kind of German cake, made of yeast dough and often frosted or filled with raisins, nuts.

LANCE: Lance baked goods, such as Lance Pecan Twirls.

LASAGNA: A baked food consisting of pasta, cheese, seasoned tomato sauce, and sometimes meat.

LEMONDROP: Small, golden, sweet. A small, hard lemon-flavored candy.

LePEEP: For the restaurant chain.

LICORICE: A candy flavored with licorice.

LITTLE CAESAR: For the pizza-chain Little Caesar's.

LITTLE SMOKIE: From Little Smokies, a brand of cocktail franks.

LOLLIPOP: Sweet. A hard candy on a the end of a stick.

LUBY: For the restaurant chain, Luby's.

MAGNUM: A large wine bottle. The last name of the private detective in the TV series "Magnum P.I."

MAI TAI: A tropical drink. An exotic pet.

MALMSEY: The name of a grape from which a strong, sweet white wine is derived.

MAPLE: Sweet; brownish colored. A syrup made from the sap of the maple tree, especially the sugar maple.

MARGARITA: An orange-flavored cocktail.

MARMALADE: A jam-like preserve made of or from

oranges or other fruits and sugar. A cat in an episode (set in Hooterville) of TV series "The Beverly Hillbillies."

MARSHMALLOW: White, puffy, soft-hearted. A soft, spongy candy made of sugar, starch, corn syrup, and gelatin. A pet that is a big softie.

MARTINI: A cocktail.

MARY JANE: A soft, taffy-like candy.

MEATBALL: Plump. A small ball of hamburger mixed with seasoning and bread crumbs.

MELBA: Melba toast, a slightly stale bread, sliced thin and toasted to a crisp, named for Australian soprano Nellie Melba.

MERINGUE: Fluffy white confection made of egg whites beaten stiff and mixed with sugar, often browned as a topping for pies and cakes.

MERLOT: (Pronounced "mer-lo,") A red wine.

MINT: Cool. Any of various aromatic plants whose leaves are used for flavoring and medicine, as peppermint.

MOCHA: A superior Arabian coffee. Brown-colored pet.

MOLASSES: A thick, dark-colored syrup. Sweet.

MONTEREY JACK: A semi-soft cheese. A big mouse in the Disney animated TV series "Chip 'n Dale Rescue Rangers."

MOO GOO: Short for the classic Chinese dish Moo Goo Gai Pan.

MORTON: A brand of salt.

MUFFIN: (Old French: "soft") A bread or cake cooked in a muffin tin.

MULBERRY: A tree or its berrylike fruit.

MULLIGAN: From Mulligan stew, a pet that has a hearty appetite and is not choosy when it comes to food.

NEHI: A brand of soft drink.

NESTLE: A brand of chocolate candies and other foods.

NOODLE, NOODLES: Flat, narrow strip of dried dough. A playful pet.

NUESKE: For Nueske's applewood smoked specialty products.

OH HENRY!: A chocolate candy.

OL' ROY: Dog food brand.

PANCHO: From Pancho's Mexican Buffet.

PAPRIKA: (Greek: "pepper")

A cooking spice.

PASTA: A pet that likes Italian food.

PAYDAY: A candy bar with caramel and peanuts.

PEACH, PEACHES: A small tree with pink blossoms that produces fruit with a fuzzy skin.

PEANUT: Small, frisky. A vine of the pea family, with brittle pods ripening underground and containing edible seeds. The name of the most rare Beanie Baby, the royal blue elephant.

PEANUT BUTTER: A tan-colored pet. A processed peanut food.

PEKOE: Dark. A black, small leaf tea of Ceylon and India.

PIE: A pastry filled with fruit or meat.

PINK LADY: Very feminine. A cocktail made of gin, brandy, lemon juice, grenadine, and the white of an egg.

PISTACHIO: A pudding flavored with the edible green nuts of the Asian pistachio tree.

PIXIE: From Pixie Stix, a powdered candy in a cardboard or plastic tube-like stick.

PIZZA: A pet that loves to eat pizza.

POPCORN: Fluffy, white. An Indian corn that pops into a white puff when heated.

PORK CHOP: A pet who loves to eat pork chops.

POUPON: The name of a gourmet mustard.

PRETZEL: An oddly shaped or puzzling pet. A hard, brittle biscuit usually in the form of a loose knot and sprinkled with salt.

PRINGLES: A brand of snack foods.

PUDDING: Soft, sweet. A boiled or baked soft food.

QUIZNO: For Quizno's Subs.

RAISIN: Small, dark, sweet. A grape of any variety that has been dried by the sun or by other means.

RALLY: From Rally's restaurant chain.

RAVIOLI: Pasta in the shape of a small case filled with meat or cheese. A pet that likes to eat ravioli.

RAZZLE: From Razzles, a candy with gum in the center.

RELISH: Pickles or other foods eaten to add flavor to other foods.

ROB ROY: A mixed drink. Calvin Coolidge, the 30th President of the United States, had a collie with this name.

ROLO: Chocolate covered caramel candies.

RUBIO: The restaurant chain Rubio's.

RUFFLES: A brand of snack food.

SAKE, SAKI: A Japanese beverage of fermented rice.

SALAMI: A pet that enjoys eating sausage.

SARDINE: Small fish (such as anchovy) used for food.

SAUSAGE: A pet that enjoys eating sausage or is long and lean in appearance. Great name for a Dachshund.

SCAMPI: Spicy. A shrimp dish prepared with garlic-flavored sauce.

SCHNAPPS: A variety of flavored liqueurs.

SHASTA: A brand of soft drink.

SHERBET: Cool as the frozen dessert made of fruit juice, sugar, and water.

SHONEY: The Shoney's restaurant chain.

SHORTBREAD: Sweet. A cookie made of sugar, flour and shortening.

SHORTCAKE: Sweet. A crisp biscuit or cookie.

SHRIMP: Small. A long-tailed crustacean, valued as food.

SHULA: For Shula's Steak House chain.

SIZZLER: From the steak house chain.

SKILLET: A small pot or kettle used for cooking on the hearth.

SKITTLES: From the brightly colored fruit-flavored candies.

SLAPJACK: A pancake. Any pet that enjoys pancakes or waffles.

SMOKEY BONES: From the Smokey Bones restaurant chain.

S'MORSELS: A candy resembling milk duds.

SMOOTHIE: A processed drink made of various ingredients.

SNICKERS: A candy bar with chocolate, peanuts, and caramel.

SONNY BRYAN: From Sonny Bryan's restaurants.

SORBET: A fruit-flavored ice served as a dessert or between courses to cleanse the palate.

SPAM: A processed-meat food in a can.

SPICE: Aromatic products used to season foods.

SPRITZER: A beverage of white wine and soda water.

STEAK: A slice of meat, usually beef.

STRAWBERRY: Sweet. Juicy edible red fruit.

SUEBEE: A brand of honey.

SUKI: Short for Sukiyaki, a Japanese stir fry dish.

SUNDAE: From ice cream sundae, a pet that likes to eat ice cream.

SUSHI: Raw fish - a Japanese delicacy. A pet that eats raw meat.

SWIZZLE: A mixed drink stirred with a swizzle stick until the container becomes frosted.

TABASCO: Spicy, spirited. Sauce made from hot peppers.

TACO: Tortilla filled with a mixture of seasoned meat, cheese, lettuce, etc. A pet that likes this kind of food.

TAFFY: Flattering, sweet. A chewy candy made of sugar or molasses boiled down and stretched.

TAHOE JOE: From Tahoe Joe's restaurant chain.

TANG: The orange-favored breakfast drink that went into space with the US astronauts.

TAPIOCA: A kind of pudding.

T-BONE: A kind of beef steak. A pet that eats mostly beef.

TIFFIN: In Great Britain, a light midday meal.

TIPPIN: From the Tippin's restaurants.

TOFFEE, TOFFY: Taffy, sweet. A brittle candy.

TOFFIFAY: From the hazel nut covered caramel and chocolate candy.

TOFU, TOUFU: A freeze-dried food product.

TOGO: From Togo's, the restaurant chain.

TOOTSIE: From Tootsie Roll, the taffy-like chocolate candy.

TREBORS: Hard candies of various favors with a chocolate surprise inside.

TROLLI SOUR GUMMI BEARS: A jellybean candy with a tart center.

TRUFFLE, TRUFFLES: Dark edible fungi, considered a costly delicacy.

TUBBY: From Tubby's restaurants.

TWINKIE: Shining. The name of a popular snack cake.

VITTLES: Food.

WHATCHAMACALLIT: A crispy candy bar dipped in chocolate.

WHISKAS: A brand of cat food.

WIENER: Sausage, frankfurter. A pet that enjoys this food. Great name for a Dachshund.

WYLER: From Wyler's, a brand of powdered drink mix.

XANDO: For the chain of restaurants.

YAMS: A starchy, tuberous root that grows on a vine: the sweet potato.

ZARDA: For the restaurant chain.

ZAXBY: From Zaxby's, the chain of fast-food restaurants serving chicken.

ZIMA: A beer made in America.

ZINFANDEL: A red table wine made from a small black grape.

ZOTZ: From Zotz Candy Bomb, a candy with a tart center.

Did You Know?

FALA: Franklin Delano Roosevelt, the 32nd President of the United States, had a Scottish terrier with this name.

GRIM: Rutherford B. Hayes, The 19th President of the United States, had a greyhound with this name.

MOUSTY: Pop singer Julio Iglesias' had a tabby cat with this name.

Pashmina

Chapter 20

Fashion and Accessories

The world of high fashion can inspire a glamorous or sophisticated name for a sleek cat (*Gisele*), a fashionably chic bird (*Chanel*), a trend-setting fish (*Fendi*), and a dapper dog (*Armani*), among many others!

ARAMIS: A classic cologne for men.

ARDEANA: For American fashion designer Ardeana Couture.

ARMANI: For designer Giorgio Armani.

ATTAR: Fragrant. A perfume made from the petals of flowers, as of roses.

BARBIE: Unique. The name of a popular fashion doll.

BIRKENSTOCK: A brand of footwear.

BLUSH: A facial makeup used to add color to cheeks.

BLYBLOS: For the popular Italian designer.

BUXTON: Maker of accessories.

CANOE: A brand of cologne.

CARTIER: Valuable. The famous watch and jewelry maker.

CASHMERE: Soft. A soft fabric made from fine wool.

CERRUTI: From Cerruti Image cologne.

CHANEL: French fashion designer Gabrielle (Coco) Chanel.

CHANTILLY: A delicate silk, linen or synthetic lace.

CHAPS: A brand of men's cologne by Ralph Lauren. Also, leg coverings made of leather and worn by cowboys for protection.

CHEENO: A type of slacks.

CHENILLE: Velvety, soft; fluffy. A wool, cotton, silk, or rayon yarn with a plush pile used for creating fabric (also called chenille).

CHIC: Smart elegance; clever; stylish.

CHIFFON: Shiny, soft. A silky fabric often associated with dresses and gowns for bridesmaids.

CITRONELLA: Light-colored. An oil used in perfume, soap, or candles; used to repel mosquitoes.

COCO: For French fashion designer Gabrielle (Coco) Chanel.

CONFETTI: A brand of clothing for children.

CORDELIA: For the British fashion model.

COTY: A brand of cologne.

DAMASK: A lustrous fabric made with flat patterns in a satin weave.

DENIM: Heavy cotton fabric used for making jeans and also for upholstery.

DIOR: Stylish. For fashion designer Christian Dior.

ELLE: (French: "she") For supermodel Elle McPherson. Also, the name of the character, Elle Woods, played by Reese Witherspoon in the movies *Legally Blonde* and *Legally Blonde 2.*

ELLESSE: (Pronounced "L-S") Maker of casual clothing.

FABIO: For the Italian male model who has graced the covers of numerous romance novels.

FEDORA: A soft felt hat with a creased crown. The fedora was famous as a favorite men's hat in the 1930s-40s.

FENDI: Designer clothing and accessories.

FERNANDA: For popular Brazilian-born model Fernanda Tavares.

FEZ: Tasseled. A tapering felt cap, usually red with a black tassel.

FIA: For American independent sportswear designer Fia Miami.

FINESSE: A brand of products for grooming.

FLAIR: Stylish. Sophisticated.

FLEECE: Fuzzy, warm. A type of material used for clothing and other items.

GIORGIO: For designer Giorgio Armani.

GISELE: For the popular Brazilian-born fashion model Gisele Bundchen.

GITANO: A brand of clothing, including jeans.

GIVENCHY: French fashion designer.

GOTCHA: A brand of casual wear.

GUCCI: Designer of clothing and accessories.

HALSTON: A designer perfume.

IMAN: For the popular international model, born in Somalia.

JACQUARD: A fabric of intricate weave or pattern.

JERZEE: A line of casual wear.

JOOP: *Joop!* is a brand of cologne.

JOVAN: A brand of fragrance.

KIARA: For popular Ugandan-born fashion model Kiara Kabukuru.

KIMO: Short for kimono, a garment of clothing worn by both men and women in Japan.

KIMONO: A garment of clothing worn by both men and women in Japan.

KITTY BOOTS: British fashion designer based in New York.

KNICKERBOCKER, KNICKERS: Short, loose trousers gathered at or just below the knees, now considered old-fashioned. For Diedrich Knickerbocker, the fictitious author of *Washington Irving's History of New York.*

KRIZIA: For the popular Italian fashion designer.

LACE: Beautiful, delicate.

LEVI: (Hebrew: "joined in harmony") A popular brand of jeans and other clothing.

MACY: For Macy's department store.

MANON: For the popular German fashion model Manon Von Gerkan.

MILLA: For fashion model Milla Jovovich, who became the face of L'Oréal, then went on to have roles in movies including *Zoolander* and *Resident Evil.*

MISSONI: For the popular Italian fashion designer.

MITTENS: Warmth. A pet that appears to be wearing mittens or gloves.

MOSSIMO: A brand of clothing.

MUDD: A brand of casual clothing.

NOEMIE: For the popular fashion model Noemie Lenoir, who was born in Versailles.

OSHKOSH: Oshkosh B'Gosh, a brand of children's clothing.

PACO: A brand of casual wear, especially jeans.

PANTS: A garment that starts at the waist and covers each leg to the ankles.

PASHMINA: Silk scarf or shawl.

PRADA: A designer brand of shoes.

PREPPY: Dressy, tidy. Slang for a person who attended a college preparatory school.

PUCCI: Stylish. For Italian fashion designer Emilio Pucci.

REEBOK: A brand of sportswear and sneakers.

RONNI NICOLE: A line of ladies' clothing.

SAKS: For Saks Fifth Avenue, department store.

SANDAL: A casual shoe, usually having straps, for warm weather.

SATEEN: A shiny smooth and durable fabric made of cotton.

SATIN: Silky smooth and glossy like satin.

SAVANE: A line of men's clothing.

SEIKO: A watch manufacturer.

SHALIMAR: Cologne fragrance.

SHALOM: For popular dark-haired fashion model Shalom Harlow.

SHANTIQUE: A brand of ladies' clothing.

SKIPPER: The name of popular fashion doll Barbie's younger sister.

SONOMA: A brand of clothing.

SPATS: Coverings for shoes.

SPEEDO: Fast. From the tight biker shorts.

STAFFORD: A line of clothing.

STILA: A cosmetics maker.

TABU: A brand of perfume.

TANGA: For the popular blonde fashion model Tanga Moreau.

TATIANA: For popular German-born fashion model Tatiana Patitz.

TIFFANY: Maker of fine jewelry and home decor.

TUX: Short for tuxedo, a formal suit worn by men.

TWEED: A rough woolen fabric used for suits and coats.

TWIGGY: A trendy English fashion model from the 1960s.

TWILL: A fabric with twill

weave, which has the appearance of diagonal lines.

TYSON: Explosive. For model Tyson Beckford.

VANDERBILT: For fashion designer Gloria Vanderbilt.

VELOUR: A fabric resembling velvet used for upholstery with lighter weights for clothing.

VELVET: A clothing or upholstery fabric with a furry feel.

VELVETEEN: A clothing fabric made of cotton to simulate velvet.

VENDELA: For the blonde Swedish supermodel.

VERSACE: For the late Italian designer Gianni Versace and the continuing House of Versace.

VOGUE: Always modeling, posing. A well-known fashion magazine. Also, a dance popularized by Madonna.

WINDSONG: A cologne and other products.

YVES SAINT LAURENT: Popular French designer.

Did You Know?

BOSTON BEANS: Calvin Coolidge, the 30th President of the United States, had a bulldog with this name.

GHENGIS: From Ghengis Khan, the Mongol conqueror of central Asia. Actress Zsa Zsa Gabor has a Shih Tzu named Ghengis Khan.

LIBERTY: Gerald Ford, the 38th President of the United States, had a golden retriever with this name.

Ami

Chapter 21

Foreign Language

Names of foreign origin often have a nice ring to them as well as a bit of intrigue: **Belle Fleur**, **Charro**, **Tabu**, and others.

ABRIL: (Spanish) April.
ACME: (Greek: "the top") The highest point.
ADAN: (Spanish) Lazy fellow.
AGRIO: (Spanish) Disagreeable.
AIMEE, AMY: (French) Loved one, friend.
AISHA: (African) Life.
AKEEM, AKIM: (African) King.
ALADO: (Spanish) Winged, swift.
ALBO: (Spanish) White.
ALBORADA: (Spanish) Dawn.
ALEGRE: (Spanish) Cheerful, joyful.
ALMA: (Spanish) Soul, spirit.
ALOHA: (Hawaiian: "love") A word used as a greeting or farewell.
ALTO: (Spanish) Tall.

AMADO: (Spanish) Beloved.
AMADOR: (Spanish) Loving.
AMADORA: (Spanish) Loving.
AMATISTA: (Spanish) Amethyst.
AMAZONA: (Spanish) Amazon; horsewoman.
AMI: (French) Friend.
AMIGA: (Spanish) Friend, girlfriend.
AMIGO: (Spanish) Friend, boyfriend.
AMOUR: (French) Love.
AMY: (Latin: "beloved") Dainty.
ANASTASIA: (Greek) "Of the resurrection."
ANDANZA: (Spanish) Fate, fortune.
ANGELITO: (Spanish) Little angel.
ANIMA: (Latin) Breath, soul.

ARGENT: (French: "money") Silver-colored or grayish white.

AU REVOIR: (French) "Until we meet again." Goodbye.

AVRIL: (French) April.

AYTAN: (Indian) Big, brown.

AZUL: (Spanish) Blue

BABEL: (Spanish) Messy.

BABUSHKA: (Russian) Grandmother.

BAJA: (Spanish) Lower. (Pronounced "ba-ha")

BALLENA: (Spanish) Whale.

BANSHEE: (Irish: "female fairy") A pet that howls or is otherwise noisy.

BEAU GESTE (French) Beautiful gesture.

BEAUREGARD: (Old French: "beautiful in expression") Diane L. Krueger, author of the novel *Reflections* and the series *Elusive Love & Moonbeams*, has a Westie with this name.

BEAUX YEUX: (French) "beautiful eyes."

BEBE (French) Baby.

BELLE FLEUR: (French) Beautiful flower.

BELLEZA: (Spanish) Beauty.

BETE: (French) Beast.

BETE NOIR: (French) Black beast.

BIDDY: (African) Small yellow bird.

BIJOU: (French: "jewel") Amiable.

BLANCO: (Spanish) White. Lyndon Johnson, the 36th President of the United States, had a collie with this name.

BOBO: (Spanish) Silly, naive.

BOLERO: (Spanish) Bowling alley.

BON: (French) Good.

BONET: (French) Bonnet.

BONITO: (Spanish) Pretty, handsome.

BONJOUR: (French) Good morning.

BONNE CHANCE: (French) Good luck.

BONUS: (Latin) Good.

BRIO: (Spanish) Spirit.

BRISA: (Spanish) Breeze.

BRONCO: (Spanish) Rough, wild.

BRUTO: (Spanish) Brute, beast.

BUENO: (Spanish) Good.

BUSHIDO: (Japan) "Way of the warrior."

BUSHWHACKER: (Dutch) Forest watcher.

CALLISTA: (Greek) Most beautiful.

CARLO, CARLOS: A Spanish form of Charles. Manly.

CARO: (Spanish) Beloved.

CAZADOR: (Spanish) Hunter.

CAZADORA: (Spanish) Huntress.

CELADOR: (Spanish) Watcher, guard.

CHACHO: (Spanish) Lad.

CHAMPIGNON: (French) Mushroom.

CHANSON: (French) Song.

CHAPEAU: (French) Hat.

CHAQUITO: (Spanish) Very small.

CHARLOTTA: (French) Small and womanly.

CHARRO: (Spanish) Rustic; cowboy.

CHATO: (Spanish) Flat-nosed.

CHEERIO: (British) Hello or goodbye.

CHERI, CHERIE: (French) Beloved.

CHEVAL: (French) Horse.

CHIPPER: (British) Lively, in good spirits. The name of the chipmunk Beanie Baby.

CHIQUITA: (Spanish) Little one.

CHISPA: (Spanish) Sparkle, gleam.

CHRISTAL: (Greek) Christian.

CHULA: (Spanish) Flashy girl.

CLIQUE: (French) "To make a noise."

COBA: (Spanish) Fib; neat trick.

COLETTE: (French) Victorious in battle.

CONSUELO: (Spanish) Solace, comfort.

COQUANT: (French) Little rascal.

COQUETA: (Spanish) Flirtatious.

CORAZON: (Spanish) Heart.

CORDURA: (Spanish) Wisdom, prudence.

DAGMAR: (Anglo-Saxon) Splendid.

DALAI: (Mongolian) Ocean.

DALILA: (African) Gentle.

DAMA: (Spanish) Lady, gentlewoman.

DEBONAIR: (Old French) "Of good breed."

DEKA: (Greek) Ten.

DEKE: (Greek) Ten.

DELICIA: (Spanish) Delight.

DIABLO: (Spanish) Devil.

DIOSA: (Spanish) Goddess.

DOLORES: (Spanish) "Mary of the sorrows."

DOMINGO: (Spanish) Sunday.

DONCELLA: (Spanish) Lady's maid.

DORADO: (Spanish) Golden.

DROLE: (French) Funny.

EBANO: (Spanish) Ebony.

EL DORADO: (Spanish: "the gilded") Golden.

ELEGANTE: (Spanish) Elegant, graceful.

ELLA: (Spanish) She.

ENCANTADORA: (Spanish) Enchanter, magician.

ENID: (Celtic) Spotless purity.

ENIGMA: (Spanish: "puzzling, mystery") Baffling.

ENJOYA: (Spanish) "To adorn with jewels."

EQUUS: (Latin) Horse.

ERIZO: (Spanish) Hedgehog; sea urchin.

ESCENCIA: (Spanish) Essence.

ESQUIRE: (Latin) Shield-bearer.

ESTELLA, ESTELLE: (Latin) Star.

ESTRELLA: (Spanish) Star.

ETOILE: (French) star.

FAISAN: (Spanish) Pheasant.

FELINE: (Latin) Cat.

FEMME: (French) Woman.

FIESTA: (Spanish: "feast") Festive.

FLAMENCO: (Spanish: "flame") Bright.

FLEUR: (French) Flower.

FONTAINE: (French: "fountain") An interesting name for a water pet, such as a fish or a turtle.

FRESCO: (Italian: "fresh") Refreshing.

FRIJOLE: (Spanish) Bean.

FUEGO: (Spanish) Fire.

GABARDA: (Spanish) Wild rose.

GAIA: (Greek) Earth.

GALA: (Old French: "enjoyment") Festive.

GALAN: (Spanish) Handsome fellow.

GANA: (Spanish) Desire, wish.

GANSA: (Spanish) Silly girl.

GANSO: (Spanish) Dolt.

GARÇON: (French) Young lad, servant.

GATO: (Spanish) Cat, tom cat.

GAUCHO: (Spanish: "good horseman") A cowboy of South America.

GAYO: (Spanish) Merry, bright.

GAZAPO: (Spanish) Young rabbit.

GEMA: (Spanish) Jewel.
GEMELO: (Spanish) Twin.
GEO: (Greek) The earth.
GEORGIO: (Greek: "farmer") Nature lover.
GIGANTE: (Spanish) Giant.
GIGIO: (Italian) Cricket.
GITANA, GITANO: (Spanish) Gypsy.
GLICINA: (Spanish) Wisteria.
GORDA: (Spanish) Darling.
GORDO: (Spanish) Stout, plump.
GOZO: (Spanish) Pleasure.
GRINGO: (Spanish) Gibberish.
GRISWOLD: (Old German) "From the gray forest."
GRONCHO: (Spanish) Worker.
GUNTHER: (Scandinavian) Battle army, warrior.
GUSTAVE, GUSTAVUS: (Scandinavian) "Staff of the Goths."
HADA: (Spanish) Good fairy.
HAKIM: (Arabic) Wise, learned.
HAMISH: Scottish form of James.
HARA: (Japanese) Belly.
HIJA: (Spanish) Daughter.
HIJO: (Spanish) Son.

HOMBRE: (Spanish) Man, fellow.
HONDO: (Spanish) Deep, low.
JABADO: (Spanish) White with brown patches.
JACA: (Spanish) Pony, small horse, mare.
JAI: (Spanish) Celebration.
JARDIN, JARDINIÉRE: (French) Garden.
JIAO JIAO: (Chinese) "Double charming."
JINETA: (Spanish) Horsewoman.
JINETE: (Spanish) Horseman.
JOLIE: (French) Pretty.
JOLIE COEUR: (French) Happy heart.
JONGLEUR: (Old French) A wandering minstrel of the Middle Ages in France and England.
JOSE: (Spanish) Joseph.
JOYA: (Spanish) Jewel, gem.
JUANITA: (Spanish) Joan. Gracious.
JULIENNE: (French: "a caterer") Clear.
JUNTO: (Spanish) United.
JURA: (Spanish) Oath.
JUSTO: (Spanish) Fair, right.
KAI: (Chinese) King.
KAI LUNG: (Chinese) King

dragon.

KIMIKO: (Japanese) "noble child"

KIRA: (Persian) Sun.

LABELLE: (French) Beautiful one.

LADINO: (Spanish) Wily, smart.

LAJA: (Spanish) Sandstone.

LANA: (Spanish) Wool, fleece.

LARGO: (Spanish: "long") In music, slow and stately. From the classic movie *Key Largo,* starring Humphrey Bogart and Lauren Bacall.

LAYLA: (Arabic: "darkness") The title of a popular song by English guitar great Eric Clapton. Also spelled Laylah.

LAZO: (Spanish) Bow, knot, lasso.

LENA, LINA: (Greek) Torch.

LEVEE, LEVIE: (French: "to raise") Early morning riser.

LEVERT: (French) The green.

LINDA: (Spanish) Pretty.

LOBA: (Spanish) She-wolf.

LOBO: (Spanish: "wolf") When they were kids, Michael Jackson and his brothers had a German Shepherd named this.

LOCO: (Spanish: "crazy") A name for a zany, mischievous pet.

LOLA: (Spanish) "Mary of the sorrows." A form of Dolores.

LUJO: (Spanish) Luxury.

LUNA: (Spanish: "moon") A name for a pet that stays up nights.

MADEMOISELLE: (French) Young lady.

MADRE: (Spanish) Mother.

MADRINA: (Spanish) Godmother.

MAGIA: (Spanish) Magic.

MAGIO: (Spanish) Wizard.

MAI: (French) May.

MAJO: (Spanish) Pretty, lovely, nice, handsome.

MALO: (Spanish) Bad.

MAMASITA: (Spanish) Little mother.

MANANA: (Spanish) Tomorrow.

MANITA: (Spanish) Little hand.

MANSO: (Spanish) Tame.

MARGARITA: (Spanish) Pearl.

MARINO: (Spanish) Sea.

MARIQUITA: (Spanish) Ladybird.

MARTYR: (Greek) Witness.

MASTOS: (Greek) Beast.

MAXIMUS: (Latin) Super.

MENEO: (Spanish) Shake, toss.

MERCEDES: (Spanish) "Mary of the graces."

MERCI: (French) Thank you.

MERINO: (Spanish: "shepherd") Soft, woolly.

META: (Spanish) Goal.

MIA: (Italian) Mine.

MICO: (Spanish) Monkey.

MIGNON: (French) Darling.

MIGUEL, MIQUEL: God-like. Spanish form of Michael.

MIO: (Spanish) Mine, belonging to me.

MODESTIA, MODESTO: (Spanish) Modesty.

MONA: (Greek) Solitary.

MON CHERIE: (French) My dear.

MONSIEUR: (French) Sir, mister, gentleman.

MONTAGUE: (French) Pointed hill.

MONTE: (Spanish) Mountain, wild country.

MYA: (Hawaiian) Emerald.

NANO: (Spanish) Spoiled; silly.

NATA: (Spanish) Cream.

NAUTILUS: (Greek) Sailor.

NENA: (Spanish) Baby girl.

NENE: (Spanish) Baby boy.

NERO: (Spanish: "stern") A Roman emperor.

NEVA: (Spanish) Snowy.

NEZ: (French) Nose.

NIDO: (Spanish) Nest.

NIKITA: (Russian) Victory.

NIKOLI: (Russian) Victory.

NINA: (Spanish) Little girl.

NINO: (Spanish) Little boy.

NORIA: (Spanish) Water-wheel.

NOVIO: (Spanish) Sweet-heart, bridegroom.

NUNCIO: (Latin) Messenger.

OMEGA: (Greek: "great") The last letter of the Greek alphabet.

ORSON: (Latin) Bear.

OSA: (Spanish) She-bear.

OSADIA: (Spanish) Daring, boldness.

OSO: (Spanish) Bear.

OUIJA: (French-Greek: "yes") A device used in fortune-telling, consisting of a small three-cornered board moved over a larger board (Ouija board) bearing the alphabet and other symbols.

PACO: (Spanish) Frank.

PADRE: (Spanish) Father.

PAISANO: (Spanish) Pleasant.

PAJARITO: (Spanish) Baby bird, fledgling; birdie.

PAJARO: (Spanish) Bird.

PALO ALTO: (Spanish) High Tree. Calvin Coolidge, the 30th President of the United States, had a dog with this name.

PALOMA: (Spanish) Dove.

PANDO: (Spanish) Bulging.

PANELA: (Spanish) Brown sugar, sugar loaf.

PANTERA: (Spanish) Panther, jaguar.

PANZA: (Spanish) Belly.

PANZER: (Greek) Armor.

PAPOOSE: (Native American) Baby.

PARFAIT: (French) Perfect.

PASEO: (Spanish) "to take a stroll." A formal march of bullfighters into an arena.

PAZ: (Spanish) Peacefulness, tranquillity.

PEDRO: (Spanish: "rock") Peter. Sturdy.

PEMA: (Albanian) Fruit tree.

PENCO: (Spanish) Hard-working; horse.

PERITO: (Spanish) Skillful.

PERLA: (Spanish) Pearl.

PESO: (Spanish-Latin: "something weighed") Any of the momentary units and silver coins of some Spanish speaking countries, such as Mexico.

PEZ: (Spanish: "fish") The name of a candy for kids that comes in a collectible dispenser.

PILAR: (Spanish) Milestone.

PINCHO: (Spanish) Prickle.

PINTA: (Spanish) Spot.

POETICA: (Latin) Poetry.

POIK: (Swedish) Little boy.

POQUITA: (Spanish) Little bit.

POQUITO: (Spanish) Little bit.

POTRO: (Spanish) Colt.

POZA: (Spanish) Puddle.

POZO: (Spanish) Well.

PRADO: (Spanish) Meadow, field, green grassy area.

PRENDA: (Spanish) Token.

PRESEA: (Spanish) Treasure, jewel, precious.

PRIETO: (Spanish) Blackish, dark.

PRIMICIA: (Spanish) First appearance.

PRIMO: (Italian) Firstborn.

PRISA: (Spanish) Speed.

PROA: (Spanish) Bow, bows.

PRONTO: (Spanish) Quick, prompt.

PUEBLO: (Spanish: "people") A pet that loves people.

PUELA: (Latin) Girl.

PUER: (Latin) Boy.

PUJA: (Spanish) Effort.

PUNTO: (Spanish) Spot, speckle.

QUANTA: (Spanish) Quantum.

QUEDO: (Spanish) Quiet, soft, gentle.

QUIETO: (Spanish) Still, motionless.

RABEAR: (Spanish) "To wag its tail."

RABILLO: (Spanish) "Small tail."

RABO: (Spanish: "trail") A good name for a pet that strays.

RABON: (Spanish) Short-tailed, bob-tailed, tailless.

RACHA: (Spanish) Gust of wind.

RADA: (Spanish: "roads") A pet that strays or loves to travel.

RALEA: (Spanish) Kind, sort, breed.

RAMO: (Spanish) Bouquet, bunch of flowers.

RAMOS: (Latin: "a branch") A pet that loves to climb trees.

RANA: (Spanish) Frog.

RARO: (Spanish) Rare, uncommon.

RATON: (Spanish) Mouse.

RAUDO: (Spanish) Swift.

RAZON: (Spanish) Rightness, justice.

REACIO: (Spanish) Stubborn.

REDONDA, REDONDO: (Spanish) Roundness.

REGALIA, REGALO: (Spanish) Royal; gift.

REGIO: (Spanish) Royal, regal, kingly.

REINDA: (Spanish) Reign, restraint.

REMAR: (Spanish) To row.

REMO: (Spanish) Arm, leg, wing.

RENO: (Spanish) Reindeer. Also, a city in western Nevada.

REO: (Spanish) Sea trout.

REY: (Spanish) King.

RICO: (Spanish) Wealthy, valuable, precious.

RIMA: (Spanish) Rhyme, poetry.

RIO: (Spanish) River, stream.

RISA: (Spanish: "laughter") A jovial, humorous pet.

RIZAR: (Spanish) Curl, ruffle.

ROBALO: (Spanish) Sea bass.

ROBUSTO: (Spanish) Strong, tough.

ROCA: (Spanish) Rock.

ROGARE: (Old French-Latin) "To ask."

ROJO: (Spanish) Red.

ROMO: (Spanish) Snub-nosed.

ROSA: (Spanish) Rose.

ROSALINDA: (Spanish) Pretty rose.

ROSE: (French) Pink.

ROSETA: (Spanish) Small rose.

ROUGE: (French) Red.

RUBIA: (Spanish) Blonde.

RUBIO: (Spanish) Golden.

RUFO: (Spanish) Sandy-haired, red-haired, curly-haired.

RUMBA: (Spanish: "party, celebration; a rhythmic dance") A pet with rhythmic movements.

SABIO: (Spanish) Wise.

SABU: (Spanish) Bloodhound. Short for Sabueso.

SALITA: (Spanish) Small room.

SALSA: (Spanish) Spicy.

SALVAJE: (Spanish) Wildcat.

SANTO: (Spanish) Saint.

SAPO: (Spanish) Small animal, bug, toad.

SAZON: (Spanish) Good heart.

SELVA: (Spanish) Forest, woods, jungle.

SEMPER: (Latin) Always.

SENDA: (Spanish) Path.

SENOR: (Spanish) Gentleman.

SENORITA: (Spanish) Young lady.

SENSATO: (Spanish) Sensible.

SERAFIN: (Spanish) Angel, cherub.

SERENO: (Spanish) Calm, serene.

SERIO: (Spanish) Serious, solemn.

SESENTA: (Spanish) Sixty.

SESERA: (Spanish) Intelligence.

SETA: (Spanish) Toadstool.

SHABBA: (Afican) king.

SHEREE, SHERIE: (French, from "Cheri") Beloved.

SIERPE: (Spanish) Snake.

SIESTA: (Spanish: "nap") A good name for a pet that naps or sleeps most of the time.

SIGNORINA: (Italian) Young lady.

SIGNOR: (Italian) Male.

SINO: (Spanish) Fate, destiny.

SIRENA: (Spanish) Mermaid, bathing beauty.

SITSI: (Navajo) Daughter.

SOBRINA: (Spanish) Niece.

SOBRINO: (Spanish) Nephew.

SOCORRO: (Spanish) Help,

assistance, relief.

SOL: (Spanish) Sun.

SOLEADO: (Spanish) Sunny.

SOMBRERO: (Spanish) Hat or other headgear.

SONORA: (Spanish) Loud.

SONRISA: (Spanish) Smile.

SORBO: (Spanish) Sip, gulp.

SUAVE: (Spanish) Smooth, gentle, mild, soft.

SVEN: (Swedish) Young.

TABU: (Spanish) Taboo.

TANTE: (French) Aunt.

TAO: (Chinese) "The way."

TÉA: (Spanish) Torch, fire lighter.

TEJON: (Spanish) Badger.

TELA: (Latin) Web.

TESSELLA: (Latin) Small square stone.

TIA: (Spanish) Aunt.

TIERRA: (Spanish) Earth, world.

TIGRE: (Spanish) Tiger.

TIGRESA: (Spanish) Tigress.

TINO: (Spanish) Skill, good judgment.

TIO: (Spanish) Uncle.

TODO: (Spanish) All, whole.

TOMA: (Spanish) Taking, capturing.

TOPO: (Spanish: "mole") Clumsy person.

TORDO: (Spanish) Dapple gray.

TORO: (Spanish: "bull") He-man, strong man.

TOUJOURS: (French) Always.

TREOWA: (Anglo-Saxon) Faith.

TRINO: (Spanish) Warble.

TRONCA: (Spanish) Bird.

UNO: (Spanish) One.

VARGA: (Spanish) Steepest part of the slope.

VARITA: (Spanish) Magic wand.

VARON: (Spanish) Man, boy.

VELA: (Spanish) Candle, light.

VENIA: (Latin) Grace. Also (Spanish), "pardon, forgiveness."

VENTURA: (Spanish) Happiness; luck.

VIADA: (Spanish) Speed.

VIDA: (Spanish) Life.

VIEJA: (Spanish) Old one.

VIENTO: (Spanish) Wind, breeze.

VIGIA: (Spanish) Watchman.

VIGILLA: (Spanish) Watchful.

VIN: (French) Wine.

VIOLET, VIOLETTE: (French) Purple.

VITA: (Latin) Life.

VIVA: (Spanish) Cheer.
VIVO: (Spanish) Living, alive.
VOZ: (Spanish) Voice.
VUELO: (Spanish) Flight; lace, frill.
WAHOO: (American Indian) A large shrub or tree having purple fruit and red seeds.
WAMPUM: (Algonquian) Small beads.
WASHO: (Cherokee) Lone eagle.
XENO, XENON, XENOS: (Greek) Strange, foreign.
XI WANG: (Chinese) Hope.
YANA: (Spanish) Black.
YAZ: (Spanish) Jazz.
YEDRA: (Spanish) Ivy.
YEMA: (Spanish) Egg.
YUGO: (Spanish) Yoke.
ZAFADO: (Spanish) Shameless; alert, sharp.
ZAFAR: (Spanish) Loosen; untie.
ZAFIRO: (Spanish) Sapphire.
ZAGAL: (Spanish) Boy, lad, youth, shepherd boy.
ZAGALA: (Spanish) Girl, lass, sherpherdess.
ZAMARRA: (Spanish) Sheepskin.
ZAMBO: (Spanish) Mixed breed.
ZAMBRA: (Spanish) Gypsy.

ZANGON: (Spanish) Big, lazy lad.
ZARCO: (Spanish) Light blue.
ZARPA: (Spanish) Claw, paw.
ZAZAMORA: (Spanish) Blackberry.
ZONDA: (Spanish) Hot northerly wind.
ZONZO: (Spanish) Silly.
ZORRA: (Spanish) Fox; vixen.
ZUMO: (Spanish) Juice.

Lodi

Did You Know?

ANNIE: Graceful. Known for Annie Oakley, the female rifle expert whose targets resembled punched tickets. Barbara Eden, actress and the star of the TV series "I Dream of Jeannie," has a poodle with this name.

RUTHERFORD: Herder. Known for Rutherford Birchard Hayes, who was the 19th President of the United States. Fran Drescher, the star of the TV series "The Nanny," once had a cat with this name.

SIAM: Rutherford B. Hayes, the 19th President of the United States, had a Siamese cat with this name.

Schooner

Chapter 22

Travel and Mechanical

With computers and technology playing an ever more important part in our daily lives, is it any wonder that we may now have a dog named **Robo**? Or a cat named **Tron**? Maybe a goldfish named **Munsey**? Or even a cute little canary named **Hemi**?

ALFA: For Alpha Romeo, an Italian sports car.

ASTON: For Aston Martin, the British automobile, the car driven by Agent 007 James Bond in the popular novels and movie series.

ATARI: Maker of video games

AUDI: A car made in Germany.

BENTLEY: Luxury automobile, manufactured by Rolls Royce.

BLAZER: A recreational vehicle manufactured by Chevrolet.

BOEING: Manufacturer of aircraft.

BOSCH: An electronics manufacturer.

BOXCAR: A roofed train car.

BRONCO: A recreational vehicle manufactured by Ford.

BUGGY: Any small cart for carrying heavy materials. Also, known for a baby carriage.

BULLDOZER: Strong; sturdy.

CADILLAC: Classy, large. A luxury car manufactured by General Motors.

CANOE: A narrow boat with sharp ends, usually propelled by paddles.

CARRERA: A Porsche. Sporty.

CHOPPER: Loud; hungry. Name for a helicopter.

CLIPPER: A fast sailing ship. John F. Kennedy, the 35th President of the United States, had a German Shepherd with this name.

DeSOTO: An old automobile, made by Chrysler.

DROID: Short for android, a robot. Mechanical.

DYSON: A brand of vacuum cleaner.

EDSEL: The name of a highly unsuccessful car of the 1950s.

GADGET: Small.

HARLEY: From the Harley-Davidson motorcycle, an American classic.

HEMI: In 1951, Chrysler introduced their new line of V8 motors, popularly known as the "hemi", because the combustion chamber was fully machined into the shape of a ½-dome or hemi-sphere.

HOOVER: A brand of vacuum cleaner.

HUMVEE: An all-terrain vehicle. Also called a Hummer.

JAG: Short for Jaguar, a luxury car.

JAGUAR: A luxury automobile manufactured in Great Britain.

JALOPY: An old run-down vehicle.

JEEP: Rugged. From "Eugene the Jeep," an animal in a comic strip by E. C. Segar. Also, a small, all-purpose vehicle with four-wheel drive, used by the US army and later sold as domestic vehicle as well.

JET: A fast airplane.

KAYAK, KYAK: An Eskimo canoe made of skins completely covering a wood frame except for an opening for the paddles.

LAMBORGHINI: An Italian sports car.

LASER: A device producing an intense, highly directional beam of light. A pet that is fast and intense.

LEXUS: A luxury automobile.

MASSER: Short for Masserati, a sports car. Speedy.

MECHE: Mechanical. Predictable.

MERCEDES: Mercedes Benz, a German luxury car.

MINKA: For Minka Lavery, maker of lighting products.

MUNSEY: A brand of small appliances.

NOKIA: A brand of cell phone.

PASCAL: A unit of pressure.

PIPER: Small planes manufactured in America by Piper, Inc.

PORSCHE: A sports car manufactured in Germany.

POULAN: Pronounced "polan," a popular brand of chainsaw.

REGAL: A car made by Buick.

REMINGTON: A brand of firearms.

RICKSHA, RICKSHAW: A small covered, two-wheeled vehicle for one passenger and pulled by one man.

ROBO: Short for robot. Very precise in movement.

ROCKET: To dart about swiftly. Actress Kate Jackson, the former star of the TV series "Charlie's Angels," has a Siberian husky with this name. The name of a Beanie Baby bird, a bluejay. Also, the name of musician Beck's pet rabbit.

ROLLS ROYCE: A luxury vehicle made in Great Britain.

ROOMBA: A small robotic vacuum cleaner.

RYOBI: A brand of power tools.

SCHOONER: Typically, a sailing vessel with two masts.

SEGA: A video game manufacturer.

TANK: A heavy, armored vehicle, used by the military.

TRIUMPH: A sports car made in Great Britain. Also, the name of *Triumph the Comic Dog.*

TRON: Short for electronic. A pet that is a creature of habit, mechanical.

TRUCKER: A pet that stays on the go.

TUGBOAT: Small, sturdy boat designed for towing or pushing ships.

TURBO: Fast. A car that is turbo-charged. The name of a trained stunt dog performing at Dollywood, located in eastern Tennessee.

TWEETSIE: For Tweetsie Railroad, a family attraction located in the Appalachian mountains of Blowing Rock, North Carolina.

YEBO: *Yebo!*, a wireless phone provider.

ZEPPELIN: A zeppelin is a dirigible airship with a cigar-shaped bag.

Rocket

Did You Know?

BRUTUS: Ruthless. Irrational. Fashion designer Bill Blass has a golden retriever with this name.

CINCINNATUS: Ulysses S. Grant, the 18th President of the United States, had a horse with this name.

GENERAL: John Tyler, the 10th President of the United States, had a horse named The General.

Razzleberry & Reanna

Hoops

Chapter 23

Sports and Athletes

Pets are often natural athletes and with so many gifted sports figures today as well as sports stars of the past to choose from there is sure to be a perfect name for your new pet: *Mia, Jordan, Martina, Evander,* among many others. Or maybe you have a sporting pet: Say you may have a snowboarding cat! Or a bobsledding dog! Or a surfing parakeet! Or maybe a fish that is a real swimming champ! Or any other sporting pet, maybe a pet that just likes running to and fro!

ADIDIAS: A brand of casual wear and sneakers.

AIKIDO: A Japanese art of self-defense employing locks and holds and using an opponent's own resistence against him.

ALBIE: For Atlanta Braves pitcher Albie Lopez.

ANDRETTI: For Indy racing champion Mario Andretti.

ANNIKA: For professional golfer Annika Sorenstam who won more LPGA tournaments (18) than any other player in the 1990s.

AVIA: A brand of sportswear.

BABE: Small, loved. A pet that acts like a baby. For baseball great Babe Ruth, born George Herman Ruth, the most famous player in the game's history. Also, the name of American folk hero Paul Bunyan's ox.; and the name of a talking pig who thinks he's a sheep dog in the movie *Babe.*

BEAUMONT: Known for the prestigious horse race, Beaumont Stakes.

BLITZ: A play where the defensive team sends players rushing towards the line of scrimmage as soon as the ball is snapped to try to sack the quarterback.

BO: For football great Bo Jackson, the Heisman Trophy winner.

BOCCIE, BOCCI, BOCCE: (Pronouned "bochee") A game of Italian origin and similar to lawn bowling.

BOOGIE: A brand of surf boards.

BRODIE: San Francisco Forty-Niner quarterback John Brodie.

BUTKUS: Former Chicago Bear football player Dick Butkus, All-Pro 7 of 9 NFL seasons with Chicago Bears; worked with XFL in 2001.

CHIPPER: For Atlanta Braves baseball player Chipper Jones.

COACH: Leader. To instruct.

CONSECO: For baseball great Jose Conseco.

DERBY: A horse race in Kentucky.

DiMAGGIO: American baseball player, Joseph Paul DiMaggio, better known as Joe DiMaggio, and who was married briefly to Marilyn Monroe.

DITKA: For Mike Ditka, former football player for the Chicago Bears and later the head coach.

DOMINIQUE: Of God. For Dominique Moceanu, a gymnast on the 1996 gold-winning U.S. Olympic team.

DRIBBLE: To bounce a basketball.

DUNK: In basketball, to put the ball into the basket with your hands above rim.

EARNHART: For race car driver Dale Earnhart who was a 7-time NASCAR national champion; finally won Daytona 500 in 1998 on 20th attempt; died in last lap crash at the 2001 Daytona .

EVANDER: For championship boxer Evander Holyfield.

EVEL: Daring. For stuntman and daredevil Evel Kenevel.

FLUTIE: For Doug Flutie who won Heisman Trophy with Boston College (1984) and has played in USFL, NFL and CFL.

GOOLAGONG: For Evonne Goolagong Cawley, an Australian tennis player who won Australian Open 4 times, Wimbledon twice (1971,80), French once (1971).

GUINNESS: For the *Guinness Book of World Records*, sports and miscellaneous records.

HAMM: For American-born, internationally recognized soccer champion Mia Hamm.

HOOPER: Athletic.

HOOPS: Playing basketball.

HULKSTER: Huge. Nickname for wrestler Hulk Hogan.

JABBAR: Athletic. For African-American basketball player Kareem Abdul-Jabbar.

JARRETT: For race car driver Dale Jarrett who was the 1999 Winston Cup champion; 3-time Daytona champion (1993,96,2000).

JAVELIN: Athletic.

JAVY: (Pronounced "HA-vee") For Atlanta Braves baseball player Javy Lopez.

JELENA: Russian for "shining light." For tennis star Jelena Dokic.

JOCK, JOCKO: Slang for athlete or sports lover.

JORDAN: Open-minded. For basketball great Michael Jordan.

JUJITSU: A wrestler.

JUDO: Defensive. A wrestler. From "jujitsu," a form of Japanese wrestling in which the strength and weight of an opponent are used against him.

KAREEM: Blessed. For American basketball player Kareem Abdul-Jabbar.

KATARINA: Pure. For German figure skating champion and four-time Olympic Gold medalist Katarina Witt.

KICKS: Playful prankster. A soccer bear Beanie Baby.

K.O.: In boxing, a knockout where an opponent is down for a ten-count.

MADDUX: For long-time Atlanta Braves pitcher Greg Maddux.

MAGIC: For Earvin Magic Johnson, player for the Los Angeles Lakers and 3-time MVP (1987,89-90).

MARINO: For Dan Marino who had a 17-year, record-breaking career with the Miami Dolphins. Marino holds records for throwing the most touchdown passes (420), the most passing yards (61,361), and the most completions (4,967).

MARTINA: Warrior. For tennis great Martina Navratilova.

McGWIRE: For St. Louis Cardinals' slugger Mark Mc-

Gwire, who shattered Roger Maris's season home run record in 1998.

MEADOWLARK: Any of various North American song-birds with a yellow breast. For Meadowlark Lemon, a member of the Harlem Globetrotters basketball team.

MIA: For Mia Hamm who be-came the all-time leading scorer in international soccer with her 108th goal in 1999.

MIZONA: A manufacturer of sports equipment.

MONTANA: For Joe Mon-tana, formerly a quarterback for the San Francisco 49ers and second in pass efficiency.

NADIA: Hope. For Romanian gymnast Nadia Comaneci , an Olympic medalist in the 1976 Montreal Games.

NERF: A brand of toy foot-ball.

NIKE: A brand of sportswear and sneakers.

NOLAN: For Nolan Ryan, the pitcher who holds the all-time record for strikeouts (5,714) .

OKSANA: A Russian name meaning "glory be to God." For Ukranian figure skater Ok-sana Baiul, 1993 world cham-pion at age 15 and a Olympic gold medal winner.

OLD SMOKEY: The name of the University of Tennessee sports team's, the Volunteers (Vols for short) mascot, a blue tick coon hound.

PALOOKA: An inexperi-enced boxer.

PICABO: For United States skiing champion and Olympic Silver and two-time gold medalist Picabo Street.

POCONO: The Pocono 500, a NASCAR race held in the Poconos mountains of New York.

POLO: A game played on horseback by two teams who try to drive a small wooden ball through the opponents' goal with long-handled mal-lets. Also, water polo. A suit-able name for a pony or horse.

PUCK: A rubber disk used in hockey.

PUTTER: A short, straight-faced golf club used in putting. Also, to busy oneself in an aimless way.

PUTT PUTT: An amateur golf game involving obstacles.

REBOUND: Retrieving and recovering the basketball after

a missed shot.

RIMSHOT: Athletic.

RIPKIN: For baseball great Cal Ripkin, Jr., who broke Lou Gehrig's major league Iron Man record of playing, 130 consecutive games on September 6, 1995.

ROOKIE: A player in his or her first year.

RUGBY: Active. A kind of football named for the boys' school in England at which the game was first played.

SHAQ: Short for Shaquille. Nickname for basketball great Shaquille O'Neal.

SHAQUILLE: For basketball great Shaquille O'Neal.

SHORTSTOP: A pet that is fast but often comes to an abrupt stop. In baseball, the infielder between second and third base.

SKEET: A sport in which clay targets are thrown into the air and fired upon.

SLAMDUNK: A basketball term for putting the ball through the hoop up close and quickly.

SLUGGER: Active, athletic. A term for a good hitter in a game of baseball. Also, slang for a fighter such as a boxer.

SOSA: For Sammy Sosa, the Chicago Cubs baseball slugger who surpassed Roger Maris's home run record, just after Mark McGwire did in 1998.

SOX: The name of the mascot for the Boston Red Sox baseball team.

SPAULDING: A brand of sports equipment and athletic wear.

SPEEDO: A brand of sportswear.

SPORT, SPORTY: Athletic, energetic.

SPUD: For basketball star Spud Webb, NBA Slamdunk Champion and once the smallest player in the NBA.

SUGAR RAY: The name of boxing champion Sugar Ray Leonard.

SWISH: In basketball, a shot that goes into the basket touching only the net.

TACKLE: In football, grasping and knocking a player to the ground to keep him from advancing.

TIGER: For young golf pro Tiger Woods. Also, an aggressive pet. The name of the family dog in the TV series "The

Brady Bunch." Tiger appeared in the first episode of the series chasing the girls' cat Fluffy and toppling the guests, tables, and the cake at the wedding reception for Carol and Mike.

TKO: In boxing, a technical knockout. A pet that is rowdy.

TRAP: On a golf course, an area filled with sand.

TROTTER: A runner.

TROXY: A runner.

WILSON: A brand of sporting goods.

WILT: For basketball great Wilt Chamberlain who played for the 76ers and the L.A. Lakers and led the teams to NBA titles.

XAVIER: (Arabic: "bright") For basketball star Xavier Mc-Daniel.

YAO: For Yao ming, the NBA star who was born in China and plays for the Houston Rockets basketball team.

YOGI: For baseball great Yogi Berra who holds the record for most hits in the World Series.

ZAMBONI: In hockey, the machine used to smooth the ice.

Did You Know?

BLAZE: Franklin Delano Roosevelt, the 32nd President of the United States, had a mastiff with this name.

MUSHKA: The dog on one of the first Russian space flights had this name.

SAUDI: When they were a couple, Brad Pitt and Jennifer Aniston had a dog with this name.

Mandalay

Addie & Aria

Chapter 24

Unusual Names

OK. I admit it. This chapter is *just* an excuse to lump together a lot of miscellaneous names, but in the chapter's defense, they *are* some petty unusual names! Imagine a cat named *Alodi*! A dog named *Bluegrass*! A bird named *Frisket*! A fish named *Dokken*! And don't even get me started on the armadillo named *Ming Poo*!

ABRA: Short for Abracadabra.

ABRACADABRA: Magical word; a word magicians use when performing their tricks.

ABUNDANCE: Wealth.

ADAGIO: Musical.

ADDIE: Musical.

AGIS: Pure.

AHMAD: Highly praised.

AHMET: Praised.

AIRELL: In charge.

AIRLA: Ethereal.

AIRLIA: Ethereal.

ALLISE: Well-known.

ALMIRA: Exalted.

ALODI: Prosperous.

ALONA: Strong as an oak.

ALONDRA: Single; alone.

ALPHA: The first letter of the Greek alphabet. The first of anything.

AMABEL: Easy to love.

AMBROSINA, AMBRO-SINE: Immortal.

AMYRA: Loved.

ANASAZI: Ancient.

ANTHEA: A flower. Expressive.

APOLLA: Musical.

ARIANNA, ARIANNE: Graceful melody.

ARIKANA: Eater of corn.

ARIOSO: A melody.

ARISTA: The best.

ARKY: Refuge.

ARNON: Strong.

ASTIN: Fortunate.

ATHEA: Healing.

AVENA: A pet who comes when called.

AYDA: Maiden. Pronounced "ah-da."

BABA: Self-sufficient.

BAKER: In the 1959 space program, a squirrel monkey survived a ballistic rocket flight.

BANNER: In command. The real name of the poodle who played Barbara Ann in the movie *Good Boy!*

BAPTISTA: Purity.

BARBAROSA: Cowboy.

BARD: Poetic.

BEVA: Trendy.

BLESSING: Gift.

BLUEGRASS: Country-bred. A pet that enjoys the simple life, the outdoors.

BLUME: Bloom, flower.

BOGARD, BOLEGARD: Beautiful expression.

BONITA: Good; pretty.

BOOTLES: Valuable.

BOUQUET: Fragrant flowers.

BOURGEOIS: Respectable.

BROTHER: Male.

BUENA: Good.

BURGESS: Citizen.

BUTCHER BOY: Ulysses S. Grant, the 18th President of the United States, had a horse with this name.

CARIA: Quiet as a whisper.

CARISSE, CARISSA: Creative.

CARMAN: The name of a dog, a Jack Russell Terrier, in Purina Dog Chow Incredible Dog Team, precision-trained dogs that travel the country performing at halftime shows, on television programs and a variety of other public events.

CARMEL: (Hebrew) Garden.

CARMELITA: (Hebrew) Little garden.

CARTER: A digger.

CASH: Valuable.

CASHA: Valuable.

CASSIETTA: Pure.

CATFISH: The name of columnist Lewis Grizzard's dog.

CEDRIC: In control.

CHAN: Short for Chancellor.

CHANTAL: A melody.

CHARISMA: Popular.

CHARMAINE: A charmer.

CHASTA: Pure.

CHASTAIN, CHASTINE: Pure.

CHASTITY: Decent, pure.

CHATERLAINE: The lady of the castle, mistress of the chateau.

CHAY: Resting.

CHIQUITO: Boy.

CHOICE: The best; carefully chosen.

CIPANGO: Poetic word for Japan.

CLORINDA: Popular.

CLU: Mysterious.

COCHISE: Chief.

COLE, COLLANE: Victorious.

COLUMBELLA: Female.

CONCITA: Prosperous.

CONCORDIA: Old-fashioned.

CONRAD: Bold advisor.

COPIA: From cornucopia, an abundance.

COQUETTE: Female, flirtatious.

CORD: Strong.

CORDELL: Strong.

CRAFTY: Skilled. Clever.

CRAVEN: Desired.

CRINGLE: Often used in Chris Cringle, another name for Santa Claus.

CRUMB. CRUMBS: A messy pet.

CUFF: An item encircling the wrist or ankle.

CURRAN: Hero.

CYTHEREA: Venus.

DACK: Clumsy.

DAELA: (Pronounced "DAY-la") "Of the day."

DAI: Day. Bright.

DAINTRY: Delicate.

DAMOISELLE: Damsel.

DAMSEL: Maiden.

DANICA, DANNA: Judged.

DARIA: Queenly.

DARICE: Elegant.

DARK KNIGHT: Mysterious.

DEBANY: Good breeding.

DELANE: Restful.

DESIREE: Desire.

DESSIE: Wanted.

DEVANE: Patriotic.

DILLARD: Sour.

DOKKEN: A pet that likes to swim.

DOLLA: A gift.

DOLLAR: Of value; money.

DOM: Homebody.

DOMBEY: Homebody.

DOMENIA: Homebody.

DOMI: Homebody.

DONACELLA: A maiden.

DORAE: A gift.

DORO: A gift.

DOSIA: A gift.

DOTRICE: A gift.

DRAGAN: Creative.

DRAGANA: Creative.

DRAGO: Short for dragon, a large mythical monster, usually represented as a large reptile with wings and claws, breathing out fire and smoke.

DRENA: Thirsty.

DULCE, DULCIE: Charming.

DUTCH, DUTCHIE: Unusual.

EANO: Belonging.

EGBERT: Bright sword.

EGERTON: Homebody.

ELITA, ELITE: The best.

ELMIRA, ELMYRA: Celebrated.

ELRENA: Maiden.

ENRICA: Homebody.

EPSILON: The fifth letter of the Greek alphabet.

ERSTINE: Old-fashioned.

EUPHEMIA: Well-known.

EXCELLENCY: Excellent.

FAME, FAMELLE: Known.

FARA: Exotic.

FEDARA: Special.

FELLER: Harry S. Truman's, the 33rd President of the United States, personal physician had a dog with this name.

FEODOR: Special.

FIDELIA, FIDELLA: Faithful.

FLAG: Honorable, loyal.

FLEETWOOD: Top of the line, the best.

FLETCH: Short for Fletcher.

FLETCHER: The "maker of arrows."

FLORINA: Healthy.

FLORRIE, FLORRY: A flower.

FLOYCE: A show-off.

FOGGY: Easily overwhelmed, confused.

FOGY: Old-fashioned; chubby.

FOLKSY: Old-fashioned.

FORTUNA: Fortunate.

FORTUNE: Valuable; lucky.

FRAGILE: Delicate.

FRANZ: Sharing.

FRISKET: A masking device or material used in printing and graphic arts.

FUDDY: Short for fuddy duddy. Fussy; old-fashioned.

FUSTY: Old-fashioned.

GAGE: Secure.

GAINELLE: Graceful; prosperous.

GAL: Slang for girl.

GALIVANT: Gallant.

GALLANT: Brave and noble; grand; stately.

GAMIEL: Reward.

GANGSTER: Intimidating. A pet that is usually up to no good. Actor Sylvester Stallone has a boxer with this name.

GARIBALDI: Patriotic.

GAVIN: Giver.

G-BOY: Short for government

boy. G-Boy was the name of J. Edgar Hoover's Cairn Terrier.

GEEZER: Eccentric; old man.

GEISHA: A Japanese dancing girl.

GEM: Precious, valuable.

GEMMA: Precious, valuable.

GENIA: Well-born.

GENTELLE: Genteel, affectionately refined.

GENTRY: Well-bred.

GERELLE: Graceful.

GERMAINE: Akin.

GEZA: Eccentric.

GHOST: Spooky; elusive.

GIRL: Female.

GODWIN: Godly friend.

GRADY: (Latin: "step") A pet that is always on the go.

GRAECO: Greek.

GRATEFUL: Pleasing. Thankful.

GRAZELDA, GRAZELLE: A pet that likes to eat, especially a pet that feeds on vegetables and grasses.

GUIDO: (Italian) Forest dweller.

GWAR: Unique.

HAMBONE: Imitator.

HAMISH: Homebody.

HAMLIN: Hearty.

HAVEN: Refuge.

HEIRESS: Woman or girl of great wealth.

HENSLEY: Follower.

HEPHZIBAH: Pleasurable.

HEPSY: A pleasure.

HERMENIA: Messenger.

HERMERA: Worldly.

HERMIE: Messenger.

HERMIT: Solitary.

HESPER: The evening star.

HESPERUS: The evening star.

HEXUM: Charming.

HIGHNESS: Purebred.

HOAGY: Lover of music.

HO HUM: Ordinary, familiar.

HUMBUG: Tricky one.

HUMDINGER: Excellent.

HUTCH: Homebody.

IDONA: A worker.

IMPERIAL: Magnificent.

INDEPENDENCE: Self-reliant.

INNOCENCE, INNOCENT: Naive, playful.

IONA: Radiant.

ISIDORA, ISIDORE: A gift.

ISOLDE: Pleasant.

IVA: Skilled.

IVAR: Skillful.

IVON: Skillful.

IVOV: Skillful.

JACINTHA: Precious.

JACO: Pronounced "jay – CO." Aggressive.

JAECKEL: Like a jackal.
JAMA: Daughter.
JAMAL: Son.
JAMELLA: Supplanter.
JAMYMA: Homebody.
JARE: Descent.
JEMINA: Homebody.
JENGA: For the stackable game.
JERE, JEREE: Appointed.
JESSAMINE: Jasmine.
JESSENE: Wealthy.
JESSIAH: Wealthy.
JILLETTE: A girl or young
JILLIE: A girl or young lady.
JOBE: Magnificent.
JOBETH: Magnificent.
JOBINA: Thoughtful.
JOCOBINA: Clever.
JONEA: Well known.
JOSSI: God-like.
JOYCELYN: Merry.
JUBAL: Jubilation.
JURLEE: Illustrious.
JURLENE: Illustrious.
KANOA: Creative.
KAPPA: The tenth letter of the Greek alphabet.
KASPAR, KASPER: Priceless.
KASS: Valuable.
KEETA: Lighthearted.
KESTER: Clever.
KILLIAN: Irish.

KILO: In the metric system, a prefix meaning one thousand.
KINARA, KYNARA: Akin.
KINDRED: Akin.
KIRKLE: Given to divinity.
KIRKLEE: Given to divinity.
KITTA: Kittenlike. Betty White, star of "The Golden Girls" and other TV series and movies, has a Golden Retriever with this name.
KOTO: Homebody.
KREME: Cream. The best.
KRESS, KRESSA: Sneaky.
KUDO: From kudos, meaning "praise, glory."
LABYRINTH: A maze, confusingly intricate.
LADY LUCK: Lucky.
LAHOMA: Homebody.
LARKIN: Musical.
LAROSA: Rose.
LATIMER: Homebody.
LATINA, LATYNE: Blessed.
LAVELLE: Clean.
LAVINIA: A winner.
LEANDER: Hero.
LECHEE: Greedy.
LEETHA: Having a good sense of direction.
LENDORA: Lighthearted.
LENOX, LENNOX: In charge.
LETTA, LETTIE: Gladness.

LEVON: Praise worthy.

LEXINA: Defender of man.

LILITH: Demon. Devilish.

LILLIBET: Lily.

LINC: Short for Lincoln. Crucial link as in "the chain."

LINK: Attachment, bond.

LISE: Healthy.

LISELLE: Healthy.

LODI: Prosperous.

LOFTY: Grand.

LOGY: Idle, slow moving.

LOLANDA: Clear-headed.

LORA: A winner.

LORAN: A winner.

LORD: Powerful.

LORE: Traditional; intelligent.

LOREL: Traditional; intelligent.

LOREN: A winner.

LOUDEN: Loud.

LOURDES: Divine. The name of singer-actress Madonna's daughter.

LUCE, LUCERO: (Latin) Light, lightbringer.

LUDLOW: Regal.

LUGENE: Elegant.

LUGH: Mythical.

LUGO: Mythical.

LUXOR: For luxury, comfortable.

LYCIA: Proud.

LYSANDRA: Freedom.

MACARONI TEX: John F. Kennedy, the 35th President of the United States, had a pony with this name.

MACHEN: Of German origin. Good name for a German shepherd.

MADAM: Lady.

MAGEE: From the Janis Joplin song "Bobby Magee."

MAGINNIS: Scottish.

MAGNIFICO: Nobleman.

MAGNUS: Great.

MAIA: Maiden.

MAIDEN: Sweet and fair; a young girl.

MAJESTA: Majestic.

MAJESTY: Dignified.

MALINA: Skilled.

MALLORY: Visionary.

MAMA: A mother; nurturing.

MAMMY: Mother.

MANDAN: White chief.

MANFRED: Serene.

MANLEY: Strong, masculine.

MANNA: Sweet; miraculous.

MANNERS: Well-behaved.

MANVILLE: Valued.

MARISKA: A Russian name.

MARKKA: Nickled bronze coin of Finland.

MARNIE: Kind.

MARTA: Ladylike.

MARTIKA: Lady.
MARTINE: Warrior.
MARVELLA: A miracle.
MARX: Shield.
MASON: A builder.
MAXI: Great.
MAYDA: Maiden.
MAYER: Helper.
MAZEL: (Hebrew, from mazel tov) Congratulations.
McCOY: From the real McCoy, meaning genuine, not a substitute.
McTAVISH: Old-fashioned.
MECCA: Center of activity.
MEDALLION: Valuable.
MEGANA: Great.
MELICENT: Strong worker.
MERCY: Compassionate.
MERIT: Excellent.
MERRICK: Deserving.
MERVIN: Sea friend.
MERWIN, MERWYN: A friend.
MICAELA: Divine.
MIKA: Divine.
MILADY: Gentlewoman.
MILLA: Elegant; pure.
MIMSY: Superficial.
MINA: Skilled.
MING POO: Exotic.
MINION: Favorite, prince.
MIRACLE: Blessing.
MIRELLA: Blessing.

MISHKA, MISKA: Gift.
MISS: Female.
MISTER: A gentleman, a man.
MIZZY: A lady.
MOGOLLON: Intriguing.
MOM CAT: Motherly.
MOMMY: Motherly.
MOMPET: Motherly.
MONETA: Valuable.
MONNY: Solitary.
MONTU: Solitary.
MONY: Solitary.
MONZI: Solitary.
MOONSTONE: A gem.
MORGANA: Sea lover.
MORLY: Prosperous.
MORVIN: Sea lover.
MOTIF: A dominant idea. The real name of the Italian greyhound who played Nelly in the movie *Good Boy!*
MOZELLE: Ladylike.
MUMBO: From Mumbo Jumbo, protector from evil.
MUMSY: Motherly.
MYKEL: Godly.
MYKEN: Godly.
NAIDA: Of the water.
NAKIA: Defenseless. friend.
NANKO: Abraham Lincoln, the 16th President of the United States, had a pet with this

name.

NANNY: A child's nurse. A nurturing pet. Abraham Lincoln, the 16th President of the United States, had a goat with this name.

NASTASSIA: Blessed.

NATHANIA: Gift.

NEWBIE, NEWBY: Any new pet.

NICOL: Victory.

NICOLA: Victory.

NIKKA: Victory.

NINNY: Innocent.

NIOBE: A mother.

NIRVANA: Blessed.

NITA, NITE: Hungry.

NUI: Aggressive.

OBLIGE: A favor of kindness.

ODELE: Impressive.

ODELIA: Highly valued.

ODELIA: Impressive.

ODESSA: Distant.

ODETTA, ODETTE: Impressive.

OLAF: Saint.

OMEN: Perceptive.

ORACLE: Of great wisdom.

ORASTUS: Disruptive.

ORPHAN: Abandoned.

OSBORN: Divine.

OSGOOD: Divine.

OSWALD, OSWOLD: Powerful.

OTTO: Prosperous.

PALMER: Divine.

PAMONA: Meek one.

PARADOX: Contradictory.

PARAMOUR: A sweetheart.

PARNASSUS: Creative. Poetic.

PASSION: Excitement, enthusiasm.

PATRIOT: Home-loving.

PEACEFUL: A calm, serene pet.

PEARLENA, PEARLENE: A pearl.

PENDRAGON: Leader.

PENNYWISE: Thrifty.

PEPITA: Producing many young.

PEPITO: Producing many young.

PERSIS: Short for persistent.

PETAL: Flower.

PETRA: To become rock. Solid, sturdy.

PETRO: Rock, stone.

PHANTASM: Deceptive likeness, illusive.

PHERES: Perceptive.

PHILBERTA: Happy.

PINELLA: Yearning desire.

PLACIDA: Calm, quiet.

PLACIDO: Calm, quiet.

PLEASANT: Pleasing, merry.

PLESENCE: Pleasing.
POET: Imaginative, thoughtful.
POETESS, POETESSA: Poetic.
POL: Short for Polly. Andrew Jackson, the 7th President of the Unites States, had a pet parrot with this name.
PRAISE: Worthy.
PRIMAL: Original, primeval.
PRODIGAL: Extremely generous or wasteful.
PRODIGY: Extraordinary.
PROTEGÉ: One who needs guidance or protection.
PRU: Prudent.
PRUDENCE PRIM: Calvin Coolidge, the 30th President of the United States, had a collie with this name.
PRUDY: Prudent.
PRUNELLA: Old-fashioned.
PURDELL: Pure, chaste.
PURDENE: Pure, chaste.
PURITY: Pure, chaste.
PUSHINKA: John Kennedy, the 35th President of the United States had a dog named this while in the White House.
QUILA: The name of a dog, an Australian Shepherd/Border Collie Mix, in Purina Dog Chow Incredible Dog Team, precision-trained dogs that travel the country performing at halftime shows, on television programs and a variety of other public events.
QUINTANA, QUINTINA: The fifth, as in quintuplets.
QUITO: A nickname for Achilles.
RADIANCE: Shining.
RALSTON: Prosperous.
RAOUL: Shield.
RASMA, RASMUS: Native one.
RAZZLEBERRY: Sweet and funny.
RAZZLE DAZZLE: A state of confusion or hilarity.
RAZZMATAZZ: Double talk.
REAGLE: Regal. The name of a dog, a Australian Shepherd, in Purina Dog Chow Incredible Dog Team, precision-trained dogs that travel the country performing at halftime shows, on television programs and a variety of other public events.
REATHA: The best.
RIA: Goddess.
RIETTA: Home ruler.
ROCKNE: Strong.
ROLENA, ROLENE:

Renowned.
ROLLANDE: Renowned.
ROMAINE, ROMAYNE: Gypsy man.
ROMANY: A gypsy.
ROMLEY: Manly.
RONDEL: Poetic.
RONNA: Strong ruler.
ROSWELL: Mighty.
RUBY ROUGH: Calvin Coolidge, the 30th President of the United States, had a collie with this name.
SACHET: Perfumed.
SAGA: Heroic.
SAGACITY: Quality.
SAILOR BOY: Theodore Roosevelt, the 26th President of the United States, had a Chesapeake Bay retriever with this name.
SAMPSON: Shining.
SANATHA: Saintly.
SANCTUARY: A place of refuge or protection. Peaceful.
SARDOR: The name of a horse presented to Jacqueline Bouvier Kennedy, then wife of the 35th President of the United States John F. Kennedy, by Ayub Khan of Pakistan.
SCHMALTZ: Slang for anything very sentimental.
SEARLE: A lord.

SEBASTIONA: Majestic.
SECUNDA: The second.
SELANA: Musical.
SELESE: Musical.
SEMAR: Shy one.
SEPTIMA: The seventh child.
SERENE: Clear, calm, and honorable.
SERENELLA: Clear, calm, and honorable.
SERENITY: Serene.
SERPENTINE: Snake-like.
SEXTUS: The sixth.
SHALAMAR: Exotic.
SHAMAN: Blessed. A magician or healer.
SHAVONNE: Praise worthy.
SHELBY: A homebody.
SHINOLA: For the shoe shine product.
SIBONE: All knowing.
SIBYL: Perceptive. Prophetess.
SIGRID: Heroic.
SIGUE: Heroic.
SIROCCO: Hot wind.
SISTER: Nurturing companion.
SOJOURN: Brief stay.
SOLONA: Peaceful.
SOOTHSAYER: Perceptive.
SORCERER: Wizard.
SORCERESS: Female wizard.

SOUBRETTE: A lady's maid; a pretty or flirtatious young lady.
SOVEREIGN: Supreme.
SPLENDOR: Shining.
SPONGE, SPONGEE: Soaking up influences.
SPYRO, SPYROS: Nosy.
SQUIRE: A lady's companion.
STAFFORD: Watchful.
STIL: Quiet, motionless, peaceful.
STILLY: Quiet, motionless, peaceful.
STILTON: Quiet, motionless, peaceful.
STYLES: Sophisticated.
SUZERAIN: Lordly, sovereign.
SWAMI: Master.
TACA: The 40th President of the United States, Ronald Regan, had Siberian husky with this name.
TALISMAN: Lucky; bringer of good fortune.
TALITHA: Innocent maiden.
TALLIS: Reverent.
TERENA: Jovial.
TERESSA: Jovial.
TEREVA: A dreamer.
TESIA: Worker.
THADDEA: A princess.

THEA: Watchful.
THEDA: Divine.
THEOBALD: A prince.
THEODIS: Gift.
THEODORA: Gift.
THEODOSIA: Gift.
THERRELL: Rewarding.
THESA: A treasure.
THOROUGHGOOD: Well-bred.
TINGSLEY: Stimulating.
TOINETTE: Valuable.
TOMAHAWK: (Algonquian: "a light ax with a head of stone") Tool and weapon used by Native Americans.
TORIA: Winner.
TRELLA: A star.
TREV: Wise.
TRINITY: Divine unity.
TRIUMPH: Victorious.
TROGDEN: Crude, primitive.
TRUEBRED: Well-bred.
TRUXTON: Very mobile.
TUNICA: Family-oriented.
TURK: Inexperienced.
TYANNA: Gracious; worker.
TYLA: Worker.
TYLEN: Worker.
UDELE: Flourishing.
ULA: Jewel of the sea.
ULAILI: (Pronounced "u-lay-lee") Sea jewel.
ULI: Sea jewel.

ULLIS, ULISSA: Sea jewel.
ULRICA: Wealthy.
UNITY: United, oneness.
UTOPIA: Sanctuary.
VAN: Of the Dutch.
VANCE: Sharing.
VAQUERO: In the southwest, a cowboy.
VARDEN: A shepherd.
VARINA, VERINA: Wise.
VEAH: Humble.
VEDA: Intelligent.
VENETIA: Easygoing.
VERGIL: Flourishing.
VINEY: Clinging.
VINT: Short for Vinton.
VINTON: Drinker.
VIOLETTA: Purple, full of passion.
VIRTUE: Worthy.
VITO: Life.
WEARY: Tired.
WEATHERLY: Moody.
WICKLIFFE, WYCK-LIFFE: "From the white cliff."
WILLETA, WILLETTE: Wistful.
WILLONA: Wishful; lioness.
WINDEMERE: Windy waters.
WINSTON: (Old English: "from the friendly town") The name of a teddy bear known as the fertility bear, made by Nickerbocker Bears.
YARDLEY: A shepherd.
YASMINE: Jasmine.
YEARDLY: From the enclosed meadow.
YOLANDO: Worthy.
YONEX: Tennis great Martina Navratilova has a dog with this name.
YOUNGBLOOD: Youth; strong, vital.
YUKI: Lyndon Johnson, the 36th President of the United States, had a mutt with this name.
YUL: Yule, of the Christmas season.
YUMA: Chief's son.
ZAZZLE: Beyond dazzling.
ZEA: Enthusiastic.
ZENA: Female.
ZENAS: Worthy.
ZENITH: The highest point.
ZENOBIA: A good role model.
ZETA: The sixth letter of the Greek alphabet.
ZULEIKA: Perfect.

Mozart

Did You Know?

PAL: The real name of the collie who played Lassie in the first movie "Lassie Come Home," based on the book of the same title.

SIZI: The name of Albert Schweitzer's cat during his time as a medical missionary in Africa.

TINY TIM: Calvin Coolidge, the 30th President of the United States, had a chow with this name.

Dilly & Dally

Cuff + Link

Chapter 25

TERRIFIC TWOSOMES!

On that rare occasion (thank goodness!) when you have two new pets to name, pairs of names (like *Samson and Delilah, Arlo and Janis, Simon and Garfunkel*, and others) can really come in handy. This chapter offers many well-known pairs drawn from history and pop culture, so you'll be sure to find a great pair of names for your terrific twosome!

ABBOTT AND COSTELLO: The American comedy team (Bud) Abbott and (Lou) Costello.

ADAM AND EVE: In the Bible, Eve gave Adam the forbidden fruit, and as a result, they were expelled from the Garden of Eden.

ALEX AND EMMA: For the movie of the same name about the writer with writer's block and the stenographer he hires.

AMOS AND ANDY: Characters played by Spencer Williams (Andy) and Alvin Childress (Amos) in the old radio and later TV series "Amos & Andy."

ANTONY AND CLEOPATRA: Egyptian queen Cleopatra and Roman General Antony comprise one of the great romantic duos of all-time.

ARLO AND JANIS: The couple in the syndicated comic strip "Arlo & Janis" by Jimmy Johnson.

ASTERIX AND OBELIX: A tiny warrior and his best friend in the comic book series, *Asterix,* set in Roman times under the rule of Caesar.

BARNEY AND BETTY: For the Rubbles, neighbors of the Flintstones in the 1960s animated TV series, "The Flintstones."

BARON AND BARONESS: A nobleman and his wife.

BATMAN AND ROBIN: The caped crusader and his sidekick.

BEAVIS AND BUTTHEAD: The dimwitted friends in the 1990s animated MTV series of the same name.

BEN AND JERRY: For the creators of "Ben & Jerry's Ice Cream."

BERNARD AND MISS BIANCA: The handsome little brown mouse (voiced by veteran comedian Bob Newhart) and the beautiful white mouse (voiced by Eva Gabor) in the Disney animated movie *The Rescuers* and the sequel *The Rescuers Down Under.*

BERT AND ERNIE: The friends from "Sesame Street."

BLONDIE AND DAGWOOD: The husband and wife in the syndicated comic strip titled "Blondie."

BLUE AND JEAN: Bluejean.

BOGIE AND BACALL: For actors Humphrey Bogart and Lauren Bacall who starred together in *Key Largo.*

BORIS AND NATASHA: Russian bad guys from the animated TV series "Rocky and Bullwinkle."

BRAD AND ANGELINA: For celebrity couple Brad Pitt and Angelina Jolie.

BUNNY AND CLAUDE: For the cartoon spoof of Bonnie and Clyde.

BUTCH AND SUNDANCE: Outlaws in the western movie *Butch Cassidy and the Sundance Kid*, starring Robert Redford and Paul Newman.

CAGNEY AND LACEY: The two female cops and partners in the TV series of the same name.

CALVIN AND HOBBES: The boy (Calvin) and his cat (Hobbes) in the comic strip "Calvin and Hobbes."

CAPTAIN AND TENNILLE: The husband and wife musical duo who scored big hits in the 1970s with "Love Will Keep Us Together" and other love songs.

CHEECH AND CHONG: The irreverent 1970s comedy duo.

CHIP AND DALE: The playful chipmunks in many Disney

cartoons including the animated TV series "Chip 'n Dale Rescue Rangers."

CLARK KENT AND LOIS LANE: Superman's alter ego and his beloved and fellow reporter, Lois Lane.

COFFEE AND CREAM: One light-colored pet; one dark-colored pet.

COPPER AND TOD: Unlikely friends, a fox cub and a hound pup, in the Disney animated film *The Fox and the Hound.*

CUFF AND LINK: The name of the turtles in the reality TV series "Big Brother 4."

DAISY AND DONALD: Donald Duck and his girl friend, Daisy Duck.

DAVEY AND GOLIATH: In the Bible, the giant (Goliath) who was killed by much smaller Davey.

DAY AND NIGHT: Two pets as different as day and night.

DICK AND JANE: The boy and girl in the old children's book series of the same name.

DILLY AND DALLY: Dilly Dally.

DONNY AND MARIE: Known for the brother and sister singing duo.

DUKE AND DUCHESS: A nobleman and his wife.

DYNA AND MITE: Dynamite.

DYNA AND MO: Dynamo.

EMPTY AND FULL: Playful name for pets who are total opposites.

FELIX AND OSCAR: The roommates in the 1970s TV series "The Odd Couple."

FIGARO AND CLEO: A cute and cuddly kitten (Figaro) and a cute little goldfish (Cleo) in Disney's *Pinocchio.*

FISH AND CHIPS: For the food.

FLAP AND JACK: Flapjack.

FRAISER AND NILES: The somewhat stiff brothers in the long-running TV series "Fraiser."

FRANK AND ERNEST: Friends in the comic strip "Frank and Ernest" by Bob Thaves.

FRED AND ETHEL: Neighbors of the Ricardos in the 1950s TV series "I Love Lucy."

FRED AND GINGER: For Fred Astaire and Ginger Rogers, called the most famous dancing duo ever paired.

FRED AND WILMA: The husband and wife from the 1960s animated TV series "The Flintstones."

GARFIELD AND ODIE: The lovable but mischievous cat and the naive dog in the animated TV series "Garfield and Friends."

GEORGE AND GRACIE: For the highly successful comedy team, George Burns and Gracie Allen, who were husband and wife.

GOOBER AND GOMER: Off-beat cousins in the 1960s TV series "The Andy Griffith Show."

HALF AND HALF: One half milk; one half cream. Two pets with the same name.

HANSEL AND GRETEL: A young boy and girl in the Grimm's fairy tale "Hansel and Gretel."

HAROLD AND MAUDE: Odd couple in the cult movie classic *Harold and Maude*.

HECKLE AND JECKLE: From the cartoon TV series about two magpies.

HIM AND HER: Female and male.

HOMER AND MARGE: The unconventional parents in the long-running animated TV series "The Simpsons."

HOPE AND FAITH: For the bickering sisters in the TV series starring Kelly Ripa and Faith Ford.

HOT AND COLD: Pets with opposite temperaments.

HOT AND SPICY: Two temperamental pets.

HUGS AND KISSES: Loving, affectionate pets.

ITCHY AND SCRATCHY: The cartoon cat and mouse within a cartoon in the TV series "The Simpsons."

JACK AND JILL: The boy and girl who tumbled down a hill in the children's nursery rhyme.

JORINDA AND JORINGEL: The names of the beautiful maiden and the handsome youth in Grimm's fairy tale "Jorinda and Joringel."

KATIE AND MATT: Former co-hosts of the NBC morning series "Today."

KAZAA AND KAZAM: Magical.

KEN AND BARBIE: The

popular fashion doll and her boyfriend.

KING AND QUEEN: The royal ruler and his wife.

KIT AND KABOODLE: The whole thing.

LADY AND TRAMP: The name of the female and male dogs in the animated Walt Disney movie *Lady and the Tramp.*

LAUREL AND HARDY: For the American film comedy team Stanley Laurel and Oliver Hardy.

LAVERNE AND SHIRLEY: The slapstick friends and roommates in the TV series of the same name.

LEATHER AND LACE: Tough and tender.

LILO AND STITCH: The name of the spirited little girl (Lilo) and her alien friend (Stitch) in the Disney animated movie of the same name.

LORD AND LADY: A royal couple.

LOVE AND KISSES: Affectionate pets.

LUCY AND ETHEL: The wacky duo of neighbors Lucy Ricardo and Ethel Mertz from the 1950s TV series "I Love Lucy."

LUCY AND RICKY: From the 1950s TV series "I Love Lucy," starring real-life husband and wife comedians Lucille Ball and Desi Arnaz as married couple Lucy and Ricky Ricardo.

MARY AND RHODA: Best friends and neighbors in the 1970s TV series "The Mary Tyler Moore Show."

MICKEY AND MINNIE: For the world's most famous mouse, Disney's Mickey Mouse and his girlfriend Minnie.

MILK & HONEY: Soothing.

MILO AND OTIS: From the unlikely friends Milo (a cat) and Otis (a dog), in *The Adventures of Milo and Otis.*

MISS PIGGY AND KERMIT: Jim Hensen's top Muppet stars, Miss Piggy and Kermit the Frog.

MISTER AND MISSUS: A title for a male and a female.

MONET AND MATISSE: For artists Claude Monet and Henri-Emille-Benoit Matisse, Monet an Impressionist and Matisse a modern artist.

MUTT AND JEFF: A pair of

comical performers in the 1800s and later the basis for a comic book series.

MYRT AND MARGE: Popular soap duo (mother, Myrtle Vail and her daughter Marge) in the radio serial of the same

NEAT AND TIDY: Two very clean and orderly pets.

NICE AND NAUGHTY: One saintly pet; one devilish pet.

NIGHT AND DAY: Pets that are extreme opposites in personality and behavior.

OZZIE AND HARRIET: For "The Adventures of Ozzie and Harriet," the old TV series about the Nelson family.

PEACHES AND CREAM: Delicious fruit and topping.

PEANUT BUTTER AND JELLY: Processed peanut food and fruit preserves used primarily for sandwiches and sweets, candies and cookies.

PERDITA AND PONGO: The mom and pop of the pups in the Disney animated movie *101 Dalmatians*.

PODO AND KODO: The names of a pair of ferrets in the TV series "Beastmaster."

RAGGEDY ANN AND RAGGEDY ANDY: The beloved rag dolls in the children's book *The Raggedy Ann Stories* by Johnny Gruelle.

REN AND STIMPY: The Chihuahua (Ren) and cat (Stimpy) in the animated TV series of the same name.

RISE AND SHINE: Early risers.

ROCK AND ROLL: Rowdy music lovers.

ROCKY AND BULLWINKLE: From the animated TV series starring a moose (Bullwinkle) and his sidekick, a flying squirrel (Rocky).

ROMEO AND JULIET: The ill-fated couple in William Shakespeare's tragic play of the same name.

RUFF AND RUMBLE: Rowdy.

RUFF AND TUFF: Rough and tough.

SAMSON AND DELILAH: In the Old Testament, Delilah was Samson's lover, who betrayed him to the Philistines by cutting his hair, which was the source of his power.

SI AND AM: The two Siamese cats in the Disney animated movie *Lady and the Tramp*.

SIEGFRIED AND ROY: For the Las Vegas entertainers who include tigers in their act.

SIMON AND GARFUN-KLE: Paul Simon (later a highly successful solo recording artist) and Art Garfunkle, a 1960s musical duo best known for their soundtrack recording for the movie *The Graduate.*

SIR AND MADAME: Titles for a male and female.

SKEETER AND SCOOTER: The twins in Jim Henson's Muppets.

SLAM AND DUNK: Slam-dunk.

SNIFF AND GROWL: One pet that is friendly; one pet less friendly.

SONNY AND CHER: The husband and wife singing duo of the 1960s.

STARKSY AND HUTCH: The detectives in the TV series of the same name.

ST. ELSEWHERE AND CHICAGO HOPE: Two TV medical dramas. The name of two dogs in an episode of the TV series "Will and Grace."

SUGAR AND SPICE: Sweet and hot-tempered.

SUN AND MOON: Two pets who are total opposites.

SWEET AND SOUR: One pet with a good temperament; one pet with a bad disposition.

TARZAN AND JANE: Edgar Rice Burroughs' character known as the Lord of the Jungle and his city-born romantic interest, Jane.

TEENY AND TINY: Two very small pets.

THELMA AND LOUISE: Daring duo. For the characters in the movie of the same name.

TINTIN AND SNOWY: From the children's books and TV series "Adventures of Tintin," an animated series about a boy reporter and his dog, Snowy.

TOM AND JERRY: The mischievous cat (Tom) and mouse (Jerry) in the popular cartoon series.

TONY AND ANGELA: The unlikely couple in the TV series "Who's the Boss."

TRYPHENA AND TRYPHOSA: (Derived from Greek *tryphe:* "softness, delicacy") Companions in the New Testament.

TUCK AND ROLL: The

names of the Hungarian pill bugs in the Disney animated movie *A Bug's life.*

TWEEDLE DEE AND TWEEDLE DUM: From "tweedle dee and tweedle dum," meaning two persons or things so much alike that they are nearly indistinguishable. The obnoxious identical twin brothers is Lewis Carroll's classic book *Alice In Wonderland.*

VANILLA AND CHOCO-LATE: A light colored and dark colored pet.

VENUS AND MARS: Women are from Venus, Men are from Mars.

WAYNE AND GARTH: The comical duo in the *Wayne's World* movie series.

WIGGLE AND GIGGLE: The name of a children's game.

WILL AND GRACE: The roommates in the comedy series of the same name.

WILYKAT AND WILYKIT: Characters from the 1980s cartoon series "Thundercats."

ZEUS AND APOLLO: The names of the two Doberman's in the long-running TV series "Magnum, P.I.," starring actor Tom Selleck.

Did You Know?

BLANCHE: (Old French: "white, fair") Actress Delta Burke, star of the TV series "Designing Women," has a small pooch with this name.

RICKY: Short for Richard. The name of singer Gloria Estafan's Dalmatian.

SOJAH: Soldier. Actress and recording artist Tisha Campbell, who stars the TV series "Martin" and "My Wife and Kids," has a tan-colored chow named Sojah.

ABOUT THE AUTHOR

Eugene Boone, a native South Carolinian, has spent over a decade researching pet names while compiling **The Big Book of Pet Names.** Mr. Boone has written for national and international magazines including *Women's Circle, Fate, The Professional Poet, Writer's Lifeline, The Poet*, among others. He is the author of several books including: **Writing To Be Published** *(Exploits Publications*, Canada, 1984) and **Markets For Writers** *(RSVP Press*, 2nd Edition, 1987).

For several years, Mr. Boone was a columnist for *Published! Magazine*.

Mr. Boone's biographical information appears in **Contemporary Authors, The International Authors & Writers Who's Who** (Cambridge, England), **The Working Press of the Nation, Who's Who of North American Poets**, and other reference resources.

CPSIA information can be obtained at www.ICGtesting.com
Printed in the USA
LVOW10s0325261114

415613LV00002BB/268/P

9 780930 865542